SEX THERAPY IN BRITAIN

Open University Press
Psychotherapy in Britain series
Series Editor: Windy Dryden

TITLES IN THE SERIES

Individual Therapy in Britain
Windy Dryden (ed.)

Marital Therapy in Britain: Volumes I & II
Windy Dryden (ed.)

Forthcoming

Family Therapy in Britain
Eddy Street and Windy Dryden (eds.)

Group Therapy in Britain
Mark Aveline and Windy Dryden (eds.)

Sex Therapy in Britain
Martin Cole and Windy Dryden (eds.)

Related titles

Cognitive – Behavioural Approaches to Psychotherapy
Windy Dryden and William Golden

Therapists' Dilemmas
Windy Dryden

SEX THERAPY IN BRITAIN

Edited by
Martin Cole and Windy Dryden

OPEN UNIVERSITY PRESS
MILTON KEYNES · PHILADELPHIA

Open University Press
Open University Educational Enterprises Limited
12 Cofferidge Close
Stony Stratford
Milton Keynes MK11 1BY

and
242 Cherry Street
Philadelphia, PA 19106, USA

First Published 1988

Copyright © 1988. Editorial and selection material © Martin Cole and Windy Dryden. Individual chapters © as credited.

All rights reserved. No part of this publication may be reproduced, stored in a retrieval system or transmitted in any form or by any means, without written permission from the publisher.

British Library Cataloguing in Publication Data

Sex therapy in Britain.
1. Great Britain. Man. Sexual disorders.
Psychotherapy
I. Cole, Martin II. Dryden, Windy
III. Series
616.6′906914

ISBN 0-335-09838-X
ISBN 0-335-09828-2 Pbk

Library of Congress Cataloging-in-Publication Data

Sex Therapy in Britain / edited by Martin Cole and Windy Dryden.
p.cm. — (Psychotherapy in Britain series)
Includes index
1. Sex Therapy 2. Sex Therapy — Great Britain. I. Cole, Martin II. Dryden, Windy. III. Series
RC 557.S44 1988
616.85′83′00941 — DC19 88-12449 LOC.

ISBN 0-335-09838-X
ISBN 0-335-09828-2 Pbk

Typeset by Inforum Ltd, Portsmouth
Printed in Great Britain by Biddles Ltd., Guildford and Kings Lynn

To the memory of the Departments of Biological Sciences (1966–1985) and Educational Enquiry (1970–1983) (now deceased) at the University of Aston in Birmingham, to whom we owe a debt. R.I.P.

CONTENTS

Part 3 Sex therapy with specific groups

Part 4 Research and training

THE EDITORS

MARTIN COLE

Martin Cole began his professional career as a biologist. He spent four years in Africa working initially for the (then) Tanganyika Government and finally in Nigeria as a lecturer at University College, Ibadan. In 1961 he obtained a post in the College of Advanced Technology, Birmingham, later to become the University of Aston, where he remained until 1984 lecturing in genetics and social and reproductive biology.

After his return to Britain he became increasingly involved in sex education, sex therapy and fertility control both from an academic and political standpoint. He became an active member of the Abortion Law Reform Association in the early 1960s and was cofounder of the Birmingham Brook Advisory Centre in 1964. He founded the Birmingham Pregnancy Advisory Service, later to become the British PAS, in 1966, and the Institute for Sex Education and Research in 1969. He has made a number of films on sex education and sex therapy and written numerous articles and papers for magazines and journals. He was coauthor (with Philip Cauthery) of *The Fundamentals of Sex* (W.H. Allen, 1971). Currently he is practising sex therapy privately in Birmingham.

WINDY DRYDEN

Windy Dryden is Senior Lecturer in Psychology at Goldsmiths' College, University of London. He is the author of *Rational-Emotive Therapy:*

Fundamentals and Innovations (Croom Helm, 1984), *Therapists' Dilemmas* (Harper & Row, 1985) and *Counselling Individuals: The Rational-Emotive Approach* (Taylor & Francis, 1987). He is series editor of the *Psychotherapy in Britain* series published by Open University Press and series editor of the forthcoming *Counselling in Action* series to be published by SAGE Publications. He is a Fellow of the British Psychological Society, serves on the editorial boards of several international journals, including the *British Journal of Guidance and Counselling* and is coeditor of the *Journal of Cognitive Psychotherapy: An International Quarterly*. At present he practises part-time as an Honorary Psychotherapist in the Department of Psychiatry, St Thomas's Hospital, London, and part-time for the Raphael Counselling Centre in London.

THE CONTRIBUTORS

Charmian Bollinger: Consulting Clinical Psychologist in Private Practice, London

Paul T. Brown: Consulting Clinical and Occupational Psychologist in Private Practice, Partner, Gwynn & Brown, London

Grahame F. Cooper: Psychotherapist and Sex Therapist; Counselling and Psychotherapy Services, Birmingham

Patricia d'Ardenne: Principal Clinical Psychologist, District Department of Clinical Psychology, Tower Hamlets Health Authority

Mary Davies: Education Consultant and Trainer; former Education and Training Officer for The Association To Aid the Sexual and Personal Relationships of People with a Disability (SPOD)

Dennis Friedman: Director, Psychiatric Unit, Devonshire Hospital, London, W1. Formerly Honorary Lecturer in Sexual Medicine, St Bartholomew's Hospital, London, EC1

Peter Gordon: Sex Therapist; also Training and Development Officer, Family Planning Association, London

Lisa Kayata: Psychologist, Institute of Psychiatry, London

Anna Leeming: Research Psychologist and Director of Leeming Research Ltd, Nottingham

Derek Perkins: Top Grade Clinical Psychologist, Broadmoor Hospital, Crowthorne, Berkshire

Alan J. Riley: Physician in Sexual Medicine, London and Saffron Walden. Editor of the *British Journal of Sexual Medicine* and coeditor of *Sexual and Marital Therapy*

Elizabeth J. Riley: Sexual and Marital Therapist, London and Saffron Walden

Jean Smith: Senior Clinical Psychologist, South Glamorgan Health Authority, Cardiff

Eddy Street: Clinical Psychologist, South Glamorgan Health Authority, Cardiff

David Szydlo: Psychologist, Institute of Psychiatry, London

Glenn D. Wilson: Senior Lecturer in Psychology, Institute of Psychiatry, University of London

PREFACE

This book provides an up-to-date overview of the state of the art of sex therapy in Britain. The contributors, all established experts in their own specialisms, together provide a broad interdisciplinary account of sex therapy as it is practised in Britain today.

The book is divided into four sections. In the first section entitled 'Sexual Dysfunction', we begin by providing a brief outline of the different sexual dysfunctions. One of us (Martin Cole) then considers the frequencies and incidences of 'normal' and dysfunctional sexual behaviour. These two opening chapters set the scene for Chapters 3–5 where the sociobiological, endocrinological and psychological bases of sexual dysfunction are addressed. Finally, a chapter on diagnostic procedures is presented which provides an assessment-treatment link between the first two sections.

The second section considers 'General Therapeutic Approaches and Issues'. In Chapter 7, Grahame Cooper provides a comprehensive review of the psychological methods of sex therapy as practised in Britain. He bases his overview on a survey of the therapeutic practices of British sex therapists which was conducted especially for inclusion in this volume. In Chapter 8, Alan Riley outlines the place of drugs in the treatment of sexual dysfunction, having set the scene for this discussion in Chapter 4 in the first section. In the remaining chapters in this section a range of treatment issues are considered – the role of the group treatment of sexual dysfunction, how sexual problems may reflect relationship difficulties and the fact that sexual dysfunction must be considered in a transcultural setting.

In the third section, 'Sex Therapy with Specific Groups', contributors were asked to discuss briefly their work with specific groups. The chapters in this section are designed to *reflect* the range of work that sex therapists are doing in Britain rather than to provide a comprehensive account of such work – an endeavour which would have necessitated a second volume.

In the final section, 'Research and Training', two chapters bring the volume to a close. First, in Chapter 17, certain salient issues are discussed which concern the training of sex therapists. This is followed by an account of four training courses that are currently offered in Britain. In the concluding chapter, a research overview is presented which places sex therapy in its empirical context.

It is apparent then that sex therapy in Britain embraces a wide range of perspectives from the endocrinological to the transcultural and thus, as noted above, a wide variety of disciplines are involved in its study. This has necessarily meant that it has been quite difficult for us as editors to achieve a common tone and level in this volume. This should be viewed in context since it inevitably reflects the heterogeneous nature of sex therapy in Britain. Nonetheless, we consider that this volume is the most comprehensive that has been produced to date on sex therapy in its British context.

Martin Cole, Birmingham
Windy Dryden, London

ACKNOWLEDGEMENTS

We wish to acknowledge Consella Parkinson for her painstaking assistance in the preparation of this book and Jonathans' Restaurant, Oldbury, West Midlands, where the project was conceived, nourished and brought to fruition.

PART 1

SEXUAL DYSFUNCTION

CHAPTER 1

SEXUAL DYSFUNCTION: AN INTRODUCTION

Martin Cole and Windy Dryden

Human sexual behaviour is highly variable making it extremely difficult to be able to judge whether a particular response should be classified as *normal* or *dysfunctional*. Both males and females exhibit considerable variation in drive, performance and specific needs so that mean or modal behaviours often have little significance (see Chapter 2 by Cole). For example, there are some men who have never masturbated to orgasm nor have they any wish to do so, whilst others may masturbate several times a day for long periods. Some men will have had hundreds of sexual partners during the course of their lives whereas others may have had only one or indeed may never have had any experience of intercourse. Within the marital unit intercourse may continue until the ninth decade or cease very much earlier, sometimes after only a few years of marriage. And when practised, intercourse may last for less than a minute or so or for as long as an hour or more, resulting in one or more orgasms for the woman, always in some instances and never in others. None of these behaviours can be regarded as intrinsically problematical, however rare, *except* when an individual, or his or her partner, perceive them to be so.

Of course, there are many instances when intercourse, for various reasons, is either not possible or is sufficiently unrewarding that help is sought. In these circumstances where specific problems can be identified, naturally they have been widely described and given names (e.g. Bancroft, 1983). The taxonomy and classification of these so-called disorders or sex dysfunctions have evolved over the years and the summary presented in Table 1.1 represents a generally agreed format and one which as far as possible is followed in this book.

Table 1.1 A classification of the sexual dysfunctions

Disorder	*In men*	*In women*
Desire (or) Drive (or) Interest (or) Appetite	Impaired sexual desire	Impaired sexual desire
Arousal (or) Excitement	Erectile dysfunction	Impaired sexual arousal
Orgasmic	Premature ejaculation Retarded ejaculation	Orgasmic dysfunction
Other	Dyspareunia Sexual phobias	Vaginismus Dyspareunia Sexual phobias

Essential as it is to have a single and widely accepted nosology of the sex dysfunctions it is also important to resist succumbing to the slavish use of the medical model without some awareness of the pitfalls that may arise as a consequence. Problems must always be perceived in the context in which they appear and one should try to avoid labelling patients with their condition. Although it is critically important that an accurate diagnosis is made, effective 'treatment' and 'cures' are not always possible. Often it is just as important to help the individual or couple to see their 'problem' in a different perspective so that they can avoid unrealistic expectations either of themselves or of their partners (Cole, 1985).

Sexual dysfunctions are defined either as *primary* when they have been present throughout the sexual life of an individual or *secondary* where they have appeared subsequently after an initial period of normal function. A sexual disorder may also be described as *situational* when it occurs only in some circumstances but not in others and a disorder is defined as *total* or *global* when it occurs in all situations.

In the following section a brief description of the main sex dysfunctions is provided.

THE SEXUAL DYSFUNCTIONS

Impaired sexual desire

A total indifference to sexual activity in itself may not, of course, be a problem. For example, one may have a partner who is equally unconcerned and sex may never have played a significant part in the relationship. Deficiencies in sexual desire usually only become a problem when difficulties arise as a result of dissatisfaction in one's partner, when perhaps sexual responses are not thought to be adequate to initiate a new relationship, or when a person's behaviour falls short of his or her own expectations.

This lack of sexual appetite is commonly found in women though less so in men (Hawton, 1985). The lack of desire is usually total so that she may not even masturbate nor wish to have intercourse with other partners. However, occasionally, blocks in sex desire may be partial and self-masturbation or perhaps even sex with another partner may be rewarding. When desire dysfunctions occur in men they are rarely total and usually only express themselves in specific situations such as with a particular partner.

The reasons for the absence or loss of a sexual appetite are highly complex and those who present for help with impaired sexual desire probably include a wide range of quite distinct conditions. For example, in many women impaired sexual interest will have been caused by the negative effects of early childhood experiences where sex may never have been openly discussed in the home and where the overt and covert expression of sexual feelings was regarded as unacceptable. Then there are those women (and men) who, instead of showing lack of interest or desire in their partners, experience a positive aversion to the prospect of sexual intimacy. They will actively *avoid* sex and are repelled by the thought of any sexual contact.

A further group of men and women will simply have a low sex drive and their problem may simply be that they have a partner with whom they are sexually incompatible. Finally, though less well-defined, is a significant group of men and women who might be described as having become sexually habituated to their partners – that is they are no longer interested in them because of a loss of attraction or because of familiarity and boredom. A low sex drive may also be a consequence of alcohol, tobacco or drug abuse or may result from a number of medical conditions such as multiple sclerosis or depression.

Superficially all these groups may present with a similar symptom of impaired sexual desire though causally the categories of behaviour are quite distinct and may demand different treatment approaches.

Erectile dysfunction

Erectile dysfunction describes a condition where a man finds that his erection is not strong enough to penetrate the vagina in intercourse. It is probably the commonest specific sex disorder in men in the Western world. Like many other conditions it can be primary, secondary or situational and the loss of erection may be complete or only partial. About one third to one half of those who present with erectile dysfunction have a condition which is likely to be caused by physical or organogenic factors (Melman *et al.*, 1984; Spark *et al.*, 1980). These are medical conditions which affect, for example, either the blood or nerve supply to the penis or perhaps result in an alteration in the sex-hormone balance. In the remainder, psychological factors will be largely implicated in a relationship where, for example, 'sex-stress' in the form of problems in a relationship, performance anxiety or remote effects from childhood-rearing will precipitate the disorder in vulnerable individuals. Ultimately, whatever the cause, the poor erection is brought about by insufficient blood flowing and being held in the erectile tissues of the penis.

Impaired sexual arousal in women

When a man fails to become sexually aroused the consequences are usually obvious, for amongst other things he fails to get an erection. The outward signs of similar blocks in the sexual responses of a woman are naturally less conspicuous. However, there are many women who, whilst experiencing normal sex desire, fail to become aroused sexually when stimulated by their partners and clearly their sexual responses are blocked to a greater or lesser degree. The mechanisms that prevent a woman becoming sexually aroused are probably largely psychogenic though there will undoubtedly be some instances when, as with men, these blocks will have a physical basis.

One of the specific signs of a lack of arousal in women is the absence of vaginal lubrication, a response which incidentally is physiologically identical to that of erection in the man and moreover, like erection, it is also a response over which the individual has no control. However, normally associated with dryness of the vagina would be other more striking deficiencies in arousal as shown by an absence of whole body responses normally present in the sexually stimulated woman. Thus, a woman who has impaired sexual arousal would not show the expected constellation of responses such as flushing of the face, an increase in spontaneous body movements, vocalization and of course a parallel increase in heart and respiratory rates.

Impaired sexual arousal may be associated with blocks in sexual desire, and where both exist together it may not be easy to distinguish between them. However, these areas of the sexual response cycle are thought to be quite distinct and clearly blocks in the one can and do occur independently of blocks in the other.

Premature ejaculation

Premature ejaculation is not easy to define precisely so perhaps it is best to describe it as a condition where a man reaches orgasm and ejaculates quickly, so quickly that in fact neither he nor his partner are satisfied. Quick ejaculation is a real problem for many couples and it is usually the second most frequent presenting problem at sex dysfunction clinics. Though it is a very distressing condition in its severest form, that is, when ejaculation takes place before, at the point of, or shortly after penetration, there are obviously many men who can last up to a minute or so or even longer but who would not regard the condition severe enough to seek treatment. This is in contrast to those men who have erectile difficulties who usually seek help sooner or later. This may be because premature ejaculation appears to be tolerated better than erectile problems, for example, it does not interfere with fertility so dramatically (Cole, 1986) and so the actual frequency of premature ejaculation may be much more common than is suggested by clinic presentations.

The quick ejaculator differs from a man who can postpone his orgasm in having a very sensitive ejaculatory reflex, a kind of ejaculatory 'hair trigger' though the actual mechanisms which distinguish him from others not distressed by this condition are ill-understood. Similarly the causes of this disorder are not really known. Various hypotheses have been proposed but there is no general agreement, and neither early experiences nor the nature of the current relationship provide adequate explanations.

It is probably true to say that as with almost all sex dysfunctions there is a large biogenic or organogenic element involved in the causation of premature ejaculation, linked possibly to the way in which the neurohormonal mechanisms which control ejaculation operate. Such innate predispositions to quick ejaculation may be exacerbated by a poor relationship where, for example, for whatever reason, a man is anxious about his sexual performance.

Retarded ejaculation

A relatively rare condition, retarded ejaculation occurs in only about 1 per cent of men (see Chapter 2) and describes a situation where a man finds it difficult or impossible to reach orgasm and ejaculate. The problem may be primary or, rarely, secondary where, for example, the difficulty may appear temporarily in a new and unsatisfactory relationship. The condition may be absolute in the sense that ejaculation is not possible either in masturbation or in intercourse or it may only be partial where ejaculation can be achieved in self-masturbation but not in coitus. In some men ejaculation may take place only after a very long period of stimulation (an hour or more) and in practice is rarely achieved. Like premature ejaculation this condition can cause considerable distress in a relationship and moreover can prevent the couple from having children.

Little is known about the causes of this condition or of the psychological mechanisms which determine whether orgasm will be delayed in a person or not. It is clear that the retarded ejaculator in contrast to the premature ejaculator has a high inertia in his ejaculatory reflex and that he requires levels of stimulation which are not normally available to him in coitus. As with premature ejaculators there do not appear to be any obvious factors in the histories of retarded ejaculators to account for their condition in terms of early experiences and it is likely that there are certain innate factors which predispose them to their condition.

Orgasmic dysfunction

Between one third and a half of all sexually active women have never experienced an orgasm in intercourse without some form of additional stimulation (see Chapter 2). This fact has led many sex therapists to the conclusion that the absence of coital orgasm in women cannot be reasonably regarded as a sex disorder because the condition is so frequent. Be that as it may, the great difficulty that many women experience in achieving a climax in intercourse does distress them and their partners so much that many seek help. In these women the desire and arousal mechanisms are usually intact but they block before achieving orgasm. In most of these women orgasm probably can be achieved in self-masturbation if this form of stimulation is found to be acceptable. The block in the orgasmic response does not therefore appear to be physiological and it is more likely that the tactile input from the act of penile thrusting is insufficient to induce orgasm in intercourse. Added to this is the distraction of intimacy in coitus which may interfere with sexual arousal.

To make matters more complicated there is an ongoing debate about the dual nature of female orgasm. Masters and Johnson (1966) claim that there is only one type of female orgasm, arguing that only the clitoris needs to be stimulated for this orgasm to be achieved and that the so-called 'vaginal orgasm' was a myth. However, there is much evidence to the contrary and many women report quite different types of orgasm and sites of stimulation, which can be roughly divided into the 'clitoral-vulval' and the 'vaginal-uterine' (Fisher, 1973; Singer, 1973; Bentler and Peeler, 1979), though Levin (1981) reports that however the orgasm is described the same physiological responses appear to be involved. Reports from the literature do not help one to identify a particular type of woman who is likely to find it difficult to achieve coital orgasm of either kind and once again one is led to the inevitable conclusion that there are certain innate anatomical and psychophysiological characteristics which make coital orgasm more difficult for some women than others.

Vaginismus and dyspareunia

Normally during sexual arousal the entrance to the vagina relaxes and dilates spontaneously and the penis enters with little difficulty. However, in some women the muscles surrounding the lower third of the vagina constrict reflexively when penetration is attempted and intercourse becomes either impossible or, at best, extremely painful and distressing. The phobic response of a woman who develops this psychosomatic defence against intercourse is called *vaginismus*. Associated with, and sometimes indistinguishable from vaginismus, is an allied condition called *dyspareunia*. Strictly this refers to the pain or discomfort experienced within the vagina once penetration has been achieved. These feelings may be described as aversive sensations within the vagina or as more generalized feelings, say, of nausea. Some young women may develop a transient vaginismus at the beginning of their sex lives but this normally resolves itself without recourse to treatment.

Vaginismus and dyspareunia are often caused by physical factors. For example, very rarely a tight hymen may cause pain or a previous obstetric history or more frequently an infection may be responsible. On the other hand both vaginismus and dyspareunia can be largely psychogenic and represent good examples of a psychosomatic response.

Unlike many other sex disorders it is usually not difficult to detect in a woman's history early experiences which are likely to have predisposed her to defend herself against intercourse. For example, a history of child abuse, an experience of early attempted or successful rape or a family background in which strict antisexual values predominated, all predispose to vaginismus. However, it is abundantly clear that not all women who have had these negative sexual experiences develop vaginismus and clearly once again it is likely that there are innate neurophysiological conditions which predispose some women, but not others, to this response as a defence against sexual intercourse.

Dyspareunia may also occur in the male during intercourse: this pain may be caused, for example, by an infection, a tight foreskin, or rarely the cause may have a psychological basis.

Sexual phobias

A few men, but rather more women, present with a number of specific sexual phobias. For example, in women there may be an aversion to touching her partner's penis or even rarely a fear of having her vulva stimulated by his hand. More common is an aversion in women to semen and of course oral sex, when the woman takes the penis into her mouth, is often totally unacceptable. Vaginismus, already discussed, is a further good example of a specific phobic response in a woman. Specific phobias in men are less common though a fear of the foreskin being retracted is a good example of one.

Heterophobia

Strictly speaking heterophobia is not a sex disorder but a condition which, as the name suggests, prevents heterosexual intercourse being accomplished at all. Because of the high levels of anxiety triggered by the prospect of any heterosocial experience, anxiety, which is also often accompanied by a marked deficiency in social and in particular sexual skills, imposes a block often very early on in the courtship-coitus sequence of behaviours thus preventing not only intercourse but effective relationship-formation.

Heterophobic behaviour may, or may not, be associated with other sexual problems though often the desire, arousal and orgasm phases of sexual behaviour are intact. Heterophobia is found in men and women though more commonly in men where the biosocial pressures for him to be more innovative and assertive in courtship and sex play increase performance anxiety in the male. The corresponding condition in homosexuals, homophobia, may also prevent homosexual intimacy, but here it is complicated by the fact that some men are uncertain of the direction of their sex drive until they have had a sexual experience, an uncertainty that adds to their already high levels of anxiety.

Heterophobia has been overlooked as an important behavioural problem because most sex therapists know that the treatment of such a condition is not likely to be easy without a partner.

REFERENCES

Bancroft, J. (1983) *Human Sexuality and Its Problems*, Churchill-Livingstone, London.

Bentler, P.M. and Peeler, W.H. (1979) Models of female orgasm, *Archives of Sexual Behavior*, Vol. 8, pp. 405–24.

Cole, M.J. (1985) Sex therapy – a critical appraisal, *British Journal of Psychiatry*, Vol. 147, pp. 337–51.

Cole, M.J. (1986) Socio-sexual characteristics of men with sexual problems, *Sexual and Marital Therapy*, Vol. 1, No. 1, pp. 89–108.

Fisher, S. (1973) *The Female Orgasm*, Basic Books, New York.

Hawton, K. (1985) *Sex Therapy: A Practical Guide,* Oxford University Press, Oxford.

Levin, R.J. (1981) The female orgasm – a current appraisal, *Journal of Psychosomatic Research*, Vol. 25, No. 2, pp. 119–33.

Masters, W.H. and Johnson, V.E. (1966) *Human Sexual Response*, Little, Brown & Co., Boston.

Melman, A., Kaplan, D. and Redfield, J. (1984) Evaluation of the first 70 patients in the center for male sexual dysfunction of Beth Israel Medical Center, *Journal of Urology,* Vol. 131, No. 1, pp. 53–5.
Spark, R.F., White, R.A. and Connolly, P.B. (1980) Impotence is not always psychogenic, *Journal of American Medical Association*, Vol. 243, pp. 750–5.
Singer, I. (1973) *The Goals of Human Sexuality*, Wildwood House, London.

CHAPTER 2

NORMAL AND DYSFUNCTIONAL SEXUAL BEHAVIOUR: FREQUENCIES AND INCIDENCES

Martin Cole

HUMAN SEXUAL BEHAVIOUR INVESTIGATED

In this chapter I seek to provide a summary of the results of the most important surveys into the incidences and frequencies of human sexual behaviour (see Table 2.1). The distinction between normal and dysfunctional sex is somewhat invidious and often misleading but it is used here to conform to the conventions adopted in later chapters.

This book is about sex therapy in *Britain*. However, much valuable research into the nature and pattern of human sexual behaviour has been conducted overseas, and to omit this would be a great loss. Therefore it was decided to include all the relevant published data that could be located so that the information provided would help the reader put human sexual behaviour in its widest perspective and in addition provide a convenient collection of base-line data for reference purposes.

There are three obvious problems which face those who seek information about human sexual behaviour. First, there is the difficulty experienced in trying to arrive at an agreed classification and *definition* of the behaviours under investigation (e.g. What do we really mean by premature ejaculation?). Second, there are the many obstacles to be overcome to ensure that the participants in any survey *respond* adequately and honestly to the questions put to them. Finally, there are the often insurmountable difficulties experienced in trying to obtain a representative *sample* to question.

Definitions

Therapists do not always agree on how to classify sexual disorders: each has his or her own way of doing this which either leads to the omission of some categories altogether or to the creation of new disorders depending upon the motivation of the therapist or the nature of the sample. For example, both Masters and Johnson (1970) and Kaplan (1974) agree that orgasmic dysfunction was the commonest presenting sex disorder in women, yet other studies (see Table 2.9) recognized blocks in arousal to be more bothersome to women. This kind of discrepancy must have arisen from a difference in interpretation rather than in the nature of the sample. Again, Cole (1982; 1986), because he was working with a group of predominantly single men, recognized the category of heterophobia, a condition where, largely as a result of anxiety about heterosexual relationships, the individual was totally inexperienced sexually. The heterophobic was my second largest category of presenting males, yet other workers had neither met with nor identified this problem category at all.

Naturally as our understanding of human sexual problems increases so new concepts will evolve. An example of this is the recognition of blocks in sex drive or desire (Kaplan, 1979). So far, however, there have been no published reports of the incidence of this group of patients and presumably hitherto they have been put into other categories even though problems associated with 'frequency dissatisfaction' in couples are probably as common, if not more so, as any other difficulty experienced.

Definitions also need to be as precise as possible. For example, to say that 7 per cent of the male population suffer from erectile disorders (possibly one of the most readily defined dysfunctions) in fact says very little. More information is required. What is the age structure of the sample? Are primary, secondary and situational erectile problems included? Does the definition include those who can achieve intercourse but only with a partial erection? It is often said that at some time or another all men will experience difficulties with erection – it would be nice to know whether this in fact was true or not.

Responses

Responses that are given by those participating in surveys may not of course be reliable. First, they may reply in a way they think is expected of them, denying those aspects of their sex lives which they might regard as unacceptable. For example, homosexual fantasies, a visit to a prostitute or regular masturbation in marriage might not be easily disclosed. Second, the answers might be unreliable because of a poor memory. Who can recall with any degree of accuracy when they first masturbated to orgasm?

Sampling

Statistical theory nowadays is sufficiently sophisticated to ensure that a representative sample can be drawn from the population under investigation.

Table 2.1 Major surveys of human sexual behaviour

Reference	*Characteristics of sample*	*Sampling technique*	*Final sample size*	*Response rate*
Kinsey *et al.* (1948; 1953)	US adult men and women; majority of subjects from Indiana Strong bias towards higher socioeconomic groups	Unique group sampling	5,300 ♂♂ 5,900 ♀♀	Unique group sampling 25% of groups gave 100% response Remainder only partially sampled groups
Gebhard and Johnson (1979) [from Kinsey *et al.* (1948; 1953)]	Re-analysis of the Kinsey data	The data have been 'cleaned' by the removal of those who were believed to have a sexual bias, e.g. those with criminal records, mental hospital patients etc.	Maximum: 5,637 ♂♂ 5,609 ♀♀	As above
Chesser (1956)	UK women – bias towards higher socioeconomic groups	Patients of UK GPs (? random)	6,000	30–40%
Schofield (1965)	Unmarried UK aged 15–19 of both sexes	From NHS patients' lists and market research agency – random	934 ♂♂ 939 ♀♀	15% refusal
Gorer (1971)	UK men and women aged 16–45	Stratified random sample from electoral register	949 ♂♂ 1,037 ♀♀	65% 18% refusal Remainder unobtainable
Kantner and Zelnik (1972) and Zelnik and Kantner (1977)	US women aged 15–19: 92% unmarried	National probability sample	4,239 1,886	Not reported

Sorenson (1973)	US adolescents of both sexes	Random sample	393	47%
Hunt (1974)	US men and women	A representative but not random sample	1,044 ♀♀ 982 ♂♂	Approximately 20%
Miller and Simon (1974)	US (from Illinois) white adolescents of both sexes aged 14–17	Random stratified sample	2,064	75%
Vener and Stewart (1974)	US white students of both sexes	Total sample of students in population	4,220	98.4%
Frenken (1976)	Dutch married men and women, largely middle class	Random: supplied from the Dutch census	500	85%
Hite (1976)	US women	Non-random sample of respondents to questionnaire in magazines, women's organizations and personal contacts	c. 3,000	3% (!)
Pietropinto and Simenauer (1977)	US men	General public requested to participate from booths in public places	c. 4,000	c. 50%
Tavris and Sadd (1977)	US women aged 25% <25 52% 25–34 23% >35	Total sample of respondents to questionnaire in *Redbook* magazine	100,000	—

Table 2.1 (contd.)

Reference	*Characteristics of sample*	*Sampling technique*	*Final sample size*	*Response rate*
Farrel (1978)	UK teenagers aged 16–19 of both sexes (94% single)	Random from electoral register	1,556	74% 16% refusal 10% not available
Garde and Lunde (1980)	Danish women all aged 40	Random sample from the Danish census	227	94% of an 88% sample
Hite (1981)	US men	Non-random sample of respondents to questionnaires in magazines and men's groups	7,239	6%
Sanders (1985)	UK women married and unmarried aged 16–60	'Random' stratified sample for age and location	'Random', 4,000 taken from 15,604 completed questionnaires volunteered by readers	—

Problems start, however, when selected individuals refuse to co-operate and therefore cannot be replaced without distorting the results. For example, the extrovert rather than the introvert is more likely to agree to participate in a sex survey and those with sexual problems may regard such an investigation with considerable suspicion and drop out as a result, a group of course which needs to be properly represented.

These difficulties are illustrated in the differing reports obtained by MORI (1984) and Sanders (1985) where they sought information on the age of first intercourse. Sanders had the advantage of a large (15,600) sample of voluntary respondents who anonymously completed a questionnaire in the magazine *Woman*. However, her sample, large as it was, was unlikely to be either random or representative of all women and was therefore biased. MORI on the other hand had obtained their information from a small quota sample (n = 513) which was likely to be more representative but suffered the disadvantage that the answers on intimate matters were obtained by personal interview, which may have inhibited the interviewees. The former report probably overestimated sexual activity whilst the latter is likely to have underestimated it. This state of affairs is obviously unsatisfactory. Because sex is such a private behaviour, because people are not practised in talking about their sex lives and because guilt and anxiety surround the whole subject, the exact nature and extent of human sexual response becomes an imponderable – it is by its very nature often unknowable. No doubt with the passage of time the situation will change as sexual taboos diminish, but by then inevitably sexual behaviour will also have changed so that the exact truth about what people actually did might never be known.

Bancroft (1983) has provided a particularly good account of the problems confronting those engaged in surveys into sexual behaviour to which the reader is referred. He points out that in spite of their limitations, surveys of this kind are particularly useful in providing base-line data and establishing norms for different groups of people. The results of surveys also help those concerned to make realistic policy decisions in education and health care. They enable false myths to be challenged, and above all they may influence public opinion, though this of course can be for the better or for worse.

'NORMAL' SEXUAL BEHAVIOUR–INCIDENCES AND FREQUENCIES

Preadolescent sexual activity

There are very few reports on the sexual behaviour of preadolescent youngsters which is surprising considering the fact that it is probable that at least 1 in every 2 preadolescent boys and 1 in every 3 girls engages in some

Table 2.2 Preadolescent sexual activity

Reference	*Activity*	*White males*	*White females*
Gebhard and Johnson (1979) [from Kinsey *et al.* (1948)]	None	49%	68%
	Sex play up to but excluding attempted and successful coitus	37%	27%
	Attempted or successful coitus	14%	5%

form of genital sex play before puberty (see Table 2.2). Attempted or successful coitus is a natural progression from manual stimulation and genital touching, but it is only reported by a minority (Gebhard and Johnson, 1979). Kinsey *et al.*'s (1948) original data suggest a much higher incidence of coitus in the preadolescent boy. For the 10-year-old he reports that as many as 11 per cent achieved coital penetration though probably the real estimate from a random sample is half this value. Most of this sexual activity takes place between the ages of 8 and 13, although for some it occurs from earliest childhood.

Whatever the real figures are they reflect the need of the growing boy and girl to learn and explore in an unstructured way (subject to individual variation) the developing awareness of his or her sexuality. Much of this preadolescent exploratory behaviour is homosexual. In boys homosexual behaviour is reported more frequently than are heterosexual experiences; whilst in girls about one third report prepubertal homosexual activity (Gebhard and Johnson, 1979). This would suggest that homosexual activity also plays an important part in the child's development.

Adolescent and postadolescent sexual behaviour

When Michael Schofield first published his report on the sexual behaviour of young people in 1965 he and his colleagues spent a considerable amount of time lecturing to audiences throughout Britain. Little was known then about adolescent sexual behaviour in Britain and those audiences (I was there) were fascinated (and often horrified) with what they heard. The same lecture given today, even if it were updated, would hardly draw an audience. However, then, the whole subject of premarital sex was charged emotionally almost to breaking point when the arguments were, amongst other things, about providing the unmarried with contraception, where nowadays it is about providing under-16s with contraception.

In the 1920s there was a significant increase in premarital sexual activity (Bell, 1966) but thereafter reportedly little change until the 1960s. Then over the last two decades there has been a further clearly defined change in the sexual behaviour of young people in the Western world which is documented by a large number of independent studies (see Table 2.3). Three trends are evident. First, there has been a significant and dramatic increase in premarital sexual activity, so much so that the concept of premarital sex has now lost much of its meaning. Second, some of the differences in sexual behaviour between the sexes, which in the 1960s were clearly evident, are slowly disappearing (Miller and Simon, 1974; Vener and Stewart, 1974 and later workers) though many remain such as the motives for intercourse (Carroll *et al.,* 1985). Third, differences in sexual behaviour between the social classes and some ethnic groups are also becoming less distinct.

The reasons for this recent increase in adolescent sexual activity in the early 1960s (see Figure 2.1), an increase reported throughout the Western world, are complex. An obvious candidate was thought to be the advent of the contraceptive pill but profound changes of this magnitude in human sexual behaviour cannot be so readily explained (Reiss, 1977). One contributory factor may have been that this generation of adolescents was the product of those marriages immediately following the Second World War. At this time there were changes in the attitudes of parents to discipline and sexuality, much of it due to a reaction against the arbitrary discipline they had received as children and which would have affected the way in which these post-war babies were reared. One of the consequences of this more permissive upbringing was the earlier and more overt expression of these youngsters' sexual behaviour after puberty.

As long ago as 1974 Farrel (1978) reported that roughly 1 in 2 16-year-old boys and 1 in 4 16-year-old girls in the UK had experienced intercourse, and by the time they were 18 nearly three quarters of the boys and over half the girls were coitally experienced. This contrasts dramatically with Schofield's (1965) estimates ten years previously when only 1 in 3 boys and 1 in 6 girls had reportedly had intercourse. It is not known what the figures might be now in 1988, but it would not be unreasonable to assume that at 18 *probably at least 75 per cent of boys and 60 per cent of girls are having intercourse.*

One must, however, continue to be conscious of the fact that the magnitude of the errors involved in collecting information of this kind is unknown and probably unknowable. For example, a comparison of the two recent surveys already referred to, namely that of MORI (1984) and that of Sanders (1985), reveal quite considerable differences in the age of first intercourse in young women (see Table 2.3), the latter reporting first intercourse at a much earlier age than the former. These differences can almost certainly be explained by the way in which the data were collected and highlight the

Table 2.3 Adolescent and postadolescent sexual behaviour – proportion who have experienced intercourse

Reference	*Male*	*Female*	*Comment*
Schofield (1965)	34% at 18	17% at 18	In 1964: (UK) almost certainly underestimates (see below*)
McCance and Hall (1972)	—	33% at 18	In 1971 (UK)
Kantner and Zelnik (1972)	—	18% at 16 32% at 18 } 1971	A comparison of sexual experience in roughly comparable samples in 1971 and 1976 of white girls in USA
Zelnik and Kantner (1977)	—	22% at 16 42% at 18 } 1976	
Hunt (1974)	Married (18–24) 95%	Married (18–24) 81%	In 1972 (US)
Tavris and Sadd (1977)	—	49% at 16–17 82% at 18–19	In 1974 (US)
Farrel (1978)	47% at 16 70% at 18	28% at 16 55% at 18	In 1974 (UK)

		♂		♀		
Gebhard and Johnson (1979) [from Kinsey *et al.* (1948, 1953)]		16	18	16	18	1938–1963 US males and females
	White college	15%	31%	3%	10%	
	White non-college	29%	44%	10%	24%	
	Black college	53%	70%	17%	37%	
Hite (1981)	30% at 16 56% at 18	—				In 1975 (US)
MORI (1984)	—	5% under 16 18% at 16–17 22% at 18–19 19% at 20–21		(cf. Sanders)		Quota sample (n = 513 UK women, 18+) April 1984
Sanders (1985)	—	♀♀ Now 22–25		♀♀ Now 41–60		* UK frequencies for the older women suggest that Schofield's (1965) data are underestimates
		20% under 16 45% at 16–18 25% at 19–21		10% under 16 35% at 16–18 30% at 19–21		

Figure 2.1 Accumulative incidence of sexual intercourse by age amongst UK teenagers for 1964 and 1974 (data from Schofield, 1965 and Farrel, 1978).
Girls are represented by circles: outline, 1964; solid, 1974.
Boys are represented by squares: outline, 1964; solid, 1974.
(Reproduced with permission from Bancroft, J. (1983) *Human Sexuality and Its Problems*, Churchill-Livingstone.)

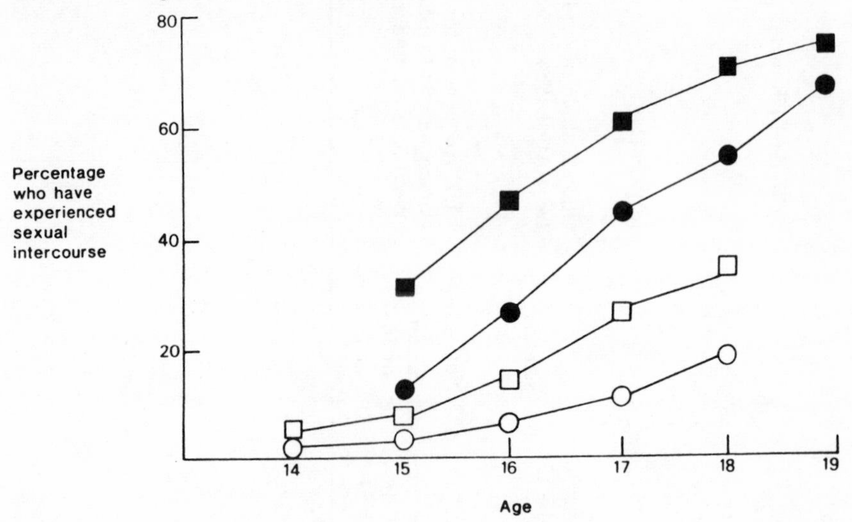

difficulties likely to be experienced in this sensitive area of data collection. However, any reservations that one might have about the reliability of these data do not conceal the fact that a very substantial number of young people are embarking on their sex lives much earlier than was the case a decade or so ago.

Many of the ethnic differences may however remain, notably the differences between the US blacks and the US whites (Gebhard and Johnson, 1979). There are also more subtle differences between northern and southern Europeans in their sexual behaviour and attitudes (Kinsey *et al.*, 1953; Littlewood, 1978) but one would predict that eventually, as with other trends discussed in this chapter, it will be the needs of the *individual,* rather than the characteristics of the *group* from which he or she is drawn, which will determine his or her sexual behaviour.

Intercourse – extramarital experience and number of partners

A few years ago any information on the incidence and frequency of extramarital intercourse would have commanded considerable attention. Today this kind of information has much less impact since extramarital sex is becoming a not infrequent event (see Table 2.4). Indeed, with the changing status of marriage, a corresponding increase in cohabitation and an increase in the prevalence of divorce (now at 42 per cent, OPCS Monitor [1985]) the concept of extramarital sex has (like that of premarital sex) lost much of its meaning.

Even without the benefit of any surveys the incidence of divorce and remarriage itself will provide a rough minimum estimate of the extent of extramarital sex in couples (or more precisely the expectation of extramarital sex). Table 2.4 gives a fuller picture from various cultures at various times. This information suggests that well over a third of men and perhaps between a tenth and a quarter of women had extramarital sexual experiences five to ten years ago. More recently Sanders (1985) reported that 30 per cent of her sample of UK women have had at least one affair since they were married and that 10 per cent were having one at the present time. Men appear to be more sexually adventurous than women but the interesting question is whether this will remain true following the impact of feminism.

A more detailed analysis from Hite (1981) is of some interest (see Table 2.4). She reports that whereas the mean incidence of extramarital intercourse amongst men was 66%, after two years of marriage this rose to 72%. However, after that the incidence remained more or less constant possibly suggesting that the increased risk of extramarital sex as a marriage lengthens has been more or less offset by the more inhibited behaviour of the older cohorts.

Quite obviously some of those who are described as having engaged in extramarital intercourse may have simply had one experience on a business trip, or on the other hand, they may have had a number of transient but meaningful affairs throughout their married lives yet both would appear as the same statistic. Symons (1979), quoting data from Hunt (on females) and Rubens (on males), sheds some further light on the extent of extramarital intercourse. Men had more extramarital sexual partners than women had. The proportion of women who had had more than 6–10 extramarital experiences was 16 per cent, whereas for the man it was 35 per cent. However, the modal frequency of 2–5 extramarital partners is the same for men and women (45 per cent and 44 per cent respectively).

Finally, Tavris and Sadd (1977), from a US sample, compared the incidence of extramarital sex between employed and unemployed wives. Extramarital intercourse was much more frequent amongst the working wives, presumably because of the available opportunities (see Table 2.4).

Whichever way Western culture is examined probably there are some sections of society where extramarital sex would be unthinkable. For example, introverted couples, those with a low sex drive or those with strong religious convictions might be less likely to experiment sexually, though Bell *et al.* (1975) suggest that the best predictor of extramarital sex is the degree to which the woman rates her marriage.

Table 2.4 Intercourse: extramarital experiences

Reference	*Men*	*Women*	*Notes*
Athanasiou *et al.* (1970)	40%	31%	
Gorer (1971)	8% of couples		UK sample
Hunt (1974)	41%	18%	US sample
Bell *et al.* (1975)	—	sub-samples vary from 0–81% [see p. 23]	US wives (n = 2262): provides analysis of factors likely to predict EMI
Pietropinto and Simenauer (1977)	43%	—	
Tavris and Sadd (1977)	Under 25: 20%; 25–29: 29%; 30–34: 30%	35–39: 39%; 40+: 40%	US wives in 1974
Gebhard and Johnson (1979) [from Kinsey *et al.* (1948)]	30%	20%	US white males and females
Davis and Fabris (1980)	41%	14%	Italian sample
Garde and Lunde (1980)	—	13%	40 year olds
Hite (1981)	1st year of marriage 16% 2–5 years of marriage >6% mean (white sample) 66% mean (m. 2 years or more) 72%		US husbands (1974–79)
Sanders (1985)	—	30% of sample 10% at any one time	UK sample

Intercourse – frequency

Most, if not all, infraprimate mammals are only sexually active at specific times of the year when the female is in oestrus. Some sexual experimentation may take place between seasons but this is rare. In the *Anthropoidea* (the apes) the females (like women) come into oestrus approximately once a month and it is at this time that the males show particular sexual interest in the females. However, they are not totally ignored at other times and in the apes we see the beginnings of non-reproductive and recreational sex. For example, sexual displays and coitus may be used to establish dominance over either another male or female, and the female in turn may allow copulation to turn off the male's aggression as a gesture of appeasement. Sex may be used by the female ape as a means of distraction, for example, to obtain food, and homosexual play amongst juveniles and adults and sex in pregnancy also provide examples of non-reproductive sex. However, the full development of recreational sex is only found in humans.

Unlike other mammals intercourse is not restricted biologically in man to any great extent, taking place as it does throughout the menstrual cycle, during pregnancy, before puberty and after menopause. However, whilst there are few, if any biological constraints on coitus in humans there are in many cultures social constraints which restrict the opportunity for intercourse. In many cultures intercourse is forbidden during menstruation, pregnancy and lactation. More specifically sex is forbidden in Ramadan for Moslems and the sex life of the orthodox Jew is rigorously regulated by rules which must be strictly adhered to. For example, in orthodox Jewry intercourse may not recommence after menstruation until after ritual washing and so the woman may determine the extent of her sex life by deciding whether and when to proceed with this ritual. The strict Hindu may have as many as 100 days a year during which intercourse is forbidden and this is not untypical of many other religions. Quite apart from the significance of these taboos in reinforcing the authority of the religion they have the added advantage of going some way to prevent habituation. For better or worse these cultural restraints are disappearing and once again we see the appearance of the needs of individuals (of high and low drive) taking precedence over these exogenous cultural determinants.

It is very difficult to summarize the data presented here because of the number of variables involved and the inadequacy of the information available. Moreover, much of the data is presented as mean frequencies giving little or no idea of variances which are likely to be large (but see Gebhard and Johnson, 1979, and Figure 2.2). The reader is referred particularly to Sanders (1985), who reports in detail on the frequency of intercourse in married and unmarried women (analysed for age) from a sample of respondents to *Woman*. It is interesting to compare her data with those from MORI

Table 2.5 Intercourse: frequency

	Sanders (1985)		*MORI (1984)*
	Unmarried	*Married*	
Every day	7%	5%	2%
5–6 times a week	—	—	3%
4–5 times a week	19%	10%	2%
3–4 times a week	—	—	7%
2–3 times a week	34%	29%	15%
Once or twice a week	—	—	17%
Once a week	19%	25%	—
Once or twice a month	12%	18%	9%
Less than once a month	7%	8%	8%
Never nowadays	3%	5%	24%
Refused to say	—	—	12%

(1984) (see Table 2.5). The differences in reported frequencies of intercourse doubtless result from the differing methods of sampling and highlight the problems experienced in obtaining reliable information. By way of a summary it is probably true to say that for a large number of couples intercourse is a regular weekly or twice weekly event (Tavris and Sadd, 1977). However, for many others intercourse may follow an episodic pattern and for a further unknown number it is very rare or has ceased altogether.

The mean frequency of intercourse naturally declines with age, see Figure 2.2 (Gebhard and Johnson, 1979; Sanders, 1985) and more particularly, where these are not confounded, with the age of the relationship. However, where marital coitus is supplemented by extramarital sex the overall decline in intercourse may be less dramatic. Both men (Pietropinto and Simenauer, 1977) and women (Chester and Walker, 1980) report that they would like to have more frequent intercourse than they are actually having.

Intercourse – duration

At first sight Kinsey's estimate that approximately three quarters of all US men ejaculate within two minutes of penetration seems surprising. Yet on reflection this is not quite so remarkable a statistic. Folklore will have it that many men can extend coitus continuously for half an hour or more, but there is little evidence that this is anywhere near the norm. For example, Gebhard and Johnson (1979) report that only 4 per cent of men claim to have lasted more than 20 minutes. On the other hand, using Kinsey's 'cleaned' data (i.e.

Figure 2.2 Mean frequency of sexual intercourse per week by age as reported by married men (the Kinsey data, Gebhard and Johnson, 1979).
Non-college males are represented by outline circles; the college males, solid circles.
(Reproduced with permission from Bancroft, J. (1983) *Human Sexuality and Its Problems*, Churchill-Livingstone.)

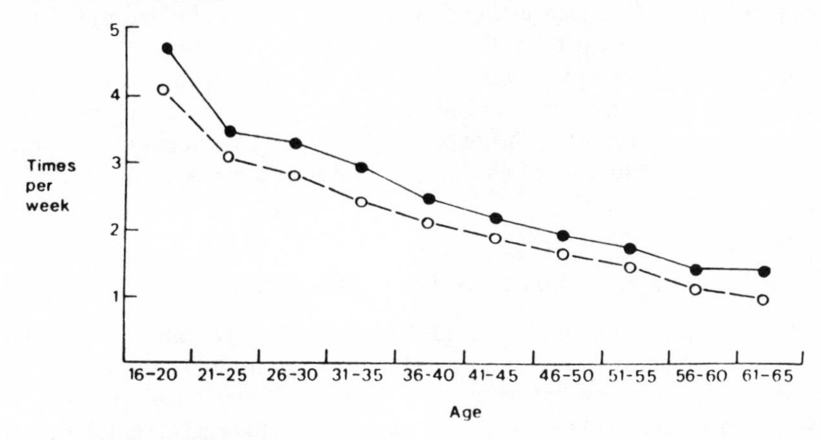

data from which has been removed those who were believed to have a sexual bias, e.g. those with criminal records, mental hospital patients etc.) their estimate of the number of men who ejaculate within 2 minutes of penetration drops to 33 per cent, with 60 per cent ejaculating within 5 minutes. Dickinson and Beam (1931) reported that 40 per cent of their sample of couples lasted less than 5 minutes though 9 per cent lasted more than half an hour. To add further confusion Hunt (1974) said that the median time for the duration of intercourse in his sample was 10 minutes. However, without a stop-watch by the bedside and a conscious and premeditated attempt to time intercourse, estimates must be inherently unreliable.

Amongst the lower mammals coitus is rarely an extended affair. In lions and the domesticated cat, for example, coitus lasts for only 5–10 seconds, as it does in bulls, stallions and elephants. When there is genital 'locking' as is found in dogs, foxes and wolves, coitus can be more protracted, but this is unusual. In the non-human primates intromission is also a brief event. This is typically shown in chimpanzees where coitus lasts for about 15 seconds and normally much less (Ford and Beach, 1965). Clearly, where the reproductive role of coitus takes precedence over its social role there is little purpose in extending its duration. Indeed, extended coitus could be a disadvantage where the animal may be at risk from predators or the female may lose interest and depart before ejaculation. In man clearly there are many social and psychological factors which would seem to favour the extension of coitus, though bearing in mind its non-reproductive significance in man it still appears to be a rather brief affair. There are few humans who could emulate the mink and sable where copulation has been known to last as long as 8 hours!

Of course, all these observations fail to take into account the simple fact that for many young couples, at least, intercourse is not simply a matter of sex play, intromission, thrusting and orgasm which can be precisely timed from start to finish. Instead coitus often consists of a leisurely sociosexual experience where sex play, conversation, penetration, withdrawal, perhaps interrupted by a cigarette or a drink, take place before one or more further penetrations and orgasm. This experience could not be meaningfully timed and of course could, and often does, extend over a considerable period of time.

Masturbation in the male

Almost all (but significantly not quite all) men have at some time in their lives masturbated to orgasm (see Table 2.6). From puberty onwards the incidence of self-masturbation increases rapidly until by the age of about 30, 94 per cent of men will have certainly masturbated to orgasm (Gebhard and Johnson, 1979). Hite (1981) reports that 99 per cent of her US sample had masturbated, but this must include those who did not masturbate to orgasm, either because it was not possible (the retarded ejaculator) or because ejaculation was not acceptable for one reason or another. Some individuals do not masturbate at all, either because of a low sex drive, wet dreams providing most of their orgasms or because intercourse from an early age provided a sufficiently fulfilling outlet. Whether some fail to masturbate simply as a result of guilt remains an open question though that explanation would seem less likely nowadays.

Hite also reports that 82 per cent of her male sample masturbated in a conventional manner, that is, stimulating the shaft or glans of the penis with their hands. The remainder usually used pelvic movements simulating intercourse on a pillow or bed (15 per cent) or rarely (1 per cent) masturbated by placing the penis between their legs. Water massage or self-fellatio made up a further 1 per cent. Cole (1986) found that in his UK sample (n = 184) of men suffering from sexual problems, 6 per cent had never masturbated and a further 10 per cent used the unconventional methods described by Hite, thereby showing little difference from the 'normal' population. This would suggest that, contrary to what had been previously suggested (Cauthery and Cole, 1971), neither the absence nor the use of unusual methods of masturbation can be regarded as a good indicator of poor psychosexual development.

In most males unsatisfied sexual needs are usually present and because available or suitable partners are not, masturbation will provide the obvious alternative outlet. However, Hunt (1974) reported that 72 per cent of young

Table 2.6 Incidence of masturbation

Reference		*Men*	*Women*
Davis (1929)		—	67%
Landis (1940)		—	54%
Schmidt and Sigusch (1972)		—	67%
Hunt (1974)	Religious	92%	51%
	Non-religious	93%	75%
Hite (1976)		—	85–90%
Tavris and Sadd (1977)		—	84% (since marriage)
Gebhard and Johnson (1979) [from Kinsey *et al.* (1948; 1953)]		94%*	62% and 40%*
Chester and Walker (1980)		—	64%
Garde and Lunde (1980)		—	47%
Nineteen (1980)		—	52%
Hite (1981)		99%	—
Sanders (1985)		—	66% unmarried 56% married
Cole (1986)		94% (dysfunctional)	—

* Masturbated to orgasm

husbands masturbated regularly with a median frequency, for a husband less than 35, of twice a month. This would suggest that masturbation is important for reasons other than a simple release from sexual tension and one of these reasons may be that masturbation provides an opportunity for sexual fantasy.

More detail on the frequency of masturbation is provided by Gebhard and Johnson (1979). As would be expected in those who masturbate the unmarried male has a higher mean frequency than the married male, this frequency falling from about three times a week at puberty to about once a week at 45. This compares to a mean frequency of rather less than once a week in the married man. Social class does not appear to have much effect.

Though some men do masturbate without accompanying sexual fantasies this is unusual (Gebhard and Johnson reported that 81–90 per cent of men fantasize during masturbation) and it is the tandem effect of erotic penile sensations and sexual fantasies potentiating each other that provides the greatest sexual reward. The role of masturbatory fantasies is twofold. They serve, in the adolescent, as an opportunity to rehearse the adult sexual repertoire (Cauthery and Cole, 1971) and throughout life can be regarded simply as normal play activity. At a physiological level the neurohormonal and secretory mechanisms involved in erection and ejaculation are kept 'tuned'. Indeed, the overall health of the prostate gland and genital apparatus may depend upon their regular stimulation and use.

There is a significant group of married men who never or rarely masturbate and when requested to do so, for example, in therapy or even exceptionally to produce a semen sample, are deeply uncomfortable about the prospect. The combination of a low sex drive, a sexually inhibited upbringing and/or a good sexual relationship with their partner probably accounts for this.

The anxiety and guilt which used to be associated with masturbation is not surprising in view of the easily available and risk-free sexual pleasure that the activity affords. Guilt of this kind, however, is less common than it was, at least in the Western world, though one should never underestimate the distress that this guilt has caused in the past.

A large number of male species of monkeys and apes regularly masturbate (Ford and Beach, 1965). Indeed, male masturbation in many other mammals is not at all rare, even when there are available females. This observation may not allay the fears of those few remaining authorities who regard masturbation as being in some way deviant, but it may help the behaviour to be seen in a more helpful perspective.

Masturbation in the female

Masturbation, whether to an orgasm or not, serves the same functions in a woman as it does in the man. It provides both a physiological and psychological release from sexual tension and in so doing exercises the appropriate neurohormonal mechanisms and gives an opportunity for sexual pleasure and play and sexual rehearsal by way of fantasy where this is present. The statistics on female masturbation (see Table 2.6) are less clear than in the male because not all authors specify whether they are referring to masturbation to orgasm or not – this being of more significance in females because of the elusive nature of their orgasms. To summarize it is probably fair to say that from the data about two thirds of women in the West have masturbated though not all will have achieved an orgasm in this way. According to Gebhard and Johnson (1979) the mean frequency of masturbation in women differs little over the lifespan. It amounts to rather less than once a week and does not appear to be affected by either marital status or social class.

Female sexual fantasies are a frequent, though not invariable, feature accompanying self-masturbation. Gebhard and Johnson found that about two thirds of women fantasize and many of these fantasies are bizarre and complex (Friday, 1976; Sanders, 1985). The techniques that women use to masturbate are much more varied than those used by men. A majority of women, perhaps nearly two thirds, mainly stimulate the clitoris and the labia to achieve arousal. Insertion of a finger or other object into the vagina is a relatively rare technique used by perhaps only 1 woman in 6. Other methods include pelvic thrusts on a pillow or mattress, crossing the legs, breast stimulation and fantasy alone. Little reliable data is forthcoming on the use of vibrators though in recent times, if sales of these and other devices are anything to go by, they must be used quite widely.

There is a large group of married women who, like men, do not masturbate (see Table 2.6), nor in many cases does the idea ever occur to them – indeed, many show a marked resistance to any suggestion that they might. This fact is particularly evident to those therapists whose task it is to treat patients with primary orgasmic dysfunction and who, it is believed, need to learn how to masturbate to orgasm as part of their therapeutic programme (Heiman *et al.*, 1976; Hooper, 1984).

No doubt with the passage of time and the increasing sexual awareness of women the incidence of female masturbation and its accompanying fantasy will increase. Any remaining differences between the sexes and between individual women will then reflect their individual needs rather than be a result of the overall effect of exogenous cultural factors.

Oral sex

Heterosexual oral sex, that is, stimulation of the vulva by the mouth of the man (cunnilingus) or stimulation of the penis by the mouth of the woman (fellatio) is clearly and unambiguously an important part of the normal sexual repertoire of men and women in the developed world (see Table 2.7), as it is no doubt also widespread elsewhere (Ford and Beach, 1965). It is less popular amongst the lower socioeconomic groups, amongst blacks and amongst those of the older generations and the long-marrieds (Pietropinto and Simenauer, 1977). Fellatio and cunnilingus appear to be more or less equally popular amongst men and women (Gebhard and Johnson, 1979), though Chester and Walker (1979) report that many women have a great desire for cunnilingus often in excess of their partner's ability to satisfy. Where differences in the practice of oral sex do exist these are likely to disappear in time, reflecting the general trend to cultural uniformity – those differences that remain once again expressing instead individual preferences.

There are obvious and clearly defined mammalian and primate precedents for oral sex where it can be readily observed in wild and domesticated animals. Its role there is clearly to do with the detection of pheromones which will, above all, indicate the state of oestrus in the female. Pheromones also act as appropriate behavioural releasers for each sex but particularly in the male. The recognition and transfer of pheromones in human oral sex is more conjectural but the popularity of these behaviours in man would suggest that they have more than a vestigial role to play.

Table 2.7 Incidence of oral sex

Reference	*Men*		*Women*	
	Cunnilingus	*Fellatio*	*Cunnilingus*	*Fellatio*
Hunt (1974)	College males in marriage 66%	College males in marriage 61%	College females in marriage 72%	College females in marriage 72%
Pietropinto and Simenauer (1977)	Enjoy it 55%	—	—	—
	Practise it to please 23%	—	—	—
Tavris and Sadd (1977) [women] Hite (1981) [men]	Do you like . . .	Do you like . . .	Often 39%	Often 40%
	Yes 88%	Yes 85%	Occasionally 48%	Occasionally 45%
	OK —	OK 5%	Once 6%	Once 6%
	No 9%	No 5%	Never 7%	Never 9%
	Never tried 3%	Never tried 5%		
Gebhard and Johnson (1979) [from Kinsey *et al*. (1948, 1953)]	College 40%	38%	50%	44%
	Non-college 26%	22%	38%	32%
	Black 14%	14%	15%	11%

Additionally, cunnilingus may conceivably play a role in partner selection there being a wide variation in the consciously perceived odour of the vulva to the male which may be 'read' as pleasant or otherwise.

Homosexual behaviour

Homosexual behaviour – that is, sexual preference for a person of one's own sex – is a significant though relatively rare feature of probably all human societies. It has been reported throughout history and from all societies. A distinction must be made between those who are exclusively homosexual and those who, on the other hand, are either to a greater or lesser extent bisexual or who report only very occasional homosexual experiences. Kinsey *et al.* (1948) dealt with this neatly in their homosexual-heterosexual ratings where they classify men on a 7-point scale: 0 representing those who are exclusively heterosexual; 6 those who are exclusively homosexual; and 3 where homosexual and heterosexual behaviours are equally balanced.

The incidence of homosexual behaviour in women is almost certainly lower than in men (see Table 2.8) and that observation is consistent with the general view that men engage in a much wider sexual repertoire than women (Wilson, 1979).

Probably about 3–5 per cent of men in Western society are exclusively or almost exclusively homosexual. That means that in the UK about half a million are active homosexuals at any one time. The number of women who are exclusively homosexual is probably only about 1 in 100. Apart from those who are regularly bisexual, additionally there are many men and women who have had at least one homosexual experience to orgasm as adults, and Kinsey puts this figure for men as rather more than 1 in 3. The corresponding proportion of women is much lower, probably about 1 in 5.

The causes of homosexual behaviour are still debated widely, and depending upon the motivation of the writer and the evidence cited the conclusions are either that it is largely biogenic, psychogenic or sociogenic (Goodman, 1986; Ruse, 1981). However, the fact that homosexual behaviour is found as a minority behaviour in almost all human societies (Ford and Beach, 1965) would suggest a biogenic element in the aetiology of homosexuality. However, the most persuasive argument in support of a genetic basis to homosexual behaviour is the fact that heterosexuality must have a high reproductive fitness value if the species is to survive. As a result the heterosexual-homosexual option could not be left to the chance effects of culture to decide. The risks would have been too high – instead the mechanism determining the direction of the sex drive would have evolved, at least in part, as a result of natural selection acting upon genetic factors.

Table 2.8 Incidence of homosexual behaviour

References	*Males*	*Females*
Kinsey *et al*. (1948)	4% white males exclusively homosexual throughout lives	Between 1–3% unmarried exclusively homosexual
and	37% had some homosexual experience (to orgasm) after adolescence	<0.3% married exclusively homosexual
Kinsey *et al*. (1953)	Approx. 50% of white males never had any homosexual experience	
Gagnon and Simon (1973)	Re-analysis of Kinsey *et al*. data (n = 2,900 college males):	Re-analysis of Kinsey *et al*. data:
	3% exclusively homosexual	<1% exclusively homosexual
	3% extensively homosexual and heterosexual	2% extensively homosexual
		6% at least one homosexual experience
Hunt (1974)	1–2% exclusively homosexual	2% single females mainly to exclusively homosexual
	17% had some homosexual experience after adolescence	
Pietropinto and Simenauer (1977)	1.3% homosexual	—
	3.1% bisexual	
Gebhard and Johnson (1979) [from Kinsey *et al*. (1948, 1953)]	c. 10% 'extensive' (>20 partners or >50 experiences) c. 63% none	c. 3.5% 'extensive' (>20 partners or >50 experiences) c. 86% none
Hite (1981)	9.0% homosexual	—
	6.0% bisexual	

'DYSFUNCTIONAL' SEXUAL BEHAVIOUR – INCIDENCES AND FREQUENCIES

Presentation at clinics

One would expect the distribution of sexual problems presenting in clinic populations roughly to reflect the frequency of these same problems in the general population and by and large this appears to be so, at least for men (see Table 2.9). Thus, problems associated with erection usually appear as the largest in clinic populations as they do also, so far as is known, in the general population. Likewise, premature ejaculation (subject to some ambiguities over definition) ranks second in most clinic samples once again corresponding to its reported incidence in a clinically recognizable form in the general population.

The situation is less clear with problems in women but the confusion arises largely as a result of difficulties over definition. For example, Masters and Johnson (1970) did not recognize the condition of general sexual dysfunction (Kaplan, 1974) but instead classified all their patients with blocks in arousal into the category of orgasmic dysfunction. Moreover, sexual disorders in women, with the possible exception of vaginismus, where intercourse is often prevented by the contraction of the vaginal muscles, are by their very nature less easily categorized because of the more complex nature of a woman's sexual responses.

There are also methodological difficulties which make the comparison of different clinic samples unsatisfactory. For example, Masters and Johnson (1970) report only *treated* cases the frequency of which may, or may not, have reflected the distribution of the cases which presented originally. Additionally, some patients will present to a clinic with a combination of problems (Bancroft, 1983) (e.g. with premature ejaculation and erectile dysfunction or general sexual dysfunction and orgasmic disorders) and the therapist may be unsure into which category to place them. The situation is further complicated when couples present with difficulties. A problem may be neglected or overlooked in one partner if the therapist considers that this problem is simply contingent upon the presenting problem in the other.

However, even with these limitations and qualifications, the distribution of presenting problems in clinics does bear a surprisingly close resemblance to what is believed to be the distribution of the same problems in the population at large – adding some credibility to the reports of incidence in the latter (see Table 2.9).

Problems with erection

There is no precise nor objective way by which one might define erectile

Table 2.9 Incidence of sexual problems presenting at clinics

Dysfunction	*Bancroft and Coles (1976)*	*Mears (1978)*	*Cole (1982)*	*Masters and Johnson (1970)*	*Heisler (1983)*	*Approximate estimate of dysfunction in general population*
Male	*(n = 98)*	*(n = 438)*	*(n = 130)*	*(n = 448)*	*(n = 553)*	
Erectile	42% (1)	37% (1)	37% (2)	55% (1)	35% (2)	7–20% ? (1) (Table 2.10)
Premature ejaculation	23% (2)	22% (2)	12% (3)	42% (2)	54% (1)	3–13% (2) (Table 2.11)
Retarded ejaculation	9% (4)	18% (3)	5% (5)	4% (3)	5% (4)	1–4% (4) (Table 2.12)
Homosexual and related problems	12% (3)	—	—	—	—	5% (3) (Table 2.8)
Deviance	9% (4)	6% (5)	2% (5)	—	—	?
Others	4% (6)	7% (4)	44%* (1)	—	6% (3)	?
Female	*(n = 102)*	*(n = 1330)*	*(n = 20)*	*(n = 342)*	*(n = 843)*	
General sexual	62% (1)	51% (1)	25% (2)	—	29% (2)	?
Orgasmic	18% (2)	22% (2)	30% (1)	91% (1)	56% (1)	5–40% (Table 2.13)
Vaginismus/ Dyspareunia	12% (3)	18% (3)	15% (3)	9% (2)	15% (3)	4% (Table 2.14)
Others	8% (4)	9% (4)	30% (1)	—	—	

* Including 51 'heterophobic' patients.
Numbers in parentheses represent the rank order.

dysfunction, though to the sufferer the impact of this disorder is dramatic and clear-cut enough. The severity of the condition may vary from a total lack of response both in self-masturbation and when attempting intercourse through various degrees of potency so that penetration may be achieved occasionally in certain circumstances but perhaps only with a partial erection.

These problems of definition make the incidence reported in Table 2.10 inherently unreliable and so it is somewhat surprising to find quite a good measure of agreement from the different sources. It appears that about 7 per cent of men are likely to develop severe erectile problems some time in their lives, though as Kinsey *et al.*'s (1948) data illustrate, since the failure of the erectile responses is highly correlated with age, the age-structure of any sample must be taken into consideration.

In human terms these figures, if they can be applied to the UK, mean that about three quarters of a million men suffer from severe erectile difficulties. These difficulties not only will dramatically affect the quality of their sex lives but may also, in many cases, affect the quality and stability of their relationships. Perhaps of even greater significance is the fact that if a man with profound erectile problems has no relationship he has a much poorer chance of ever establishing one, particularly when he is young (Cole, 1986).

Problems with ejaculation – too soon

The fact that most authors are agreed that there can be no satisfactory definition of premature ejaculation has not deterred them, more often than not, from providing their own special definitions. Such definitions fall into two categories: those which use the 'stop-watch concept' and regard the time between penetration and ejaculation as diagnostic and those which rely upon subjective reporting of satisfaction or otherwise – these subjective feelings on the part of the man may or may not take into consideration the feelings of his partner.

Masters and Johnson (1970) propose that a man should be regarded as a premature ejaculator if he could not provide his partner with an orgasm on at least 50 per cent of occasions! Whilst their attempt to involve the partner in this definition of premature ejaculation is admirable most sex therapists would regard this attempt as having gone too far – particularly since up to 70 per cent of women may be non-orgasmic in intercourse (Sanders, 1985). On the other hand, a strict adherence to a 'lasting time' is equally unsatisfactory and in a clinical situation obviously both the objective and subjective aspects of the problem must be taken into account. Kinsey *et al.* (1948) tried to achieve this. They report that three quarters of the married men they interviewed ejaculated within two minutes of vaginal penetration yet only 6 per cent of the same sample regarded premature ejaculation as a problem.

Table 2.10 Incidence of erectile dysfunction

Reference		
Kinsey *et al.* (1948)	0.1% at 20 0.8% at 30 1.9% at 40 6.7% at 50 18.4% at 60 27.0% at 70 50% at 70+	his well-known distribution curve: more or less total erectile dysfunction (mean 1.6%)
Frank *et al.* (1978)	7% 9%	'difficulty in getting erection' 'difficulty in maintaining erection'
Nettelbladt and Uddenburg (1979)	7%	failure to get an erection on at least 50% of occasions
Gebhard and Johnson (1979) [from Kinsey *et al.* (1948)]	7% 36% 57%	'more than incidental' incidental never (n = 3,331)
Catalan *et al.* (1981)	7%	

Some authors have reported that premature ejaculation is the commonest sexual problem in men and if one simply takes subjective reporting (see Table 2.11) as an indication this would appear to be so (e.g. Hite, 1981; Frank *et al.*, 1978 and Nettelbladt and Uddenberg, 1979). As many as 1 man in 3 wishes he could last longer or feels that he has ejaculated too soon. However, this is not premature ejaculation in the strict sense of the term.

Table 2.11 Incidence of premature ejaculation (PE)

Reference	
Kinsey *et al.* (1948)	Approximately 6% of men regarded PE as a problem
Frank *et al.* (1978)	36% 'ejaculated too quickly'
Gebhard and Johnson (1979) [from Kinsey *et al.* (1948)]	3.8% said they ejaculated within 1 minute of penetration <1% said they ejaculated within half a minute of penetration
Nettelbladt and Uddenberg (1979)	20–40% of married men
Catalan *et al.* (1981)	13% (patients at an STD clinic)
Hite (1981)	Do you ever have orgasm too soon after penetration? Yes 71% No 29%

Moreover, if note is taken of clinic attendance (see Table 2.9) then premature ejaculators rank usually either second or third in the presentation frequency.

Even quite severe premature ejaculation appears to be better tolerated by couples than comparable problems with erection. The divorce rate of those with premature ejaculation is lower than that of those with erectile problems and the fertility of quick ejaculators is hardly impaired at all (Cole, 1986). What appears to emerge from the reported incidences of premature ejaculation is that their range corresponds very roughly to the reported incidences for female orgasmic dysfunction (see Table 2.13). If one takes the view that these two behaviours represent the opposite tails of the distribution curve of the liability to anorgasmia (Cole, 1985) then just as it can be argued that female orgasmic difficulties should not be regarded as a dysfunction because they are so common the same interpretation might be assumed for premature ejaculation.

In spite of all this an objective measure of premature ejaculation would be very useful. It might therefore be helpful to measure the interval between penetration and ejaculation not in seconds but in 'thrusts'. At least it is easier to count thrusts than keep an eye on the clock!

Problems with ejaculation – too late

The rarity of ejaculatory (and hence orgasmic) problems in men contrasts strikingly with women when orgasmic problems are extremely frequent. Retarded ejaculation in men (Masters and Johnson, 1970, called it ejaculatory incompetence) is not always a clear-cut and qualitative lack of response. Ejaculation and orgasm may be possible in self- and partner-masturbation or in sleep but not in intercourse. In its rare and absolute form ejaculation and orgasm have never been experienced in any circumstances. On the other hand some men simply have difficulty ejaculating in some circumstances and at some times but not in others.

The reports from the published literature are sparse but all are agreed that this disorder is rare and is probably only found with any degree of severity in about 1 per cent of men (see Table 2.12).

Problems with orgasm in women

Table 2.13 provides reports from 19 studies all attempting to estimate the incidence and frequency of orgasm in intercourse in women drawn from different countries, ethnic groups, marital status and age. Only a brief glance at the table reveals a very wide variation in the reports. For example, Hite (1976) found, in a large group of US women (n = 3,000), which was

Table 2.12 Incidence of retarded ejaculation

Reference	
Kinsey *et al.* (1948)	0.15% (n = 4,108)
Hunt (1974)	4%
Frank *et al.* (1978)	Absolute 0% Difficulty in ejaculating 4%
Nettelbladt and Uddenberg (1979)	c. 4%
Catalan *et al.* (1981)	1%

admittedly heavily biased in favour of those who were single, feminist and sexually liberated, that 29 per cent had never or almost never experienced an unassisted orgasm in intercourse. Whilst in contrast Garde and Lunde (1980) report that only 4 per cent of Danish women (n = 225) were non-orgasmic. A woman's capacity to achieve an orgasm in intercourse has a multifactorial causation. Kinsey *et al.* (1953) identify at least five factors: the woman's intrinsic (biogenic) capacity to be orgasmic in coitus, her age, educational background, decade of birth and her premarital orgasmic experience. To these might also be added her marital state (Sanders, 1985), the perceived sexual status of her partner and of course whether she was using additional stimulation in coitus. In view of these complexities it is not surprising that, depending upon the composition of the sample questioned, such a large variation is found in the prevalence of so-called coital orgasmic dysfunction.

One of the most recent and comprehensive reports on the incidence of female orgasm is that of Sanders (1985) to which the reader is referred. From her final sample of 4,000 married and single women she found that 4 per cent of wives and 15 per cent of unmarried women never achieved an *assisted* orgasm in '*love-making*' (which presumably included activities other than intercourse) by any means. This difference between the married and unmarried groups was statistically significant. When the same two groups were asked about their ability to achieve *unassisted* orgasm in *intercourse* a striking 60 per cent of the wives and 80 per cent of the unmarried women reported that they had never had an unassisted orgasm, a difference which again is statistically significant. Two points emerge from this.

The first point is that 'unassisted anorgasmia' in intercourse would appear from this survey to be the 'norm', particularly in the unmarried group. This adds weight to the view that coital orgasmic dysfunction should not be regarded as a sexual disorder *per se* (Cole, 1985). Second, the observation that the unmarried (in this case single, divorced and separated) are less likely to be orgasmic than the married women would support the view that the ability to achieve orgasm may help a woman to form and maintain a stable relationship (or conversely a lack of orgasm may make it more difficult).

The observed association between the facility to form a stable bond and the ability to be orgasmic raises many questions since neither variable is likely to be causally related to the other in a simple manner. I had earlier gained the impression that this correlation did exist from clinical impressions, and it is nice to see some statistical evidence in support of it. One interpretation would be that women who found orgasms elusive would be more sexually active with a variety of partners because they were seeking out new relationships in the hope that their 'problem' would be resolved. In some cases there is no doubt that this 'adaptive' behaviour pays off but clearly even this explanation is oversimplistic.

Although Sanders' (1985) data are supported to some extent by those of Hite (1976) they give a strikingly different picture to most other reports (see Table 2.13). They must be accepted with caution and make any summary almost impossible.

It can be said, however, that if these reports do approximate to reality then there is little sense in continuing to regard 'female orgasmic dysfunction' as a sexual disorder in the accepted sense of that word. Instead the facility (or liability) (Cole, 1985) to achieve an orgasm is better regarded as a continually varying characteristic which may or may not be expressed depending upon a woman's genetic predisposition (to be orgasmic) and her experiential (remote and immediate) history. Identifying the absence of orgasm in a woman as 'dysfunctional' is not only intellectually unacceptable but it can also be therapeutically counterproductive. It will be counterproductive because it will create additional performance anxiety in those who are already concerned about the difficulties they are having obtaining an orgasm.

The data presented here, although of interest, do little to help explain why some women are orgasmic and others are not, and until some relevant causal factors can be firmly identified treatment programmes will only have limited success (Cole, 1985).

Masters and Johnson (1970) believe that a woman is absolutely certain when she has had an orgasm; moreover, they also believe that her partner could also be equally certain of her orgasmic behaviour. This is not a view that I think many would hold nowadays; indeed, many women themselves often report that they do not know whether they are orgasmic. If women are uncertain about their orgasms it does little to increase one's confidence in the data presented here and the assumption, if it is still held, that orgasm in women is an all or nothing event must be challenged. Indeed, even some men report being unsure of any clear-cut sensory reward at ejaculation. There is therefore likely to be in both sexes, though particularly in women

Table 2.13 Incidence of female orgasmic dysfunction

Reference	Sample	Incidence of orgasm in intercourse				
		Never or almost never	*Sometimes*	*Usually*	*Usually with assistance*	*Always or almost always*
Dickinson and Beam (1931) p. 63	Clinical sample of US married couples and singles (n = 422)	26% (+ 14% rarely)	15%	2%	3%	40%
Terman (1951)	800 middle-class married couples	8%	22%	—	—	—
Kinsey *et al.* (1953)	Kinsey *et al.* sample (n = 8,000)	12%	16%	27%	—	45%
Chesser (1956)	English married women (n = 200)	5% (+ 10% rarely)	26%	45%	—	22%
Athanasiou *et al.* (1970)	Approx. 10,000 US ♀ respondents to *Psychology Today*: maj. <30 yrs.	20%	20%	15%	—	45%
Tavris and Sadd (1971)	10,000 married US women	7% (+ 11% rarely)	19%	48%	—	15%
Fisher (1973)	300 US married women in early to middle 20s	5%	—	—	57%	38%
Hunt (1974)	Married white US women	7%	8% (25% of occs.)	32% (50–70% of occs.)	—	53%
Kaplan (1974)	US couples	—	—	—	—	35%
Hite (1976)	3,000 US women (only 38% married)	29%	22%	—	19%	30%

Levine and Yost (1976)	30–39 year old black ♀♀ att. gyn. clinic for non-sexual complaints	17%	24% (33–50% of occs.)	59% (67–100% of occs.)	—	—
Pietropinto and Simenauer (1977)	Representative sample US men (n = 4,066) (reported by male!)	5% (0–10% of occs.) N.B. 13% not sure	26% (10–60% of occs.)	26% (60–90% of occs.)	—	30%
Frank *et al*. (1978)	White, well-educated happily married couples (n = 100)	15%	—	—	—	—
Gebhard and Johnson (1979)	Kinsey *et al*. sample (n = 2,360)	c. 12%	—	—	—	c. 37%
Chester and Walker (1980)	Married and unmarried UK women (n = 2,289)	19% (+ 17% rarely)	5% (<50% of occs.)	5% (c. 50% of occs.)	5% (>50% of occs.)	36%
Garde and Lunde (1980)	Danish women aged 40 (n = 225)	4%	15%	61%	—	19%
Catalan *et al*. (1981)	Patients at STD clinic (n = 70)	37%	—	—	—	—
Golombok *et al*. (1984)	Random sample UK women (GP patients) (n = 30)	17% (+ 13% rarely)	—	—	—	—
Sanders (1985)*	4,000 UK respond-ents to *Woman* magazine — wives:	4%	38%	43%	—	15%
	unmarried:	15%	44%	41% (usually or always)	—	—

* These figures refer to 'love-making', see text for incidence of orgasm in intercourse.

Table 2.14 Incidence of vaginismus

Reference	
Pasini (1977)	1–2%
Catalan *et al.* (1981)	4%

where orgasm is a more precarious event, not only a qualitative difference in response but a quantitative difference in frequency and in intensity.

Vaginismus

Very little is known or has been written about the incidence and epidemiology of vaginismus. Once again we are necessarily confronted with the problems of definition since it is well known that many women often experience mild symptoms of vaginismus at the beginning of their sex lives but these disappear of their own accord without treatment. However, severe vaginismus will prevent intercourse or make it intolerable because of the accompanying pain (dyspareunia) – this level of severity makes the condition qualitatively distinct from a whole range of milder symptoms. It is the incidence of this disabling spastic contraction of the vaginal musculature in preventing intercourse which is of particular interest and is described here as vaginismus.

Estimates of the incidence of this form of incapacitating vaginismus are put at about 1–4 per cent of the population (see Table 2.14), but reliable data are sparse. Kinsey *et al.* (1953), though not referring specifically to vaginismus, report that about 2 per cent of their sample had not consummated their relationship, but there may have been other good reasons for this non-consummation apart from vaginismus. Most sex therapists will have seen many more cases of vaginismus than retarded ejaculation and one might therefore assume that the former is more frequent than the latter but by how much would be, at the moment, difficult to determine.

CONCLUSION

Despite the difficulties described earlier which bedevil the collection of reliable information about human sexual behaviour it is hoped that the broad picture presented here will have provided some insight into the nature and extent of human sexual activity.

The researcher, however, is faced with an ever-changing situation and it is evident that over the last 30 years in particular very significant changes have taken place in the way in which human sexual relationships are organized. Most dramatically these changes can be seen in the phenomenal increase in adolescent sexual activity and to a lesser extent in the rise in 'extramarital' sex. These new patterns of behaviour can be seen throughout the developed world and have affected the lives of millions of individuals.

If data were available no doubt other recent secular trends could be detected in the incidence of, for example, female masturbation, oral sex and homosexual behaviour. However, these trends can only be guessed at, though one may cautiously surmise that the human species as a whole is much more innovative and sexually uninhibited overall than it has ever been before. The most serious deficiency in the presentation of data of this kind however is that by focusing on *mean* incidences and frequencies of a behaviour, the variability of the population and hence the responses of the individual are often masked and ignored.

Thus whilst comparisons between, for example, men and women, different ethnic groups, social classes or age cohorts often reveal interesting and significant differences in sexual behaviour, there is considerable evidence to show that these differences are beginning to disappear as social pressures become more relaxed. Instead one finds that the needs of the *individual* rather than the characteristics of the *group* from which he or she is drawn determine his or her sexual behaviour. This is because as environments become equalized and increasingly optimized the biological needs of the individual begin to take precedence over the masking effects of cultural pressures.

Predictions about changes in human sexual behaviour in the future, always difficult, have now become almost impossible with the arrival of AIDS (HIV). For the time being, therefore, we can only reflect upon the wholly unpredictable effect the arrival of this virus will have on mankind.

REFERENCES

Athanasiou, R., Shaver, P. and Tavris, C. (1970) Sex, *Psychology Today,* 4 July, pp. 39–52.

Bancroft, J. (1983) *Human Sexuality and Its Problems*, Churchill-Livingstone, London.

Bancroft, J. and Coles, L. (1976) Three years' experience in a sexual problems clinic, *British Medical Journal*, i, pp. 1575–7.

Bell, R.R. (1966) *Premarital Sex in a Changing Society,* Prentice-Hall, Englewood Cliffs, NJ.

Bell, R.R., Turner, S. and Rosen, L. (1975) A multivariate analysis of female extramarital coitus, *Journal of Marriage and the Family,* Vol. 37, pp. 375–84.

Carroll, J.L., Yolk, K.D. and Hyde, J.S. (1985) Differences between males and females in motives for engaging in sexual intercourse, *Archives of Sexual Behavior*, Vol. 14, No. 2, pp. 131–40.

Catalan, J., Bradley, M., Gallwey, J. and Hawton, K. (1981) Sexual dysfunction and psychiatric morbidity in patients attending a clinic for sexually transmitted diseases, *British Journal of Psychiatry*, Vol. 138, pp. 292–6.
Cauthery, P. and Cole, M.J. (1971) *The Fundamentals of Sex*, W.H. Allen, London.
Chesser, E. (1956) *The Sexual, Marital and Family Relationships of the English Woman*, Hutchinson Medical Publications, London.
Chester, R. and Walker, C. (1980) Sexual experience and attitudes of British women, in W.H.G. Armytage, R. Chester and J. Peel (eds) *Changing Patterns of Sexual Behaviour*, Academic Press, London.
Cole, M.J. (1982) Surrogates and sexual dysfunction, *British Journal of Sexual Medicine*, Vol. 9, pp. 13–20.
Cole, M.J. (1985) Sex therapy – a critical appraisal, *British Journal of Psychiatry*, Vol. 147, pp. 337–51.
Cole, M.J. (1986) Socio-sexual characteristics of men with sexual problems, *Sexual and Marital Therapy*, Vol. 1, pp. 89–108.
Davis, K.B. (1929) *Factors in the Sex Life of Twenty-two Hundred Women*, Harper, New York.
Davis, R. and Fabris, G. (1980) The sexual life cycle in a male supremacist Catholic society: the case of Italy, in R. Forelo and W. Pasini (eds) *Medical Sexology*, Elsevier/North Holland, Amsterdam.
Dickinson, R.L. and Beam, L. (1931) *A Thousand Marriages*, Williams and Wilkins Co., Baltimore.
Farrel, C. (1978) *My Mother Said . . . the Way Young People Learn about Sex and Birth Control*, Routledge & Kegan Paul, London.
Fisher, S. (1973) *The Female Orgasm: Psychology Fantasy*, Basic Books, New York.
Ford, C.S. and Beach, F.A. (1965) *Patterns of Sexual Behaviour*, Methuen, London.
Frank, E., Anderson, C. and Rubinstein, D. (1978) Frequency of sexual dysfunction in 'normal' couples, *New England Journal of Medicine*, Vol. 299, pp. 111–5.
Frenken, J. (1976) *Afkeer van Seksualiteit*, Van Loghum Slaterus-Deventer (English Summary).
Friday, N. (1976) *My Secret Garden: Women's Sexual Fantasies*, Quartet, London.
Gagnon, J. and Simon, W. (1973) *Sexual Conduct: The Sources of Human Sexuality*, Aldine, Chicago.
Garde, K. and Lunde, I. (1980) Female sexual behaviour. A study in a random sample of 40-year-old women, *Maturitas*, Vol. 2, pp. 225–40.
Gebhard, P.H. and Johnson, A.B. (1979) *The Kinsey Data: Marginal Tabulations of the 1938–1963 Interviews Conducted by the Institute for Sex Research*, W.B. Saunders Company, Philadelphia.
Golombok, S., Rust, J. and Pickard, C. (1984) Sexual problems encountered in general practice, *British Journal of Sexual Medicine*, Vol. 11, pp. 210–2.
Goodman, R.E. (1986) Genetic and hormonal factors in human sexuality: evolutionary and developmental perspectives, in G. Wilson (ed.) *Variant Sexuality: Research and Theory*, Croom Helm, London.
Gorer, G. (1971) *Sex and Marriage in England Today*, Nelson, London.
Heiman, J., LoPiccolo, L. and LoPiccolo, J. (1976) *Becoming Orgasmic: A Sexual Growth Program for Women*, Prentice-Hall, Englewood Cliffs NJ.
Heisler, J. (1983) *Sexual Therapy in the National Marriage Guidance Council*, National Marriage Guidance Council, Rugby.
Hite, S. (1976) *The Hite Report*, Macmillan Publishing Company, New York.
Hite, S. (1981) *The Hite Report on Male Sexuality*, Macdonald, London.

Hooper, A. (1984) *The Body Electric*, Unwin Paperbacks, London.
Hunt, M. (1974) *Sexual Behavior in the 1970s*, Playboy Press, Chicago.
Kantner, J.F. and Zelnik, M. (1972) Sexual experience of young unmarried women in the United States, *Family Planning Perspectives*, Vol. 4, pp. 9–18.
Kaplan, H.S. (1974) *The New Sex Therapy*, Brunner/Mazel, New York.
Kaplan, H.S. (1979) *Disorders of Sexual Desire*, Baillière Tindall, London.
Kinsey, A.C., Pomeroy, W.B., Martin, C.E. and Gebhard, P.H. (1948) *Sexual Behavior in the Human Male*, W.B. Saunders Company, Philadelphia and London.
Kinsey, A.C., Pomeroy, W.B., Martin, C.E. and Gebhard, P.H. (1953) *Sexual Behavior in the Human Female*, W.B. Saunders Company, Philadelphia and London.
Landis, C. (1940) *Sex in Development*, Hoeber, New York.
Levine, S.B. and Yost, M.A. (1976) Frequency of sexual dysfunction in a general gynecological clinic: an epidemiological approach, *Archives of Sexual Behavior*, Vol. 5, pp. 229–38.
Littlewood, B. (1978) South Italian couples, in M. Corbin (ed.) *The Couple*, Penguin, London.
Market and Opinion Research International (MORI) (1984) Sex, love and marriage, *British Public Opinion*, Vol. VI, No. 4, pp. 6, 7 (on behalf of the *Sunday Times*).
Masters, W.H. and Johnson, V.E. (1970) *Human Sexual Inadequacy,* J.A. Churchill, London.
McCance, C. and Hall, D.J. (1972) Sexual behaviour and contraceptive practices of unmarried female undergraduates at Aberdeen University, *British Medical Journal*, ii, pp. 694–700.
Mears, E. (1978) Sexual problem clinics: an assessment of the work of 26 doctors trained by the Institute of Psychosexual Medicine, *Public Health,* Vol. 92, pp. 218–33.
Miller, P.Y. and Simon, W. (1974) Adolescent sexual behavior: context and change, *Social Problems,* Vol. 22, pp. 58–76.
Nettelbladt, P. and Uddenberg, N. (1979) Sexual dysfunction and sexual satisfaction in 58 married Swedish men, *Journal of Psychosomatic Research*, Vol. 23, pp. 141–7.
Nineteen (1980) *The Nineteen Survey*, April.
Office of Populations, Censuses and Surveys (OPCS) Monitor (October 1985) *Divorces, 1984*, Government Statistical Service, London.
Pasini, W. (1977) Unconsummated and partially consummated marriage as sources of procreative failure, in J. Money and H. Musaph (eds) *Handbook of Sexology*, Elsevier/North Holland, Amsterdam.
Pietropinto, A. and Simenauer, J. (1977) *Beyond the Male Myth. A nationwide survey*, Times Books, New York.
Reiss, I.L. (1977) Changing sociosexual mores, in J. Money and H. Musaph (eds) *Handbook of Sexology*, Elsevier/North Holland, Amsterdam.
Ruse, M. (1981) Are there gay genes? Sociobiology and homosexuality, *Journal of Homosexuality*, Vol. 6, No. 4, pp. 5–34.
Sanders, D. (1985) *The* Woman *Book of Love and Sex*, Sphere, London.
Schmidt, G. and Sigusch, V. (1972) Changes in the sexual behavior among young males and females between 1960 and 1970, *Archives of Sexual Behavior*, Vol. 1, pp. 293–308.
Schofield, M. (1965) *The Sexual Behaviour of Young People*, Longmans, London.

Sorenson, R.C. (1973) *Adolescent Sexuality in Contemporary America*, World Publishing, New York.

Symons, D. (1979) *The Evolution of Human Sexuality*, Oxford University Press, Oxford.

Tavris, C. and Sadd, S. (1977) *The Redbook Report on Female Sexuality*, Delacorte Press, New York.

Terman, L.M. (1951) Correlates of orgasm adequacy in a group of 556 wives, *Journal of Psychology*, Vol. 32, pp. 115–72.

Vener, A.M. and Stewart, C.S. (1974) Adolescent sexual behavior in middle America revisited 1970–73, *Journal of Marriage and the Family*, Vol. 36, pp. 728–35.

Wilson, G. (1979) The sociobiology of sex differences, *Bulletin of the British Psychological Society*, Vol. 32, pp. 350–3.

Zelnik, M. and Kantner, J.F. (1977) Sexual and contraceptive experience of young unmarried women in the United States, 1976 and 1971, *Family Planning Perspectives*, Vol. 9, pp. 55–71.

CHAPTER 3

THE SOCIOBIOLOGICAL BASIS OF SEXUAL DYSFUNCTION

Glenn D. Wilson

Our sexual behaviour is controlled by phylogenetically ancient parts of our brain and therefore is best understood at the level of instinct, within the concepts of ethology and sociobiology. In fact, the 'reproductive imperative' is the ultimate principle underlying all human behaviour, since animals survive in proportion to their breeding success. As I have argued previously (Wilson, 1981a), evolutionary analysis can throw a great deal of light on sexual behaviour, both normal and 'problematical'.

Ethology (the study of instincts) is a long-standing branch of biology. Sociobiology is not an entirely new discipline but an extension of ethology towards the evolutionary explanation of apparently complex social behaviour such as competition, altruism and mating (Wilson, 1975). A major impetus to sociobiology came from the recent recognition that the primary unit of survival is not 'the good of the species', or even the individual animal, but the actual genes (Dawkins, 1976). It is now widely accepted among biologists that animals are just transitory machines designed by evolution for optimal replication of genes. In a sense, genes 'strive to reproduce themselves as much as possible' using the body and behaviour of the carrier animal in their service.

This insight produced great gains in the understanding of social behaviour. For example, the occurrence of altruism can now be predicted on the basis of the proportion of genes shared by the helper and the helped. When it comes to the analysis of mating behaviour, sex is discovered to be a divisive influence, containing the seeds of a great deal of the marital conflict and clinical phenomena that we observe so frequently (Wilson, 1975; Wallace, 1979).

PARENTAL INVESTMENT

The key to understanding male and female sexuality, and especially the difference between them, is to be found in the concept of 'parental investment' (Trivers, 1972). The idea is that females produce eggs, which are large and few in number and therefore at a greater premium than male sperm, which are small and plentiful. In the human case, for example, a woman produces only a few hundred eggs in her lifetime, whereas a man produces millions of sperm with each ejaculation, and this may occur several times a day. The result is that females 'invest' more time and energy in the care and upbringing of their offspring than do males, and this difference is held to be basic to most of the gender differences in body, brain and behaviour that are common to nearly all primates and mammals. These are summarized in Table 3.1; for complete documentation see Ellis (1986).

Perhaps most relevant for present purposes is the predatory nature of male sex drive, as contrasted with female selectivity. For the male, with his almost unlimited supply of sperm the optimal reproductive strategy (from the point of view of 'the selfish gene') is to impregnate many females simultaneously, hence his interest in multiple mates of breeding age. From the female point of view, no advantage is gained from multiple partners – only one pregnancy can occur at a time. Rather, the survival of the offspring depends upon the quality of the father and his willingness to support them – hence the coyness of women and their need to build relationships.

Another important difference between eggs and sperm is that eggs are

Table 3.1 Gender differences expected on the basis of evolutionary theory and observed empirically

	Males	*Females*
Physical:	Greater size and strength	Lesser size and strength
	Capacity for short-term energy output	Capacity for endurance
Mental:	Spatial and mathematical skills	Verbal and social skills
	Rationality	Empathy
Temperamental:	Sexual initiation and exploration	Sexual selectivity and relationship seeking
	Aggression	Nurturance
	Independence	Attachment
	Psychopathy	Emotionality
	Dominance	Submission

Source Wilson, 1987a.

present in the female's body from birth and are therefore susceptible to environmental damage of one sort or another, such as radiation or chemical interference. This means that as a woman gets older there is an increased chance that her offspring will be deformed in some way. While mutations are occasionally beneficial to the species as a whole, the majority of them are detrimental, so any individual woman is generally better off having her babies when young. A man's sperm are little altered by his age since they are manufactured afresh on each occasion. As he gets older he becomes slightly less virile and less fertile because his ejaculate is less concentrated and his orgasms more widely spaced, but he remains theoretically capable of producing healthy children until his dying day. The best-known example of genetic damage to human babies, Down's syndrome, is much more likely to occur if the mother is approaching menopause, whereas the age of the father is fairly irrelevant.

These two important differences have led to clear differences in the typical mating behaviour of men and women. Although there is much overlap between the sexes, men are more inclined towards casual sex, and youth and novelty in partners, whereas women are more interested in stable and loving relationships in which devoted attention is paid to them (Symons, 1979; Wilson, 1981a). This difference is illustrated in a comparison of the frequency of various themes appearing in the sexual fantasies of men and women (Table 3.2). Group sex themes and visual 'turn-ons' predominate in men, whereas women are more likely to incorporate their partner in the fantasy and attend to details of the setting.

Parental investment theory comfortably explains the differences between men and women as regards what attracts them in the opposite sex (Wilson and Nias, 1976). Men are typically seeking what they describe as physically attractive women, by which they mean indications of 'fertile ground in which to plant their seed'. The woman should be young (so her eggs have not deteriorated), she should have clear eyes and an unblemished complexion (indicating health), she is more desirable with proportionately large breasts and hips (the better to bear children), and the narrow waist is attractive because it signifies that she is not already pregnant (no sense in wasting time and semen if she is).

Women are seeking evidence that a man is superior breeding material, which means physical strength and skills relevant to defence and provision and willingness to share the burden of child-rearing. Since the evolutionary history of *Homo sapiens* is parallel with a shift of emphasis from brute strength to intelligence most women today are more impressed with the latter. To some extent, each sex shares the interests of the other, for there are also evolutionary limits set on the degree of divergence between the sexes.

Table 3.2 Main elements of anonymously reported sexual fantasies (percentages)*

	Men (*n = 291*)	*Women* (*n = 409*)
Group sex	31	15
Voyeuristic/fetishistic	18	7
Steady partner incorporated	14	21
Identified people (other than partner)	8	8
Setting romantic/exotic	4	15
Rape/force	4	13
Sadomasochism	7	7
No fantasies	5	12
Everything	3	0
No answer	21	19

* Columns add up to more than 100 because categories are not mutually exclusive.
Source Wilson, 1987b.

MALE COMPETITION, DOMINANCE AND PARAPHILIA

A major postulate to be derived from parental investment theory is that males will be driven by their polygamous desires to compete assiduously for females. In many species vicious battles do occur between males for access to territory and females. Ideally, this should not be necessary, since there are an equal number of females and males and therefore enough to go around. The trouble is that the males want more than their fair share of the females, or at least to impress and monopolize the young and attractive ones among them (which usually means also the healthiest and best breeders). This might be the primitive basis for the male interest in competitive sports like tennis and boxing and perhaps also the motivational power underlying much of big business, crime and war. Since those males with the most competitive instinct have in the past succeeded best in passing their genes to following generations, certain aggressive and psychopathic tendencies appear to have become highly developed in men.

So long as males compete with one another for access to as many females as possible, it is inevitable that their degree of success will be uneven. Some males will gain control of several females, while others will necessarily miss out altogether. Studies of several species have confirmed such an effect. Males show much greater variability in reproductive success, measured either by the number of partners copulated with or the number of offspring that result, than do females. While nearly all females manage to mate somehow or another, many male animals, especially those that are small and submissive, do not manage any heterosexual contact at all. An extreme case is the North American grouse in which only about 1 in 10 of the males ever get to mate. Studies of free-range Rhesus monkeys reveal that the top 20 per cent of males perform about 80 per cent of the copulations and at least half hardly ever achieve copulation, apparently because of social inhibition. Similar rates of male success are observed in polygynous human tribes such as the Yanamamo in the jungles of Brazil and Venezuela (Freedman, 1979).

We now see why variant sexuality (paraphilia) is an almost entirely male phenomenon. If successful men monopolize more than their share of young women, others are bound to miss out and will need to find substitute sexual outlets. Take the late King Sobhuza II of Swaziland who had nearly 100 wives – this must have created a problem for about 99 Swazi men. The dominant male phenomenon may be less obvious in Western society, but nevertheless, successful men such as Paul Getty and Charlie Chaplin are more likely to have multiple wives (as well as mistresses).

Intermale competition for breeding privileges leads to notable evolutionary modifications. Darwin was among the first to note that the spectacular tail display of the peacock was probably selected because it impressed the female of the species. Experimental support for this idea comes from studies of Kenyan widow-birds in which the long tail-feathers of some males are docked and used to extend those of others. Females of the species show a striking preference for those males with elongated tails, and reject those with the pruned tail. The human male has a very much larger penis than other apes, and there is speculation that this could have arisen as a result of female preferences (Eberhard, 1985). Large penises might simply advertise maleness, but there is also the possibility that ancestral women found them more satisfying.

The male bower-bird of New Guinea has another means of impressing the female. He constructs an amazing Gaudi-style garden with colourful towers and pavements. This functions to attract females, but since it is not carried on his body, he is less conspicuous to predators. Perhaps the creativity of the human male, seen in such things as the Taj Mahal, Disneyland, Wagner's Ring Cycle and Einstein's theory of relativity, is equivalent in some way to the courtship-motivated industry of the male bower-bird. Certainly megalomania is a characteristically male trait, and accomplishment is one of the attributes that women find most attractive in men (Wilson and Nias, 1976).

When two or more males compete directly for dominance within a hierarchy, biochemical changes take place following the outcome, such that the victor is prepared for sexual activity and the losers fall into a state of relative depression that may be basic to some forms of male sexual inadequacy (Rose *et al.*, 1975; McGuire *et al.*, 1983). Indeed, a loss of sexual appetite is often noted in depressive patients, and many of the conditions that predispose to depression could be interpreted as relating to a fall in social status.

Depression is commonly regarded as an illness (and help is quite reasonably provided), but it may be adaptive in some circumstances for a male who is clearly losing a fight to withdraw from competition, at least in the short term, so he lives to fight (and possibly reproduce) another day. The fact that men have a capacity to 'turn off' libido when faced with long periods of deprivation is evidenced by a decline in sexual fantasy in men who are imprisoned and in hospital (Wilson, 1978). This probably reflects declining hormone production rather than the fabled bromide in the tea.

Assuming that sex drive is not dissipated entirely, what other adaptations are possible? One of the most obvious is masturbation – a partial solution that is very widely employed. (Women sometimes do masturbate, but for different reasons from men – usually because they are short of orgasms, not potential partners). The term *wanker* carries the connotation that a man is inadequate to the task of obtaining women. Masturbation provides short term relief, and may even have some advantages (as the advocates say 'you don't have to look your best'), but it does not provide optimal sensation and lacks the important interpersonal element. Therefore, some men elaborate with fantasy-like partial experiences such as viewing pornography, peeping at lovers in the park or women undressing in bedroom windows, flashing schoolgirls, rubbing up against women in crowds or close contact with symbolic or conditioned associations of womanhood such as high-heeled shoes and underwear.

A dominance-failure interpretation of fetishism is supported by the work of La Torre (1980), who found that ego-deflatory feedback to male students to the effect that women found them unattractive diminished their interest in women, while increasing their response to impersonal female approximations such as shoes and underwear. Also consistent with this interpretation is the work of Gosselin and Wilson (1980) showing that most types of sexually deviant men tend towards shyness and introversion (Figure 3.1).

A high proportion of fetishistic men are sexually inexperienced. Of Chalkley and Powell's (1983) clinical sample, nearly half had never had intercourse, and there was a high frequency of socially stigmatizing conditions such as psoriasis, dermatitis, epilepsy, personality disorder, anxiety and depression. Although a clinical sample is likely to exaggerate the extent of these connections, it does seem probable that perceived disadvantage is one of the predisposing factors to sexual unorthodoxy.

Paedophile men are also characterized by shyness and sensitivity (Wilson and Cox, 1983) and, on their own report, they often prefer children because they find them 'more approachable' than adults as potential sex partners. A heightened concern with dominance and submission within their construct system is revealed in repertory grid analyses of paedophiles (Howells, 1979).

Figure 3.1 Location of variant and normal groups in relation to extraversion and neuroticism.
(Source: Gosselin and Wilson, 1980.)

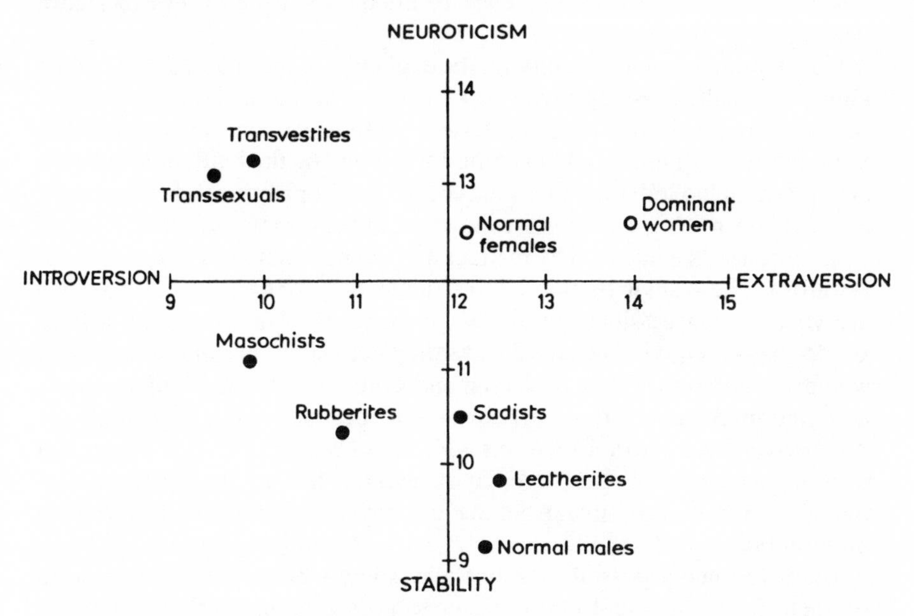

Also consistent with this interpretation is the fact that social skills training is the only treatment approach to show much promise with paedophile men (Crawford, 1981).

Another possible solution to the problem of intermale competition is to opt out and assume certain aspects of the female role. Many masochists, transvestites and transsexuals say they feel 'more relaxed' in assuming a submissive, feminine role (Gosselin and Eysenck, 1980), and this may represent relief from the stress of striving for masculine dominance.

There are plenty of animal models for this type of adaptation. A species of fish that lives in the coral reefs of the Pacific changes sex according to its position in the dominance hierarchy. Social groups consist of one male and a harem of females occupying an aquatic territory. The male suppresses any tendency of his females to change sex by aggressively dominating them, until he dies, whereupon the dominant female in the group promptly turns into a male and takes over the harem (Robertson, 1972).

Much of the homosexual behaviour that occurs among animals in the wild also appears to be dominance-related. In one species of tree lizard, mature males maintain territories containing several females. Smaller males may copulate with the females of the harem, but if the larger male comes around they must themselves assume the female role in copulation (Trivers, 1976).

Intermale battles in mountain sheep often end with the loser being mounted by the victor (Geist, 1971), and male monkeys use the female presentation position as gesture of acquiescence to a superior male (Eibl-Eibesfeldt, 1971).

Not all human homosexuality can be explained in these terms, but certain kinds, especially those occurring in all-male environments such as prisons, public schools, ships and monasteries, often have such overtones. The ancient Greeks operated a kind of 'buddy system' on the battlefield in which an older man looked after all aspects of the development of a teenage lad – hence the term *Greek love*; however, most of these men were heterosexual by preference as evidenced by the fact that women (not boys) were given as rewards for heroism in battle. In the Arabian State of Oman, where women are virtually inaccessible outside of marriage, what is essentially a third gender has emerged. The *Xaniths*, as they are called, are biological males who dress differently from both men and women, with intermediate-length hair and make-up. They work in servile occupations and assume the submissive role in sexual relations with men (Wikan, 1977). Thus a great deal of excess male libido is tapped off without female involvement, even though much of this sexual behaviour may be substitutive rather than preferential.

There are many possible reasons why some men might feel unable to compete for women and find it easier to pursue sexual outlets in the gay community. They may have had unfortunate early encounters with women causing them to feel incompetent or unattractive. Perhaps they were savagely punished for heterosexual play in childhood. Perhaps they hated their mother and generalized this attitude to women at large. For whatever reason these men decide to opt out of the heterosexual 'rat race' and take their pleasure with others of their own gender.

From the point of view of survival of the species, it matters not that some males are removed from the breeding pool by their pursuit of non-reproductive sexual outlets. All the females can be (and usually are) fertilized by the remaining males. However, if women were to adopt deviant sexual practices that did not lead to impregnation, there would be an irrecoverable loss of reproductive efficiency to the species. Perhaps it is partly for this reason that this does not happen to any extent. Almost any woman, however unattractive, is able to persuade some man to service or even marry her. The result, as I have noted, is that human females breed fairly evenly while men are more variable with respect to the number of children they sire.

The dominance theory may also help to explain why sadomasochistic practices such as slavery and humiliation are more common within gay male circles than within the 'straight' heterosexual population (Spengler, 1977; Kamel, 1980). Assuming that some degree of social dominance is necessary for adequate performance of the male sexual role (erection and insertion) then heterosexuals have less of a problem because male dominance over females is readily assumed (whether for social or biological reasons). When two men are preparing for the sex act, the matter of their relative dominance is usually more ambiguous, and so role-playing games, such as master-slave, doctor-patient, headmaster-pupil or torturer-victim, may be contrived to assist in the turn-on. Of course, many heterosexual couples also experiment with fantasy games of this kind, but they are seldom so preoccupied by them.

Also consistent with the dominance interpretation is the discovery that fetishists, sadomasochists and transvestites share many common interests (Gosselin and Wilson, 1980). When members of clubs catering to these three male variations were surveyed with respect to their sexual fantasies and behaviour, there emerged a considerable degree of overlap among them. The outstanding common elements were enjoyment of impersonal sex objects, such as clothing, instruments and materials (e.g. 'being excited by rubber', 'wearing clothes of the opposite sex') and a desire to take a submissive role in social and sexual encounters (e.g. 'being forced to do something', 'being tied up', 'being whipped or spanked'). It appeared that choice of membership of the particular society was to some extent arbitrary, and that the sexual interest of these men was directed either towards inanimate objects (where the issue of dominance does not arise) or a deliberate, unmistakable reversal of the normal dominance relationship such that they become child-like victims (thus averting the competitive struggle).

THE GENETICS OF HOMOSEXUALITY

The fact that male sex orientation is found to have a genetic factor (accounting for about half of the variance) has posed a paradox for evolutionary theorists. To explain how genes that promote non-reproductive sexuality survive through generations, various hypotheses have been put forward, such as heterozygote advantage and kin selection (Kirsch and Rodman, 1982; Mellen, 1981). Yet the genetic basis of homosexual behaviour may be no more specific than that underlying the multiplicity of factors which influence an individual's position in the dominance hierarchy. Clearly it is impossible for all the males in a group to be simultaneously dominant, since dominance is a relative concept. Low intelligence, which is partly genetic, presumably survives in the population for the same reason.

Incidentally, none of the preceding is incompatible with the Gay Lib argument that homosexuals choose their lifestyle freely, on the basis of preference, rather than because of any psychological or biochemical illness. There are many possible benefits of the gay life: there is no risk of pregnancy or entanglement with a person of the opposite sex who, in certain intellectual and temperamental ways, may seem like an alien being; no risk of the radical change of lifestyle that seems to reduce many heterosexual people to slaves of their family. Men might find other men more compatible in terms of sex drive and adventurousness, while women might find others of their own gender more tender, sensitive and faithful as lovers. Instinct theorists allow that behaviour is 'pulled' as well as 'pushed'.

My intention is not to denigrate variant sexual preferences, but to point out that their appearance is inevitable given that young women are a scarce commodity. Religion, traditional morality and some branches of feminism have tried to promote a system of universal monogamy which would ensure an equal distribution of sexual resources, and the aim is admirable, but they have to contend with an instinctive tendency towards polygyny which seems impossible to override completely.

This being the case, the hope that sexual deviation can be eliminated from the population, like smallpox or syphilis, is forlorn. There seems little to be gained from combating mild sex deviations by legal strictures or medical 'cures' unless substitutes such as pornography and prostitution are freely available or the social skills required for heterosexual success are taught in their place.

DIFFICULTIES WITH ORGASM

One female problem that sex therapists are frequently called upon to treat is that of orgasm failure. A high proportion of women have difficulty in this respect at some time in their lives and there is no evidence that openness of discussion has made any difference to the young generation. Table 3.3 shows the proportions of British men and women reporting various sexual difficulties, divided into two generations (under and over 30). For all the articles in *Cosmopolitan* and other 'liberated' women's magazines concerning sexual initiative and fulfilment, nearly half of today's women find orgasm elusive.

Following Masters and Johnson (1970) most sex therapists have presumed that this is a pathological state of affairs, reflecting a repressive upbringing of women in Western society. Inhibitions such as childhood punishment and religious guilt-induction are cited as causes of anorgasmia and treatment is aimed at relaxation and 'permission-giving'.

However, evidence supporting repression theory is entirely lacking. In Table 3.3, guilt, fear and disgust are much less often reported as problematic than boredom and disinterest. Table 3.4, which is previously unpublished but based on the same large sample, suggests that the role of punishment in childhood is minimal. Memories of having been punished for sex play or the

Table 3.3 Percentages of men and women, under and over 30 years old, reporting various sexual difficulties*

	Male (n = 1,862)		*Female (n = 2,905)*	
	<30	*>30*	*<30*	*>30*
Impotence	25	29	6	7
Orgasm too quick	59	53	12	14
Inability to have orgasm	23	23	44	41
Painful intercourse	18	13	45	37
Disgust	5	4	8	9
Guilt	15	13	19	18
Anxiety/fear	14	14	19	16
Boredom/disinterest	21	17	35	36

* Terminology used here is that which was presented to respondents.
Source Wilson, 1981b.

fact of whether or not the parents kept a special instrument for punishment in the house, such as a strap or cane, did not have any appreciable effect on sex problems, male or female. My own large-scale surveys and those of others (Fisher, 1973) have failed to find any connection between orgasm difficulty and either the type or the devoutness of religion. Attempts to implicate anxiety as a personality trait, the personality or behaviour of male partners, even traumatic experiences such as rape or assault in childhood have also produced inconsistent and mainly negative results. Whatever it is that impedes women's orgasm, anxiety does not appear to be a major factor (Norton and Jehu, 1984).

Table 3.4 Punishment history related to sexual difficulties (percentages reporting; n = 4,767)

	Punished for sex play		*Special instrument for punishment*	
	Yes	*No*	*Yes*	*No*
Impotence	22	14	17	14
Orgasm too quick	38	29	33	29
Inability to have orgasm	33	35	34	36
Painful intercourse	30	32	36	31
Disgust	11	7	8	7
Guilt	22	17	15	18
Anxiety/fear	19	17	15	17
Boredom/disinterest	25	29	28	29

Animal and cross-cultural studies are illuminating. In other primates female orgasm does not seem to occur in the wild, but the fact that it can be produced by laboratory stimulation of the clitoris proves that the neurological apparatus is available (Symons, 1979). Similarly, in most primitive cultures, intercourse proceeds too quickly for female orgasm. There are, however, one or two societies which provide special training in love-making for teenagers, with female orgasm as the goal (and this is usually achieved).

When women are asked about the importance of orgasm to their sexual satisfaction, great variations are revealed. Some consider intercourse without orgasm to be frustrating; others enjoy intercourse but place little value on achieving orgasm. Hite's (1976) sample of women cited feelings of affection and intimacy as the main reason for enjoying intercourse, regardless of whether they were orgasmic, and the favourite physical sensation during intercourse was not orgasm but the moment of penetration. So it is doubtful whether orgasm should be regarded as an essential aspect of normal female sexuality. For many women it is just 'icing on the cake'; for others it is an exceptional, exciting, and perhaps also frightening, event.

In evolutionary terms, there seems to have been no strong tendency for orgasmic capacity to be selected for in women. Orgasm might function to reward women for engaging in intercourse, which would seem to have survival value, but there is the possible disadvantage that women who arrived at orgasm too easily, would terminate intercourse prematurely (as men often do), and escape from their male partner before insemination has occurred. Another evolutionary disadvantage to easy female orgasm is that women would lose their ability to control the timing of intercourse and to choose partners with discretion. This is the plight of the so-called 'nymphomaniac' – intercourse is so attractive and rewarding that she loses the power that most women wield with the sparing disbursement of sexual favours.

Various theories have been put forward to explain how the human female might have evolved greater orgasmic capacity than other primates (e.g. the pair-bond consolidation theory popularized by Morris [1972]) but it now seems probable that female orgasm has no evolutionary function at all. Symons (1979) argues that the potential for orgasm is there simply as a spin-off of the fact that females share most of their neurology with males. For the sake of embryological simplicity, the neurological blueprints of male and female are left as similar as possible without incurring reproductive disadvantage. A female canary has all the mechanisms for singing but does not do so unless injected with male hormones. The human male has vestigial nipples which are useless to him and not erotically sensitive unless he is given oestrogen. The clitoris is a vestigial penis and, as such, is rather small and not located in such a place that intercourse is the optimal method of stimulation. If sufficient clitoral stimulation is given, orgasm will occur, but a great deal of manual, oral, or mechanical attention may be necessary in addition to, or instead of, intercourse.

This theory puts new light on the Masters and Johnson observation that the vaginal spasms of female orgasm are timed at 0.8 of a second, the same as the muscular contractions that propel ejaculate through a man's urethra. Symons (1979) suggests that this has come about not because male and female genitals are designed for the ultimate compatibility of simultaneous orgasm, but simply because the wiring of nerve to muscle is the same for the two sexes. Multiple orgasm is possible for women because they do not actually ejaculate – a capacity that exists in some prepubertal boys for the same reason.

I have described the treatment implications of this spin-off or 'artifact' theory of female orgasm previously (Wilson, 1987c). If anxiety is not the cause of orgasm difficulty one would not expect anxiolytic drugs to be effective in the treatment of anorgasmia, whereas testosterone might well enhance female responsiveness because of its masculinizing effect. Such evidence that is available supports both expectations. For example, Figure 3.2 shows the results of a study by Carney *et al.* (1978) which compared the efficacy of diazepam and testosterone as treatments for female orgasm difficulty. Post-treatment and follow-up scores show testosterone is

Figure 3.2 A comparison of the effects of male sex hormone and an anxiolytic drug on the sexual functioning of unresponsive women.
(Modified from Carney *et al.*, 1978.)

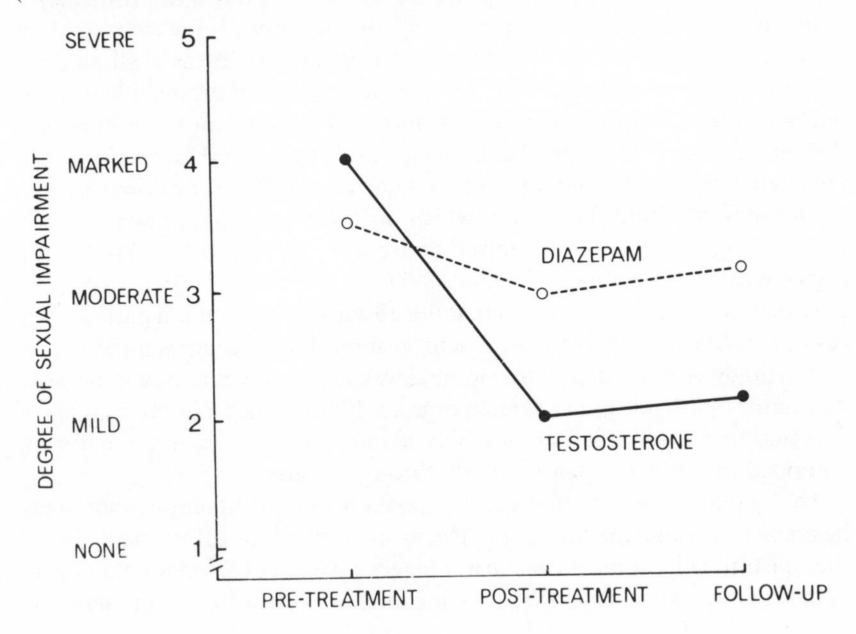

Figure 3.3. A schematic distribution of female orgasm difficulty, each position to the right subsuming those to the left.
No position on this curve need be regarded as 'pathological' and a particular woman may shift along the horizontal axis to the right as she gains skill and experience in love-making.
(Modified from Kaplan, 1974.)

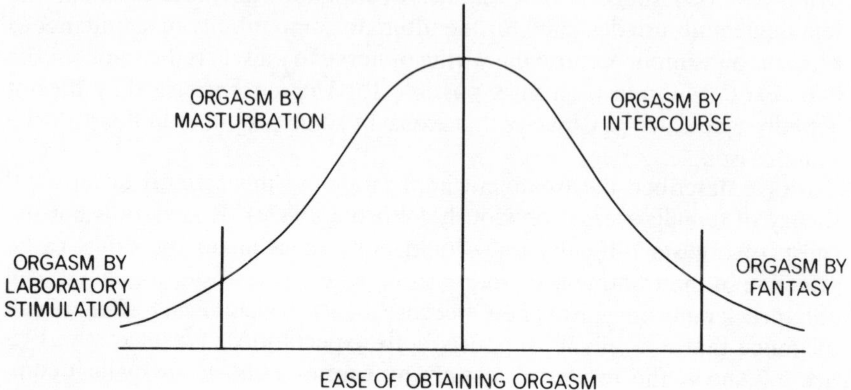

effective while diazepam is not. More recently, Riley and Riley (1986) have shown that diazepam impairs the sexual responsiveness of non-anxious women in a dose-related manner. Thus there is a possibility that anxiolytics may be counterproductive in the treatment of female orgasm difficulty.

Behavioural methods for promoting orgasm may be summarized as raising libido, allowing sufficient time, and engaging in forms of stimulation that are as masculine as possible. More specific suggestions include increasing background arousal by fantasy, erotica and role-playing games in which the female partner is assigned dominance, using prolonged foreplay, including manual and oral stimulation of the clitoris, and sexual positions such as female-superior and 'flanquette' which maximize clitoral contact.

These suggestions are recognized as useful by many practising sex therapists regardless of theoretical persuasion (e.g. Gillan and Gillan, 1976). But note that none of them assumes that the absence of orgasm is a pathological condition, that anxiety is a major factor responsible for orgasm difficulty, or that orthodox intercourse is the optimal way for a woman to obtain orgasm. The natural distribution of female orgasm difficulty is probably roughly as depicted in Figure 3.3. Perhaps only about half of women are naturally equipped to enjoy orgasm regularly through intercourse.

To say that orgasm is, biologically speaking, a male function, should not be taken to devalue the female orgasm in any way, or the efforts made by sex therapists to help women achieve it. Fingers have not evolved for playing the piano, but we can learn to do so, giving ourselves and others a great deal of pleasure in the process. Likewise, many women who have not experienced orgasm can learn the skill, and their male partners can learn to help. To this end it would help if we abandoned the myth that men and women are 'made for each other' – constructed in such a way that in the absence of any pathology they will naturally enjoy simultaneous orgasm during intercourse. Orgasm is natural for men in every sense of the term, but for women it is a variable capacity that can be developed with appropriate training and experience.

PREMATURE EJACULATION

Sex therapists often receive complaints that the male partner's ejaculation occurs too quickly. If it happens so fast that the man has not reached the point of penetration (or even got his trousers off) then it would appear to be his problem. However, there is an increasing tendency among sex therapists to define premature ejaculation in terms of the failure of intercourse to continue long enough for female orgasm to occur. Viewed this way, it simply becomes the flip side of female orgasm difficulty, with the 'blame' transferred from the female to the male partner. Again, this merely illustrates the fact that, for the evolutionary reasons previously outlined, female sexual arousal moves more slowly towards orgasm than that of the male, with the result that men can be more certain of achieving orgasm than women can during intercourse (or any other kind of sexual activity).

As men get older, premature ejaculation is less common as a problem, whereas there is an increasing possibility of retarded ejaculation. It may be partly for this same reason that many women find sexual intercourse more satisfying as they get older. What is so often attributed to experience and increasing libido may simply be due to having sex with older male partners who take more time in love-making and are therefore more compatible with the female arousal pattern.

Manuals of sex therapy normally prescribe the 'start-stop' or 'squeeze' techniques for treatment of premature ejaculation. But there is a rather more obvious and practical form of treatment that ought to be tried first – one that takes account of the differing arousal patterns of men and women. This is based on the simple fact that most men can be rearoused for a second orgasm after a rest period of 20 minutes or so (even if they do not know it themselves) and the second time around usually takes a great deal longer. The rearousal process may well require some assistance from the female partner, and erotica and lubricating oils come in handy for this purpose. If the man can be induced to repeat intercourse fairly soon after his first attempt he is less likely to have a problem with premature ejaculation (if so he could always try for a third – he is bound to slow down some time).

As a variation on this method a couple might adopt a pattern of masturbating the man about half an hour before having intercourse, the interval between being filled by foreplay in which the woman is kissed, caressed and stimulated. This routine could be called 'his and hers' or 'one for him and one for her'. A similar strategy is reported by experienced male orgy-goers who arrive at the party late having masturbated at home just before departure; to the chagrin of the spent males they delight and amaze the merely warmed-up women with their staying power.

Of course, not all premature ejaculators can be dealt with in this way. Cases do appear in the clinic in which guilt or anxiety seem to play a role. Some men, especially those who have sex very infrequently, and then usually in 'illicit' circumstances, have intercourse only when their libido builds up sufficiently to override their inhibitions, but immediately after the deprivation pressure has been released their guilt returns with a vengeance and their need is to terminate proceedings as quickly as possible (so they grab their trousers and run). If premature ejaculation is connected with this pattern, then a more traditional therapeutic approach delving into upbringing, attitudes, and lifestyle, and using behavioural techniques such as desensitization and the 'squeeze', may be indicated. But my impression is that this clinical syndrome is relatively uncommon and that, as with female orgasmic dysfunction, the role of anxiety in male sex problems has been overestimated.

Anxiety has also been cited as a cause of retarded ejaculation, but premature ejaculation is about 40 times as common (Gebhard and Johnson, 1979). To a large extent, therefore, premature ejaculation may be understood as an inevitable result of the fact that young men are more quickly and easily brought to orgasm than young women are.

DISORDERS OF DESIRE

Another problem that seems to be restricted largely to one sex is that of insufficient libido or desire. In recent years this has become recognized as a common problem among women – perhaps as common as orgasm failure (Kaplan, 1979). Again, provided we abandon the myth that men and women are much the same by nature, this should come as no surprise. Putting aside ancient (not just Victorian) wisdom concerning female indifference to sex, modern surveys in which men and women are asked to rank their pleasures show repeatedly that, whereas sex has first priority for most men, a great many women say they prefer knitting and gardening. Leading some group discussions recently among ordinary British women concerning their attitudes towards sex, I was amazed how often clichés like 'my husband's very good – he doesn't bother me too often these days' cropped up. This sex difference in desire is also apparent in Table 3.3, with twice as many women as men reporting boredom and disinterest as a problem.

As with orgasm difficulty and premature ejaculation, lack of desire for sex appears as a major problem because average male and female arousal patterns are poorly synchronized. Typical male sexuality includes ready arousal to a wide variety of stimuli, starting from visual stimuli alone. Men may become sexually aroused just by looking at women, whereas most women need something more than this – usually the addition of olfactory and tactile cues (not to mention favourable emotional circumstances).

The reason is clear to the sociobiologist: while it is advantageous for males to be turned on easily by the mere sight of females, since this serves gene proliferation, quick arousal is disadvantageous for females because it interferes with their strategy of careful mate-appraisal.

Since lack of desire occurs as a result of a male-female discrepancy in sexual inclination, it may be asked why it is defined more as a female problem than male. After all, if the male partner was equally disinterested in sex there would be no problem, so it is really as much his 'fault' as hers. The answer probably is that libido cannot easily be reduced except by chemical or surgical means, whereas an interest in sex can be developed by the use of erotica, fantasy, role-playing, subtle foreplay and other forms of psychological stimulation. Thus the female partner is more usually seen as a suitable case for treatment.

Finally, I should mention a 'disorder of desire' that affects men more strikingly than women – the boredom that arises from repetitive sex with the same partner. In the animal laboratory this is known as 'the Coolidge effect', after an anecdote concerning the visit of President and Mrs Coolidge to a government farm. On discovering that the rooster performed his duty dozens of times a day, Mrs Coolidge said, 'Tell that to the President.' President Coolidge was initially dumbfounded, but then astutely enquired, 'Was that with the same hen?' 'Oh no, Mr President, a different hen each time' was the reply. 'Tell that to Mrs Coolidge,' he said.

The tendency for males to be sexually recharged by novel females has been observed in most mammals (Bermant and Davidson, 1974) and is another manifestation of their reproductively optimal 'promiscuity strategy'. This presents a problem, for men especially, over the course of a long marriage and is responsible for a great deal of adultery. Progressive 'contempt due to familiarity' (at least as regards sexual excitement) is an almost inevitable outcome of sexually exclusive marriage. It is not unusual for sex therapists to see men who are unable to achieve erection with their wives but perfectly capable of stud-like prowess with their new secretary. Once again, what is observed is not a disease but a normal biological phenomenon, and realistic solutions must be sought.

CONCLUSION

In this chapter I have tried to show how the common sexual problems that afflict men and women can be better understood in the context of the evolutionary divergence of the two sexes. One effect of this analysis has been to 'normalize' conditions like female orgasmic dysfunction and premature ejaculation, by pointing out that they arise not primarily because there is anything wrong with individual 'patients' but because of inevitable incompatibilities in the sexual responsiveness of men and women. As Cole (1985) notes, this information alone may be of considerable help and reassurance to people in sex therapy, even though it implies an element of fatalism. A great deal of harm has probably been done by the myth that has been propagated by church and medical authorities, and more recently by some feminists, that monogamous marriage ought to be unmitigated bliss and that men and women are 'designed' to make each other happy.

It may be necessary to repeat that the male-female differences discussed here apply only on average and that there is a great deal of overlap between the sexes. A good model to keep in mind is that of height, where it is true that men are taller than women, but *only as a generalization* – there are plenty of short men and tall women. It is necessary to keep in mind the image of two overlapping normal distributions, the means for men and women being displaced in relation to each other. This same state of affairs prevails with respect to behavioural tendencies such as sexual predatory behaviour, ease of visual arousal and speed of orgasm. The average differences between men and women tell us nothing certain about the disposition of any individual person, but they do predict the frequency of various sexual difficulties and partner incompatibilities.

It hardly seems earth-shattering to assert that men and women are different, yet this ancient wisdom is often lost sight of by therapists raised within the recent environmentalist *zeitgeist*. For the best of political motives, social learning theorists and feminists have sought to minimize the role of genetic differences in human behaviour and promote the belief that social conditions can be adjusted to make us more alike. This viewpoint has led to the correction of many injustices, but at the same time has added some confusion to the theory and practice of psychology.

Summary

Sexual dysfunction has generally been considered within the context of a medical/pathological model that is inappropriate. Just as conventional sexual behaviour can be explained in evolutionary terms, so too can a great deal of sexual behaviour that is 'problematic'. Paraphilias that entail oblique sex targets are almost entirely male, and may be understood as inevitable reactions to anticipated lack of success in competition among men for access to women. As such they are adaptive behaviours which cannot easily, and often should not, be eliminated. Similarly, female orgasm difficulty and deficiency of desire is a predictable outcome of the separately evolved optimal female strategy for reproduction. Such problems are therefore normal rather than pathological. Sex therapy could be sharpened considerably if the ethological basis of these difficulties was acknowledged.

REFERENCES

Bermant, G. and Davidson, J.M. (1974) *Biological Basis of Sexual Behavior*, Harper and Row, New York.

Carney, A., Bancroft, K. and Mathews, A. (1978) Combination of hormonal and psychological treatment for female sexual unresponsiveness. A comparative study, *British Journal of Psychiatry*, Vol. 132, pp. 339–46.

Chalkley, A.J. and Powell, G.E. (1983) The clinical description of forty-eight cases of sexual fetishism, *British Journal of Psychiatry*, Vol. 142, pp. 292–5.

Cole, M. (1985) Sex therapy – a critical appraisal, *British Journal of Psychiatry*, Vol. 147, pp. 337–51.

Crawford, D.A. (1981) Treatment approaches with paedophiles, in M. Cook and K. Howells (eds) *Adult Sexual Interest in Children*, Academic Press, London.

Dawkins, R. (1976) *The Selfish Gene*, Oxford University Press, Oxford.

Eberhard, W.G. (1985) *Sexual Selection and Animal Genetalia*, Harvard University Press, Cambridge, MA.

Eibl-Eibesfeldt, I. (1971) *Love and Hate: On the Natural History of Basic Behaviour Patterns*. Methuen, London.

Ellis, L. (1986) Evidence of neuroandrogenic aetiology of sex roles from a combined analysis of human, nonhuman primate and nonprimate mammalian studies, *Personality and Individual Differences*, Vol. 7, pp. 519–52.

Fisher, S. (1973) *The Female Orgasm. Psychology, Physiology, Fantasy*, Basic Books, New York.

Freedman, D.G. (1979) *Human Sociobiology: A Holistic Approach*, Free Press, New York.

Gebhard, P.H. and Johnson, A.B. (1979) *The Kinsey Data: Marginal Tabulations of the 1938–1963 Interviews Conducted by the Institute of Sex Research*, W.B. Saunders, Philadelphia.

Geist, V. (1971) *Mountain Sheep: A Study in Behavior and Evolution*, The University of Chicago Press, Chicago.

Gillan, P. and Gillan, R. (1976) *Sex Therapy Today*, Open Books, London.

Gosselin, C.C. and Eysenck, S.B.G. (1980) The transvestite double image: A preliminary report, *Personality and Individual Differences*, Vol. 1, pp. 172–3.

Gosselin, C.C. and Wilson, G.D. (1980) *Sexual Variations: Fetishism, Transvestism and Sadomasochism*, Faber and Faber, London.

Hite, S. (1976) *The Hite Report*, Macmillan, New York.

Howells, K. (1979) Some meanings of children for paedophiles, in M. Cook and G.D. Wilson (eds) *Love and Attraction: An International Conference*, Pergamon, Oxford.

Kamel, G.W.L. (1980) Leather sex: meaningful aspects of gay sadomasochism, *Deviant Behaviour*, Vol. 1, pp. 171–91.

Kaplan, H.S. (1974) *The New Sex Therapy*, Brunner/Mazel, New York.
Kaplan, H.S. (1979) *Disorders of Sexual Desire*, Baillière Tindall, London.
Kirsch, J.A.W. and Rodman, J.E. (1982) Selection and sexuality: the Darwinian view of homosexuality, in W. Paul *et al.* (eds) *Homosexuality: Social, Psychological and Biological Issues*, Sage, Beverly Hills, CA.
La Torre, R.A. (1980) Devaluation of the human love object: Heterosexual rejection as a possible antecedent to fetishism, *Journal of Abnormal Psychology*, Vol. 89, pp. 295–8.
Masters, W.H. and Johnson, V.E. (1970) *Human Sexual Inadequacy*, J.A. Churchill, London.
McGuire, M.T., Raleigh, M.J. and Johnson, C. (1983) Social dominance in adult male vervet monkeys: behaviour-biochemical relationships, *Biology and Social Life*, Vol. 22, pp. 311–28.
Mellen, S.L.W. (1981) *The Evolution of Love*, Freeman, Oxford.
Morris, D. (1972) *Intimate Behavior*, Random House, New York.
Norton, G.R. and Jehu, D. (1984) The role of anxiety in sexual dysfunctions: a review, *Archives of Sexual Behaviour*, Vol. 13, pp. 165–8.
Riley, A.J. and Riley, E.J. (1986) The effect of single-dose diazepam on female sexual response induced by masturbation, *Sexual and Marital Therapy*, Vol. 1, pp. 49–53.
Robertson, D.R. (1972) Social control of sex reversal in a coral reef fish, *Science*, Vol. 177, pp. 1007–9.
Rose, R.M., Bernstein, I.S. and Gordon, T.P. (1975) Consequences of social conflict on plasma testosterone levels in Rhesus monkeys, *Psychosomatic Medicine*, Vol. 37, pp. 50–61.
Spengler, A. (1977) Manifest sadomasochism in males: results of an empirical study, *Archives of Sexual Behavior*, Vol. 6, pp. 441–56.
Symons, D. (1979) *The Evolution of Human Sexuality*, Oxford University Press, New York.
Trivers, R.L. (1972) Parental investment and sexual selection, in B. Campbell (ed.) *Sexual Selection and the Descent of Man*, Aldine, Chicago.
Trivers, R.L. (1976) Sexual selection and resource-accruing abilities, *Anolis Garmani Evolution*, Vol. 30, pp. 253–69.
Wallace, R.A. (1979) *The Genesis Factor*, Morrow, New York.
Wikan, U. (1977) Man becomes woman: transsexualism in Oman as a key to gender roles, *Man*, Vol. 12, pp. 304–19.
Wilson, E.O. (1975) *Sociobiology: The New Synthesis*, Harvard University Press, Cambridge, MA.
Wilson, G.D. (1978) *The Secrets of Sexual Fantasy*, Dent, London.
Wilson, G.D. (1981a) *Love and Instinct*, Temple Smith, London.
Wilson, G.D. (1981b) Cross-generational stability of gender differences in sexuality, *Personality and Individual Differences*, Vol. 2, pp. 254–7.
Wilson, G.D. (1987a) An ethological approach to sexual deviation, in G.D. Wilson (ed.) *Variant Sexuality: Research and Theory*, Croom Helm, London.
Wilson, G.D. (1987b) Male-Female differences in sexual activity, enjoyment and fantasies, *Personality and Individual Differences* (in press).
Wilson, G.D. (1987c) Biological and social aspects of female sexual functioning, in E. Karas (ed.) *Current Issues in Clinical Psychology*, Vol. III, Plenum, New York.
Wilson, G.D. and Cox, D.N. (1983) *The Child-Lovers: A Study of Paedophiles in Society*, Peter Owen, London.
Wilson, G.D. and Nias, D.K.B. (1976) *Love's Mysteries: The Psychology of Sexual Attraction*, Open Books, London.

CHAPTER 4

THE ENDOCRINOLOGY OF SEXUAL FUNCTION AND DYSFUNCTION

Alan J. Riley

Hormones are chemical messengers. Reproductive function in both sexes is dependent on a delicate balance of interacting hormonal processes. A role for hormones in the control of sexual function has been the subject of much debate for a long time but it was not until sensitive methods for measuring hormones in blood became available that the endocrinology of sexual function could be studied in depth. There is still much to be learned about the hormonal control of sexual function and the way that disturbed hormonal mechansisms can cause sexual dysfunction.

Although in the past the incidence of hormonally induced sexual dysfunction may have been overemphasized there can now be no doubt that endocrinopathy is an important cause of sexual problems. Very much more is known about the endocrinopathy of sexual dysfunction in men than in women but our understanding of hormonally induced female sexual difficulties is increasing. In a series of male patients attending a medical outpatient clinic who were discovered on screening to have erection inadequacy, hormonal factors were considered to be the cause of the sexual dysfunction in 29 per cent (Slag *et al.*, 1983). In another series of sexually dysfunctional men, many of whom had been previously considered to have psychogenic erection failure, 35 per cent were found to have abnormal hormone levels (Spark *et al.*, 1980).

Since the majority of hormone disturbances can be effectively treated it is important that endocrinopathy is considered in the differential diagnosis of sexual dysfunction. In this chapter the role of hormones in human sexual function is discussed with particular reference to hormonal factors in the cause and management of sexual dysfunction.

ANDROGENS

Androgens are hormones that promote masculinization. They are essential at all stages of development, including fetal life, for the development of male sexual characteristics and the evolution of male gender identity.

In men the main circulating androgen is testosterone, which is mainly produced by the Leydig cells of the testes under the control of a luteinizing hormone secreted by the anterior pituitary gland. Small quantities of testosterone are also secreted by the adrenal cortex. In some tissues testosterone has to be converted to 5 dihydrotestosterone to have an effect and this change is produced by the enzyme 5-α reductase. Congenital absence of this enzyme results in male pseudohermaphroditism with severe ambiguity of the external genitals. These children are often raised as girls and they may change to male gender identity at puberty when substantial increases in androgen production occur (Imperato-McGinley *et al.*, 1979).

In women androgens are synthesized by both the ovaries and the adrenals. The principal circulating androgens are dihydroepiandrosterone (DHEA) and its sulphate (DHEA-S) both secreted predominantly by the adrenal, androstenedione, secreted in approximately equal amounts by the ovary and adrenal, and testosterone. Half of the plasma testosterone is secreted by the adrenal cortex (major source) and ovary. The other half is derived from the conversion of androstenedione (major source) and DHEA. This conversion occurs mainly in the liver but also in peripheral tissues.

Some androgens are converted to oestrogens. The fact that some androgens act as prohormones for oestrogen synthesis in peripheral tissues complicates the assessment of the effects of androgens on female sexual behaviour. It could be suggested, for example, that the behavioural effects observed after the administration of testosterone result not from the androgen but from oestrogen derived from it. There are conflicting reports on the effects on human sexual behaviour of the administration of androgens that are not capable of being metabolized to oestrogens, for example, mesterolone, fluoxymesterone and dihydrotestosterone. In men, at least, such androgens are probably capable of stimulating sexual behaviour.

Sexual effects of androgens in men

Although an association between the testes and sexual function has been accepted for thousands of years only in relatively recent times has the actual role of androgens in human male sexuality been defined. Even now, there are fairly substantial gaps in our understanding of the way androgens influence male sexual behaviour. Surgical castration which removes the major source of androgens results in decreased interest in sex, a reduction in sexual activity and sometimes erectile inadequacy (Sturup, 1968; Luttge,

1971). However, some men remain sexually active for many years after castration (Bremer, 1959). Since androgens are also secreted by the adrenal cortex castration does not totally abolish androgen production and it seems likely that in some men low levels of androgens are sufficient to maintain sexual function whereas other men require higher levels of androgen secretion.

Many investigators have attempted to correlate sexual activity in normal men with plasma testosterone levels. In the majority of these studies there does not appear to be a significant association between these two parameters when the testosterone levels are within the normal range (Raboch and Starka, 1973; Bowen *et al.*, 1978). However, the results of one study suggest that plasma testosterone levels were significantly correlated with magnitude of erection and the speed of development of sexual arousal induced by erotic films (Rubin *et al.*, 1979).

Studies on the effects of androgen replacement therapy in androgen-deficient men have helped to demonstrate the effects of androgen on male sexual function (Skakkebaek *et al.*, 1981). When androgen is withdrawn there is first a reduction in self-rated interest in sex. Then ejaculation becomes difficult and fails and finally sexual activity decreases. The reintroduction of androgen results first in increased interest, then improved ejaculation and then increased sexual activity. A relationship between plasma testosterone level and frequency of erections has been observed in hypogonadal men during androgen replacement treatment (Davidson *et al.*, 1979). Laboratory studies have shown that hypogonadal men who experience loss of interest in sex and reduced or abolished sexual activity continue to attain erection in response to sexually explicit films (Bancroft and Wu, 1983). However, erection in response to fantasy was reduced in the hypogonadal men but was restored by androgen treatment. Thus androgens appear to have a role in cognitive processes involved in initiation of sexual fantasy. Since an important factor in maintaining erection is the feedback of being aware of sexual arousal, which depends at least partly on cognitive factors, patients with androgen deficiency may develop erection inadequacy.

Another way to study the effects of androgens on male sexual function is by the use of antiandrogens. These are drugs which block the effect of androgens on the cell-androgen receptors and some antiandrogens, for example, cyproterone acetate, also suppress the secretion of luteinizing hormone thereby reducing the secretion of testosterone. Treatment with antiandrogens results in reduced interest in sex and decreased sexual activity but erection response to erotic films is maintained (Bancroft *et al.*, 1974). Nocturnal erections and daytime spontaneous erections do appear to be dependent on androgens (Kwan *et al.*, 1983). Cimetidine, a drug used to reduce gastric acid production, also possesses antiandrogenic activity.

Erection inadequacy is a recognized side effect of this drug. Erection failure was demonstrated by nocturnal penile plethysmography in a group of patients treated with high doses of cimetidine. Erection was restored when either cimetidine was withdrawn or replaced with ranitidine, another drug that reduces gastric-acid production by the same mechanism as cimetidine, but which does not exhibit antiandrogenic activity (Jensen *et al.*, 1983).

Treatment of male sexual dysfunction with androgens

There is no evidence to support the use of androgens as a panacea for all sexually dysfunctional male patients. In a double-blind placebo controlled study injections of testosterone esters (Sustanon 100) fortnightly for six weeks did not improve erection in a group of ten erectile dysfunctional men with normal pretreatment circulating testosterone levels (O'Carroll and Bancroft, 1984). Indeed since androgen administration is not without risk to the patient the empirical use of androgens should not be encouraged. The main indications for androgen therapy in men are:

Hypogonadism
There is now good experimental evidence that androgen replacement therapy restores sexual function in the hypogonadal man (Bancroft and Wu, 1983; Kwan *et al.*, 1983; Skakkebaek *et al.*, 1981) and that the response to treatment is dose-related (Davidson *et al.*, 1979). The administration of testosterone in men whose hypogonadism is secondary to hyperprolactinaemia (increased prolactin secretion) may not improve sexual function until the level of plasma prolactin is reduced to normal levels.

Low sexual interest
Men complaining of low sexual interest who have normal levels of circulating testosterone may benefit from testosterone treatment. O'Carroll and Bancroft (1984) demonstrate a significant increase in sexual interest during treatment with Sustanon 100 fortnightly for six weeks, in a group of ten men whose presenting complaint was loss of interest in sex not secondary to erectile failure or physical or mental illness.

The ageing man
The significant reduction in frequency of intercourse, orgasm and morning erections in ageing men, particularly after the age of 70 (Davidson *et al.*, 1983) is associated with a decline in total and free testosterone and loss of normal circadian rhythm in testosterone secretion (Bremner *et al.*, 1983). The amount of androgens required to stimulate sexual behaviour may increase with age reflecting, perhaps, increasing androgen receptor insensitivity, but this suggestion lacks experimental confirmation at the present

time. There is some evidence that elderly men who remain sexually active have higher circulating testosterone levels than those whose sexual activity is greatly restricted (Vermeulen, 1979).

Some elderly men who have had an enforced break in their sexual outlet, such as through illness or death of their spouse, are unable to resume sexual activity because of lack of interest and erection inadequacy, when they have the opportunity to do so even when there does not appear to be any psychological reason for their sexual inadequacy. These men tend to have plasma testosterone levels in the lower quartile of the normal range. Although data obtained from controlled studies is lacking, clinical experience with men who have failed to respond to behavioural approaches suggests that these men may benefit from a short course of androgen supplementation.

Androgen receptor insensitivity

Circulating androgens have to be taken up by receptors in the androgen-sensitive cells, passed through the cytoplasm and enter the nucleus to cause an androgen effect. There are conditions in which the androgen receptor is defective and fails, to varying degrees, to take up androgen. These conditions give rise to the androgen insensitivity syndrome.

The most florid condition is when androgen receptor function is totally absent. This is known as *complete androgen insensitivity syndrome* (CIAS) or *testicular feminization syndrome* (TFS). The patient is chromosomally male, has testes which secrete normal or increased amounts of testosterone but because the cells do not respond to the androgenic stimulation the external genitalia and secondary sexual characteristics develop along female lines. These patients appear to have normal sexual interest and responses (Money and Ehrhardt, 1972).

Less marked forms of the syndrome, collectively known as *partial androgen insensitivity syndrome* (PAIS), may give rise to ambiguous genitals, infertility, and, as the following case demonstrates, sexual dysfunction.

CASE EXAMPLE

This fairly well-built, 19-year-old male presented with primary erection inadequacy and very low interest in sex. He had never masturbated nor had he experienced nocturnal ejaculation. His genitals were typically male and he had experienced slight penile growth at the age of 14 and at the same time began to grow downy hair on his face but his voice had not totally broken. He had scanty pubic hair. Endocrine screening revealed elevated plasma testosterone and LH levels (48 nmol/1 and 25 mIU/ml) respectively. A diagnosis of partial androgen insensitivity was made and he was treated with high doses of testosterone. Within three months of starting this treatment he had further penile growth, deepening of his voice and improved beard growth. These changes were followed by development of interest in sex then spontaneous nocturnal ejaculation and eventually erection. Testosterone treatment was continued for ten months and then gradually withdrawn. He continues to be sexually active without further androgen supplementation.

Sexual effects of androgens in women

There are accumulating data to support an effect of androgens on female sexual behaviour. Removal of the ovaries (oophorectomy) reduces the production of androgens and oestrogens by about 50 per cent without significantly affecting the ratio of the sex hormones. Some, but not all, women experience decreased interest in sex following an oophorectomy, but this may be secondary to the effects of oestrogen deficiency on the genital tract rather than a direct effect on central sex desire-producing mechanisms. However withdrawal of adrenal sex hormones in the oophorectomized woman by either adrenalectomy (Waxenberg *et al.*, 1959) or hypophysectomy (removal of the pituitary gland) (Schon and Sutherland, 1960) results in a profound decline in sexual desire which can be restored by androgen treatment.

Administration of testosterone has been reported to stimulate sex drive markedly in women with a variety of gynaecological disorders (Greenblatt, 1943), 'endocrine disorders' (Salmon and Geist, 1943) and in the treatment of carcinoma of the breast (Willson *et al.*, 1975). On the basis of such observations from uncontrolled studies as these, Salmon and Geist (1943) suggest that androgens have a threefold action on female sexuality, they increase: (a) the susceptibility to psychosexual stimulation; (b) the sensitivity of the external genitals and (c) the intensity of sexual gratification.

Further evidence for a stimulating role of androgens in female sexual behaviour has come from studies which have attempted to correlate plasma androgen levels with various measures of female sexual function. Frequency of intercourse in a group of married women was found to be significantly correlated with mid-menstrual cycle plasma testosterone levels (Persky *et al.*, 1978b). Also found in this study was that the women's self-rated sexual gratification scores were significantly related to their average testosterone level across the entire menstrual cycle and that high base-line testosterone level was significantly correlated to the ability to form good interpersonal relationships. Subjective measures of sexual desire, excitement, initiation and responsivity in women (assessed on various scales) were found to be correlated with plasma levels of androstenedione and testosterone (Persky *et al.*, 1982).

Significant positive correlation between average plasma testosterone levels and ratings of sexual interest has also been found in women using oral contraception, but only in those who were free from sexual problems (Bancroft *et al.*, 1980). An interesting study examines the relationship between average or mid-cycle testosterone levels and the average levels of sexuality through the menstrual cycle (Sanders and Bancroft, 1982). The results were dichotomized according to whether or not the subjects masturbated. There was no difference in testosterone levels between the women who masturbated and those who did not. In the women who masturbated there was a significant correlation between testosterone level and frequency of masturbation, but there was no relationship between testosterone level and sexual feelings or between testosterone level and frequency of partner-orientated sexual activity. In the women who did not masturbate there was a significant negative correlation between testosterone level and sexual feelings. It is apparent therefore that testosterone is not the only determinant of sexual behaviour in women.

If androgens do have some part to play in the stimulation of sexual desire in women, blocking the effects of androgens might be expected to impair female sexual function. The antiandrogen cyproterone acetate, which reduces sexual interest and activity in men (Bancroft *et al.*, 1974), is now being used in women to treat such androgen-dependent conditions as acne and hirsutism. It is usually administered in combination with ethinyl oestradiol. Cittadini and Barrace (1977) reported loss of sex drive during treatment with cyproterone acetate. The incidence of this side effect increased with duration of treatment, from 11 per cent at one to three months, to 21.7 per cent at four to six months. Between seven and nine months a third of the patients reported loss of sex desire. The incidence of reported sexual side effects of cyproterone acetate in women has ranged from 1.2 to 44 per cent (Appelt and Strauss, 1984). Interestingly, in one study 4.5 per cent of women reported increased interest in sex during treatment with this antiandrogen (Cittadini and Barrace, 1977). This may have resulted from amelioration of their primary affliction leading to improved body image.

Treatment of female sexual dysfunction with androgens

There have been few studies undertaken to evaluate the effect of androgen treatment in women presenting with sexual problems. More than 40 years ago Greenblatt and his colleagues (1942) reported on the use of implanted testosterone propionate (25–400 mg) in women aged 22 to 53, who complained of loss of sexual desire in addition to other gynaecological symptoms. Of the 55 women treated, 34 reported definite increase in sexual desire and 3 had a temporary increase. In a group of gynaecological patients treated with either oral methyltestosterone or testosterone propionate injections there were 29 patients who had always had low or absent sexual desire and of these 24 noticed improved sexual desire during the hormone treatment (Salmon and Geist, 1943). There was also a group of 29 women who had recently lost their sexual desire and of these 24 responded favourably to the hormone treatment. Salmon and Geist (1943) also reported that sexual desire could be enhanced by testosterone in those women whose pretreatment sexual desire was regarded as normal.

Two more recent controlled studies on the use of testosterone in the treatment of sexual problems in women appear at first to provide contradictory results. Both studies used Testoral® 10 mg daily a sublingal preparation of testosterone. The first was a comparative study comparing Testoral with diazepam (10 mg) as an adjunct to counselling in patients with sexual unresponsiveness (Carney *et al.*, 1978). Although both treatment groups improved Testoral proved to be significantly better than diazepam. In the second study, the same dose of Testoral® was compared against a placebo in 48 women with low sex desire and unresponsiveness (Mathews *et al.*, 1983). The patients with their partners also received behavioural treatment based on Masters and Johnson techniques. The results of this study showed Testoral® to be no better than the placebo. The difference in the results of the two studies can be explained by an inhibitory effect of diazepam on female sexual functioning (Riley and Riley, 1986). The conclusion therefore is that Testoral® 10 mg is ineffective in the treatment of low sexual difficulties in women. Increasing the dose of Testoral® to 30 mg daily did not produce a benefit over the placebo (Kellett, 1984). It is probable that this dose of testosterone is insufficient because those physicians who use higher doses of testosterone, usually administered intramuscularly, report beneficial effects in the treatment of women with low levels of sexual desire (Goodman, personal communication, 1983; Riley, 1983). Controlled evaluation of high depot doses of testosterone is awaited.

The synthetic androgen mesterolone has been claimed on the basis of uncontrolled study to improve sexual desire in women (Häflinger and Hauser, 1973). A beneficial effect was obtained in 63 per cent of women who received intermittent therapy with mesterolone 20 mg daily from the fifth to the twenty-fourth day of the menstrual cycle but long-term treatment with 10 mg daily was relatively ineffective. The promoting effect of this androgen on sexual desire is interesting as mesterolone is not metabolized to oestrogen and therefore supports the contention that androgens have a direct effect on sexual interest in women.

CASE EXAMPLE

TP was a 32-year-old, happily married woman. She had had two normal pregnancies, the last being four years before she presented at a sex therapy clinic. She had never been interested in sex. She was able to experience sexual arousal and could attain orgasm though it frequently took her a long time to do so. There were no psychological factors to account for her lack of interest in sex. Counselling over the course of a year had been unsuccessful. Examination showed her to be a healthy woman with dry skin and hair. The labia and clitoris were poorly developed. Thyroid function tests were normal and she did not have a raised prolactin level. She was given Sustanon® 100 (testosterone esters), by deep intramuscular injection. Within two weeks of this injection she experienced sexual desire for the first time in her life. Two further injections at monthly intervals were given and she continued to show interest in sex. After the third Sustanon® injection she continued to have an acceptable level of sexual desire which was still present when she presented for a follow-up assessment three months later. Although this could have been a placebo effect, it was felt that this was unlikely in view of the delay between the first injection of Sustanon® and the increase in sexual desire.

OESTROGENS

Oestrogens are hormones which promote the development of secondary female sexual characteristics. The most important oestrogens are 17β oestradiol and oestrone. The activity of oestrone is probably dependent on its conversion to 17β oestradiol. In premenopausal women the principal source of oestrogens is the ovary although some is secreted by the adrenal cortex. In males, although both the testis and adrenal gland produce some oestrogen, the most important source is the extragonadal metabolism of androgens, particularly testosterone and androstenedione. This is also the case in women.

Sexual effects of oestrogens

Women

There is no convincing evidence that oestrogens have a direct effect in controlling sexual function in women. No correlation between plasma oestradiol levels and measures of sexual arousal, frequency of intercourse and sexual gratification were found in a group of premenopausal women (Persky *et al.*, 1978a).

Oestrogens can be considered to have a facilitating role on female sexual functioning. They are responsible for the functional integrity of the vagina. Oestrogen deficiency may result in atrophic changes in the lining of the vagina and impaired vasocongestive response during sexual arousal leading to lubrication inadequacy. These changes can be ameliorated with oestrogen treatment.

Studies in the Rhesus monkey have revealed correlation between oestrogen levels and the presence of male sex attractants (pheromones) in vaginal secretions. These are a series of short-chain fatty acids. Short-chain fatty acids have also been detected in the vaginal secretion of sexually aroused women and the amount of these was 7.56 times lower in women who were taking the oral contraceptive preparation Ortho-Novum 1.50® (Sokolov *et al.*, 1976). The role of pheromones in human sexual behaviour is not known but a group of couples increased the frequency of intercourse when vaginal secretions rather than a placebo were applied to the wife (Morris and Udry,

1975). Clinical experience has shown that some men experience improved sexual functioning when their postmenopausal partners receive oestrogen replacement therapy. Whether this is a pheromonal effect remains to be shown.

Men

The role, if any, that endogenous oestrogens have in the control of sexuality in men is unknown. There have been suggestions that the behavioural effects of androgens are dependent on their metabolic conversion to oestrogen, and there is evidence for this in several animal species. However, this does not appear to be the case in man since androgens that are not capable of conversion to oestrogens, for example, mesterolone and dihydrotestosterone appear to have the same behavioural effects in man as those androgens that are metabolized to oestrogens. Furthermore the administration of the anti-oestrogen tamoxifen to men does not impair sexual behaviour (Gooren, 1982).

Oestrogens have been used for many years in the treatment of carcinoma of the prostate but the treatment induces feminization; breast growth (gynaecomastia) is particularly marked. This is brought about by the direct stimulating effect of oestrogen on target organs and by the oestrogen-suppressing gonadal function and therefore testosterone secretion through inhibition of gonadotrophin release. As a result, oestrogen therapy may be associated with loss of interest in sex, ejaculatory dysfunction, reduced seminal volume and impaired erection. For this reason, oestrogens have been used to suppress sexual activity in sex offenders. The large doses of oestrogen required for this treatment have unpleasant side effects and antiandrogens such as cyproterone acetate are probably more useful treatments (Bancroft *et al.*, 1974).

PROLACTIN

Prolactin is a peptide hormone which is secreted by the anterior pituitary gland. Phylogenetically it is a very old hormone with many identified functions in different animals. In women prolactin is essential for the initiation and maintenance of lactation, an action which is dependent on prestimulation of the breast by oestrogen and progesterone. Prolactin also acts as a modulator of ovarian and testicular hormone production. It has weak growth-promoting activity and may be involved in calcium and salt and water metabolism. The most important factor that regulates the secretion of prolactin is dopamine which reaches the anterior pituitary from the hypothalamus via the portal venous system. Dopamine inhibits the secretion of prolactin, and it is for this reason that drugs possessing antidopaminergic activity cause increased circulating prolactin secretion (hyperprolactinaemia). The introduction of bromocriptine, a drug which inhibits the secretion of prolactin by acting with dopamine, has revolutionized the management of hyperprolactinaemia.

Hyperprolactinaemia

Men

Erection inadequacy and loss of interest in sex are well-recognized complaints in hyperprolactinaemic men (Perryman and Thorner, 1981). In one report it was these symptoms that prompted 20 of 22 patients, subsequently found to have hyperprolactinaemia, to seek medical attention (Carter *et al.*, 1978). Eight cases of hyperprolactinaemia were discovered in a series of 105 consecutive men presenting with erection failure (Spark *et al.*, 1980). In another series of men found on screening at a medical outpatient clinic to suffer from erection failure there was a 4 per cent incidence of hyperprolactinaemia (Slag *et al.*, 1983). Thus hyperprolactinaemia is an infrequent cause of sexual problems in men presenting at a sex therapy clinic. However since hyperprolactinaemia is amenable to treatment determination of plasma prolactin should be included in the evaluation of men presenting with erection inadequacy and low sexual desire.

There is probably more than one mechanism by which elevated prolactin levels impair sexual function. Hyperprolactinaemia is frequently associated with reduced plasma testosterone levels which increase when the prolactin level is normalized (Carter *et al.*, 1978; Spark *et al.*, 1980). However not all hyperprolactinaemic men who complain of erection inadequacy and impaired desire have significantly reduced plasma testosterone levels. Furthermore treatment with testosterone does not improve sexual function until the prolactin level is reduced to near normal levels (Carter *et al.*, 1978), suggesting a direct inhibiting effect of prolactin on sexual functioning.

Women

Hyperprolactinaemia is an important cause of infertility occurring in 15 to 20 per cent of non-pregnant amenorrhoeic women (Jacobs, 1976). In one report, 64 per cent of hyperprolactinaemic women complained, on direct questioning, of sexual difficulties but there was no difference in prolactin levels between those who experienced sexual difficulty and the women who did not (Merceron *et al.*, 1978). In another study, all 11 women with hyperprolactinaemic amenorrhoea suffered from low sexual desire and reduced sexual activity which resolved during treatment with bromocriptine (Fioretti *et al.*, 1977).

Few studies have investigated the incidence of hyperprolactinaemia in female patients who present with sexual difficulties. Moderate elevation of plasma prolactin level (18–50 ng/ml) was found in 5.6 per cent of a series of 133 women who presented with 'idiopathic frigidity' (Buvat *et al.*, 1978). The nature of the sexual difficulties were not described and the use of the word *idiopathic* means this cause was unknown. Riley (1984) reported an 18.4 per cent incidence of elevated prolactin levels in women who complained of reduced or absent interest in sex and/or arousal dysfunction. The patients who complained of only reduced or absent interest had significantly lower prolactin levels than those who also suffered arousal dysfunction. Eighty per cent of the patients in this series had consulted other sex therapists and therefore the patients in this study formed a selective group which was biased to a higher incidence of non-psychogenic sexual dysfunction. However, included in this series were 21 patients who had not consulted a sex therapist before and of these 4.8 per cent were found to have elevated prolactin levels. It is probable, therefore, that about 5 per cent of non-amenorrhoeic women presenting to a sex therapist with low interest and/or arousal dysfunction will have eleveated plasma prolactin levels.

Hypoprolactinaemia

Deficiency of prolactin secretion is very rare. Cases of erection inadequacy and premature ejaculation have been claimed to be associated with deficient prolactin secretion (Deutsch and Sherman, 1979). It is most likely that the sexual dysfunction in these cases is caused by disturbances in central neurotransmitter activity which also inhibits prolactin secretion rather than by a direct result of low circulating prolactin levels. I have seen three men who presented with erection inadequacy who had prolactin levels too low to measure. In none of these was there any other endocrinologic disturbance and their prolactin levels increased with thyroid releasing hormone and metoclopramide. Treatment with oral metoclopramide for eight weeks, which maintained their prolactin levels to or slightly above the normal range, did not resolve their sexual problem.

THE POSTMENOPAUSAL WOMAN

Sexual dysfunction is a common complaint in perimenopausal and postmenopausal women. Studd and Thom (1981) reported dyspareunia and decreased interest in sex are common presenting symptoms in patients attending a menopause clinic occurring in 45 per cent of women. The dyspareunia results from atrophic changes in the vagina and inadequate production of coital lubrication which are features of oestrogen deficiency. Loss of sexual desire may be secondary to the dyspareunia although many postmenopausal women who complain of decreased sexual interest and pleasure have apparently well oestrogenised vaginae (Studd and Thom, 1981). The menopause is associated with depression and irritability in some patients and in many women occurs around the time of socioeconomic changes in their life, factors which conceivably could influence sexual behaviour. Can the decrease in interest in sex be a direct result of changes in androgen production that occur in the postmenopausal women?

Persky *et al.* (1982) compared the androgen status and measures of sexual function of a group of regularly menstruating women (age range 21–31) with a group of postmenopausal women (age range 50–60). They found that the level of each of four androgens (DHEA, androstenedione, testosterone and dihydrotestosterone) was significantly lower in the postmenopausal women than in the younger subjects. However, the levels of self-rated sexual desire and degree of sexual arousal were not significantly different between the two groups although the younger women engaged in more frequent intercourse. Both groups experienced the same rate of orgasm, regardless of coital frequency, but the postmenopausal women reported feeling less sexually satisfied than the younger subjects. The authors questioned 'whether this was a consequence of the higher expectations of intimacy on the part of the older women as reflected in their equal levels of desire and arousal, or to some deficiencies on the part of their husbands' (p. 316).

Morrell *et al.* (1984) have studied the effect of age and hormonal status on sexual responses to erotic films and fantasy determined by vaginal photoplethysmography. Three groups of women were studied: young women (mean age 31 years) with regular menstrual cycles; older (mean age 51 years) premenopausal women; and postmenopausal women (mean age 57 years). The plasma oestrogen level of the postmenopausal women was less than 20 per cent of the level in the premenopausal women. The results of this study show that the postmenopausal women had significantly lower vaginal pulse amplitude responses to erotic films than either of the two groups of premenopausal women. The magnitude of difference amounted to only about 16 per cent. There were no significant differences in vaginal pulse amplitude responses to fantasy among the three groups. Furthermore there was no difference in self-reported sexual behaviour between the premenopausal and postmenopausal women.

Studies on the use of oestrogens and androgens in the management of the postmenopausal sexually dysfunctional patient have provided conflicting results. A confounding issue in assessing the effects of treatment is a highly significant placebo effect on ratings of coital satisfaction (Campbell and Whitehead, 1977). Fedor-Freyberg (1977) reported that oestrogen therapy improves sexual desire, sexual activity, orgasmic capacity, sexual satisfaction and pleasure, and sexual fantasies. These observations are supported to some extent by the results of study that compared oestradiol, progestogen and placebo (Dennerstein *et al.*, 1980). In this study oestrogen had a significant effect on vaginal dryness, sexual desire and orgasmic frequency. However, the extensive experience of Studd and his colleagues led them to report that oestrogen therapy improves sexual satisfaction only in women with dyspareunia secondary to atrophic vaginitis (Studd *et al.*, 1977a; 1977b). Oestrogen was without a significant sex desire-promoting effect in women with loss of desire and the absence of dyspareunia. These patients, however, gained significant improvement in sexual desire from the combined administration of oestradiol (50 mg) and testosterone (100 mg) implant.

More recently, Dow *et al.* (1983) compared implants of oestradiol (50 mg) alone with oestradiol (50 mg) combined with testosterone (100 mg) in postmenopausal women who were experiencing reduced sexual interest. Both treatments significantly improved sexual interest and responsiveness even in patients who denied any pretreatment dyspareunia. There is some evidence that oestrogen treatment may stimulate the production of adrenal androgens (Abraham and Maroulis, 1975).

THYROID DYSFUNCTION

The thyroid hormones influence sexual development and reproductive function in both sexes both by a direct effect of the hormones on metabolic processes and by an indirect effect mediated through changes in sex steroid hormones. In hypothyroidism the secretion of androgens is decreased but since there is also a decrease in the production of sex-hormone-binding globulin the amount of free testosterone may be actually increased. Hyperthyroidism is associated with an increase in sex-hormone-binding globulin and therefore a decrease in free testosterone.

In one study of hyperthyroid men 71 per cent experienced reduced interest in sex and 56 per cent suffered erection inadequacy (Kidd *et al.*, 1979). It has been claimed that 80 per cent of hypothyroid men show reduced interest in sex (Kolodny *et al.*, 1979). Eighty per cent of hypothyroid women experience arousal dysfunction of whom 50 per cent are anorgasmic (Kolodny *et al.*, 1979). Treatment of both hyperthyroidism and hypothyroidism usually results in improved sexual functioning.

The sex therapist must be aware that only slight changes in thyroid function may cause sexual difficulties in the absence of the more usual clinical features of thyroid dysfunction.

SEXUAL DYSFUNCTION AND HORMONAL CONTRACEPTION

Hormonal contraception in the female depends upon the administration either of a combination of oestrogen and progestogen or of progestogen alone. The different preparations of oral contraceptives currently available have differing relative oestrogenic/progestogenic potencies. Sexual problems are frequently reported by women using oral contraception (Kay, 1974). Other studies on the effect of this method of contraception on sexual behaviour have provided conflicting results with some studies showing enhanced and others suggesting impaired sexual desire and performance.

It has been suggested that reduced sexual desire in users of oral contraception is related to the progestogen content either by a direct inhibiting effect or indirectly by the progestogen inducing depression. The latter hypothesis is unlikely because not all women who complain of reduced sexual desire on oral contraception are depressed and the empirical use of antidepressants does not always cure the problem. Leeton *et al.* (1978) in a controlled study found a decrease in sexual response but no increase in depression index during treatment with an oral contraceptive. Furthermore, Cullberg (1972) found no correlation between changes in sexual desire and increases in progestogen content of oral contraceptives. Another explanation for reduced sexual desire may be reduced circulating levels of free testosterone resulting from oral contraception-induced increase in sex-hormone-binding globulin production (Pogmore and Jequier, 1979).

However, clinical experience suggests that changing women who complain of loss of interest in sex during oral contraception to a preparation with a higher oestrogen/progestogen ratio frequently alleviates the problem. This change of preparation is also helpful for women who experience vaginal dryness on this method of contraception.

It must be remembered that patients using oral contraception can experience sexual dysfunction totally unrelated to this method of contraception even when a temporal association between starting oral contraception and the reporting of the sexual problem suggests a causal relationship.

LUTEINIZING HORMONE RELEASING HORMONE

Luteinizing hormone releasing hormone (LHRU) is produced by the hypothalamus and stimulates the anterior pituitary gland to secrete gonadotrophin. Long-acting analogues of LHRH are now available. The administration of LHRH has been evaluated in the treatment of men suffering erection inadequacy (Benkert *et al.*, 1975; Davies *et al.*, 1976; Moss, 1978). Results have been equivocal, particularly in patients who are endocrinologically normal. In patients with hypogonadism secondary to hypothalamic-pituitary dysfunction LHRH has produced a significant improvement in sexual function even before the increase in testosterone secretion occurred

(Mortimer *et al.*, 1974). This observation may suggest that LHRH may have a direct effect on the sex centre in the brain. Evans and Distiller (1979) studied the acute effect of LHRH on sexual arousal induced by erotic stimuli in normal men. Although there was a trend towards an enhancing effect of LHRH on sexual arousal statistical significance was not achieved.

OXYTOCIN

Oxytocin is a hormone that is released from the posterior lobe of the pituitary gland. Its main functions are to stimulate contractions of the uterus during labour and the ejection of milk during lactation. There is a growing literature suggesting that oxytocin may be involved in sexual behaviour in animals.

There is a significant increase in circulating oxytocin levels after orgasm in women (Fox and Knaggs, 1969) and ejaculation in men (Ogawa *et al.*, 1980). In lactating women the increased oxytocin secretion may cause the release of milk during sexual orgasm. Oxytocin stimulates smooth muscle contraction including the vas deferens and uterus, but the actual role that oxytocin has in the physiology of the sexual response is not known. Nipple stimulation, which reflexly promotes oxytocin secretion appears to be essential in some women for the initiation of orgasm during love-making and in other women nipple stimulation facilitates the attainment of orgasm (Riley and Riley, in press).

Nasal administration of synthetic oxytocin in doses up to 8 units failed to facilitate the attainment of orgasm during genital stimulation in four anorgasmic women or to stimulate ejaculation in two men with retarded ejaculation (Riley and Riley, in press).

Oxytocin is inactivated by oxytocinase and an increase in circulating oxytocinase levels has been reported in men with erection inadequacy (Lidberg, 1972a). Synthetic oxytocin was claimed to be of some benefit in the treatment of a small group of such men (Lidberg, 1972b) but this observation awaits confirmation from other studies.

VASOACTIVE INTESTINAL POLYPEPTIDE

Vasoactive intestinal polypeptide (VIP) is a chemical that is released by some nerves and stimulates a response in adjacent cells. The genital organs, especially the erectile tissue, of both men and women are richly innervated by VIP containing nerves (Polak *et al.*, 1981; Ottesen *et al.*, 1982). Levels of VIP in the deep dorsal vein and corpus cavernosus of the penis in animals are increased during sexual stimulation (Dixson *et al.*, 1984) and during penile erection in man (Virag *et al.*, 1982). In the human female clitoral stimulation increases circulating VIP levels (Ottesen *et al.*, 1982). VIP relaxes penile smooth muscle and intracavernosal injection of VIP induces erection (Virag *et al.*, 1983). In the female it inhibits myometrial activity and increases myometrial blood flow. It is likely that VIP is involved in the initiation of the genital vascular changes that characterize the sexual response in both sexes. Penile VIPergic nerves have been reported to be reduced in a diabetic man suffering from erection inadequacy (Crowe *et al.*, 1983).

PRACTICAL CONSIDERATIONS

Which patients should be screened for hormone abnormalities?

The overall number of patients presenting to the sex therapist who are found to have endocrine abnormalities is small. However, since the majority of hormone abnormalities is treatable the likelihood of an endocrine cause for sexual dysfunction should be considered early in the clinical evaluation of the patient. There are possibly two exceptions to this: premature ejaculation and sexual dysfunctions which are obviously situational are unlikely to have a hormonal cause.

Since hormone tests are expensive and not readily available to all sex therapists it may not be practical to undertake hormone-screening of all patients. One solution is to screen patients only when they have failed to respond to behavioural approaches within a reasonable period of time. There are, however, some clinical presentations which make the presence of hormonal abnormalities more likely and in these patients it may be advantageous to undertake endocrine evaluation early in the patient's assessment, so that appropriate treatment can be investigated before the patient becomes demotivated by unsuccessful psychotherapy.

Men

1. All cases of primary erection and ejaculatory failure and low sexual desire.
2. Secondary ejaculatory failure, not related to drugs.
3. Secondary low sexual desire, particularly in the absence of total erection failure.
4. Sexual dysfunction (except premature ejaculation) in patients who have a history of alcohol abuse.
5. Sexual dysfunction (except premature ejaculation) in patients who have other symptoms or signs suggesting hormone imbalance, for example, infertility, gynaecomastia.

Women

1. Low sexual desire and/or arousal dysfunction in association with menstrual disturbances and/or infertility.
2. Arousal dysfunction and loss of sexual desire in the perimenopausal and postmenopausal woman.
3. Postpartum loss of sexual desire and/or arousal dysfunction.

Although in some patients with endocrine sexual dysfunction the correction of the hormone imbalance results in a dramatic amelioration of the sexual difficulty, other patients may have a superimposed psychogenic sexual dysfunction which may persist after the primary endocrine disturbance has been treated. Patients who are found to have an endocrine induced sexual difficulty must therefore receive appropriate behavioural therapy in addition to medical treatment for the endocrine disturbance.

ACKNOWLEDGEMENT

The author is very grateful to Wendy Phillips for the preparation of the manuscript.

REFERENCES

Abraham, G.E. and Maroulis, G.B. (1975) Pregnenolone, cortisol, and androgen in post-menopausal women, *Obstetrics and Gynaecology,* Vol. 45, pp. 271–7.

Appelt, H. and Strauss, B. (1984) Effects of anti-androgen treatment on the sexuality of women with hyperandrogenism, *Psychotherapy and Psychosomatics,* Vol. 42, pp. 177–81.

Bancroft, J., Davidson, D., Warner, P. and Tyrer, G. (1980) Androgens and sexual behaviour in women using oral contraceptives, *Clinical Endocrinology,* Vol. 12, pp. 327–40.

Bancroft, J., Tennent, T., Loucas, K. and Cass, J. (1974) Control of deviant sexual behaviour by drugs: behavioural effects of oestrogens and anti-androgens, *British Journal of Psychiatry*, Vol. 125, pp. 310–5.

Bancroft, J. and Wu, F.C. (1983) Changes in erectile responsiveness during androgen replacement therapy, *Archives of Sexual Behaviour*, Vol. 12, pp. 471–9.

Benkert, O., Jordan, R., Dahlen, H.C., Schneider, H.P.G. and Gammel, G. (1975) Sexual impotence: a double blind study of LHRH nasal spray versus placebo, *Neuropsychobiology*, Vol. 1, pp. 203–10.

Bowen, W.A., Monti, P.M. and Corriveau, D.P. (1978) Serum testosterone levels and sexual activity and interests in men, *Archives of Sexual Behavior*, Vol. 7, pp. 97–103.

Bremer, J. (1959) *Asexualization: A Follow-up Study of 244 Cases,* Macmillan, New York.

Bremner, W.J., Vitiello, M.V. and Prinz, P.N. (1983) Loss of circadian rhythmicity and blood testosterone levels with aging in normal men, *Journal of Clinical Endocrinology and Metabolism,* Vol. 56, pp. 1278–81.

Buvat, J., Buvat-Herbaut, M., Lemaire, A., Racadot, A. and Fossati, P. (1978) La prolactinemie dans 854 cas de dysfonctions sexuelles cliniquement idiopathiques, *Nouvelle Press Medicale*, Vol. 11, pp. 3543–6.

Campbell, S. and Whitehead, M. (1977) Oestrogen therapy and the menopausal syndrome, *Clinics in Obstetrics and Gynaecology,* Vol. 4, pp. 31–47.

Carney, A., Bancroft, J. and Matthews, A. (1978) Combination of hormonal and psychological treatments for female sexual unresponsiveness – a comparative study, *British Journal of Psychiatry*, Vol. 132, pp. 339–46.

Carter, J.N., Tyson, J.E., Tolis, G., Van Vliet, S., Faiman, C. and Friesen, H.G. (1978) Prolactin-secreting tumors and hypogonadism in 22 men, *New England Journal of Medicine*, Vol. 299, pp. 847–52.

Cittadini, E. and Barrace, P. (1977) Use of antiandrogens in gynecology, in L. Mertini and M. Motta (eds) *Androgens and Antiandrogens*, Raven Press, New York.

Crowe, R., Lincoln, J., Blacklay, P.F., Pryor, J.P., Lumley, J.S. and Burnstock, G. (1983) Vasoactive intestinal polypeptide-like immunoreactive nerves in diabetic penis. A comparison between streptozotocin-treated rats and man, *Diabetes*, Vol. 32, pp. 1075–7.

Cullberg, J. (1972) Mood changes and menstrual symptoms with different gestagen/estrogen combinations, *Acta Psychiatrica Scandinavica* (Suppl.), Vol. 236, pp. 1–84.

Davidson, J.M., Camargo, C.A. and Smith, E.T. (1979) Effects of androgens on sexual behavior in hypogonadal men, *Journal of Clinical Endocrinology and Metabolism*, Vol. 48, pp. 955–8.

Davidson, J.M., Chen, J.J., Crapo, L., Gray, G.D., Greenleaf, W.J. and Catania, J.A. (1983) Hormonal changes and sexual function in aging men, *Journal of Clinical Endocrinology and Metabolism,* Vol, 57, pp. 71–7.

Davies, T.F., Mountjoy, C.Q., Gomez-Pan, A., Watson, M.J., Hanker, J.P., Besser, G.M. and Hall, R. (1976) A double blind cross over trial of gonadotrophin releasing hormones (LHRH) in sexually impotent men, *Clinical Endocrinology*, Vol. 5, pp. 601–7.

Dennerstein, L., Burrows, G.D., Wood, C. and Hymen, G. (1980) Hormones and sexuality: effect of estrogen and progestogen, *Obstetrics and Gynecology,* Vol. 56, pp. 316–22.

Deutsch, S. and Sherman, L. (1979) Hypoprolactinaemia in men with secondary sexual impotence and men with premature ejaculation, Endocrinology Society Meeting, *Abstracts*, p. 350.

Dixson, A.F., Kendrick, K.M., Blank, M.A. and Bloom, S.R. (1984) Effects of tactile and electrical stimuli upon release of vasoactive intestinal polypeptide in the mammalian penis, *Journal of Endocrinology,* Vol. 100, pp. 249–52.

Dow, M.G.T., Hart, D.M. and Forrest, C.A. (1983) Hormone treatments of sexual unresponsiveness in post-menopausal women: A comparative study, *British Journal of Obstetrics and Gynaecology,* Vol. 90, pp. 361–6.

Evans, I.M. and Distiller, L.A. (1979) Effects of luteinizing hormone releasing hormone on sexual arousal in normal men, *Archives of Sexual Behavior,* Vol. 8, pp. 385–96.

Fedor-Freyberg, P. (1977) The influence of oestrogens on the well-being and mental performance in climacteric and post-menopausal women, *Acta Obstetricia et Gynecologia Scandinavica* (Suppl.), p. 64.

Fioretti, P., Corsini, G.U., Murru, S., Medda, F. and Genazzini, A.R. (1977) Depression and sexual behaviour in hyperprolactinaemic amenorrhoea. Effect of bromoergocriptine treatment, *Acta Endocrinologica,* Vol. 85, p. 141.

Fox, C.A. and Knaggs, G.S. (1969) Milk-ejection activity (oxytocin) in peripheral venous blood in man during lactation and in association with coitus, *Journal of Endocrinology*, Vol. 45, pp. 145–6.

Goodman, R. (1983) Personal communication.

Gooren, L. (1982) Aromatization of testosterone to estradiol is not required for maintenance of sexual behavior in the male, *Proceedings of the 5th World Congress of Sexology*.

Greenblatt, R.B. (1943) Testosterone propionate pellet implantation in gynecic disorders, *Journal of the American Medical Association*, Vol. 121, pp. 17–24.

Greenblatt, R.B., Montama, F., Torpin, R. and Augusta, G.A. (1942) Sexual libido in the female, *American Journal of Obstetrics and Gynecology,* Vol. 3, pp. 235–8.

Häflinger, O. and Hauser G.A. (1973) Therapeutic trial of Proviron in frigidity, *Therapeutische Umschau,* Vol. 30, pp. 533–6.

Imperato-McGinley, J., Peterson, R.E., Gautier, T. and Sturla, E. (1979) Androgens and the evolution of male-gender identity among male pseudohermaphrodites with a 5 α reductase deficiency, *The New England Journal of Medicine,* Vol. 300, pp. 1233–7.

Jacobs, H.S. (1976) Prolactin and amenorrhoea, *New England Journal of Medicine,* Vol. 295, pp. 954–6.

Jensen, R.T., Collen, M.T., Randoc, S.J., Allende, M.D., Raufman, J.P., Bissonnette, B.M., Duncan, W.C., Durgin, P.L., Gillin, J.C. and Gardner, J.D. (1983) Cimetidine-induced impotence and breast changes in patients with gastric hypersecretory states, *New England Journal of Medicine*, Vol. 309, pp. 883–7.

Kay, C.R. (1974) *Oral Contraceptives and Health: An Interim Report from O C Study,* Pitman Medical, Manchester.

Kellett, J.M. (1984) Testosterone: a treatment for low libido in women, *British Journal of Sexual Medicine*, Vol. 11, pp. 82–7.

Kidd, G.S., Glass, A.R. and Vigersky, R.A. (1979) The hypothalamic-pituitary-testicular axis in thyrotoxicosis, *Journal of Clinical Endocrinology and Metabolism,* Vol. 48, pp. 798–802.

Kolodny, R.C., Masters, W.H. and Johnson, V.E. (1979) *Textbook of Sexual Medicine*. Little, Brown, Boston.

Kwan, M., Greenleaf, W.J., Mann, J., Crapo, L. and Davidson, J.M. (1983) The nature of androgen action on male sexuality: a combined laboratory self-report study on hypogonadal men, *Journal of Clinical Endocrinology and Metabolism,* Vol. 57, pp. 557–62.

Leeton, J., McMaster, R. and Worsley, A. (1978) The effects on sexual response and mood after sterilization of women taking long-term oral contraception: Results of a double-blind cross-over study, *Australian and New Zealand Journal of Obstetrics and Gynaecology*, Vol. 18, pp. 194–7.

Lidberg, L. (1972a) Oxytocinase levels in patients suffering from impotence, *Hormones*, Vol. 5, p. 273.

Lidberg, L. (1972b) The effect of syntocinon on patients suffering from impotence, *Pharmakopsychiatry,* Vol. 5, p. 187.

Luttge, W.B. (1971) The role of gonadal hormones in the sexual behavior of the Rhesus monkey and human: a literature survey, *Archives of Sexual Behavior*, Vol. 1, pp. 61–8.

Mathews, A., Whitehead, A. and Kellett, J. (1983) Psychological and hormonal factors in the treatment of female sexual dysfunction, *Psychological Medicine*, Vol. 13, pp. 83–92.

Merceron, R.E., Raymond, J.P., Courreges, J.P. and Klotz, H.P. (1978) Sexualité et hormones gonadiques au cours de l'hyperprolactinemie dans les deux sexes, *Annales de Médecine Interne*, Vol. 129, pp. 681–6.

Money, J. and Ehrhardt, A.A. (1972) *Man and Woman: Boy and Girl. Differentiation and Diphorphism of Gender Identity from Conception to Maturity*, Johns Hopkins University Press, Baltimore.

Morrell, M.J., Dixen, J.M., Carter, C.S. and Davidson, J.M. (1984) The influence of age and cycling status on sexual arousability in women, *American Journal of Obstetrics and Gynecology,* Vol. 148, pp. 66–71.

Morris, N.M. and Udry, J.R. (1975) *An Experimental Search for Pheromonal Influences on Human Sexual Behavior*, Eastern Conference on Reproductive Behavior, Nags Head NC.

Mortimer, C.H., McNeilly, A.S., Fisher, R.A., Murray, M.A.F. and Besser, G.M. (1974) Gonadotrophin releasing hormone therapy in hypogonadal males with hypothalamic or pituitary dysfunction, *British Medical Journal*, Vol. 4, pp. 617–21.

Moss, R.L. (1978) Effects of hypothalamic peptides on sex behavior in animal and man, in M.A. Lipton, A. Dimascio and K.R. Killman (eds) *Psychopharmacology: A Generation of Progress*, Raven Press, New York.

O'Carroll, R. and Bancroft, J. (1984) Testosterone therapy for low sexual interest and erectile dysfunction in men: a controlled study, *British Journal of Psychiatry,* Vol. 145, pp. 146–51.

Ogawa, S., Kudo, S., Kitsunai, Y. and Fukuchi, S. (1980) Increase in oxytocin secretion at ejaculation in male, *Clinical Endocrinology*, Vol. 13, pp. 95–7.

Ottesen, B., Ulrichsen, H., Fahrenkrug, J., Larsen, J.J., Wagner, G., Schierup, L. and Søndergaard, F. (1982) Vasoactive intestinal polypeptide and the female genital tract: relationship to reproductive phase and delivery, *American Journal of Obstetrics and Gynecology,* Vol. 143, pp. 414–20.

Perryman, R.L. and Thorner, M.O. (1981) The effects of hyperprolactinemia on sexual and reproductive function in man, *Journal of Andrology*, Vol. 5, pp. 233–42.

Persky, H., Charney, N., Lief, H.I., O'Brien, C.P., Miller, W.R. and Strauss, D. (1978a) The relationship of plasma estradiol level to sexual behavior in young women, *Psychosomatic Medicine*, Vol. 40, pp. 523–35.

Persky, H., Lief, H.I., Strauss, D., Miller, W.R. and O'Brien, C.P. (1978b) Plasma testosterone level and sexual behavior of couples, *Archives of Sexual Behavior*, Vol. 7, pp. 157–73.

Persky, H., Dreisbach, L., Miller, W.R., O'Brien, C.P., Khan, M.A., Lief, H.I., Charney, N. and Strauss, D. (1982) The relationship of plasma androgen level to sexual behaviors and attitudes of women, *Psychosomatic Medicine*, Vol. 44, pp. 305–20.

Pogmore, J.R. and Jequier, A.M. (1979) Effect of varying amounts of ethinyl oestradiol in the combined oral contraceptive on plasma sex hormone binding globulin capacity in normal women, *British Journal of Obstetrics and Gynaecology*, Vol. 86, pp. 563–7.

Polak, J.M., Gu, J., Mina, S. and Bloom, S.R. (1981) Vipergic nerves in the penis, *Lancet*, Vol. ii, pp. 218–9.

Raboch, J. and Starka, L. (1973) Reported coital activity of men and levels of plasma testosterone, *Archives of Sexual Behaviour*, Vol. 12, pp. 309–15.

Riley, A.J. (1983) Androgens and female libido, *British Journal of Sexual Medicine*, Vol. 10, No. 96, pp. 5–6.

Riley, A.J. (1984) Prolactin and female sexual function, *British Journal of Sexual Medicine,* Vol. 11, pp. 14–17.
Riley, A.J. and Riley, E.J. (1986) The effect of single dose diazepam on female sexual response induced by masturbation, *Sexual and Marital Therapy*, Vol. 1, pp. 49–53.
Riley, A.J. and Riley, E.J. (In press) Oxytocin and coitus, *Sexual and Marital Therapy*.
Rubin, H.B., Henson, D.E., Falvo, R.E. and High, R.W. (1979) The relationship between men's endogenous levels of testosterone and their penile responses to erotic stimuli, *Behaviour Research and Therapy*, Vol. 17, pp. 305–12.
Salmon, U.J. and Geist, S.H. (1943) The effects of androgens upon libido in women, *Journal of Clinical Endocrinology,* Vol. 3, pp. 353–8.
Sanders, D. and Bancroft, J. (1982) Hormones and the sexuality of women in the menstrual cycle, *Clinics in Endocrinology and Metabolism*, Vol. 11, No. 3, pp. 639–59.
Schon, M. and Sutherland, A.M. (1960) The role of hormones in human behavior. III: changes in female sexuality after hypophysectomy, *Journal of Clinical Endocrinology,* Vol. 20, pp. 822–41.
Skakkebaek, N., Bancroft, J., Davidson, D. and Warner, P. (1981) Androgen replacement with oral testosterone undecanoate in hypogonadal men: a double blind controlled study, *Clinical Endocrinology,* Vol. 14, pp. 49–61.
Slag, M.F., Morley, J.E., Elson, M.K. *et al.* (1983) Impotence in medical clinic outpatients, *Journal of the American Medical Association,* Vol. 249, pp. 1736–40.
Sokolov, J.J., Harris, R.T. and Hecker, M.R. (1976) Isolation of substances from human vaginal secretions previously shown to be sex attractant pheromones in higher primates, *Archives of Sexual Behavior,* Vol. 5, pp. 269–76.
Spark, R.F., White, R.A. and Connolly, P.B. (1980) Impotence is not always psychogenic: newer insights into hypothalamic-pituitary-gonadal dysfunction, *Journal of the American Medical Association*, Vol. 243, pp. 750–5.
Studd, J.W.W., Chakravarti, S. and Oram, D. (1977a) The climacteric, *Clinics in Obstetrics and Gynaecology,* Vol. 4, pp. 3–29.
Studd, J.W.W., Collins, W.P., Chakravarti, S., Newton, J.R., Oram, D. and Parsons, A. (1977b) Oestradiol and testosterone implants in the treatment of psychosexual problems in the post-menopausal woman, *British Journal of Obstetrics and Gynaecology*, Vol. 84, pp. 314–5.
Studd, J.W.W. and Thom, M.H. (1981) Ovarian failure and ageing, *Clinics in Endocrinology and Metabolism,* Vol. 10, No. 1, pp. 89–113.
Sturup, G.K. (1968) Treatment of sexual offenders in Herstedvester Denmark. The rapist, *Acta Psychiatrica Scandinavica* (Suppl.), Vol. 204, pp. 5–6.
Vermeulen, A. (1979) Decline in sexual activity in aging men: correlation with sex hormone levels and testicular changes, *Journal of Biosocial Science* (Suppl.), Vol. 6, pp. 5–18.
Virag, R., Ottensen, B., Fahrenkrug, J., Levy, C. and Wagner, G. (1982) Vasoactive intestinal polypeptide release during penile erection in man, *Lancet*, Vol. ii, p. 1166.
Virag, R., Ottensen, B., Wagner, G. and Fahrenkrug, J. (1983) VIP as neurotransmitter in penile erection, *Regulatory Peptides*, Vol. 6, p. 301.
Waxenberg, S.E., Drellich, M.G. and Sutherland, A.M. (1959) The role of hormones in human behaviour. I: Changes in female sexuality after adrenalectomy, *Journal of Clinical Endocrinology,* Vol. 19, pp. 193–202.
Willson, R.J., Beecham, C.T. and Carrington, E.R. (1975) *Obstetrics and Gynecology*, Mosby, St Louis.

CHAPTER 5

THE PSYCHOLOGICAL BASIS OF SEXUAL DYSFUNCTION

Anna Leeming and Paul T. Brown

What is sexual dysfunction? Hawton (1985) defines it as 'the persistent impairment of the normal patterns of sexual interest or response' (p. 30). But this perhaps fails to convey the subtleties of sexual difficulties – a problem can be intermittent and yet perceived as severe, and the wide variety of sexual practices and preferences challenges any clear-cut description of *normality*. The onus of definition may lie very particularly with the individual: What does functioning effectively mean to the *person*? and What actually represents a 'problem'?

Sexual disorders may stem from medical rather than psychological factors. Kaplan (1974) estimated that about 10 per cent of her patients' sexual difficulties could be related to a physical cause like diabetes, alcohol abuse or neurological disease, whereas in other estimates the figures ranged from 3–20 per cent. However, this chapter is concerned only with the *psychological* factors which most commonly underlie sexual disorder.

In discussing the broad range of sexual activity we are indebted in the first instance to the work of Masters and Johnson (1966; 1970) in the US, who devised therapy techniques aimed at helping couples – partners within a relationship, as opposed to individuals in isolation. They described sexual function in terms of a four-phase cycle of sexual response common to both sexes. Initial stimulation began the *excitement* phase, and the individual then moved progressively through the *plateau* and *orgasmic* phases to the *resolution* phase, during which the body returned to the unstimulated state following orgasm.

Kaplan (1974) modified this model and described instead a biphasic model of sexual response consisting of *excitement* (or *arousal*) and *orgasm* (or *response*) phases. Later she added a third stage to this description – that of *sexual desire* (Kaplan, 1979). It is this final model which will be used in this chapter as a framework for the discussion of disorders.

In her triphasic model, Kaplan (1979) describes how similar processes are experienced by both sexes during sexual activity, but particular disorders are specific to each sex and related to each stage of the cycle. In the male there are disorders of desire, erectile function and ejaculation. In the female the disorders are of desire, capacity to become aroused and orgasm.

A distinction must be made between those people who have experienced difficulty ever since they became sexually active, and those who present with a problem which has suddenly or gradually developed. The first group are considered to have a 'primary' disorder, and the latter a 'secondary' disorder (Masters and Johnson, 1970). The psychological factors contributing to each may be very different.

Similarly Masters and Johnson (1970) identified a distinction between disorders which occurred in all situations and those which occurred selectively. Is a woman orgasmic when she masturbates, but not with a partner (a 'situational' problem)? Does a man experience premature ejaculation with all extramarital partners as well as with his wife (a 'total' or global problem)?

Detailed history-taking is essential to piece together an accurate picture of the disorder itself and its impact on the individual(s) concerned. If psychological rather than medical causes are indicated, these may be acting in three different ways. First, as *predisposing* factors; past experiences may be predisposing the individual to respond in a sexually dysfunctional way: second, as *precipitating* factors; past experiences may determine that an individual's reaction to a crisis includes an adverse effect on his or her sexual functioning: third, as *maintaining* factors; a sexual difficulty arises and, instead of being transient, persists because intervening psychological factors prevent its resolution (Hawton, 1985).

Who is vulnerable? Arentewicz and Schmidt (1983) point out that individuals who are ambivalent about close relationships, that is, have a strong need for but at the same time a strong fear of intimacy, are likely to develop sexual difficulties.

Barlow (1986) suggests that some individuals may be predisposed towards sexual dysfunction because of their negative perceptions or expectations in a sexual situation, which may lead to avoidance of erotic cues. Moreover, he notes the finding – perhaps an example of the negative perceptions previously described – that dysfunctional men tend to underrate their level of sexual arousal, and to underestimate their ability to suppress or control it.

Contrary to the prediction of psychoanalytic theory, neuroses and personality disorders do not invariably lead to sexual difficulties. However, individuals with obsessive reactions are particularly vulnerable to performance anxiety. Furthermore, the sexual interest of their partners may become impaired as the obsessive behaviour becomes increasingly 'turning-off' (Kaplan, 1983).

Kaplan (1979) puts forward the view that a person's physical response to stress is as unique and unchanging as his or her thumbprint – some individuals will always react with muscle tension, others with increased stomach acidity, and yet others with changes in the genital blood vessels. Moreover, the individual's specific response pattern is a major factor determining which symptom he or she may develop. Thus, if sexual activity evokes anxiety, this may lead in one individual to reduced sexual desire, in another to erectile dysfunction and in yet another to orgasmic difficulties. It may therefore be difficult to predict predisposition towards any particular sexual dysfunction without clear insight into an individual's unique experience of and response to stress.

THE NATURE OF SEXUAL FUNCTION

Any discussion of sexual *dysfunction* requires prior reference to sexual *function*. We describe briefly Kaplan's triphasic model of desire, excitement and orgasm (Kaplan, 1979) as a description of sexual function, so that sexual dysfunction can subsequently be explored in the same light.

Desire

Sexual desire is an appetite or drive akin to hunger and thirst. It may not directly involve the genital organs, but is a sensation activated in the brain which prompts the individual to seek fulfilment – either by initiating or by responding to sexual activity.

Excitement (or arousal)

Sexual excitement is characterized by complementary changes in the genital organs of both sexes. Dilation of the blood vessels causes the penis to enlarge and harden in order to penetrate the vagina, and similarly the vagina reacts by swelling and moistening in order to accommodate the penis.

Orgasm (or response)

In both sexes orgasm consists of a series of reflex contractions of the genital muscles. The male experiences two distinct phases – emission and ejaculation – while the female experiences only one, rhythmic contractions comparable to those experienced by the male during ejaculation.

Although the sexual activity of the well-functioning individual usually incorporates all three stages from initial desire to orgasm, they are not irrevocably bound in sequence. For example, the reflexes of arousal and orgasm may be evoked by stimulation even in a person with low sex drive; or an individual may experience both desire and excitement, but fail to achieve ejaculation or orgasm.

THE NATURE OF SEXUAL DYSFUNCTION

Disorders can occur at each stage of the response cycle. They may be serving several purposes – for example, as a defence against anxiety or an expression of conflict within a relationship. Frequently, there is no single determinant: a variety of experiences throughout the life history serve to promote a particular dysfunction.

However, Kaplan (1974) makes a clear differentiation between *immediate* and *remote* psychological causes of sexual dysfunction. The former operate in the present to inhibit the sexual response as it occurs; examples include fear of failure and communication difficulties between partners. The latter are more deeply rooted in the individual's past – for instance, unconscious conflicts related to childhood or marital experience. Nevertheless, notwithstanding this differentiation, Kaplan adopts a multicausal approach to assessment and treatment – she stresses that sexual dysfunction may relate to a variety of factors, and consequently may require a variety of therapeutic techniques.

Moreover, presenting symptoms rapidly become divorced from their original identifiable causes as they begin to be self-reinforcing – for example, an incident of sexual failure leads to fear of repeated failure and perhaps increased demand from the partner; this fear inhibits performance on the next occasion which further augments the anxiety and stress. The dysfunction becomes autonomous and increasingly dissociated from any deeper psychological causes which may exist (Arentewicz and Schmidt, 1983).

SPECIFIC DISORDERS AND THEIR CAUSES

The desire phase

Kaplan (1979) describes dysfunction in this early stage as the consequence of the interaction between anxiety and sensation. Sexual awakening provokes anxiety which in turn provokes repression – turning off the sexual response. It is the individual's defences against anxiety which interact with the sexual response to present the symptom. This is characterized by an apparent low interest in sex, and little inclination either to pursue sexual fulfilment or to take advantage of any sexual opportunity that arises.

Impaired sexual desire (male)
It is unusual for a man to present with impaired sexual interest as a primary disorder. More often it is accompanied by a performance difficulty such as erectile or ejaculatory dysfunction. When it occurs as a secondary disorder in the absence of any medical cause, and is evidenced by a noted reduction or absence of desire, it is usually indicative of relationship difficulties. These may be characterized by anger or resentment between partners: such feelings, possibly of diverse origin, tend to be incompatible with an individual's normal sexual response (Bancroft, 1983).

Impaired sexual interest is a common symptom of depression and it can also occur as a side effect of antidepressant drugs. Other psychiatric disorders such as mania and schizophrenia may also be accompanied by reduced drive. Another frequent link is with alcoholism (Hawton, 1985): not only is a high level of alcohol likely to have an inhibiting effect in any sexual encounter, but the consequences of alcohol abuse tend to be severe in interpersonal terms – often leading to the development of sexual difficulties which are then maintained within the relationship.

Impaired sexual desire (female)
Lack of interest or enjoyment is the most commonly presented problem amongst women (Bancroft, 1983). A distinction needs to be made between whether a woman's impaired sexual interest is total (and primary), whereby she rarely engages in masturbation or fantasy; or situational whereby she may be attracted to other men but no longer to her partner (secondary or situational). Similarly, her impairment may be only partial in that she is able to respond to sexual stimulation but would have no inclination to initiate sex spontaneously. A total lack of interest is likely to have its roots in childhood experiences, whereas a reduction or absence of desire for a partner is more likely to reflect relationship difficulties or be related to recent events such as childbirth, or the onset of depression (Hawton, 1985). Radical surgery of a disfiguring nature is especially likely to trigger sexual difficulties: Maguire *et al.* (1978) found that 56 per cent of mastectomy patients developed medium- or long-term sexual problems, compared with only 8 per cent of controls.

Uncertainty about gender identity (traditionally referred to by psychoanalysts as 'penis envy') can have an inhibitory influence upon both desire and arousal by promoting a negative body image, especially where the sexual organs are concerned. A general insecurity thus impinges upon sexual function, especially in circumstances when gender identity is felt to be under threat as a result of external circumstances such as career setbacks or the onset of menopause.

Impaired sexual desire (male and female)
In both men and women impaired sexual appetite may be linked to

personality factors in that the individual has a tendency to avoid pleasurable activities in general or specifically sexual pleasure (Bancroft, 1983). What causes the anxiety which can inhibit desire? The psychoanalytic view relates it to childhood experiences. For example, if the basic demands for food, warmth and comfort in infancy are frustrated or unfulfilled, this may lead to expectations of disappointment in adulthood, whereby sexual desire promotes fear of unfulfilment. Dysfunction then occurs as a defence against anticipated disappointment (Arentewicz and Schmidt, 1983).

Some individuals have developed negative attitudes towards their body and sexual functions. Or a poor self-image may lead to unease with sexual activity (Bancroft, 1983). Feeling bad about oneself or one's body encourages inhibition during sexual activity because an atmosphere of trust and security are less readily achieved. Self-consciousness about physical attributes is more characteristic of women. Nevertheless, a man who is experiencing problems at work may feel less potent as a man and develop reduced desire or performance difficulties in consequence. Similarly, fears of failure in performance or rejection by one's partner may be linked to low self-esteem – or doubts about sexual competence and attraction to others.

Alternatively, individuals may experience a fear of loss of control which can inhibit sexual response at different stages. The psychoanalytic view relates this to the anal stage. If the pleasure experienced by infants in excretory functions conflicts with parental demands, this may be expressed in adulthood in a reluctance to lose control or 'let go' (Arentewicz and Schmidt, 1983).

The closeness implicit in the sexual relationship can also be perceived as intensely threatening, and again dysfunction may occur as a defence against this anxiety. Attachment in childhood may be associated with loss or overdependency. Loss through the death or physical absence of a parent may engender such insecurity that intimacy in adulthood is beset with anxiety. Conversely, in childhood, overdependency on the parent of opposite sex may result in the identification and unfair comparison of all future partners with that parent. From the psychoanalytic viewpoint, this Oedipal fixation also arouses fears of early incestuous desires. Either may lead an individual to avoid sexual involvement. Where adult relationships are entered into, a balance between closeness and distance is established within the partnership; however, events can occur to upset the equilibrium – for instance, if the dependency of one partner is suddenly increased – and these may lead to the withdrawal of closeness by the other as demonstrated by sexual withdrawal.

Some partnership difficulties may stem from lack of communication, either related specifically to sexual needs and anxieties or concerning the relationship in more general terms. As Hawton (1985) points out, the absence of clear expression can set in motion a cycle of guesswork, misconception, resentment and continuing disharmony.

Anxieties which relate to sexuality may be associated with morality. For example, if in childhood sexual interest is met with punishment or sexual development is denied, the individual may come to see sexual activity in terms of good and bad. And conflict may occur subsequently when early taboos coincide with the more liberal attitudes of adulthood. Again sexual dysfunction may develop as a defence against the anxiety which this conflict generates (Arentewicz and Schmidt, 1983).

The excitement (arousal) phase

Kaplan (1979) argues that disorders of this middle phase of the sexual cycle are not consequences of the defences against anxiety previously described, but instead direct consequences of the anxiety itself, the defences against which have failed to be effective – for example, the fear of sexual failure (or performance anxiety) as a common cause of impotence. On the other hand, Barlow (1986) points out that anxiety does not invariably have an adverse effect on sexual functioning: some recent studies show *increased* arousal in response to experimentally induced stress (Beck and Barlow, 1984; Norton and Jehu, 1984). Barlow (1986) suggests that a negative or positive reaction may be determined in part by the existing quality of the individual's sexual functioning – in comparing functional and dysfunctional males, he found that anxiety (artificially induced by threat of shock) increased arousal in the former and decreased it in the latter. This evidence suggests that, while the genesis of an existing dysfunction may remain unclear, anxiety may act as one of its maintaining factors.

Impaired sexual arousal (female)

Impaired sexual arousal is rarely seen in isolation in the female – it is more often accompanied by impaired sexual interest which in turn inhibits the usual physiological responses of vaginal swelling and lubrication. It can occur, however, after childbirth or menopause as a result of hormonal changes (Hawton, 1985).

Impaired sexual arousal (male)

Erectile dysfunction. A total inability to achieve an erection is rare, except when the causes have a medical basis. When it did occur amongst Masters and Johnson's patients, the psychological causes could be traced in most instances either to a severely religious background or to an initial sexual experience of a traumatic nature (Belliveau and Richter, 1970). In the former case, guilt and ignorance combined to bring about erectile failure; in the latter, an experience such as a humiliating episode with a prostitute led the individual to perceive sexual activity as degrading and, consequently, something to be avoided.

The more commonly presented problem, however, is when a man is able to become erect during masturbation, but is unable to achieve or maintain an erection with a partner. This 'situational' difficulty usually has a psychological rather than a medical base (Hawton, 1985).

Erectile function is particularly vulnerable to anxiety. A common cause of anxiety is performance fear – the man fears that he will be unable either to achieve an erection or to maintain it long enough to penetrate and satisfy his partner. He tries to 'will' or control his erection, which only serves to inhibit his own natural sensitivity and pleasure. The consequence is that he *is* unable to achieve or maintain his erection – his concentration on his performance has confirmed his fears and will strengthen them the next time a sexual opportunity occurs. A vicious circle develops when there is anticipation of failure: the well-functioning partner may react by making increasing demands, tension grows, the anticipated failure becomes actual failure. The problem either persists or deteriorates to the extent that sexual activity ceases altogether.

What does performance fear originate from? The male is extremely sensitive to such fears: even one failure to achieve erection can be sufficient to make a man doubt his masculinity – that is, his ability to perform 'like a man'. The anxiety this generates can lead to undue concern with his physical performance on the next occasion. Even if there is a rational cause for failure – such as an excessive amount of alcohol – the fact that the failure occurred may be enough to begin the vicious circle.

Alternatively, performance fear already present in the premature ejaculator may increase gradually until the individual develops secondary erectile difficulties in addition to his ejaculatory problems. Masters and Johnson (1970) noted how the premature ejaculator's desperate attempts to hold back can lead to the 'spectatoring' which inhibits sexual response – in these circumstances preventing erection. More recently, a study by Abrahamson *et al.* (1985b) reports how the levels of arousal in sexually dysfunctional men are not adversely affected by the presentation of distracting stimuli unrelated to sexual performance. Barlow (1986) suggests that this may be because sexually dysfunctional men are effectively distracted already – that is, their usual response pattern is inhibited to some degree by the interference of other competing thoughts and concerns. Focusing on non-sexual matters is an effective way of dissociating oneself from physical sensation and therefore reducing erotic sensitivity (Bancroft, 1983).

The partner of a premature ejaculator may have considerable influence on how the disorder develops – if she subjects him to ridicule or criticism or if she reacts with increased sexual demands because of her own growing frustration, the progression from premature ejaculation into secondary erectile difficulties may be hastened. Several studies indicate that sexually dysfunctional men tend to become markedly less aroused than sexually functional men when presented with performance related stimuli (e.g. a film showing a woman in a state of high arousal) (Beck *et al.*, 1983; Heiman and Rowland, 1983; Abrahamson *et al.*, 1984a).

The orgasm phase

Kaplan (1979) sees disorders of orgasm in both sexes as deriving either from inadequate stimulation or from obsessive concentration on performance. As with premature ejaculation 'spectatoring' is undertaken as an unconscious defence against anxiety by attempting to control it, but in reality the conscious attention which is focused upon the orgasmic reflex only serves to inhibit it.

Female dysfunction

Orgasmic dysfunction. This can be a primary and total disorder in which a woman has never achieved orgasm. In some cases it may be linked to arousal difficulties; in others, women may be highly arousable and yet unable to reach orgasm. Or it can be secondary and situational whereby a woman achieves orgasm in some circumstances but not in others, for example, during masturbation but not during intercourse, with one partner but not with another. However, as Fisher (1973) points out, women who are capable of orgasm do not invariably experience one, and their satisfaction in love-making is not dependent upon the consistency of their response. Perhaps in this area more than any other, the definition of *dysfunction* must take account of the attitudes and expectations of the person concerned.

Women who have never achieved orgasm frequently express negative attitudes towards sex. Even in today's society females are subjected to a double standard: whereas men are encouraged to accept and exploit their sexual feelings, promiscuity remains a stigma amongst women. At the same time, some women experience a home background where sexual matters are denied or repressed (perhaps with the support of religious sanction which equates sex with sin). Thus a woman may develop a highly restrictive and negative value system which subsequently affects her ability to function sexually (Belliveau and Richter, 1970).

Alternatively, primary orgasmic dysfunction may be related directly to the partner of the woman concerned. In reality, negative attitudes towards sex may reflect negative feelings towards him as a person – she may see him as 'second-best' in some way or otherwise feel disillusioned with her choice. Or the woman's symptom may be a reflection of her partner's own sexual inadequacy, whereby *her* concern with *his* performance inhibits her own sexual response – this is illustrated by the common association of orgasmic difficulties in the female with premature ejaculation in the male (Belliveau and Richter, 1970).

Negative feelings may also relate selectively to aspects of sexual activity: for example, a woman brought up to consider touching as sinful may be able to achieve orgasm through intercourse but not through masturbation or oral-genital contact (Belliveau and Richter, 1970).

Secondary orgasmic dysfunction is also associated with a negative attitude towards a partner. It may be that a woman has ceased to see her partner in a positive light – perhaps as the result of changes in his behaviour (e.g. in cases of infidelity or alcoholism) – and her negative feelings towards him are expressed in her diminishing sexual response.

Male dysfunction

Premature ejaculation. What do we mean by 'premature'? Apart from ejaculation which occurs either before or immediately after vaginal penetration, which must generally be considered premature, as Hawton (1985) points out, it is 'the extent to which the couple feel that the man's ejaculatory control is sufficient to allow intercourse which is satisfactory for them both' (p. 37) which should be the decisive factor.

Premature ejaculation can occur as either a primary or a secondary disorder, but it is more commonly the former. It may stem from sexual experience in adolescence: not only is rapid ejaculation a biological characteristic of relative sexual immaturity, there are circumstances in which it may be considered particularly desirable, for example, in an encounter with a prostitute or during covert sexual activity where there is a risk of detection. Masters and Johnson (1970) argue that it can take only a few such episodes for speedy ejaculation to become a habit then perceived as undesirable and dysfunctional in the sexual relationships of adulthood.

Alternatively, premature ejaculation may occur because an individual has not learned to control the speed of his adolescent response. The feeling that ejaculation is imminent can only be controlled if it is perceived, and it is possible for anxiety to block the perception of this sensation (Kaplan, 1974), though not all authors agree that this is so.

What causes the anxiety which interferes with the learning of adequate ejaculatory control? In one individual it may be performance fear related to loss of erection or anticipation of the now familiar rapid response; in another it may stem from feelings of guilt provoked by pleasurable sensations; in yet a third it may reflect hostility or anger towards the partner. The result in any event is likely to be even quicker ejaculation and a less intense orgasm (Bancroft, 1983).

When premature ejaculation occurs as a secondary disorder it may be in response to stresses of unrelated origin or as a reaction in the male to primary sexual dysfunction in the woman. Alternatively, it may reflect difficulty in both partners in achieving sexual understanding and compatibility; while sexual adjustment is still taking place, premature ejaculation occurs and slowly becomes established, promoting further dysfunction in its wake.

Premature ejaculation may be associated with other types of disorder: erectile problems in the male and desire or orgasmic difficulties in his partner. Treatment therefore must concern itself with which dysfunction developed first and how the two are interwoven.

Retarded ejaculation. Retarded ejaculation is not a common disorder. It can take the form of a total inability to ejaculate under any circumstances; or an individual may be able to ejaculate during masturbation but not with a partner; or ejaculation may just be extremely difficult, requiring an excessive amount of stimulation. Total failure is more likely to have a medical base (Hawton, 1985), although Masters and Johnson treated some men whose complete inability to ejaculate could be traced to severe parental reaction to masturbation and wet dreams (Belliveau and Richter, 1970).

Where partial or delayed ejaculation occurs, Kaplan (1974) suggests that this may be a symptom of the individual being unable to 'let go'. This may arise from an excessive need within the individual to maintain control. Alternatively, it may be a reflection of relationship difficulties – feelings of hostility, fear of impregnation – which are causing the man, consciously or unconsciously, to hold back from full intimacy. However, as Bancroft (1983) points out, there have been no satisfactory research studies to date to prove these links.

OTHER SEXUAL DISORDERS

There are some sexual disorders which Kaplan (1979) does not relate to any specific phase of the response cycle. First, there are dysfunctions which occur as a result of involuntary muscle spasms.

Involuntary muscle spasms

Dyspareunia (male)

Dyspareunia in the male is characterized by pain on or immediately after ejaculation. It is a rare disorder and usually has a medical cause (Hawton, 1985). However, Kaplan (1979) suggests that in some instances it can derive from anxiety about ejaculation, which causes an involuntary and painful spasm of the genital muscles. Kaplan suggests that the psychological cause is usually deep-rooted, but it may be mild or severe – ranging from guilt about masturbation to profound sexual conflicts.

Dyspareunia (female)

Dyspareunia is pain on intercourse, either on initial or deep penetration. If medical causes such as vaginal infections have been ruled out, the most common cause is lack of arousal (Hawton, 1985).

Vaginismus

For women presenting with this condition, intercourse is often impossible because of spasm of the vaginal muscles which prevent penetration. Often women with vaginismus are sexually responsive in other ways, and perceive their reaction to be involuntary. Usually a primary disorder, vaginismus can nevertheless develop as a result of, for example, childbirth or sexual assault, where pain once experienced leads to future expectation of pain. A psychosomatic circle is thus established, caused by a fear of penetration. Duddle (1977) explores reasons for this anxiety and suggests that sexual ignorance or misinformation may be one contributory factor. Fear of penetration may also be linked to early experiences such as painful experiments with tampons or negative perceptions of the female sexual organs, rooted in childhood learning (Hawton, 1985).

Bancroft (1983) suggests that vaginismus may persist because of the opportunity it affords for 'secondary gain' – for example, a way of avoiding sexual intercourse which is perceived as threatening because it confirms an individual's adult or marital status. The individual is thus able to maintain a childlike or single role, perhaps denying the responsibilities which are actually hers. In such cases, the anxiety underlying the condition is indicative of a personality disorder which may be difficult to treat.

Alternatively, vaginismus may be indicative of collusion between partners as a mutual defence against sexual anxiety. Arentewicz and Schmidt (1983) point out that the partners of women presenting with vaginismus are frequently inexperienced and undemanding sexually. The condition offers a rationale for the avoidance of sexual activity which is unconsciously sought by both parties.

Sexual phobias

Other disorders which Kaplan (1979) puts into a separate category are sexual phobias. These can be specific, for example, an aversion to penile stimulation, or more general, like an aversion to any kind of foreplay. Sometimes they present in isolation and sometimes they accompany other types of sexual dysfunction. They are usually related to some traumatic sexual experience such as incest or rape (Hawton, 1985).

CONCLUSION

In conclusion, although sexual disorders *per se* are relatively definable and few in number, less so are the psychological factors from which they stem. Like most of human behaviour, sexual dysfunction can rarely be attributed to a single, simple cause. Immediate and past experiences interweave to impinge upon effective functioning. Moreover, the variety of personality is such that the same symptom in two individuals may be traced back to a very different cause or combination of causes.

The key to effective therapy, therefore, must lie in the accurate unravelling or diagnosis of the psychological processes which are contributing to the presenting condition. There are no clear-cut causal links between experience and dysfunction. Appropriate treatment is dependent upon an understanding of both the patient and the disorder in their widest perspective.

REFERENCES

Abrahamson, D.J., Barlow, D.H., Beck, J.G., Sakheim, D.K. and Kelly, J.P. (1985a) The effects of attentional focus and partner responsiveness on sexual responding: replication and extension, *Archives of Sexual Behavior*, Vol. 14, pp. 361–71.

Abrahamson, D.J., Barlow, D.H., Sakheim, D.K., Beck, J.G. and Athanasiou, R. (1985b) Effects of distraction on sexual responding in sexually functional and sexually dysfunctional men, *Behavior Therapy*, Vol. 16, pp. 503–15.

Arentewicz, G. and Schmidt, G. (eds) (1983) *The Treatment of Sexual Disorders*. Basic Books, New York.

Bancroft, J. (1983) *Human Sexuality and Its Problems*, Churchill-Livingstone, London.

Barlow, D.H. (1986) Causes of sexual dysfunction: the role of anxiety and cognitive interference, *Journal of Consulting and Clinical Psychology*, Vol. 54, No. 2, pp. 140–8.

Beck, J.G. and Barlow, D.H. (1984) Current conceptualizations of sexual dysfunction: a review and an alternative perspective, *Clinical Psychology Review*, Vol. 4, pp. 363–78.

Beck, J.G., Barlow, D.H. and Sakheim, D.K. (1983) The effects of attentional focus and partner arousal on sexual responding in functional and dysfunctional men, *Behaviour Research and Therapy*, Vol. 21, pp. 1–8.

Belliveau, F. and Richter, L. (1970) *Understanding Human Sexual Inadequacy*. Hodder & Stoughton, London and Aylesbury.

Duddle, C.M. (1977) Etiological factors in the unconsummated marriage, *Journal of Psychosomatic Research*, Vol. 21, pp. 157–60.

Fisher, S. (1973) *The Female Orgasm: Psychology, Physiology, Fantasy*, Allen Lane, London.

Hawton, K. (1985) *Sex Therapy: A Practical Guide*, Oxford University Press, Oxford.

Heiman, J.R. and Rowland, D.L. (1983) Affective and physiological sexual patterns: the effects of instructions on sexually functional and dysfunctional men, *Journal of Psychosomatic Research*, Vol. 27, pp. 105–16.

Kaplan, H.S. (1974) *The New Sex Therapy*, Ballière Tindall, London.

Kaplan, H.S. (1979) *Disorders of Sexual Desire and Other New Concepts and Techniques in Sex Therapy*, Brunner/Mazel, New York.

Kaplan, H.S. (1983) *The Evaluation of Sexual Disorders*, Brunner/Mazel, New York.

Maguire, G.P., Lee, E.G., Bevington, D.J., Kuchemann, C.S., Crabtree, R.J. and Cornell, C.E. (1978) Psychiatric problems in the first year after mastectomy, *British Medical Journal*, i, pp. 963–5.

Masters, W.H. and Johnson, V.E. (1966) *Human Sexual Response*, J.A. Churchill, London.

Masters, W.H. and Johnson, V.E. (1970) *Human Sexual Inadequacy*, J.A. Churchill, London.

Norton, G.R. and Jehu, D. (1984) The role of anxiety in sexual dysfunctions: a review, *Archives of Sexual Behavior*, Vol. 13, pp. 165–183.

CHAPTER 6

ASSESSING THE BASIS OF SEXUAL DYSFUNCTION: DIAGNOSTIC PROCEDURES

Dennis Friedman

The diagnostic procedures involved in the evaluation of sexual dysfunction in the male and female are the focus of this chapter. Most of the research into sexual failure so far seems to relate to the male. Apart from early studies (Masters and Johnson, 1970) describing the physiology of the female genital response, very little investigative work unique to the female has been reported. However, orgasm and libido probably obey the same neurological, endocrine and psychological laws in both sexes and there is no evidence to suggest that the neurotransmitters concerned in the female genital response are any different from those in the male. Women who are not interested in sex are usually investigated by means of a base-line endocrine profile and a gynaecological examination is carried out if pain during intercourse is complained of.

Failure to attain or maintain erection, uncontrolled or delayed ejaculation in the male, and desire dysfunction, anorgasmia and vaginismus/dyspareunia in the female, are also discussed in this chapter.

At the initial interview an attempt is made to discriminate between psychogenic and organic dysfunction. All patients with sexual problems will be assessed by a suitably qualified professional whose aim is to identify and manage pathology and to initiate investigations where needed. Saypol *et al.* (1983) referring to erectile dysfunction believe that a firm diagnosis may be made from the history, but others, notably Schiavi *et al.* (1982), find this unreliable since anxiety is often present even when organic factors predominate.

There is a glossary of medical terms at the end of this chapter.

The causes of dysfunction in both sexes are usually multifactorial. Until recently it had been assumed that psychological factors accounted for about 90 per cent of all cases of erectile dysfunction. This figure was based on reports dating from the 1950s by Simpson (1950) and Strauss (1950). Current reports suggest that between 30 per cent and 70 per cent of cases of erectile difficulty may have an organic basis (May *et al.*, 1969; Michal, 1982, and Melman *et al.*, 1984); however, the pendulum may have swung too far. In my experience, when reliable screening tests have been used, such as the measurement of night-time penile tumescence, (Karacan *et al.*, 1976), the incidence of erectile problems with an organic basis falls.

The genital response is stimulated by a signal from the cortex of the brain evoked by fantasy and/or manual stimulation of the genitals. The sensory pathway for this signal enters the spinal cord via the pudendal nerve. The brain stimulus emerges peripherally in the autonomic nervous system via the second, third, and fourth sacral nerve roots (Pick, 1970).

Psychological factors that may inhibit the cortical stimulus include feelings of anxiety, disgust, relationship problems, depression, using the spouse as a scapegoat for unresolved hostility with the parent of the opposite sex, or incompatible sexual needs. However, if lesions in the nerve supply or in the blood supply to the genitals are discovered, or if the sex hormone levels are inadequate then organic dysfunction is diagnosed. In the male, erection results only when intact cortical centres supply an excitatory stimulus via normal autonomic pathways leading to regulatory mechanisms in penile erectile tissue. Blood-flow changes then occur in the vascular spaces in the penis providing there is no significant obstruction to the arterial inflow (Blacklay *et al.*, 1984a).

Neurotransmitters are concerned with the transmission of the nervous signals. Those that may be involved in sexual mechanisms include: acetylcholine, adrenaline, dopamine, 5-hydroxytryptamine, nor-adrenaline, prostaglandins and vasoactive intestinal polypeptide (VIP) (Blacklay *et al.*, 1984b). Some drugs may block receptors in the sexual tissues thus inhibiting the neurotransmitters and therefore the sexual response.

If there is no evidence of testicular shrinkage on clinical examination sex hormone deficiency as a cause of erectile difficulty is unlikely. Endocrine factors in erectile dysfunction probably have an incidence of less than 2 per cent (Friedman *et al.*, 1986). Disorders that influence hormonal control may also affect target organ responses. Androgens are the sex steroids generally considered in both sexes to be the hormones of the sex drive. When blood androgen levels are low, the hypothalamic-pituitary-gonadal axis is investigated and enquiries are made regarding the ingestion of those drugs which affect hormone levels. Dopamine is the neurotransmitter which inhibits prolactin. If high levels of prolactin are present in the blood, gonadal function is suppressed (Spark *et al.*, 1982).

For erection to occur, the penile vascular bed must achieve a critical increase in blood flow in combination with the appropriate neural stimulation. This causes an increase in blood volume in the erectile spaces in the penile shaft. These spaces are called the corpora cavernosa which are paired structures parallel to each other and which extend the length of the shaft and the corpus spongiosum which occupies the ventral surface of the penis, encloses the penile urethra, and forms the glans penis.

The filling of these blood spaces depends on the absence of obstruction in the penile arteries and the presence of an adequate blood pressure in them. To estimate whether sufficient blood reaches the penile blood spaces through the arterial supply, the rate of blood flow and the blood pressure in the terminal branches of the internal pudendal artery are assessed. Techniques based on ultrasonography and the monitoring of the increase in penile circumference during sleep have not always proved reliable (Britt *et al.*, 1971; Ginestie and Romieu, 1978; Michal and Popsichal, 1978; and Michal, 1982). Recently, however, Blacklay *et al.* (1984a) using isotope studies have shown that delay in arrival time correlates with abnormal penile filling of the blood spaces and may be a more accurate non-invasive test. The aim of these non-invasive screening tests is to identify those subjects who will undergo invasive assessment of the internal iliac arterial system by arteriography prior to reconstructive surgery.

In addition to assessing the arterial blood flow into the penile blood spaces, identification of leaks in the veins draining the corpora cavernosa are investigated by X-raying these spaces, while introducing a radiopaque solution and papaverine into them. An artificial erection is induced by papaverine but this cannot be maintained if venous leakages are present. The results may be recorded on ciné film (Lewis and Puyau, 1986).

DISORDERS IN THE MALE – ERECTILE DYSFUNCTION

Historically, the term *impotence* has been used for erectile failure, although some authors, notably Newman and Northrup (1981) also include the inability to achieve orgasm (since the nervous pathways involved are common to ejaculation and orgasm as well as erection). The usual definition of erectile dysfunction is, however, an inability to attain and maintain an erection adequate for sexual intercourse.

Psychogenic erectile failure

History-taking

Questions are asked to discriminate between *psychogenic* and *organic* erectile failure. A psychological cause is likely if erection occurs on awakening, in the absence of coital opportunity, either in the presence of fantasy or when alone, or with one partner but not with another. The sex drive may be absent or reduced and the onset is often sudden.

An organic cause will be suspected if a partial erection occurs during sexual activity with ejaculation and orgasm unaffected. The onset is likely to be gradual and the sex drive intact. Other questions are asked concerning ejaculation. Is it premature, controlled, or delayed?

Other disorders which may be contributory are: diabetes, neurological disease (e.g. multiple sclerosis, progressive muscular atrophy); vascular disease (e.g. myocardial ischaemia, hypertension or claudication); alcoholism; psychological illness (e.g. depression or schizophrenia). Finally, details of medication are asked for.

Performance anxiety. Those who are anxious to succeed are liable to erectile failure during sexual activity. Performance anxiety is common in those who have had an upbringing in which they learned to expect more approval if they were pleasing. Children become the victims of parents who regard them as sources of love for them. Such parents may themselves have had insufficient love in childhood, and parenthood may be seen as an opportunity for them to obtain the love that they themselves were denied. Such children overvalue performance in their efforts to gain approval. 'I will love you if' is a common theme in their childhood: 'If you are good'; 'If you do well at games'; 'If you are polite and well-behaved', etc. In the sexual situation the desire to please causes him to lose touch with his feelings. He comes to adopt the role of an observer, seeing the sex act through his partners eyes.

Inappropriate partner choice. Relationship breakdown and loss of sexual interest will occur if a partner is chosen for the wrong reasons. Object choice may follow a pattern acquired during the early relationship with the mother. When the 'falling in love' phase of the relationship ends, the partner is perceived more clearly. Falling in love is a phenomenon based on the re-enactment of the early relationship with the mother. The more imperfect the original relationship the more the need for it to be idealized. Idealized expectations, if transferred onto another adult, obscure negative character traits. However, when the transference eventually breaks down, disappointment as well as hostility result.

Analytic psychotherapy is concerned with uncovering the authentic feelings experienced with the mother during early life. Reactive hatred, envy and jealousy, greed or loss of control may have been suppressed when it would have been appropriate for the infant to express such feelings. Because the infant fears losing parental love, he complies with their demands and their expectations. Recalling his childhood he believes that everything was perfect and beautiful. It is only when he relives this early commitment in a new partnership that the long suppressed feelings may surface. When they do, hostility finds its target in a partner who becomes a scapegoat for the earlier more powerful partner whose wishes were seldom questioned and always obeyed.

Ambivalent sexual orientation. If an opposite sex partner is chosen by someone who is uncertain of his sexual orientation, erectile failure may eventually result. A heterosexual relationship may be entered into for social or cultural reasons instead of a preferred homosexual one. Enquiries should be made concerning masturbation fantasies. If they are exclusively or even partly homosexual, same sex partners may be sought leading to the disruption of the opposite sex partnership.

Organic erectile failure

History-taking

For organic erectile failure to be diagnosed, a lesion must be demonstrated in the penile circulation or in the nerve supply to the penis. There should be adequate levels of circulating sex steroids. Disorders which may affect erectile function are:

Diabetes. The nerve supply and blood supply to the penis may be affected by one of the complications of diabetes (Fairburn, 1981). The diagnosis may be made if there is evidence of peripheral or autonomic neuropathy or impairment of the penile circulation. The clinical symptoms of autonomic disturbance are: abdominal distension after eating and/or vomiting; altered bowel habit with nocturnal diarrhoea, dizziness, muscle weakness, painless urinary retention, and gustatory sweating.

Neurological disease. Erectile failure results from a variety of lesions involving both the central and peripheral nervous system. Disorders include: multiple sclerosis; syphilitic involvement of the spinal cord (tabes dorsalis); tumour or injury to the lower end of the spinal cords; lesions involving the autonomic nervous system (autonomic neuropathy); motor neurone disease.

Vascular disease. Erectile failure results from reduction in blood pressure, flow rate and blood volume in the arterial bed supplying the penile cavernous bodies. It will also occur if there is a high venous outflow. Arterial risk factors include tobacco, diabetes, and hypertension (Newman and Northrup, 1981).

Alcohol. Alcohol may affect sexual performance by altering liver metabolism. Raised liver enzymes increase the rate of conversion of testosterone to oestradiol. Oestradiol acts as an antiandrogen by competing with testosterone at the androgen receptors in the sexual tissues. Alcohol has a direct suppressant effect on gonodal function and may also eventually lead to a peripheral neuropathy.

Drugs. The following groups of drugs may cause problems with erection. Antihypertensives are used in the treatment of raised blood pressure and cause erectile dysfunction by either inhibiting adrenergic neurones (e.g. debrisoquine, guanethedine and bethanidine); decreasing alpha throughput (e.g. clonidine); blocking dopamine receptors thus leading to hyperprolactinaemia and therefore gonadal suppression (e.g. Alpha-methylodopa and reserpine) or by blocking beta adrenoreceptors (e.g. propranolol and related drugs). (Most beta-blockers used as antihypertensive agents are now selective beta-blockers in which the incidence of erectile failure is low [see Chapter 8].)

Antiemetics are used in the treatment of nausea and vomiting and may block dopamine receptors (e.g. metoclopramide and domperidone) or block androgen receptors (e.g. cimetidine).

Psychoactive drugs are used in the treatment of psychosis and may also block dopamine receptors (e.g. sulpiride, phenothiazines and butyrophenones).

Calcium antagonists are used to lessen the contractibility of heart muscle and to dilate arteries. They are a rare cause of erectile failure (e.g. verapamil and nifedipine).

Anticonvulsants are used in the treatment of epilepsy. They increase blood levels of sex-hormone-binding globulin (SHBG), thus reducing blood levels of available androgen (e.g. carbamazepine and phenytoin). Antiandrogens, one of which may be used to reduce sexual arousal in convicted sex offenders (cyproterone acetate) include spironolactone, oestrogen, cimetidine, digoxin and alcohol.

Endocrine disease. Testosterone is one of several sex steroids produced in the testis and is the hormone responsible for the maintenance of the sex drive. It is bound to the sex hormone binding globulin (SHBG) and carried in the blood to the sexual target tissues, where the free unbound fraction is converted to its bioactive metabolite dihydrotestosterone. Testosterone blood levels show a diurnal variation with high concentrations in the morning and lower ones in the evening. Adult levels are reached with the puberty surge and these levels remain more or less constant until the mid-fifties after which they slowly decline. At about the same age, plasma levels of sex-hormone-binding globulin increase (Anderson, 1975).

Hypogonadism is a condition in which the gonodal secretion of testosterone is reduced. Gonodal failure may be either a primary or secondary event.

In primary hypogonadism the lesion is in the gonad and the low levels of testosterone secreted fail to initiate the negative feedback between the gonad and the pituitary. This causes the gonadotrophic hormones from the pituitary (FSH and LH) to be hypersecreted. This is known as hypergonadotrophic hypogonadism.

Primary hypogonadism when prepubertal is found in:

1. Klinefelter's syndrome – a genetic disorder in which there is an extra X chromosome (i.e. 47XXY).
2. Untreated cryptorchidism. Testicular degeneration occurs at puberty if failure of testicular descent has not been treated surgically by bringing the undescended testes from the abdomen or the inguinal canal to the scrotum.
3. Sertoli-cell-only syndrome. A rare genetic gonadal disorder.

Primary hypogonadism when postpubertal is associated with viral infections (mumps or Coxsackie orchitis); gonorrhoea (acute orchitis may follow gonorrhoea); leprosy (chronic orchitis); radiation (there is germinal cell destruction, therefore sterility, but Leydig cells are more resistant to radiation); myotonia dystrophica (testicular atrophy occurs in 80 per cent of cases with reduction in androgen production); chemotherapy (cytotoxic drugs); ageing (Leydig cell function may decline gradually in a small percentage of ageing males).

Secondary hypogonadism is due to a failure of gonadotrophic secretion and is caused by: lesions of the hypothalamus (e.g. Kallman's syndrome – a genetic disorder in which puberty is delayed); pituitary tumours, including pituitary dwarfism, necrosis, infection, or trauma and failure of LHRH or LH production.

Examination

A full physical examination will include:

Inspection. An eunuchoid body build with the hair and fat distribution characteristic of the female and with excessive breast development suggests prepubertal hypogonadism. The patient will have long arms and a span exceeding his height. The most common example of this is Klinefelter's syndrome (47XXY karyotype). There may be an increased conversion of androgen to oestrogen (an antiandrogen) in adipose tissue.

Examination of cardiovascular function. Evidence of atherosclerotic changes are sought if there is a history of claudication, ischaemic heart disease or hypertension.

Examination of the genitals. Lesions of the penis should be looked for.

These include epispadias or hypospadias, skin lesions, phimosis and Peyronie's disease in which hard areas may be felt in the penile shaft. The testes should be examined and assessed for size and consistency. Small shrunken testes suggest a deficiency in androgen secretion.

Neurological Examination. The sexual reflexes. The following reflexes should be tested:

1. The Bulbocavernosus Reflex. Pinching the glans penis leads to contraction of the bulbocavernosus muscle, which is felt with the finger pressing on the perineum behind the scrotum. This reflex is supplied by the third and fourth sacral nerves.
2. The Scrotal Reflex. The application of cold to the scrotum leads to a slow contraction of the dartos muscle.
3. The Cremasteric Reflex. Scratching the inner aspect of the thigh causes elevation of the testicle on that side. This reflex is supplied by the first and second lumbar nerves.

Special Investigations

Endocrine function tests. A base-line endocrine profile consists of the measurement of hormone blood levels. Blood ideally should be taken at 8 a.m. and assayed for testosterone, oestradiol, follicle stimulating hormone (FSH), luteinizing hormone (LH), prolactin and sex hormone binding globulin (SHBG).

Low testosterone levels may be due to hypogonadism. Low FSH and LH are due to hypogonadotrophic hypogonadism. Raised FSH and LH are due to hypergonadotrophic hypogonadism. Raised oestradiol may be due to an oestrogen-secreting tumour, alcohol or antiandrogen medication. Raised SHBG can be caused by ageing or high oestrogen blood levels. Raised prolactin is due to a prolactin secreting tumour or to the ingestion of drugs which block dopamine receptors. X-ray investigation of the pituitary fossa may be required if a pituitary tumour is suspected. However, it should be mentioned that blood levels of prolactin have to be very high before they effect sexual response and that stress itself will raise prolactin, for example, when the blood sample is being taken. Other pituitary function tests may be carried out. For example, synthetic gonadotrophin releasing hormone (GRH) stimulates the release of gonadotrophins from the normal anterior pituitary gland if it is given by rapid intravenous injection. Plasma LH fails to rise if pituitary failure is present. Clomiphene may also be used to initiate gonadotrophin release by blocking oestrogen receptors in the hypothalamus thus preventing negative feedback.

Insulin tests anterior pituitary function by inducing hypoglycaemia and is used as a stress agent.

Myocardial autonomic function tests. Autonomic function tests are usually carried out on the heart or with more difficulty on the bladder. The results are then extrapolated to the penis. There are no autonomic tests specific to the penis although the integrity of the reflex spinal pathway may be tested with a vibrator resulting in erection if it is intact. The following are tests of myocardial autonomic function:

1. The Valsalva Manoeuvre. The patient is asked to blow against a resistance, usually 40 mm of mercury in a manometer. This produces a fall in cardiac output which is followed by a rise above the normal when the resistance is released. The reflex heart rate changes are a tachycardia during the manoeuvre and a bradycardia upon release (Levin, 1966).
2. Sinus Arrhythmia. The heart rate normally increases during expiration and decreases during inspiration: a variation of less than 10 heart beats per minute is said to be indicative of myocardial autonomic impairment (Ewing and Clarke, 1982).
3. Blood Pressure Changes on Standing. Blood pressure falls on standing which is normally immediately corrected by an increase in heart rate and constriction of peripheral vessels. Blood pressure recordings are made while lying and after standing for one minute. A fall of more than 30 mm of Hg is pathological (Ewing *et al.*, 1980).

Bladder function tests. If there is a disturbance in the autonomic nerve supply to the bladder, abnormalities in outflow will occur that may be demonstrated by cystometrography. Bladder innervation and penile innervation are closely linked: by inference dysfunction in one suggests dysfunction in the other.

Vascular function tests

1. Doppler Ultrasonography. Three paired arteries supply the penis. They are the right and left dorsal, the right and left cavernous and the right and left spongiose arteries. They are derived from the internal pudendal artery which is a terminal branch of the internal iliac artery. The dorsal arteries are located on either side and proximal to the glans penis and the cavernous arteries over the mid-lateral aspect of the shaft. The spongiose arteries are on either side of the penile urethra on the ventral surface.

   The penile circulation is evaluated with a Doppler Ultrasound flow detector (Abelson, 1975). A Doppler probe with a frequency of 9.5 MHz is placed over the arterial pulses using electrode jelly to ensure good connection. An audible signal from the flow meter (Parks Electronics Model 811) demonstrates patency in the artery. The quality of the penile circulation is based on the measurement of penile blood pressure and comparing it with the brachial blood pressure.

2. Measurement of Penile Blood Pressure (PBP). A 2 cm inflatable Velcro cuff is placed around the base of the penile shaft and connected to a sphygmomanometer. The cuff is inflated (with the probe in place over each arterial pulse in turn) until the audible signal is cut off. The pressure upon return of the signal represents the systolic pressure in that artery. The brachial blood pressure (BBP) is then taken and the penile blood pressure index (PBPI) determined. The penile blood pressure index $(\text{PBPI}) = \frac{\text{PBP}}{\text{BBP}} \times 100$. A ratio of less than 65 per cent is strongly suggestive of arterial inflow obstruction (Virag *et al.*, 1985a).
3. Intracavernous Injection of Vasoactive Drugs. Papaverine or other vasoactive drugs when injected into the corpora cavernosa induce erection if significant arterial occlusions or venous leakages are absent. Artificially induced erection is therefore used to discriminate between neurogenic and psychogenic erectile dysfunction on the one hand and vascular dysfunction on the other (Stieff *et al.*, 1986).
4. Photoelectric Plethysmography. A photosensor is taped to the penile shaft and, for comparison, another sensor is taped to the ear lobe. A penile strain gauge is linked via a plethysmeter to a chart-recorder. The patient is then exposed to either visual erotic stimuli (VES) or anoxic stress induced by inflating the penile blood pressure cuff to above the systolic pressure for 5 minutes. A greater hyperaemic response occurs in the absence of vascular disease. Selected video records of erotic material relating to the patient's masturbation fantasies provide the VES. If the VES content is tailored to each individual's fantasy, full neurophysiological responses may be expected in the non-impotent subject since psychological inhibition of the cortical signal will be eliminated. The wave form of the PPG ear-lobe sensor does not alter significantly showing that the blood-flow changes are not due to a generalized autonomic reflex but a neurologically mediated haemodynamic response confined to the penile tissue (Blacklay *et al.*, 1984c). Anoxic stress may be used as an alternative to VES as a stimulus but the PPG sensor may only be an accurate monitor of penile blood flow if the anoxia induced is prolonged for longer than 5 minutes.
5. Isotope Scanning. This is a minimally invasive procedure which identifies delay and deformation in blood flow between the aortoiliac and penile vascular beds. The radioisotope in the blood is scanned by a gamma camera positioned over the aortoiliac and penile areas after the intravenous injection of 2 ml of 15 mega Bequerels of technetium 99 labelled human serum albumin. Delay in arrival time of the isotope at the penile area of interest may prove to be one of the most accurate screening indices for vasculogenic erectile dysfunction.
6. Arteriography. Arteriography is an invasive procedure and is carried out

when there is strong evidence that the patient has vasculogenic erectile failure. Usually this is performed by retrograde femoral artery catheterization. Contrast media is introduced into the internal iliac arteries via selective catheters. The arteriogram requires specialized techniques for catheterization, infusion and interpretation (Ginestie and Romieu, 1978).

Nocturnal penile tumescence tests. Penile erection occurs as a neurophysiological phenomenon in all potent males from puberty to senescence during paradoxical or REM (rapid eye movement) sleep (Karacan *et al.*, 1976). The monitoring of this response is therefore a useful screening test which helps to discriminate between psychogenic and organic erectile dysfunction. The patient is admitted to hospital overnight. Two mercury in rubber strain gauges are placed around the penile shaft, one just below the glans and the other at the base of the penis. Each is linked via a plethysmeter to a twin channel chart-recorder. The resistance changes resulting from changes in penile circumference in each strain gauge are converted into electrical signals which are recorded on the chart (Karacan, 1969).

An increase in penile circumference of more than 2.4 cm lasting for more than 5 minutes implies a normal result. Full tumescence however is not necessarily correlated with rigidity which is also critically important and although several instruments have been introduced to measure rigidity, none is completely reliable (Wein *et al.*, 1981; Virag *et al.*, 1985b).

DISORDERS IN THE MALE

Retarded ejaculation

Retarded ejaculation can be defined as an inability to ejaculate when needed. There are two stages in the male orgasm. The first stage, emission, occurs when seminal fluid is present in the posterior urethra. The second stage, ejaculation, represents the expulsion of the seminal fluid via the penile urethra to the exterior.

Emission results from contraction of the smooth muscles of the vas deferens, the seminal vesicles and ejaculatory ducts and contraction of the prostate. Ejaculation or expulsion of the seminal fluid stimulates clonic spasm of the bulbocavernosus and ischiocavernosus muscles. A lesion of the sympathetic division causes impairment of ejaculation. Overactivity of the sympathetic division leads to premature ejaculation and/or poor erection.

History-taking

A patient who complains of delayed ejaculation may give a history of ingestion of drugs which either block the alpha adrenoreceptors or which have anticholinergic side effects. Examples of drugs which cause alpha adrenoreceptor blockade are phenoxybenazamine and phentolamine. Drugs with anticholinergic side effects are the tricyclic antidepressants, the monoamine oxidase inhibitors (MAOI) and the phenothiazines. Retrograde ejaculation, that is, into the bladder, is caused by bladder neck surgery or drugs which block alpha adrenoreceptors. Orgasm however is unaffected.

In psychogenic retarded or absent ejaculation, the diagnosis will be made on the history alone. The disorder may reflect one aspect of poor communication. Ejaculation is usually not delayed during masturbation but only when coitus is attempted. Typically the non-ejaculator is overcontrolled and withholds his feelings.

Examination

Retrograde ejaculation may be confirmed by demonstrating the presence of sperm in the urine after orgasm either by inspection (the urine will be cloudy) or by microscopy.

Premature ejaculation

Premature ejaculation is due to overactivity of the sympathetic branch of the autonomic nervous system. The resulting imbalance may also lead to erectile difficulty. This may also be explained by a dissociation effect as attempts are made to reduce arousal in order to control ejaculation.

The patient's complaint is that ejaculation cannot be controlled and that ejaculatory incontinence may occur at any time from initial genital stimulation to penetration or soon afterwards. Exceptionally, fantasy may be sufficient to initiate the reflex. The diagnosis is made on the history alone and the cause is invariably psychogenic (Friedman, 1977).

DISORDERS IN THE FEMALE

Sexual dysfunction presents as loss of sexual interest, anorgasmia, or vaginismus with or without dyspareunia (coital pain). The diagnosis is made on the history, on examination and by investigation. The causes of sexual dysfunction are either psychogenic or organic.

Sexual desire dysfunction

Sexual desire dysfunction has many features in common with psychogenic erectile dysfunction. The diagnosis is made from the history. The causes are similar to those for erectile impotence. Suggested questions are: Have sexual responses ever been present? Is depression or other mental illness present? Are feelings commonly suppressed? Is vaginal lubrication present during sexual activity? Are the circumstances in which sexual activity occurs conducive to it? Is the relationship a good one? What sexual fantasies occur?

Psychogenic sexual desire dysfunction is diagnosed if the mood or affect is consistently flattened due to depression or if feelings are suppressed due to involvement in emotional conflicts outside the relationship, for example, with parents or with another partner. Preoccupation with adverse living conditions may also prevent the enjoyment of sexual activity. Incongruity of sexual orientation (i.e. when a same sex partnership is preferred) also causes sexual apathy.

Loss of sex drive may result from a reduction in androgen levels, certain drugs, chronic illness, pregnancy and lactation. Enquiries are made concerning the contraceptive pill; antihypertensive therapy; antiemetics (used in the treatment of nausea and vomiting); psychoactive drugs (used in the treatment of mental illness); cytotoxic drugs (used in the treatment of cancer); radiotherapy; early and late pregnancy; breast-feeding; chronic illness such as tuberculosis, multiple sclerosis and renal disease; surgical operations.

Since androgen is the hormone of libido, drugs which are antiandrogenic result in a reduction in libido. The contraceptive pill causes an increase in circulating sex hormone binding globulin (SHBG) thereby reducing the amount of androgen available for target organ response. Cyproterone acetate is an antiandrogen used in the treatment of excessive body hair which is a feature of the polycystic ovary syndrome. The use of cytotoxic drugs in malignant disease, pelvic irradiation, and surgery aimed at inhibiting hormone production in hormone dependent cancers (hypophysectomy and oophorectomy), results in loss of erotic feelings.

Drugs which induce hyperprolactinaemia suppress the gonads. These are the antiemetics such as metoclopramide, and the neuroleptics such as chlorpromazine and haloperidol. Breast-feeding is associated with high levels of prolactin which persists until weaning takes place. Chronic illness and fatigue make sexual responses less vigorous, although certain neurological disorders (e.g. multiple sclerosis) interfere with the sympathetic and parasympathetic outflow from the spinal cord. Some surgical procedures have the same effect. A pelvic clearance for cancer of the cervix or an abdominoperineal excision of the rectum leads to loss of libido. Mastectomy and hysterectomy may adversely affect self-esteem and sexuality.

A hormone profile will confirm the endocrine changes due to drug therapy and radiotherapy. Hormones measured are oestradiol, FSH, LH, testosterone, prolactin and SHBG.

Anorgasmia

Absent orgasm in the female is the neurophysiological equivalent of absent ejaculation in the male.

As in the male the diagnosis is made from the history. The causes are psychogenic or organic. The following questions are asked: Does orgasm occur by manual stimulation either alone or with a partner? Has orgasm occurred with other partners? Are any drugs being taken? Is there a history of chronic illness, for example, diabetes?

In some women the presence or absence of an orgasmic response may be difficult to evaluate. Much depends on the emotional climate, fantasies, memories and expectations. Orgasm can be a sensitive barometer of the state of the relationship. A full response may occur with one partner and not with another. Physiological responses may occur but the 'psyche' may fail to identify the sensations correctly.

Organic causes of anorgasmia are as those for delayed or absent ejaculation.

Anticholinergic drugs, alpha adrenergic receptor blockers, ganglion-blocking drugs and one of the thioxanthines (thioridizine) delay orgasm. Some women complain of anorgasmia on thiazide diuretics, and in diabetics neuropathy of the sensory nerves of the clitoris can impair orgasm (Kaplan, 1979). Apart from excluding diabetes, no investigation is needed.

Vaginismus

A fear of vaginal penetration results in an involuntary spasm of the vaginal muscles when intercourse is attempted. The diagnosis of penetration phobia is made from the history and confirmed by examination. No investigations are required. Questions asked include: Has intercourse ever taken place? Can tampons or a vaginal examination be tolerated? Are pleasurable feelings present in the absence of attempts to penetrate?

In severe cases non-consummation is invariably the rule, but erotic responses including orgasm occur during love-play. The patient does not suffer from a loss of libido. Underlying neurotic determinants are often of a hostile nature with the partner acting as a scapegoat for conflicts arising out of earlier loving relationships usually with parents.

Examination

Any attempt at vaginal examination is resisted by contracting the vaginal muscles and sometimes the long adductor muscles of the thighs.

Dyspareunia

The causes of dyspareunia are either psychogenic or organic. The diagnosis is made from the history combined with examination, and sometimes investigations.

Psychogenic dyspareunia is often diagnosed from the history alone. Questions asked are: Does it occur with every partner? In spite of the pain, is intercourse enjoyable? Have digital vaginal examinations or instrumental examinations been painful? Is there a history of frequent abdominal surgery or sexually transmitted disease?

Where the cause is psychogenic the problem is usually to be found in the relationship. If pleasurable feelings occur during coitus, warmth is felt for the partner. Clearly if speculum examination is painless, then she regards intercourse with her partner as a 'painful' experience. When it accompanies vaginismus the cause is usually psychogenic due to absence of lubrication associated with the phobic response.

Examination

Vaginal and speculum examination are done. Examination should be concerned with introital, vaginal and pelvic pathology.

Dyspareunia is likely to be due to organic factors if on examination the following is found:

1. At the introitus: vulval lesions; vulval dermatoses; vulvitis; intact hymen.
2. In the vagina: trauma; malignant disease; vaginitis; urethral caruncle; urethritis; postmenopausal atrophy; vaginal dryness; allergies.
3. In the pelvis: pelvic inflammatory disease; endometriosis; pelvic cancer; prolapsed ovaries; constipation; Crohn's disease.

Investigations

Investigation of the organic causes of dyspareunia should include one or all of the following: hormone profile; deep vaginal swab for thrush, trichomonas, or other infection; examination under anaesthetic; laparoscopy.

The hormone assay is to detect changes in gonadal function and the presence of vaginal lubrication. Hormones assayed are the gonadotrophins (FSH and LH), oestradiol, testosterone and prolactin. FSH and LH will be raised in gonadal failure, either premenopause or postmenopause. Oestradiol will be low if vaginal dryness is the cause of the dyspareunia, as occurs after the menopause. Testosterone may be raised in the polycystic ovary syndrome although this does not cause dyspareunia. Hyperprolactinaemia causes gonadal suppression and frequently dyspareunia.

A vaginal swab for pathogens will exclude vaginal infections but an examination under anaesthetic may be necessary when pelvic pathology is suspected. Further investigation by laparoscopy will allow for a direct view of the pelvic organs.

CONCLUSION

Sophisticated techniques for the evaluation of sexual dysfunction are now available. This is particularly so for erectile impotence leading to improved opportunities for treatment. It is now possible to identify abnormalities in the arterial blood supply to the penile shaft as well as in the venous drainage from it. Revascularization of the arterial supply and the ligation of venous leakages are becoming routine surgical procedures. Hormonal evaluation for gonadal hypofunctioning allows for replacement of the sex hormones and restoration of sexual activity. Accurate diagnosis eliminates the possibility of patients with organic disorders being treated by psychosexual counselling, probably accounting for the poor response to treatment of erectile impotence before opportunities for full assessment were available (Friedman and Emerson, 1984).

GLOSSARY

abdominoperineal	A dual surgical approach to the rectum via an incision through the abdomen and through the perineum.
adrenergic neurone	A nerve which on stimulation releases adrenaline.
anoxic	Lack of oxygen.
aortoiliac	The point at which the abdominal aorta branches into the two iliac arteries.
arteriography	A radiological technique for the imaging of arteries.
atherosclerotic	Arterial narrowing due to a thickening wall usually associated with ageing.
brachial blood pressure	The blood pressure in the brachial artery in the upper arm.
bradycardia	A heart rate below 50 beats per minute
claudication	Muscular pain on exercise due to impaired blood flow.
clonic spasm	Involuntary repetitive contraction and relaxation of muscle.
corpora cavernosa	Paired vascular spaces in the penile shaft.

cryptorchidism	A condition whereby the testes are found either in the inguinal canals or in the abdomen due to failure of descent into the scrotum.
cystometrography	The measurement of pressure within the bladder.
cytotoxic	The destruction of abnormal cells by drugs.
dermatoses	Disorders of the skin.
endometriosis	The presence of uterine lining tissue outside the uterine cavity.
gustatory sweating	Reflex facial sweating caused by eating spicy food.
hyperaemic response	An increase in blood flow due to a stimulus such as oxygen deficiency.
hypospadias	A congenital abnormality in which the urethral opening is located on the undersurface of the penis.
hypothalamic-pituitary-gonadal axis	The hormonal link between the brain and the gonads (testes and ovaries).
iliac	An artery which carries blood to the penis via the internal iliac arterial system.
introitus	The entrance to the vagina.
karyotype	The DNA complement of the cell.
laparoscopy	Endoscopic inspection for diagnostic purposes of the pelvic organs through a small incision in the abdominal wall.
myocardial ischaemia	An impairment of the blood supply to the heart muscle due to coronary artery disease.
neuropathy	A disease process in nerves.
papaverine	An opiate derivative which when injected directly into the penile blood spaces causes an increased blood flow and therefore erection.
phimosis	An inability to retract the foreskin.
polycystic ovary syndrome	Multiple small ovarian cysts associated with excess male-hormone secretion and excess body hair.

prolactin	A hormone secreted by the pituitary gland which if secreted in excess suppresses gonadal function and hence sexual response.
pudendal nerve	The nerve that carries sensory impulses (sensation) from the penis and clitoris to the brain.
sacral	That part of the spinal cord from which the nerve roots are derived which carry the stimulus from the brain to the sex organs.
tachycardia	Rapid heart rate.
ultrasonography	The assessment of arterial blood flow using sound waves.
urethral caruncle	A painful swelling at the urethral opening leading to painful intercourse in females.

REFERENCES

Abelson, D. (1975) Diagnostic value of the penile pulse and blood pressure: a doppler study of impotence in diabetics, *Journal of Urology*, Vol. 113: 636–9.

Anderson, D.C. (1975) Sex hormone binding globulin, *Clinical Endocrinology*, Vol. 3, pp. 69–96.

Bayliss, P.H. (1986) Drug-induced endocrine disorders, *Adverse Drug Reaction Bulletin*, Vol. 116, pp. 432–5.

Blacklay, P., Nimmon, C., Carroll, M., Lumley, J. and Britton, K. (1984a) Radionucleide studies in the measurement of penile blood flow, in R. Virag and H. Virag (eds) *Proceedings of the First World Meeting on Impotence*, pp. 143–5, Editions du CERI, Paris.

Blacklay, P., Crow, R., Lincoln, J., Pryor, J. and Burnstock, G. (1984b) Vasoactive intestinal peptide and other neurotransmitter agents in the diabetic penis, in R. Virag and H. Virag (eds) *Proceedings of the First World Meeting on Impotence*, pp. 205–9, Editions du CERI, Paris.

Blacklay, P., Friedman, D. and Lumley, J. (1984c) Penile skin blood flow measurement using photoplethysmography (PPG): the effect of anoxia and visual erotic stimulation, in R. Virag and H. Virag (eds) *Proceedings of the First World Meeting on Impotence*, pp. 129–32, Editions du CERI, Paris.

Britt, D.B., Kemmerer, W.T. and Robinson, J.R. (1971) Penile blood flow determination by mercury strain gauge plethysmography, *Investigative Urology*, Vol. 8, pp. 673–8.

Ewing, D.J., Campbell, I.W. and Clarke, B.F. (1980) Assessment of cardiovascular effects in diabetic autonomic neuropathy and prognostic implications, *Annals of Internal Medicine*, Vol. 92, Part 2, pp. 308–11.

Ewing, D.J. and Clarke, B.F. (1982) Diagnosis and management of diabetic autonomic neuropathy, *British Medical Journal*, Vol. 285, pp. 916–8.

Fairburn, C. (1981) The sexual problems of diabetic men, *British Journal of Hospital Medicine*, Vol. 25, No. 5, pp. 484–91.
Friedman, D. (1977) Psychological aspects of impaired male sexual function, in J. Money and H. Musaph (eds) *Handbook of Sexology*, Elsevier/North Holland. Biomedical Press, The Netherlands.
Friedman, D. and Emerson, T. (1984) Psychosexual problems: is therapy effective? *British Journal of Sexual Medicine*, Vol. 2, No. 105, pp. 61–3.
Friedman, D., Clare, A.W., Rees, L.H. and Grossman, A. (1986) Should impotent males who have no clinical evidence of hypogonadism have routine endocrine screening? *The Lancet*, Vol. i, p. 1041 (letter).
Ginestie, J.-F. and Romieu, A. (1978) *Radiologic Exploration of Impotence*, Martinus Nijhoff Medical Division, London.
Kaplan, H.S. (1979) *Disorders of Sexual Desire*, Baillière Tindall, London.
Karacan, I. (1969) A simple and inexpensive transducer for quantitative measurement of penile erection during sleep, *Behaviour Research Methods and Instrumentation*, Vol. 1, pp. 251–2.
Karacan, I., Salis, P.J., Thornby, J.I. and Williams, R.L. (1976) The ontogeny of nocturnal penile tumescence, *Waking and Sleeping*, Vol. 1, pp. 27–44.
Levin, A.B. (1966) A simple test of cardiac function based upon the heart rate changes induced by the Valsalva maneuver, *American Journal of Cardiology*, Vol. 18, pp. 90–9.
Lewis, P.W. and Puyau, F.A. (1986) Dynamic cavernosography: results in 150 studies, *Proceedings of the Second World Meeting on Impotence*, Prague.
Masters, W.H. and Johnson, V.E. (1970) *Human Sexual Inadequacy*, Little, Brown & Co., Boston.
May, A.G., DeWeese, J.A. and Rob, C.G. (1969) Changes in sexual function following operation on the abdominal aorta, *Surgery*, Vol. 65, No. 1, pp. 41–7.
Melman, A., Kaplan, D. and Redfield, J. (1984) Evaluation of the first 70 patients in the Center for Male Sexual Dysfunction of Beth Israel Medical Center, *Journal of Urology*, Vol. 131, pp. 53–5.
Michal, V. (1982) Arterial disease as a cause of impotence, *Clinics in Endocrinology and Metabolism*, Vol. 2, No. 3, pp. 725–48.
Michal, V. and Popsichal, J. (1978) Phalloarteriography in the diagnosis of erectile impotence, *World Journal of Surgery*, Vol. 2, pp. 239–47.
Newman, H.F. and Northrup, J.D. (1981) Mechanism of human penile erection: an overview, *Journal of Urology*, Vol. 126, pp. 399–408.
Pick, J. (1970) *The Autonomic Nervous System, Morphological, Comparative Clinical and Surgical Aspects*, Lippincott, Philadelphia.
Saypol, D.C., Peterson, G.A., Howard, S.S. and Yazel, J.J. (1983) Impotence: are the new diagnostic methods a necessity? *Journal of Urology*, Vol. 130, pp. 260–2.
Schiavi, R.C., Fisher, C., White, D., Beers, P., Fogel, M. and Szechter, R. (1982) Hormonal variations during sleep in men with erectile dysfunction and normal controls, *Archives of Sexual Behavior*, Vol. 11, No. 3, pp. 189–200.
Simpson, S.L. (1950) Impotence, *British Medical Journal*, i, pp. 692–7.
Spark, R.F., Wills, C.A., O'Reilly, G., Ransil, B.J. and Bergland, R. (1982) Hyperprolactinaemia in males with and without pituitary macroadenomas, *Lancet*, Vol. ii, pp. 129–31.
Stieff, C.G., Gale, H., Batren, W., Scherb, W., Thou, W.F. and Altwein, J.E. (1986) The meaningfulness of vasoactive drugs in the diagnosis of erectile dysfunction, *Proceedings of the Second World Meeting on Impotence*, Prague.

Strauss, E.B. (1950) Impotence from the psychiatric standpoint, *British Medical Journal*, i, pp. 697–9.
Virag, R., Brouilly, P. and Friedman, D. (1985a) Is impotence an arterial disorder? *Lancet*, Vol. i, pp. 181–4.
Virag, R., Virag, H. and Lajujie, J. (1985b) A new device for measuring penile rigidity, *Urology*, Vol. 132, pp. 80–1.
Wein, A.J., Fishkin, R., Carpiniello, V.L. and Malloy, T.R. (1981) Expansion without significant rigidity during nocturnal penile tumescence testing: a potential source of misinterpretation, *Journal of Urology*, Vol. 126, pp. 343–4.

PART 2

GENERAL THERAPEUTIC APPROACHES AND ISSUES

CHAPTER 7

THE PSYCHOLOGICAL METHODS OF SEX THERAPY

Grahame F. Cooper

In describing and exploring the main approaches to psychological sex therapy currently practised in Britain, I look at the methods, origins and concepts of each approach. The allocation of space to each approach is largely in accord with the frequency of use in Britain as shown by a recent survey of 145 sex therapists (Cooper, 1986). In recognizing the dynamic state of the art of sex therapy, which manifests itself as a constant shift and development, I consider the part played by therapist personality variables and, through this and other aspects, the case for an effective and positive eclectic approach will be made.

Sexual functioning is considered here using a four-phase model, namely *desire* phase, *arousal* phase, *orgasm* phase, *resolution* phase. This differs from the four stages of human sexual response described by Masters and Johnson (1966): excitement stage, plateau stage, orgasm stage and resolution stage. It also differs from Kaplan's (1979) triphasic concept of human sexual response in which she describes desire phase, excitement phase and orgasm phase.

This chapter is addressed primarily to the methods available for dealing with sexual problems of psychological origin, but as will be shown, it is not always possible to make a very clear distinction between organogenic and psychogenic problems.

The main problems covered are:

Sexual dysfunctions affecting both males and females: (a) disorders of the desire phase, and (b) disorders of the resolution phase, which consist of dysphoria due to guilt and/or anxiety, aversive reactions to sexual secretions or aversive reactions to a partner's orgasmic behaviour.

Sexual dysfunctions affecting females: (a) disorders of the arousal phase, and (b) disorders of the orgasm phase.
Sexual dysfunctions affecting males: (a) disorders of the arousal phase – partial or total erectile dysfunction – and (b) disorders of the orgasm phase – premature ejaculation and retarded or absent ejaculation.

In the past, if physical investigations failed to provide a reason for sexual dysfunction, particularly erectile dysfunction, then it was common practice to assume it to be of psychological origin and treatment was offered accordingly. Considerable advances during the last decade have increased the armamentarium of physical investigations (Kaplan, 1983), and physical causes can now be detected for cases which previously would have been assumed to be 'psychogenic'. This progress is likely to continue and it is unreasonable to assume that failure to detect a physical cause automatically means that there is a psychological one. The sexual dysfunction can only be taken as 'not proven' to be of physical origin. All sexual dysfunctions of psychological origin can be seen as psychosomatic disorders – a point emphasized by the approach of the Institute for Psychosexual Medicine, which sees the physical dysfunction and the response to physical genital examination, as giving important indicators of the underlying conflict.

As LoPiccolo and Stock (1986) state, the issue of organic versus psychological origins of sexual dysfunctions should not be considered on a bipolar unidimensional scale. It is best considered as having two orthogonal dimensions, which means that organic and psychological factors can vary independently of each other, and hence it is possible for both factors to be important simultaneously, or for either one to be important whilst the other is insignificant. However, this model does not preclude the possibility of interaction between organic and psychological factors.

Goals of sex therapy

According to Cooklin (1984) the practitioner has to see the problem as the clients'* response to a combination of stimuli from themselves and from the environment (including the partner). In tackling the problem, the goals of sex therapy need to be considered in terms of the individual and the couple. Is the goal to be increased personal sexual satisfaction? Is it to be enhanced 'sexual performance' leading to greater satisfaction for the partner? Is it to be a better communication of love between the partners? Is it to be a greater level of understanding and acceptance within the partnership? Some of these goals are issues relating to the boundary between sexual problems and marital problems (considered further in Chapter 10), but since, as Masters

* The term *client* is used throughout this chapter, not 'patient'. Patient has, by definition, connotations of passivity inappropriate to sex therapy.

and Johnson (1970) say, it is the relationship which is the primary focus of sex therapy, the two can never be completely separated.

Indeed, it is my experience that it is very unusual for a 'pure sex problem' to be found which does not somewhere have roots in the interactions between the couple. This, of course, does not mean that 'pure sex problems' are not presented. It is quite common in the early stages of therapy for there to be a request that the sex problem be simply cured by the therapist, without involving the complexities of the partner's feelings and the relationship between them.

The majority of acts of sexual intercourse takes place for individual or mutual pleasure rather than for purposes of procreation. Most psychological sexual dysfunctions arise in relation to the communication and pleasuring aspects of sexual intercourse, which are more affected by ignorance. The communication of love and affection through sexual interaction is largely acquired by learning and therefore open to all the hazards of learning processes, such as being mislearned, being misapplied, or not being learned at all.

When, for example, premature ejaculation is viewed in terms of the goals of sexual intercourse, the distinction can be clearly seen and it has been argued (Hong, 1984) that from an evolutionary point of view, premature ejaculation has a survival value. In goal-setting, therefore, it may be necessary to clarify whether the aim is the hope of increased mutual pleasure or more efficient deposition of sperm at the cervix.

THE NEW SEX THERAPIES

The term *new sex therapy* is being used here to cover an approach which has its roots in the work of Masters and Johnson (1970) and Kaplan (1974; 1979).

Before Masters and Johnson (1966) began publishing their research findings and their methods of sex therapy (1970; 1976), most sex therapy, where it was available, was based on a psychoanalytic approach which viewed sexual problems as arising from deep intrapsychic conflicts. There was also some behavioural therapy, in particular the work of Wolpe (1958), which was based on classical learning theory and deconditioning. The initial achievement of Masters and Johnson was the publication for the first time of scientific observations of human sexual functioning, including the physiological measurement of the responses of human beings during sexual arousal.

What then emerged was a new therapeutic methodology which could be seen to be partly behavioural in its concepts and origins, partly educational and partly 'permission-giving'. The last was made possible by the special nature of the relationship which was built with the therapists. It was the combination of these three aspects which gave, for the first time, a hope of a way of working with people with sexual problems which was not mysterious and hidden but was explicable and open, so that the clients themselves were really participating members of the therapeutic team. This was in marked contrast to the opacity of the psychoanalyst and the analytical approach. (There is an analogy here between an approach to sex and sexuality which is open, freely giving of information and one which is secretive and closed off, giving rise to dark fantasies.)

Masters and Johnson did not deny that transference to the therapists would take place, but it was not encouraged or used as it would have been in the analytical situation. Stanley (1981a), writing on sex problems in practice, says:

> Until quite recently it was thought that all sexual problems were purely the expression of deep intra-psychic conflict arising from traumatic experiences in infancy and childhood, which only prolonged psychoanalysis could resolve. Fortunately it is now understood that most sexual difficulties are far simpler in origin and can be resolved using brief forms of intervention that require little more than common sense once the causative facts are understood. (p. 1042)

Bancroft (1983) has given a commendably clear and straightforward account of his treatment approach to couples with psychogenic sexual problems. His account acknowledges the commonsense element, but lays much more emphasis on the psychotherapeutic aspects than do Masters and Johnson. In common with other therapists, he believes that Masters and Johnson seriously understate the psychotherapeutic component of their work. Here then can be seen the rationale for considering the new sex therapies as a different approach to the behavioural, even though the new sex therapies do have a considerable behavioural component.

Kaplan (1974) in *The New Sex Therapy* rectified the apparent deficit of the psychotherapeutic component in the Masters and Johnson approach, and produced an extremely well-balanced method of working which utilized the behavioural and educational aspects, and at the same time made good use of appropriate opportunities for deeper insight provided by the clients' responses in the treatment programme. These two aspects are also embodied in her concepts of 'remote' and 'immediate' causes. Another of Kaplan's contributions was her description of human sexual response as triphasic, as opposed to the four-stage model of Masters and Johnson. This introduced a clarification and simplification that was also much more in accord with common experience. This was particularly emphasized in her *Disorders of Sexual Desire* (1979) (designated as Volume 2 of *The New Sex Therapy*) which brought out the important distinction between disorders of desire and disorders of arousal or excitement.

The new sex therapies are thus an approach to psychological sexual problems which originated and was developed in the US. It was then brought to the UK, partly through the literature, but mainly through practitioners who went to America to train. The basic concepts and principles have been introduced into Britain virtually intact but there have been major modifications in terms of methods of practical application, particularly in the time-scale and intensity of the treatment programme. A major influence here was the initiative taken in introducing this therapy into Britain through the establishment of the 'marital sexual dysfunction clinics' of the National Marriage Guidance Council*. A training programme (initiated under the direction of Paul Brown) has led to the widespread availability of this therapy through local Marriage Guidance Councils (Brown, 1976; 1980).

As far as I am aware, no one has ever attempted exactly to replicate Masters and Johnson's therapy in Britain. It has been modified in various ways, partly because of the needs of a different culture and social structure, but also because of the personality variables and individual beliefs of the practitioners. Cole (1985) notes that 'While considerable variation in emphasis exists, with only a few notable exceptions, most sex therapists claim at least to follow a "quasi-eclectic modified Masters and Johnson × Kaplan hybrid programme" ' (p. 341). This statement has been confirmed by preliminary data from a survey I conducted (Cooper, 1986). Of the 33 respondents who indicated a sole main method upon which their work was based, 27 (82 per cent) listed the method as Masters and Johnson/Kaplan. A further 111 respondents indicated that they used an eclectic approach involving two or more methods and 105 of these (95 per cent) gave Masters and Johnson/Kaplan as one of the methods.

Clinical practice

To illustrate the application of the methods of the new sex therapies in Britain, work carried out in my practice with couples presenting with a variety of psychogenic sexual dysfunctions will now be described. Some clients come as individuals and some couples are homosexual, but heterosexual couples who have been screened to eliminate physical causes for their problems are being taken here to illustrate the principles and practice.

The initial consultation

Preparation. When making the first appointment and again at the first session, the couple are told that the session will provide an opportunity for exploration of their difficulties so that a clear assessment can be made of the nature of the problem and decisions made about the best way of moving forward towards resolution. They are also told that, during the course of the session, they will each be seen by the therapist individually as well as together. Almost invariably, the couple are seen by only one therapist.

* Now known as Relate: National Marriage Guidance

Therapist's goals. In this initial session the therapist is seeking to clarify the nature of the problem in two different ways. First, I will be observing the interaction between the couple whilst they discuss their difficulties, to help you to clarify and explore whether this is primarily a sexual problem or if the presenting sexual problem is really symptomatic of deeper difficulties and conflicts within the marital relationship. Second, I will remain alert for possible undiagnosed physical factors which may be contributing to the presented problem. The therapist will discuss with the couple their expectations of therapy and their hopes for the outcome. The strength of motivation will be explored and the importance of this will be clarified, since at times sex therapy can arouse uncomfortable feelings. I will observe the interactions between the couple by, for example, throwing questions 'into the air' and observing how they are picked up and by whom. Such a question might be, 'What is the main difficulty that you are bringing here today?'

At all times the therapist will be attending closely to the *couple* and by empathic responding will encourage the exploration of their feelings as well as of the factual information they are bringing. In this way I work to build a rapport with the couple so that they will gain both a positive sense of being understood, and a hope that their problems may be resolved. This leads to the development of a therapeutic alliance so that effective work can be done within the contract which will be agreed, usually by the end of this first session.

Individual consultations. During the session each of them will be given an opportunity for an individual consultation with the therapist. It is emphasized that anything they discuss with the therapist at this stage is confidential to the *therapist* and will not be divulged by the therapist to the other partner unless specific permission is given to do so. However this is not intended to raise any barriers to communication between them and, of course, they are totally free to discuss between them any of the issues raised in solo consultations. Indeed, it is pointed out that issues which, owing to the high levels of anxiety, need to be raised in confidence with the therapist initially, may then be much more easily shared with the partner afterwards.

The contract. Near the end of the initial session the therapist will offer the couple a summary of the major issues which have been raised, a preliminary diagnosis, an outline of a treatment programme and the details of a therapeutic contract for them to consider. The contract will include issues of therapist's and clients' responsibilities, duration of sessions (usually 1¼ hours), frequency of sessions (usually weekly or fortnightly), probable number of sessions (commonly 6–12) and details of fees, methods of payment, cancelled appointments, etc.

Each of them is given a form to take away and fill in which gives the basic factual information about themselves, their families of origin and present family, states of health, details of any medication, etc. and they are asked to bring or send this before the next session.

In most cases, this work can be completed in a single session but occasionally it takes a further session. Like Bancroft (1983), I do not take a highly detailed sexual and case history at this time, but the information received about the problem and circumstances is taken as a starting point for the work, and may be subject to modification and enlargement as the therapeutic programme progresses.

Sensate Focus 1

Like Masters and Johnson (1970) and Kaplan (1974; 1979) I offer the couple homework assignments which have the intention of minimizing anxiety by reducing or eliminating performance goals.

The couple are asked, in the following manner, to agree to a total ban on sexual intercourse: 'During the next few weeks, no matter how sexually excited either or both of you may become and no matter how loving either or both of you may feel towards the other, under no circumstances will you have, or attempt to have, sexual intercourse.'

The response of the clients to this can provide very important information as it may be greeted with relief, anger, disdain, or sadness. The therapist then immediately explains what is being offered instead – which is a modified version of Masters and Johnson's sensate focus programme.

Instructions. The couple are given clear and precise instructions as to what is involved. They are to set aside a period of time when they can ensure that their privacy will not be interrupted and they can be somewhere which feels warm, comfortable and safe for both of them but is not necessarily in the bedroom. In this environment where they can be naked together, they are to take turns in giving pleasure to, and receiving pleasure from, each other. This physical pleasuring is intended to be sensual and not specifically sexual, that is, they are instructed to avoid the genital areas, breasts and nipples and other erogenous zones. Outside of these limitations they are free to touch, stroke, massage, hold, explore the whole of the partner's body. They are instructed that if sexual arousal occurs in either or both of them, that they may be aware of it but remain clear that they are going to 'do nothing with it' and that in time the arousal will subside.

The recipient of this physical pleasuring is in charge of the process and by monitoring his or her physical and emotional feelings is able to give the partner feedback on what is pleasurable. At this stage the feedback is always given in positive terms such as, 'I like that,' 'I would like you to move more slowly,' 'I would like you to move on to my arm or feet or. . . .' In order to encourage the partner who is giving the pleasure, it is important not to give negative feedback, such as 'Don't do that,' 'You are not pushing hard enough,' 'Don't do it there.' The partner who is giving the pleasuring is instructed to monitor his or her emotional feelings during this process as well as noting the physical sensations of the texture of the various parts of the body and so to learn for future use what he or she and the partner find particularly pleasurable, both in giving and receiving.

I find it important for the couple to be instructed in this way in the initial confidence-building stages, particularly when either of them have felt themselves to have been sexually used by the partner or others. Having a period of time in which they are in control of their own bodies is an important part of confidence restoration as well as allowing learning and the development of clear communication to take place. At a later stage, it may be appropriate for the giver of the pleasuring to be more in charge and in Masters and Johnson's words to 'give-to-get'. Both may then also be encouraged to express any negative feelings. Many authors, for example, Stanley (1981c), Greenwood and Bancroft (1983), and Hawton (1985), appear to follow the original concepts more closely and to encourage the open expression of negative feelings from the start.

After an agreed period of time the couple reverse roles and they are encouraged to discuss afterwards as honestly as they can their reactions to the whole process. In my practice all these instructions are given verbally. Some other practitioners give their instructions for this work as printed instruction sheets for the clients (e.g. Fairburn *et al.*, 1983).

Monitoring. Again, it is of the utmost importance to monitor the couple's emotional reaction to these instructions, which may need to be modified accordingly. Thus, where there are high levels of anxiety, mistrust, or a degree of hostility, or where there has been a strong aversion to physical contact, it may be necessary to limit the work of the first homework assignment, for example, simply to holding hands whilst fully clothed and to being aware of physical feelings and emotional reactions to that activity.

The continuing programme. At the beginning of the second and all succeeding sessions, the couple will be seen together and the therapist watches closely for early signs, both verbal and non-verbal, of the interactions going on between them. This can provide valuable background information as they report their specific experiences, both physical and emotional, in carrying out the homework assignments and in terms of their life together in the interval since the previous session. As Kaplan (1974; 1979) emphasizes, it is not just the work that is done in the sessions and in the homework assignments which forms the material of therapy, but just as important is dealing with the resistances which are often thrown up by the homework assignment.

Sensate focus 1 as described may achieve its goals by the beginning of the second session. In some cases it may be appropriate to continue it for longer. There are wide variations in the reactions and interactions of couples to this work and these must always be taken into account. As Bancroft (1983) states:

> Sometimes inexperienced therapists lose the confidence of the couple if they stick too rigidly to the prescribed behavioural programme and fail to respond appropriately to the couple's particular needs or difficulties in carrying out assignments. (p. 253)

When the couple have achieved optimum learning from sensate focus 1, then the therapist introduces sensate focus 2.

Sensate Focus 2

The absolute ban on intercourse remains as before and the importance of sustained privacy with freedom from interruptions is re-emphasized. The difference is that the couple are not now prohibited from including genital areas, the breast, nipples and other erogenous zones in their pleasuring of each other. It is emphasized that the objective at this stage is not the achievement of sexual arousal or the achievement of orgasm, although either of these may actually occur. In many ways stages 1 and 2 represent what is commonly referred to as 'foreplay' or 'sex play' but in parallel with the desirability of not drawing a sharp distinction between 'foreplay' and 'intercourse', the pleasuring of stage 2 includes, and develops from, the pleasuring of stage 1 and is not a substitute for it.

Education. Learning to integrate foreplay and intercourse, perhaps for the first time, is an important educative component of the new sex therapies and it helps to correct the misconception that foreplay is something that the man does to the woman in order to get her ready for him to penetrate her in sexual intercourse. Rather, the aim is to achieve a level of physical and emotional interaction between the couple, enhanced by open communication, which will lead to increased pleasure for both of them in the course of which the woman will become sufficiently sexually aroused for *acceptance* of the penis into her vagina to occur comfortably and pleasurably. For the man, it is hoped that the increased pleasure will lead to sufficient erection of the penis for it to be contained and retained within the vagina during the movements of sexual intercourse. This statement does not preclude the possibility that some couples achieve their sexual pleasure without genital intercourse, nor does it exclude the fact that genital intercourse is perfectly feasible with a flaccid penis, provided that the woman is in a sufficient state of sexual arousal to be able and willing to *accept* it vaginally.

The vocabulary
Many of the couples who present with sexual problems have barriers to communication about sex which are simply due to the lack of an appropriate vocabulary. This lack can itself be a cause of sexual difficulties; it can exacerbate a sexual difficulty through lack of discussion, and it can be a considerable barrier to effective therapy.

In the early stages of therapy the therapist always explores whether or not the couple have a vocabulary which they can use comfortably. If not, specific homework assignments may be needed which will enable the couple to explore and agree on a mutually acceptable vocabulary.

It is arrogant for therapists to assume that everybody should be using medical terms and be comfortable with them. This problem arises because, as McConville and Shearlaw (1985) state, 'We have little or no freedom of language for our sexual relationships, no respectable non-medical names which we can use freely in any company' (p. 7).

The 'Word Game'
In this context I may use the 'Word Game' to encourage the development of a suitable vocabulary. The couple are instructed to write, individually and privately, lists of the synonyms they know for words of agreed sexual significance, for example, vagina, penis, breasts, testicles, anus, intercourse, masturbation, etc. They then share their individual lists with each other, one subject at a time, in the way they prefer and which does not raise undue anxiety. After sharing their lists for a particular item, they discuss which words feel comfortable and which ones feel uncomfortable. In this way most couples are able to find words which can be used comfortably in therapy and in their future life together. Sometimes the difficulties are overcome by inventing totally new words!

Provision of factual information
Ignorance of the sexual anatomy and physiology of self or partner is another all-too-common factor in the origin, exacerbation or continuation of sexual dysfunctions. This is not purely a question of a lack of 'sex education' in its formal sense, but is frequently linked, in both men and women, with a restrictive or moralistic view of sex and sexual functioning in the family of origin which makes factual information emotionally inaccessible to the individual or couple, even in adult life.

An important function of the therapist here is not only the provision of such information, but, by example, the giving of permission for such information to be acquired, discussed openly and hence utilized. I give information by talk and discussion, by the use of books, drawings and photographs, flipchart and pens. Where appropriate, details are also given of books which may be obtained by the clients for their own use (e.g. Ward,

1976; Zilbergeld, 1980; Kitzinger, 1985). Other available methods include the use of slides, models, video and films. I do not use the sexological examination (i.e. the close examination and discussion of the genital area of each partner in the presence of the other) but this is an important aspect of the methods of treatment of some authors (Frank, 1982; Stanley, 1981d).

Specific sexual dysfunctions

Whilst the preceding is not and cannot be a total description of the work of the early sessions, simply because of the variability of the couples, it does represent a fair statement of the groundwork which has to be done with almost every couple regardless of their specific sexual dysfunction. It must be recognized that this groundwork is both diagnostic and therapeutic and that these two facets of the work will constantly intermingle as the work progresses. The trust between therapist and clients develops as the therapeutic alliance strengthens and as the expectations of the outcome of the therapeutic contract become clearer.

The work so far has focused on the couple and has emphasized the strengths and weaknesses which each of them brings to the relationship. The very format of the work has emphasized Masters and Johnson's (1970) dictum that 'there is no such thing as an uninvolved partner in any marriage in which there is some form of sexual inadequacy' (p. 2). Therapy is a couple activity because, even though only one partner may be showing a 'symptom', there is likely to be distress for both of them and the work is most likely to be successful if it is approached as a co-operative venture. The couple are helped to move away from blame and retribution, which are destructive, towards the more constructive modes of learning, insight and assertive statement of need. However, as will be seen in the consideration of the specific dysfunctions, there are sometimes tasks and assignments to be carried out by the individual to assist her or his own learning and development, in addition to the mutual assignments for the couple.

Dyspareunia and vaginismus

Dyspareunia in the female (pain in the vagina during intercourse) and vaginismus can be viewed as similar problems with varying degrees of intensity. They range from a dyspareunia of mild discomfort, through serious and perhaps intolerable pain, to vaginismus where the reflex contracture of the peri-vaginal muscles effectively prevents penetration by the penis. In the most serious cases, any attempt to touch or approach the vagina leads to powerful reflex adduction of the thighs, thus precluding even the possibility of attempted penetration. My experience is that both conditions may be met where the origins and treatment are purely psychological. However, sometimes the origins can be solely due to lesions or physical trauma, while Frank (1982) sees dyspareunia as having both physical and psychological origins. (See pp. 148–9 for a description of specific treatment components for dyspareunia and vaginisms.)

Anorgasmia

Whilst the use of 'pre-orgasmia' is laudable, with its implication that all women are capable of orgasm but some have not yet achieved it, anorgasmia will be used here since it can be applied more easily to both primary and secondary inability to achieve orgasm. It recognizes that, whilst for the majority of men and women having an orgasm is a pleasurable and desirable experience, there is always the danger of it being spoken about, and seen, as a performance goal which everybody ought to achieve. There is evidence (Brindley and Gillan, 1982) that some anorgasmic women have diminished pelvic reflexes indicating a possible physiological cause.

The differences in the treatment approach to primary and to secondary female anorgasmia are more in degree than kind. In a primary anorgasmia of psychological origin it is likely that most attention will need to be paid to early learning and conditioning, whereas in secondary anorgasmia the immediate state of the relationship and possible unresolved feelings and conflicts within it warrants most attention. Kaplan (1974) refers to these as 'remote' and 'immediate' causes. (See p. 149 for a further description of specific treatment components for anorgasmia.)

Disorders of arousal

Kaplan (1979) has written extensively about inhibition of sexual desire, but distinction from disorders of arousal in the female is not always easy. Briefly, when there is inhibition of sexual desire, the woman will not be interested in getting into a potentially sexual situation and she is psychologically unavailable for arousal. On the other hand, the woman who is suffering from disorders of arousal will be interested in her sexual partner, will willingly get into a sexual situation but finds that even in those circumstances her physiological mechanisms of arousal do not function and that there is, for example, no lubrication of the vagina. If attempts are made to penetrate the vagina forcibly when it is so obviously unready to accept the penis or finger, then pain can occur, thus setting up a reflex cycle of anxiety which inhibits still further the likelihood of arousal and lubrication and continues the dyspareunia. In more severe cases, this may lead to vaginismus. From this description it can be seen that in some cases male partners may play an active and unfortunate part in setting up or enhancing the vaginismus, which is then disparagingly referred to as 'frigidity'.

By the use of the diagnostic and educational procedures and the sensate focus programme, many couples are able to overcome this difficulty with a treatment of only four to six sessions. I find it helpful to pay specific attention to understanding and gently exploring the woman's feelings and emotional responses to her situation and to the therapy situation. It is most important to allow the woman client to move forward at her own pace, however, and to ensure that the therapist does not force a way through her emotional defences into secret places that she is not ready to reveal, and thus risk emulating the behaviour of a male sexual partner who may have attempted to penetrate her before she was ready to accept him inside her.

Erectile dysfunction

As has already been indicated, erectile dysfunction may be total (when there is no significant degree of erection) or partial (when the penis becomes only partially erect or becomes erect but loses the erection before, or soon after, being accepted into the vagina). The main consideration here will be given to secondary erectile dysfunction since primary erectile dysfunction of a purely psychological origin is not very common.

I agree with Bancroft (1983) that for many couples presenting with erectile dysfunction the removal of performance anxiety combined with the learning opportunities of the initial consultation and the sensate focus programme are in themselves sufficient to restore the capacity for full erection. Perhaps even more important is gaining the understanding and belief that an erection can be allowed to subside in the secure knowledge that it will return. This reduces the frantic activity which may follow from thinking: 'Now I've got an erection, I'd better get it in quick, before it disappears.' Such frantic activity is itself likely to reduce the erection and is best avoided.

In moving on from sensate focus 2 the couple are allowed to include genital contact and genital intercourse in their love-making but without giving the man the responsibility for making a penetration. Intercourse can be best achieved by the woman moving into the superior position during mutual sensual and sexual pleasuring which has led to full arousal occurring in both of them. In this position the woman can take responsibility for accepting the erect penis into her vagina and so the man can experience this acceptance and containment without having to feel responsible for it, which will minimize the anxiety that his erection may fail.

Ejaculatory dysfunctions: premature and retarded

Premature ejaculation. The most common by far of the two ejaculatory dysfunctions is premature ejaculation. It is not a condition which can be diagnosed properly by the measurement of time from the onset of stimulation or entry to the moment of ejaculation, but can best be defined by the couple in terms of their personal satisfaction with the degree/intensity of pleasuring achieved before ejaculation occurs. Not forgetting, of course, the continuation of pleasuring which is possible *after* ejaculation. The refractory period also has to be taken into account, that is, the time taken after an ejaculation before the erectile mechanisms again become responsive to stimulation. (There is no refractory period in the female following her orgasm.)

The common groundwork of the initial consultation and the sensate focus programme will reduce the performance anxiety and improve the general level of communication between the couple but it is often not sufficient to relieve the specific symptom of the premature ejaculation.

However, a specific technique to counteract this difficulty has been evolved. Semans (1956) first described the stop-start technique, by which a man could learn to recognize the moment of ejaculatory inevitability and thus prevent ejaculation by reducing stimulation until the probability of ejaculatory inevitability had passed. This learning was achieved through manual stimulation and could then be transferred to the intercourse situation. This concept was incorporated by Masters and Johnson (1970) and developed as the squeeze technique. This technique utilizes the fact that if the penis is squeezed between thumb and forefinger, just below the head of the glans, immediately before the moment of ejaculatory inevitability, then the sensation of impending ejaculation will subside, often accompanied by some reduction in the degree of erection of the penis. The man's partner uses this fact in training him to recognize the moment of ejaculatory inevitability, and so to become able to reduce stimulation just before that moment in order to delay the ejaculation.

Clear instructions are given to the couple as follows: in addition to the mutual pleasuring given in sensate focus 2, the woman is instructed to sit astride her partner and manually stimulate the penis to just before the moment of ejaculatory inevitability. When he indicates this moment she will apply the squeeze technique until the desire to ejaculate subsides. After a few moments she will resume stimulation and again apply the squeeze at the appropriate moment. After bringing him to this point three times she then stimulates him until ejaculation occurs. When a good degree of control and delay has been achieved in this way, they are instructed to move on to the next stage in which stimulation is applied by the woman accepting the penis into her vagina whilst sitting on top of the man.

At first the penis will only be allowed to enter a short way into the vagina and she will remain absolutely still, simply containing the penis within her vagina. If he indicates the approach of ejaculatory inevitability then she lifts herself off his penis and immediately applies the squeeze technique. In this way his confidence can be built up through quiet containment of the penis within the vagina. When he has sufficient confidence in his ability to do this, he may request her to provide more stimulation by moving herself up and down on his penis. In this way he learns to control the intensity and duration of stimulation and in most cases this is successful in eliminating or reducing the tendency to premature ejaculation. Once he has gained confidence with the woman in the superior position, then other positions for sexual intercourse can be used.

Retarded ejaculation. Retarded ejaculation is much less common than premature ejaculation, and it can range from a relatively minor condition where the woman may complain 'He takes rather a long time to come, even though I do all that I know to help him,' to situations where ejaculation may be retarded indefinitely in intercourse and only achieved with great difficulty, if at all, during masturbation. It is certainly seen as a result of disease conditions such as diabetes or multiple sclerosis but also occurs as a result of psychological trauma, for example, where ejaculation has become associated with intense feelings of anxiety or guilt.

In using sensate focus to improve verbal and physical communication between the couple, the therapist may incidentally fulfil an important permission-giving function. This may be particularly true if the problem has become compounded by a resurgence of anxieties and inhibitions about masturbation, learned early in life, so that both remote and immediate causes are contributing to the dysfunction. The specific use of a behavioural desensitization technique is often required and this is described in detail in the later section on Behaviour Therapy. Individual therapy in depth is sometimes indicated for dealing with the remote causes of retarded ejaculation.

Resolution phase dysphoria

There does not appear to be a description in the literature of disorders of the resolution phase, but I have come across a number of cases. These fall into two categories: dysphoria due to guilt and/or anxiety, and aversive reactions to sexual secretions or aversive reactions to a partner's orgasmic behaviour.

Guilt and/or anxiety. Where dysphoria due to guilt or anxiety arises within a specific relationship, it is often indicative of unresolved feelings and conflicts within or about that relationship and can be treated by the improvement of communication which comes through the use of the initial consultation and sensate focus programmes. Some individual work may also be needed, if the condition is generalized and not confined to a specific partner. In these situations, it can often be traced back to traumatizing events in earlier life or childhood, or a transgression of family/cultural norms of behaviour. Acute anxiety can ensue and lead to long-lasting sexual dysfunctions in men and women after realizing that possible exposure to sexually transmitted diseases (especially AIDS) has occurred.

Aversive reactions. Dysphoria in the resolution phase also occurs when there is a feeling of revulsion to the 'mess' of sexual intercourse. This can be seen most commonly in a reaction to seminal fluid, but may also occur as a reaction to vaginal lubricant. These responses may be triggered by the sight, feel, smell or taste of either of these fluids. Again this may be a problem which cannot be successfully treated by couple therapy alone and intensive individual work is commonly needed, in my experience, as there may have been triggering events in early life. One client who had an intense aversive reaction of this type, associated it with a childhood memory of unpleasant sensations when being washed in hospital by a nurse using bare soapy hands. Serious quarrels occurred with the partner as a result of these responses.

The use of the sensate focus programme will improve communication and reduce anxiety so that these responses and their sequelae can be approached in a helpful, caring and constructive way. This work can again lead to clarification as to whether the origins of the reactions are remote or immediate and they can then be appropriately approached by individual therapy or counselling procedures.

Fundamental concepts in the new sex therapies: origins and developments

From the preceding descriptions it becomes clear that it is vitally important to recognize individual variations and to develop a therapeutic programme which matches the needs of the couple both in content and timing. However it is also apparent that there are certain principles and concepts underlying the treatment methods of the new sex therapies which are consistently adhered to, despite the variations of detail required to meet individual needs. They can be briefly summarized as follows:

First concept

It is the marital (or couple) relationship which is the focus of therapy – 'there is no such thing as an uninvolved partner in any marriage in which there is some form of sexual inadequacy.' (Masters and Johnson, 1970, p. 2).

In a continuing partnership, sexual dysfunction will lead to stress for *both* partners and it is therefore appropriate for *both* partners to participate in the therapy programme. This approach also helps to reduce the attachment of blame to the partner who is showing the symptom and that is very important.

It is interesting to note that in the early years of their work, Masters and Johnson were willing to take single people into their treatment programme, despite the above dictum. Some of these single clients brought a 'friend' as a partner for the therapy programme whilst others were provided with surrogate partners selected by the therapy team. There is an interesting tension here between the importance accorded to the *relationship* in this therapeutic approach *and* the willingness to provide surrogate or substitute partners for a single client. Later, owing to the ethical issues involved, the provision of surrogate partners was discontinued, although single clients are still encouraged to bring a 'friend' (see Chapter 16).

Second concept
Fear in the form of performance anxiety is a major factor underlying many psychological sexual dysfunctions. There is ample physiological and psychological knowledge to explain the mechanisms underlying this concept and provide the rationale for the sensate focus programme. This programme eliminates or reduces performance anxiety and its blocking effects on sexual interactions, and thus allows for the restoration of the natural sexual functioning which had been inhibited by anxiety. In this context, Masters and Johnson (1970) note:

> It should be restated that fear of inadequacy is the greatest known deterrent to effective sexual functioning simply because it so completely distracts the fearful individual from his or her natural sexual functioning by blocking reception of sexual stimuli either created by or reflected from his or her sexual partner. (p. 12)

Third concept
The use of a man-woman co-therapy team with the couple is a vital factor in the effectiveness of the treatment programmes (Masters and Johnson, 1970; 1976). Masters and Johnson have held strongly to this concept in their work, even though other workers have failed to find significant differences between the outcomes of co-therapy and single therapist practices (LoPiccolo and Stock, 1986). Masters and Johnson believe that man-woman co-therapy reduces the possibility of collusive alliances forming during the therapy. But they also demonstrate their underlying belief that only a woman can really understand the woman client's sexuality and sexual difficulties and thus be an important aid in 'interpreting' to the woman client's partner and, conversely, that only a man can really understand and interpret the male client's sexuality and sexual difficulties. This appears to demonstrate a lack of faith in the process of empathic listening and responding.

Masters and Johnson emphasize the importance of both members of the marital relationship feeling that they have an 'ally'. This is emphasized by their practice of the initial assessment being done on a same-sex basis, that is, the wife works with the female therapist and the man works with the male therapist. Perhaps it is a reflection of the fact that Masters and Johnson were not, in general, training people who were already trained counsellors since their method seems to emphasize identification through similarity of experience rather than using an empathic understanding of the patient's feelings and inner world. Most British practitioners normally work as single therapists and the co-therapy model is used relatively little (Cooper, 1986). There is not much evidence to indicate that this adversely affects the outcomes of therapy.

Fourth concept

Failure of communication is a major factor in sexual dysfunctioning. This stresses the importance of improving communications between the couple. There can be important modelling here for the clients in experiencing a therapist who is at ease in talking about sexual and related matters. For some couples it will be a question of initiating good sexual communication (both verbal and physical) for the first time rather than restoring it. Perhaps the ultimate communication is mutual pleasurable sexual intercourse.

Fifth concept

The couple have to be sufficiently motivated to commit themselves to making the treatment programme their primary activity for a specified period of time, which also may involve a period of social isolation. Masters and Johnson required the couple to be resident within the locality of the clinic for a period of three weeks (later reduced to two weeks). For many, this involved isolation from their normal social environment.

This relocation for an intensive period of therapy has not been applied in Britain. The primary aim of this residential period is to focus on the therapy, but it will *also* have the effect of focusing attention on the relationship between the couple since, being out of the normal daily routine of work and family, they will be thrown together in an intensive way which they may not have experienced for many years. It can also carry connotations of a holiday, which can induce relaxation and sharing and thus promote a healing within the relationship, in addition to the specific sexual therapy being provided.

Follow-up

After the intensive phase of the Masters and Johnson treatment programme, the majority of the follow-up work is carried out by telephone calls which, according to the information provided by Kolodny (1981) are fairly minimal, averaging some 20 minutes, four times a year for a couple of years. It is clear that the intensive phase is by far the major component of the therapy.

Adherence to the five concepts

In her development of the new sex therapies, Kaplan (1974) can be seen as sustaining the emphasis of the first, second and fourth concepts, but not the third concept. She considers that equally good results are obtained with a single therapist when compared with a man-woman co-therapy team. She agrees with the fifth concept in the sense that the couple need to be sufficiently motivated to commit themselves to the treatment programme, but she did not use the two-week intensive-therapy period which involved the social isolation of the couple from their normal family and work environment.

Similarly, current practice in Britain adheres to the first, second and fourth concepts and accepts the need for a high motivation as contained in the fifth concept, but without using a two-week intensive-therapy phase in isolation, which is costly and disruptive. The common pattern is for the couples to be seen at weekly or fortnightly intervals.

It appears to be the commonest practice in Britain for a single therapist to work with a couple (65 per cent in my survey, Cooper, 1986). Only 14 per cent indicated that they normally work with a co-therapist, either qualified or in training. This practice is validated by the failure of research to indicate that the co-therapist model is more effective than a single therapist (Crowe *et al.*, 1981; Mathews *et al.*, 1983).

Causes and change factors in the new sex therapies

In terms of psychological causes of sexual dysfunctions, apart from certain traumatic precipitating factors, Stanley (1981a) has listed the following as the three most important causes of performance anxiety which are come across in practice: (a) ignorance, (b) cultural taboos and myths, and (c) poor communications. These are seen as underlying causes which may induce and/or sustain a problem, but there are sometimes other specific precipitating factors (e.g. stress).

Stress can trigger a sexual failure, but the failure persists even when the stress is removed because of the preceding listed factors. This circle can then only be broken by a therapeutic intervention or sometimes, and sadly, by breaking the relationship and starting a new one which is 'uncontaminated'.

Figure 7.1 illustrates the relationship between the repressive blocks which precipitate or sustain negative sexual functioning and five major change factors which are involved in transforming these blocks into the new foundations for positive sexual functioning. As the lower portion of Figure 7.1 shows, there is a self-sustaining feedback between each of these blocks and sexual dysfunctioning. The upper part of Figure 7.1 shows the positive feedback loops which occur between positive sexual functioning and its appropriate foundations. These change factors which lead to the transition from block to appropriate foundation are all identifiable components of the new sex therapies.

Figure 7.1 Sexual blocks, change factors and new foundations

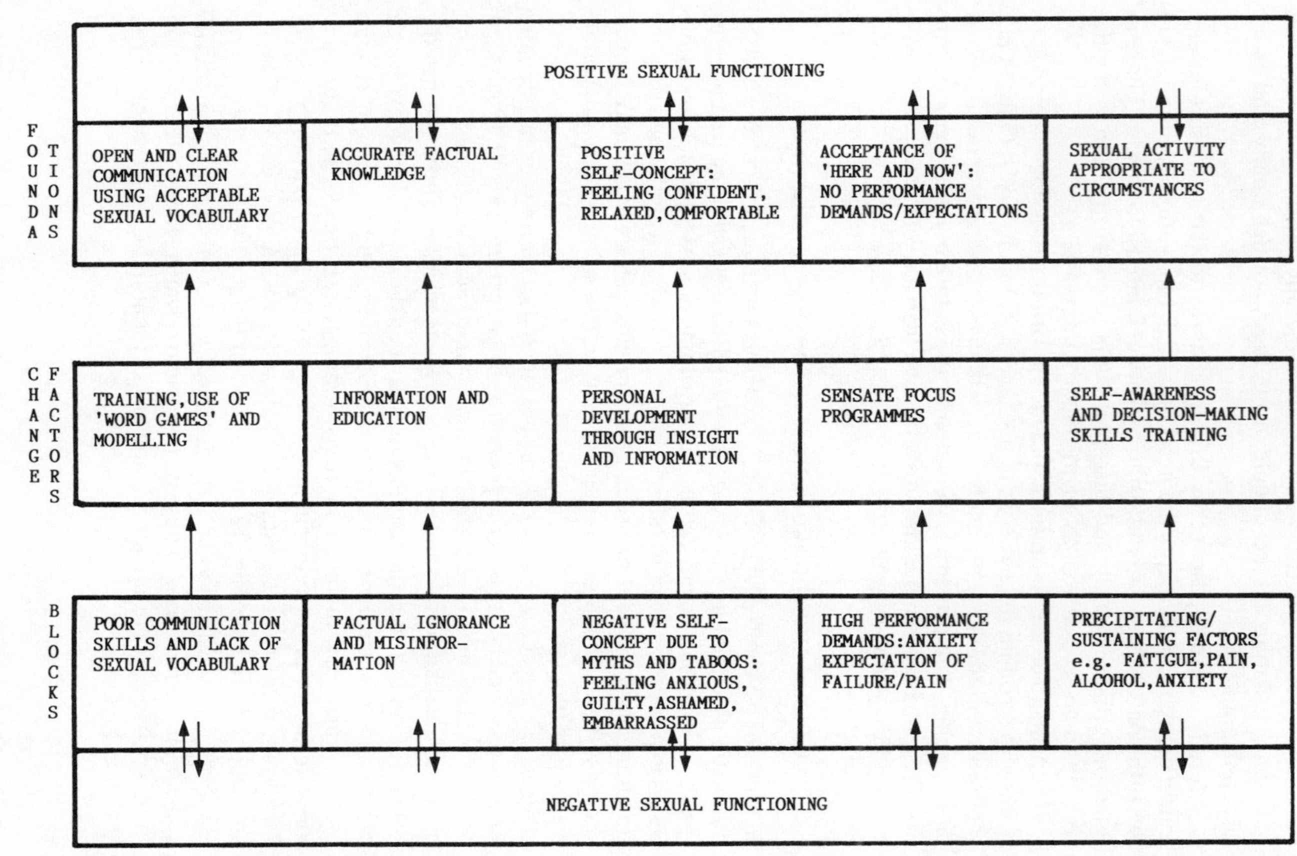

OTHER THERAPEUTIC APPROACHES

Behaviour therapy

When the work of Masters and Johnson was first published, many therapists seized on the descriptions of the sensate focus programme and the specific treatment schedules as indicating that Masters and Johnson were practising behaviour therapy. This may have been partly due to shortcomings in their writings (Bancroft, 1983; 1985) but nevertheless many authors (e.g. Frank, 1982) list Masters and Johnson's technique under behavioural methods. Bancroft (1985) sees it as a good example of what Mackay (1984) called 'behavioural psychotherapy' which is a combination of 'action and discovery'. Here, in accord with Cooklin (1984), the work of Masters and Johnson is considered under the new sex therapies and not defined as behaviour therapy.

Behaviour therapists hold that human behaviours are learned, whether they are adaptive or maladaptive. It follows from this that maladaptive behaviours can also be unlearned and replaced by the learning of more appropriate behaviours. This is a general tenet but it can be specifically applied to the area of sexual dysfunctions. The hope in behavioural sex therapy is to bring about this change of behaviour or response without necessarily exploring the underlying origins and without changing the intrapsychic structure. In the past, behavioural sex therapy has suffered from an image of being basically concerned with the 'correction' of 'deviant' sexual behaviour (Feldman and MacCulloch, 1967), rather than one of dealing with the sexual dysfunctions which are the commonest sexual problem of the general population.

As with all methods of sex therapy, however, the behavioural method will only be effective if a good therapeutic alliance is formed between the therapist and the client(s) – a process which is facilitated by the effective use of counselling skills.

A survey of 145 sex therapists working in Britain (Cooper, 1986) shows 33 who based their work upon a sole main method. Of these, 6 per cent said this method was behavioural whereas 82 per cent said it was based on the new sex therapies (Masters and Johnson/Kaplan). There were 111 respondents who indicated the use of an eclectic approach involving two or more methods and of these, 20 (18 per cent) used behavioural methods in combination with Masters and Johnson/Kaplan only, whilst a further 41 (37 per cent) used behavioural methods in other combinations.

It is clear, however, that behavioural *components* are present in the new sex therapies, in cognitive therapies and in eclectically developing therapies, and here some examples will be given of behavioural treatment of specific conditions without attempting to describe the whole field. A thorough coverage of behavioural methods of sex therapy can be found in Annon (1976) and in Jehu (1979), whilst Hawton (1982) reviews the behavioural treatment of sexual dysfunction.

The behavioural analysis is a vital preliminary in considering the treatment of specific sexual dysfunctions. This involves gathering a clear account of the problem behaviour (dysfunction), understanding the events surrounding its onset and considering the current events which are sustaining the problem behaviour, including the consequences of the behaviour itself. This information should enable the therapist to offer an hypothesis which makes the events and present situation clear to the client and allows a treatment programme to be planned.

The role of anxiety in initiating or maintaining sexual dysfunctions has already been emphasized. This anxiety may be induced by physical or emotional trauma in sexual situations, or by expectations of emotional trauma arising from irrational beliefs or unrealistic performance expectations of self or partner. Behaviour therapy techniques specifically designed for the relief of anxieties induced by physical or emotional trauma will now be considered in relation to sex therapy generally, and to some specific sexual dysfunctions.

Sexual anxieties can be reduced by systematic desensitization. In the imaginal version, the client is helped to construct a hierarchy of imagined anxiety-raising scenes. Starting with the scene at the bottom on the hierarchy, the therapist will instruct the client to alternate between the imagined anxiety-provoking sexual situation, and an imagined tranquil scene with accompanying physical relaxation. When the procedure has eliminated anxiety from the imagined scene or reduced it to a minimal level, the treatment then moves to the next imagined scene further up the hierarchy.

Disorders of arousal

Wolpe (1969) reduced clients' anxieties in situations involving sexual intercourse by instructing the couple to move slowly through a series of successive approximations to intercourse without any expectations that intercourse would actually occur. This is a process of *in vivo* desensitization which can be seen to be closely related to the principles of the sensate focus programme. Intercourse is explicitly prohibited in the early stages and only reapproached through a series of successive approximations, thus providing an extended, controlled desensitization programme which reduces anxiety.

Dyspareunia and vaginismus

Some 24 years ago Lazarus gave a detailed account of imaginal systematic sensitization with a 24-year-old woman who had been married two and a half years and who 'always experienced a violent dyspareunia during intercourse as well as disgust and anxiety at the whole messy business' (Lazarus, 1980, p. 162).

The reduction of anxiety which is vital to the treatment of this condition in women can also be achieved by an *in vivo* programme in which the woman gradually becomes accustomed to her vagina accepting and containing objects of increasing size within it. Most workers (e.g. Kaplan, 1974) advocate that the insertion should be under the woman's control whilst others advocate initial insertion by the husband (Masters and Johnson, 1970), or the therapist. There can, of course, also be a gradual progression between these two situations, but what is important is that anxiety reduction is maximal. Kaplan (1974), Frank (1982) and Fairburn *et al.* (1983) advocate the use of non-artificial objects (i.e. fingers only), whilst Masters and Johnson preferred to offer vaginal dilators in graded sizes which the couple used on their own. Stanley (1981d) prefers the term *vaginal trainer* rather than *dilator*. She maintains, rightly, that the vagina is always capable of dilating to accommodate such objects (or a penis!) and that what is required is training to achieve this acceptance and accommodation without anxiety and pain. However, she only offers these plastic trainers if the use and acceptance of fingers is not effective.

Note that it is always advisable to use a bland, water-soluble lubricant with dilators or fingers.

Anorgasmia in women

LoPiccolo and Lobitz (1972) developed a self-learning and anxiety-reducing programme for anorgasmic women. It was intended to increase knowledge of their own sexual anatomy and functioning by self-examination, and to reduce stress through becoming accustomed to seeing and touching their own genitals. It also aided the discovery of the most sensitive areas of giving pleasure, continuing for long enough to allow stimulation to trigger orgasm. The woman might later be asked to masturbate whilst her partner is watching, and to experience arousal from being stimulated by the partner under her instruction. For some anorgasmic women these processes of desensitization were helped by 'role-playing' what they believed would happen if they achieved orgasm, thus reducing anxiety about the loss of control. Later developments of this programme were published as a self-help book, *Becoming Orgasmic: A Sexual Growth Program for Women* (Heiman *et al.*, 1976). A comparable book based on the English experience is *The Body Electric* (Hooper, 1980).

Premature ejaculation

The squeeze technique for the treatment of premature ejaculation has been fully described earlier. Zilbergeld (1980) describes modifications of the exercise suitable for use without a partner. A recent article by Goodman (1986) reviews the theories of causation and gives a clear account of behavioural management of the problem, but lays undue emphasis on pain and discomfort in the procedure.

Retarded ejaculation

My usage of behavioural components can be illustrated by a case where there was a presenting problem of severely retarded ejaculation of psychological origin. In addition to the educational and permission-giving components of the therapy, the behavioural aspect was a desensitization which began as an imaginal process, but then moved on to become an *in vivo* desensitization. This was achieved by encouraging the client to begin masturbation on his own using whatever fantasy or other erotic material he wished. When he was able to achieve ejaculation in this situation he was encouraged to successively: masturbate in the presence of his wife, ejaculate whilst lying close to his wife, ejaculate onto the vulva, ejaculate into the vagina by inserting the penis after ejaculatory inevitability had been reached and so eventually move on to full intercourse with ejaculation occurring inside the vagina.

It must be added that through all of this his wife willingly and actively encouraged him since she very much wanted to resume full intercourse with ejaculation inside her vagina. Obviously there will be specific variations in the programme designed for each client, but the basic idea is to provide a series of masturbatory situations which successively approximate to the ultimate goal of ejaculation in the partner's vagina during sexual intercourse. The anxieties which might be aroused by the idea of ejaculating are overcome by the pleasurable experience of allowing and enhancing his sexual arousal. For some clients the use of a vibrator or other sexual aids may be appropriate at certain points in such a programme.

When retarded ejaculation is the presenting problem, it can sometimes be further aided if the female partner is trained to use the Kegel (1952) exercises to strengthen the contractions of the pubococcygeal muscles which constrict the vagina. This manoeuvre does not just provide extra stimulation to the penis, but increases sexual pleasure for both partners.

The sexological examination

The conduct of a sexological (genital) examination with a partner present (Stanley, 1981d) or without the partner (Tunnadine, 1970) can be seen as providing, amongst other things, a desensitizing experience through the exploration of the genitals of self or partner. The importance of the attitudes and anxieties revealed to doctor and client through this psychosomatic event is particularly emphasized in the approach of the Institute of Psychosexual Medicine (discussed further in the section on the Psychodynamic Approach).

Eclecticism and behavioural psychotherapy

It is clear then that the exercises and treatment programmes described in this section can be viewed from a purely behavioural point of view and understood in terms of the classical theories of behaviour therapy. However, when they are used and seen in the context of the new sex therapies or of other eclectic developments, they are not purely programmes for inducing behavioural change, but also serve to raise awareness of deeper feelings and responses which can be explored within the therapeutic situation to gain further insight and understanding. In this way it is likely that the client(s) will learn much more than simply acquiring a new behaviour and it is then possible for them to learn how 'to learn about themselves'. These processes of behavioural psychotherapy can be seen to be brought about by appropriate experiences of action (programmed activity) and discovery (insight into emotional responses). Thus the resources within the partnership are increased on a long-term basis and are ready for dealing with any future emotional and sexual problems.

Cognitive therapies

In the cognitive therapies, the thinking processes which form the link between stimulus and response are seen as responsible for the feeling component of the response.

Rather than using the model of stimulus-response-consequence upon which behaviour therapy is based, the cognitive therapies pay attention to the processes of cognition which are interspersed between the stimulus and the response. Thus the stimulus will be modified by erroneous interpretations or thinking patterns that constitute the cognitions, and these thinking patterns or interpretations are in turn based on the beliefs, attitudes and thoughts of the individual. Kowalski (1985) writes 'The aim in cognitive therapy . . . is therefore to enable the patient to identify the cognitive errors which usually take place instantaneously, automatically, and without . . . full awareness' (p. 64). Such identification allows change to then occur.

Kowalski has modified the model of cognitive therapy of depression (Beck *et al.*, 1979) in order to apply the principles in psychosexual therapy and counselling. He lists the following as the main cognitive errors:

Magnification. Here sexual experiences which are 'not quite perfect' are seen as being totally disastrous.

Minimization. Here any experiences which do not lead to the achievement of intercourse or orgasm are ignored, even though they have been pleasurable.

Personalization. Here the boundaries of individuality are lost and a partner takes on responsibility for the sexual pleasure of the other.

The cognitive therapies lay a heavy stress on dealing with the basic assumptions about sex which comprise the major part of the faulty thinking which disrupts normal sexual functioning. Zilbergeld (1980) elucidates many of the male myths in his highly readable book and points out how they are spread and perpetuated by popular novelists in 'sexy books'. These myths will affect men by setting up unrealistic expectations of occurrence and duration of erection, of desirable penis size and of high sexual performance without having to communicate with the woman. There is also a comparable range of myths held by women about their sexuality and sexual performance (Dickson, 1985).

It is important to note here that the effect of these myths and beliefs is to set up anxiety about performance. Tackling these irrational beliefs and myths by the giving of information and by disputation in the cognitive therapies is intended to reduce anxiety, an effect which Masters and Johnson set out to achieve by the ban on intercourse in the initial stages of the sensate focus programme.

As Kowalski (1985) points out, the cognitive therapies place a particular emphasis on dealing with the irrational beliefs and attitudes which are seen as the determinants of sexual dysfunctioning. However, the overall goal is similar to the new sex therapies in that it is intended to reduce performance anxiety, replace ignorance and irrational beliefs with soundly based anatomical, physiological and psychological knowledge and to improve communication between the partners, so that each can clearly understand what the other is experiencing, and what the other wants. In this way individual pleasure can be achieved according to what is desired on that particular occasion without assuming that every loving or sexual interaction should lead to genital intercourse and orgasm.

One aspect of the cognitive therapies which is particularly important relates to the devastating effects which are experienced by some people in the broader context of their lives when sexual dysfunction occurs. A simplified presentation of this in the case of a male client might be: 'When I went to bed with my partner for the first time, I failed to get an erection. I feel so dreadful. I am not a proper man and I daren't ask her out again. I no longer feel confident to face people and my work as a salesman is failing.'

In his work with people with sexual problems, Kowalski (1985) uses homework assignments and the giving of information in a similar way to the users of the new sex therapies. He makes a wide use of the cognitive dimension in both assessment and therapy, seeing the client's responses and interactions with the therapist as an opportunity to elucidate the underlying irrational beliefs and cognitive processes.

Rational-emotive therapy

The combination of cognitive and behavioural methods which allows patients to change and develop can be seen clearly in rational-emotive therapy (RET), one of the cognitive therapies, developed by Albert Ellis. Ellis (1975) states that much of the stimulus for the development of rational-emotive therapy came from his experiences as a sex and marriage counsellor. He also acknowledges that RET utilizes behaviour therapy as an integral part of the rational-emotive method and that it overlaps significantly with the techniques of behaviour therapists and of Masters and Johnson. He places particular importance on the use of imaging methods (using fantasy) and practical exercises which he describes as 'risk-taking' or 'shame-attacking'. Both of these are basically desensitization methods (possibly best described as 'flooding' techniques) and may involve initiating sexual behaviours outside the client's usual range or initiating explicit sexual discussions in unusual contexts. These exercises set up situations where the client survives experiences which might previously have been evaluated as 'awful'. They are part of the work which is intended to eliminate the expectation of intolerable consequences from certain client experiences or behaviours.

In RET for sexual problems Ellis (1980) uses his well-known ABC configuration, where A is the Activating experience or Activating event and C is the Consequence (client's feelings and behaviours). Between A and C is B, the Belief system by which the client functions. If the central beliefs are irrational (e.g. absolute evaluations couched in the form of 'musts', 'shoulds', 'oughts'), then this will lead to an 'awful' emotional reaction and subsequently negative behaviours. If the belief system is rational (relative evaluations couched in the form of 'desires', 'wants', 'wishes', etc.), then it will not lead to such negative consequences. This can be illustrated by taking the case of a woman who failed to achieve orgasm during intercourse with a new partner:

A – Fails to achieve orgasm with new sexual partner.
B – 'I *must* please my partner by having an orgasm.'
C – Woman feels awful, inadequate and anxious about the strength of the relationship. Unable to discuss feelings with partner.

By the processes of rational-emotive therapy, the belief system would be changed in the hope of achieving a sequence which now runs as follows:

A – Fails to achieve orgasm with new sexual partner.
B – 'It's nice to have an orgasm, but I don't have to please my partner by having one. We can share pleasure in other ways that shows our love and affection for each other.'
C – Woman is concerned but not anxious. Willing to discuss sexual feelings with partner.

Eclecticism and the cognitive therapies

As Dryden (1982) points out, RET is often criticized for its apparent lack of emphasis on the emotive modality, but this is a misconception. Like Ellis (1975), Dryden emphasizes the vital importance of the client being unconditionally accepted by the therapist as a precondition for effective treatment.

> The therapist's purpose here is to demonstrate that no matter how obnoxious the client's behaviour is, not only to the therapist, but to other people in the client's life, she accepts the client as a fallible human being, who can and often does act badly. (Dryden, 1982, p. 14)

By this reference to one of Rogers's (1961) core conditions for effective therapy and by the emphasis placed by Kowalski and Ellis on cognitive therapy as a development from the methods of behaviour therapy, it can be seen that the descriptions of clinical practice given by these authors reflect an eclectic integration of different disciplines with new approaches developed as a result of the authors' personal experiences and beliefs in specific therapeutic processes.

The psychodynamic approach

Before Masters and Johnson, such sex therapy as was available was dominated by the work and influence of Sigmund Freud and the psychoanalytic movement. Although some aspects of this are now superseded, the fundamental concepts remain as a present and pervasive factor, the importance of which is being increasingly recognized in sex therapy (Kaplan, 1974; 1979; Bancroft, 1983). Kaplan's contribution was the establishment of a balance, in which the importance of the psychodynamic aspects of the practical learning techniques was emphasized.

A clear distinction must be maintained here between classical psychoanalysis, which sought to work with underlying conflicts rather than specific dysfunctions, and psychodynamic therapy, which utilizes techniques integrating the better substantiated concepts, such as the three-tiered psyche (id, ego and super ego), conscious and unconscious processes and the mechanisms of defence, sublimation and repression.

In the work of Kaplan (1974; 1979) and others we see a recognition of the power of the unconscious processes and the mechanisms of defence, but rather than being tackled 'in abstraction', conflicts are brought to the level of consciousness through the processes of therapy (including the completion of assignments) and are thus resolved. Psychodynamic therapists argue that these unconscious processes can only be worked with effectively if the therapist has come to understand his or her own unconscious processes and conflicts through appropriate training and/or personal therapy, a view with which I concur.

Rosen (1982) drew comparisons between psychodynamic therapy and the new sex tharapy and points out that 'Both share a psychodynamic approach with the analysis of resistances to diminish anxiety; the accent being on the understanding of attitudes and conflicts interfering with personal relationships' (p. 87). He continues:

> What is significant clinically is not so much *what* is said by a sex-behavioural or psycho-therapist but the ability to listen to the patient and to understand their communications and render them intelligible in a rational, integrated way to the patient, approximating the patient's inner awareness of truth. Unconscious determinants require interpretation in the same manner. (p. 88)

The processes of psychotherapy can remove the blocks which prevent the person experiencing his or her own inner desires and their fulfilment to satisfaction.

The therapeutic alliance

A psychodynamic approach to sex therapy must always take account of the feelings occurring between client and therapist (transference and counter-transference). Unless these factors are recognized and utilized, it will be difficult to establish the rapport and sense of trust which is necessary to carry the relationship through times when the work may be painful. Dryden (1984) stresses the importance of creating this therapeutic alliance. It has been discussed from the psychoanalytic point of view by Sandler *et al.* (1970) as the treatment alliance which is regarded as

> being based on the patient's conscious or unconscious wish to co-operate and . . . readiness to accept the therapist's aid in overcoming internal difficulties. . . . there is an *acceptance* of the need to deal with internal problems and to do analytic work in the face of internal . . . or . . . external resistance. (p. 556)

There is something more than the client's wish to get better; it is an acknowledgement of the need and motivation to do the necessary work with the therapist to achieve improvement.

Application of psychodynamic concepts

My survey (Cooper, 1986) shows that only 9 per cent of those indicating a sole main method for their work listed the psychodynamic. However, of the 111 respondents who indicated that they used an eclectic approach, 22 per cent combined a psychodynamic approach with Masters and Johnson/ Kaplan, while a further 37 per cent used it in an eclectic combination with other methods. Unfortunately, data was not available from The Institute of Psychosexual Medicine (IPM). This would have made a considerable difference to the figures, since the IPM is probably the largest single organization in Britain whose members are dealing with sexual problems. Its members are medically qualified clinicians who have been trained in psychosexual medicine which is 'a precise, highly skilled, but strictly specialised method of applying psychoanalysis' (IPM *Prospectus*, p. 7) and which is 'concerned with understanding how emotional factors, not always fully conscious, interfere with sexual functions and enjoyment' (IPM *Prospectus*, p. 3).

The IPM was founded in 1974 to continue the sexual application of seminar training of doctors started by Dr Michael Balint, a psychoanalyst. The intention of these IPM seminars is to facilitate the exploration and understanding of the psychodynamic aspects of the doctor-patient relationship and thus to facilitate an in-depth understanding of the patient's sexual anxieties.

The genital examination

The importance of the genital examination is particularly stressed by the IPM, because of the emotional truths which may be revealed in addition to the physical checking. Tunnadine (1970) writes about this approach to vaginal examination, and describes it as 'the moment of truth' which

> seems to provide a kind of entrée to genuine feelings, as though layers of inhibition are shed with the clothes, and the baring of the genital area carries with it a baring of inhibitions of feelings about it. It is, of course, a moment of some desperation for the patient, as all that has been kept hidden from the outside world, by carefully built defences – modesty, civilised and moral attitudes and behaviour – is now about to be shared with another person: the doctor. (p.8)

Eclecticism and psychodynamic concepts

Frank's interesting paper (1982) discussed his work with the Marital Problems Clinic at Margaret Pyke House in London. The paper does not always draw a clear distinction between the author's practice and his assessments of papers by other workers, but it does bring out his commitment to the psychodynamic aspects of a treatment model which incorporates sensate focus and specific interventions for specific dysfunctions, combined with information-giving within a well-developed therapeutic alliance. The psychoanalytic interventions of clarification, confrontation and interpretation are important as means of bringing out the deeper issues which may underlie the presenting sexual dysfunction. The paper does, perhaps, provide an example of the difficulty of providing a succinct description of an eclectic therapeutic approach.

Like Frank (1982), both Tunnadine (1970) and Kaplan (1974; 1979) use a therapeutic approach which can be seen as eclectic. Psychodynamic elements are revealed through assignments, examinations, discussions and educative processes in which at all times the feelings are taken into account as well as the facts of the situation. The difference is that Kaplan has a background of training and experience in psychoanalysis which places heavy importance on *personal* analysis and understanding on the part of the therapist, whilst the IPM training concentrates on the dynamics of the doctor-patient relationship and does not address itself to the *personal* functioning of the doctor.

Acknowledged or not acknowledged, the unconscious will be present. It will affect individual functioning in both client and therapist, as well as the interaction betwen them and it is therefore important for the therapist to have an understanding and awareness of these psychodynamic aspects, so that the insight can be used for the benefit of the client who is seeking help.

DISCUSSION

Any discussion of the methods of psychological sex therapy must refer back to the set goals and the outcomes. The latter are considered in detail by Cole and Dryden in Chapter 18, but it is appropriate to consider some aspects here.

It is always important to explore with the couple what they mean by 'success' in therapy and how they expect their lives to be different as a result. The setting-up of unrealistic goals and performance expectations by the therapist must be avoided. In the end, even if the presenting symptoms are not reversed, sex therapy often has a profound positive effect on the relationship by increasing mutual understanding. Sexual counselling can establish an emotionally secure relationship within which normal sexual responses can occur and be enjoyed (Bancroft, 1985) but, equally important in some cases, the outcome can be a secure relationship that is not dependent on 'normal' sexual responses.

Sometimes, I find that, after a good therapeutic alliance has been established, it is helpful to raise awareness of these issues by confronting the client who is 'showing the symptom' with a simple question: 'Why to you want to have sexual intercourse with her/him?' By a continuing sequence of repetitions of the question and acknowledgements of the answers given, the client is helped to clarify the extent to which the wish to have sexual intercourse is a desire to achieve a personal sexual release/relief, or is a means of communicating a deeply held love for the partner. Through clarification of such issues, which are not necessarily mutually exclusive, some of these meanings are faced by the clients and the motivation for the therapy can be seen more clearly. It is of course essential that the therapist is aware of his or her own meanings and beliefs in this context.

The concept of levels

Thus, like the widely advertised lager, sex (and sex therapy) can touch the parts that other forms of relationships (and therapy) don't reach. It has been made clear from the earlier description of the main approaches to psychological sex therapies that some are conceived, and designed, to work at and affect the individual at different levels of the psyche. This can be illustrated by reference to Figure 7.2 which depicts a simplified model

Figure 7.2 The pyramid of human functioning, depicting psychological levels of personal and sexual functioning and target levels for therapeutic interventions. (Based on Cooper & Harvey, 1985).

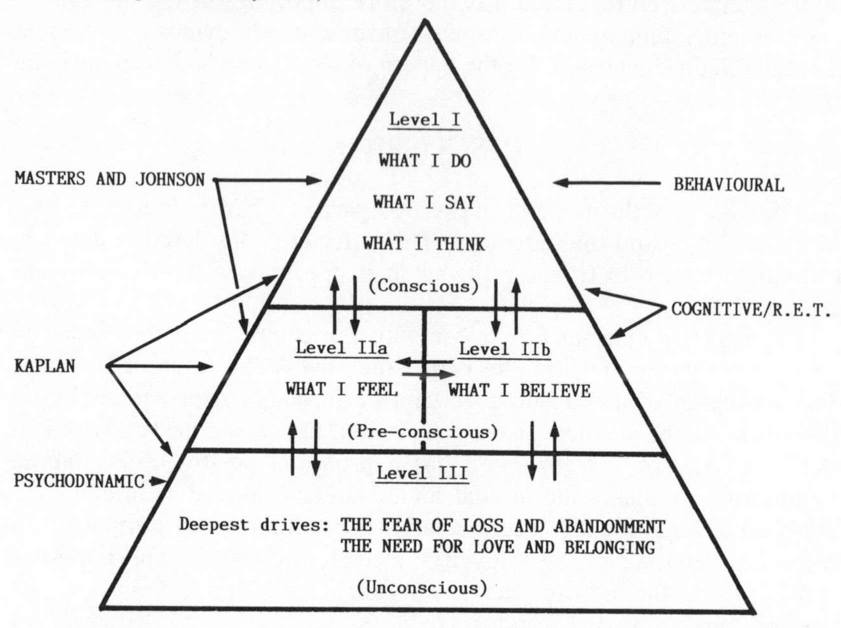

(Cooper and Harvey, 1985) of the three levels of psychological functioning which may be recognized in everyday life, as well as providing a basis for understanding sexual behaviours and the levels of therapeutic intervention under discussion here. Level 1 is the conscious interface with others, whilst Levels 2a and 2b are not always in awareness but can become so, and Level 3, the powerful drives which affect feelings, beliefs and behaviours, is not normally in awareness. Holmes (1986) considered that intervention at any one level will affect the other levels of functioning, a concept which is in accord with the Cooper and Harvey model. The bi-directional arrows at the boundaries indicate interactions between the levels. It follows that, although the diagram indicates the target levels for the various therapies, it can be expected that any behavioural task or assignment will resonate at the deeper levels. It is this effect which may result in resistance in therapy (e.g. assignments not carried out, agreed contracts broken) and which should be considered by the therapist in planning such assignments.

It could be argued, taking into account this contention, that all sex therapists should be trained in awareness of the psychodynamic concepts. In this way they would be aware of, and consciously able to work with, such material, and less likely to allow haphazard and unknown effects to occur in the process of therapy. It is because of the recognition of these concepts and effects that the Institute of Psychosexual Medicine continues to base training of doctors involved with sexual problems on the seminar method which highlights the influence of the deeper levels.

Sex therapy is not simply the application of a specific technique for the restoration of a specific function, but often involves work at different levels, and it demands, of both clients and therapists, the willingness and ability to face the existential meanings of events and relationships. The woman with children who comes into sex therapy with her husband 'because sex is no good for us', may be faced with difficult choices when it becomes clear that, whilst the marriage offers her much even though she is not orgasmic within it, she is able to achieve orgasm and sexual fulfilment within another relationship.

However, as Yalom (1980) has said, Freud's concept of the deep drives and conflicts relating to the *earliest* events in life is not the only explanation of the functioning of the psyche. Equally valid, is the existential concept that it is the awareness of ultimate concerns such as freedom, isolation, meaninglessness and death which give rise to anxiety. These issues can be of major importance in sexual dysfunction and are 'rooted' in the present.

Brief reference may be made here to the concepts of sex counselling and sex therapy, a distinction which I find it useful to draw in a practical sense. The concepts are somewhat similar to those used by Frank (1982) and Worden (1983). The processes of *counselling* are considered to be primarily educative and supportive and concerned with solving problems of immediate origin often related to the ordinary transitions of the life cycle. In contrast, *therapy* is more concerned with difficulties arising from remote causes, and the processes involve, gaining insight into, and modification of, the deeper psychic structure. In these terms, much of what is commonly referred to as sex therapy could be more accurately described as sex counselling.

Therapist development and issues of eclecticism

In the early 1950s, Rogers (1951) stated that the therapist who attempts to use methods which are not genuinely congruent with his or her own beliefs, values and attitudes is unlikely to be a successful therapist, and similarly that the therapist who has appropriate beliefs or attitudes will not fulfil his or her potential unless these are supplemented by effective therapeutic methods. In counselling and therapy generally, effectiveness is more closely correlated with the extent to which the therapist can offer the 'core conditions' of acceptance, empathy, genuineness and good communication, than to the specific therapeutic method in use (Truax and Carkhuff, 1967; Rogers 1980).

Both the method(s) used by the therapist and the client's reactions will influence the formation or otherwise of an effective therapeutic alliance. What is often overlooked, however, is the fact that the therapist's *choice* of method may be largely determined by the therapist's personality and experience. Despite Bergin and Lambert's (1978) proposal for studying outcomes with objective assessments, and systematic variations, of therapist characteristics, therapist variables are still largely unmeasured and often unconsidered in outcome studies.

Consequently, some researchers and therapists behave as if they believe that there is a method X which, if it can be discovered, will be the method to be used by *all* sex therapists with all their clients. This belief is unproductive because therapist variables are ignored, as are the limitations of present research methodology. More appropriately, research could be directed towards identifying and clarifying practices which are likely to be damaging, and recognizing that a variety of therapists use a variety of methods which are satisfactory for clients. Whatever method is chosen, the therapist will only be effective if she or he has sufficient self-understanding.

> Whether we recognize it or not, all facets of our behavior, the way we treat other people, our choices and decisions, our reactions, our values, our responsibleness or lack of it, are embedded in a philosophical base. Whether or not we are philosophically aware, we function one way or another depending upon what we believe. (Johnson and Vestermark, 1970, p.41)

This is further emphasized by Cooper (1974):

> since the personality of the therapist is, in all methods, the instrument with which he works to come to an understanding of his patient, it is essential that he should have made a sincere analytic effort to understand his own character. (p. 264)

Whilst the beginning therapist may well be advised to choose and be trained in a single clear method, it is usually found that with a growing confidence gained through experience, she or he will then want to integrate other ideas as well as developing his or her own variations. This progression can be clearly seen in the individual development of major contributors to sex therapy; a comparable progression can be seen in the overall development of all psychological therapies.

The concept of eclecticism can best be viewed against this developmental background on both the micro- and macro-levels. There is no one method or technique of sex therapy which can be proposed as 'the right one' to use in all cases. Indeed, by their very origins and nature, the new sex therapies which represent such an enormous advance in therapy during the last 20 years, are themselves evidence of this developmental model. Their strength lies partly in their broad base, but mainly perhaps in being made up of a number of different, identifiable components (such as education, communication, behaviour, psychotherapy, acquisition of insight).

In terms of the individual therapist, she or he should be able consciously to identify the needs of individual clients, and hence consciously to choose an appropriate method. To do this effectively, the therapist has to be well trained in each component and in each method of therapy under consideration, so that appropriate selections of therapeutic arena and therapeutic technique will maximize chances of success. This conscious choosing is a positive form of eclecticism as opposed to the 'hat-rack eclecticism' decried by Dryden (1984) in which the therapist, unsure of ground or progress, tries somewhat desperately with any technique that comes to mind. The concept of a 'hat-rack' of methods is not undesirable in itself, but the process by which a 'hat' is selected from the 'rack' must depend upon clearly defined criteria, not haphazard choices.

CONCLUSION

In summary then, assuming a good level of personal awareness, the most effective therapist is likely to be one who is well trained and experienced in both the principles and practice of any method which she or he might wish to use, is sufficiently flexible (both intellectually and emotionally) to be capable of selecting an appropriate method for a particular client or situation by a conscious process, and is at all times clear about the limitations of the methods and about the boundaries between self and client.

It will have become clear, from the work of this and other authors described in this chapter, that most therapists are not 'purist' practitioners of a narrow and specific method, but rather work in a broad-based way as described, and hence are practitioners who are positively eclectic, working within a developing background of positively eclectic sex therapy. Thus, for example, both Ellis (1975; 1980) and Kowalski (1985) are convinced proponents of the cognitive approach, who do not see it as an entirely separate method but rather one which is maximally effective when it is part of an eclectic matrix of differing principles and practices.

An appropriate approach is therefore flexible rather than rigid, and is based on acceptance rather than evangelical declamation. Thus Crown and d'Ardenne (1982) were able to write that 'we embed our behavioural approaches firmly in the psychodynamic attitude' (p. 72), and Bancroft (1985) that 'it is one of the achievements of modern sex therapy that it has shown a healthy eclecticism, largely breaking down the barriers between behavioural and psychodynamic approaches which otherwise lead to so much sterile polemic' (p. 79).

Perhaps much of this discussion about the relative contributions of therapist variables and chosen methods was summed up by Stanley (1981b) who, in an apt statement about the methods of sex therapy, wrote: 'As with all kinds of tools, however, it is the way that they are used rather than the actual quality of the tools that determines their effectiveness' (p. 1200).

As has already been shown, the client's intimate relationship is more than sex or sexual performance, and sex therapy may be deemed successful if the relationship is improved, even though complete sexual functioning is not restored. Similarly, sex therapy is much more than the method; it is a process, a relationship interaction which cannot be measured or defined simply in terms of the technique employed or the school of therapy followed. Both in the couple relationship and in the therapeutic relationship, it is the *meanings* which form the foundation and are therefore of paramount importance.

Singer's (1973) statement that 'man differs from all other animals, even non-human primates, in the extent to which sexual responsiveness pervades each moment and every aspect of his being' (p. 52), underlines the importance of sexuality and its meanings. It is within the committed, intimate relationship that the meaning and purpose of our existence is grappled with, a fact which may only be faced when sexual functioning is lost and the underlying issues are raised to awareness.

REFERENCES

Annon, J.S. (1976) *Behavioral Treatment of Sexual Problems – Brief Therapy*, Harper & Row, Hagerstown MD.

Bancroft, J. (1983) *Human Sexuality and Its Problems*, Churchill-Livingstone, Edinburgh.

Bancroft, J. (1985) Marital sex therapy, in W. Dryden (ed.) *Marital Therapy in Britain*, Vol. 2, Special Areas, Harper & Row, London.

Beck, A.T., Rush, A.J., Shaw, B.F. and Emery, G. (1979) *Cognitive Therapy of Depression*, New York, Wiley.

Bergin, A.E. and Lambert, N.J. (1978) Evaluation of therapeutic outcomes, in S. Garfield and A.E. Bergin (eds) *Handbook of Psychotherapy and Behavior Change*, 2nd edn, New York, Wiley.

Brindley, G.S. and Gillan, P. (1982) Men and women who do not have orgasms, *British Journal of Psychiatry*, Vol. 140, pp. 351–6.

Brown, P.T. (1976) *Report to the Counselling Advisory Board of the National Marriage Guidance Council*, NMGC, London.

Brown, P.T. (1980) Sexual function therapy after Masters and Johnson, in W.H.G. Armytage, R. Chester and J. Peel (eds) *Changing Patterns of Sexual Behaviour*, Academic Press, London.

Cole, M. (1985) Sex therapy – a critical appraisal, *British Journal of Psychiatry*, Vol. 147, pp. 337–51.

Cooklin, A.I. (1984) Interventions in family influences on sex and reproduction, *Journal of Obstetrics and Gynecology*, Vol. 4, pp. S23–S30.

Cooper, C. (1974) Short-term therapy, in V. Varma (ed.) *Psychotherapy Today*, Constable, London.

Cooper, G.F. (1986) *Survey of Sex Therapists in Britain*, Training and Consultancy Services, Birmingham.

Cooper, G.F. and Harvey, T.A. (1985) *Training Paper AT15*, Training and Consultancy Services, Birmingham.

Crowe, M.J., Gillan, P. and Golombok, S. (1981) Form and content in the conjoint treatment of sexual dysfunction: a controlled study, *Behaviour Research and Therapy*, Vol. 19, pp. 47–54.
Crown, S. and d'Ardenne, P. (1982) Controversies, methods and results, in Symposium on Sexual Dysfunctions, *British Journal of Psychiatry*, Vol. 140, pp. 70–7.
Dickson, A. (1985) *The Mirror Within*, Quartet Books, London.
Dryden, W. (1982) *The Effective Practice of Rational-Emotive Therapy*, Institute for RET (UK), London.
Dryden, W. (1984) Issues in the eclectic practice of individual therapy, in W. Dryden (ed.) *Individual Therapy in Britain*, Harper & Row, London.
Ellis, A. (1975) The rational-emotive approach to sex therapy, *The Counseling Psychologist*, Vol. 5, pp. 14–22.
Ellis, A. (1980) Treatment of erectile dysfunction, in S.R. Leiblum and L.A. Pervin (eds) Principles and Practice of Sex Therapy, Tavistock, London.
Fairburn, C.G., Dickerson, M.G. and Greenwood, J. (1983) *Sexual Problems and Their Management*, Churchill-Livingstone, Edinburgh.
Feldman, M.P. and MacCulloch, M.J. (1967) Aversion therapy in the management of homosexuals, *British Medical Journal*, ii, pp. 594–7.
Frank, O.S. (1982) The therapy of sexual dysfunction, in Symposium on Sexual Dysfunction, *British Journal of Psychiatry*, Vol. 140, pp 78–84.
Goodman, R.E. (1986) How to treat premature ejaculation, *British Journal of Sexual Medicine*, Vol. 13, 178–9.
Greenwood, J. and Bancroft, J. (1983) Appendix: counselling notes for couples in therapy, in J. Bancroft, *Human Sexuality and Its Problems*, Churchill-Livingstone, Edinburgh.
Hawton, K. (1982) The behavioural treatment of sexual dysfunction, in Symposium on Sexual Dysfunction, *British Journal of Psychiatry*, Vol. 140, pp. 94–101.
Hawton, K. (1985) *Sex Therapy – A Practical Guide*, Oxford University Press, Oxford.
Heiman, J., LoPiccolo, L. and LoPiccolo, J. (1976) *Becoming Orgasmic: A Sexual Growth Program for Women*, Prentice-Hall, Englewood Cliffs NJ.
Holmes, J. (1986) Unpublished communication to the Association of Sexual and Marital Therapists, Spring meeting.
Hong, L.K. (1984) Survival of the fastest: on the origin of premature ejaculation, *The Journal of Sex Research*, Vol. 20, pp. 109–22.
Hooper, A. (1980) *The Body Electric*, Virago, London.
Institute of Psychosexual Medicine Prospectus, IPM, London.
Jehu, D. (1979) *Sexual Dysfunctions – A Behavioural Approach*, Wiley, Chichester.
Johnson, D.E. and Vestermark, M.J. (1970) *Barriers and Hazards in Counseling*, Houghton-Mifflin, Boston.
Kaplan, H.S. (1974) *The New Sex Therapy*, Brunner/Mazel, New York.
Kaplan, H.S. (1979) *Disorders of Sexual Desire*, Ballière Tindall, London.
Kaplan, H.S. (ed) (1983) *The Evaluation of Sexual Disorders*, Brunner/Mazel, New York.
Kegel, A.H. (1952) Sexual functions of the pubococcygeus muscle, *Western Journal of Surgical Obstetrics and Gynecology*, Vol. 57, pp. 527–35.
Kitzinger, S. (1985) *Woman's Experience of Sex*, Penguin, Harmondsworth.
Kolodny, R.C. (1981) Evaluating sex therapy: process and outcome at the Masters and Johnson Institute, *The Journal of Sex Research*, Vol. 17, pp. 301–18.
Kowalski, R. (1985) Cognitive therapy for sexual problems, *British Journal of Sexual Medicine*, Vol. 12, pp. 64–6, 90–3, 131–5.

Lazarus, A.A. (1980) Psychological treatment of dyspareunia, in S.R. Leiblum and L.A. Pervin (eds) *Principles and Practice of Sex Therapy*, Tavistock, London.
LoPiccolo, J. and Lobitz, W.C. (1972) Behavior therapy of sexual dysfunction, in L.A. Hamerlynck, L.C. Handy and E.J. Mash (eds) *Behavior Change: Methodology, Concepts and Practice*, Research Press, Champaign IL.
LoPiccolo, J. and Stock, W. (1986) Treatment of sexual dysfunction, *Journal of Consulting and Clinical Psychology*, Vol. 54, pp. 158–67.
Mackay, D. (1984) Behavioural psychotherapy, in W. Dryden (ed.) *Individual Therapy in Britain*, Harper & Row, London.
Masters, W.H. and Johnson, V.E. (1966) *Human Sexual Response*, Little, Brown & Co., Boston.
Masters, W.H. and Johnson, V.E. (1970) *Human Sexual Inadequacy*, Churchill, London.
Masters, W.H. and Johnson, V.E. (1976) Principles of the new sex therapy, *American Journal of Psychiatry*, Vol. 133, pp. 548–54.
Mathews, A., Whitehead, A. and Kellett, J. (1983) Psychological and hormonal factors in the treatment of female sexual dysfunction, *Psychological Medicine*, Vol. 13, pp. 83–92.
McConville, B. and Shearlaw, J. (1985) *The Slanguage of Sex*, Futura Publications, London.
Rogers, C.R. (1951) *Client-Centred Therapy*, Houghton Mifflin, Boston.
Rogers, C.R. (1961) *On Becoming a Person*, Houghton Mifflin, Boston.
Rogers, C.R. (1980) *A Way of Being*, Houghton Mifflin, Boston.
Rosen, I. (1982) The psychoanalytical approach, Symposium on sexual dysfunction, *British Journal of Psychiatry*, Vol. 140, pp. 85–93.
Sandler, J., Holder, A. and Dare, C. (1970) Basic psychoanalytic concepts: II: The treatment alliance, *British Journal of Psychiatry*, Vol. 116, pp. 555–8.
Semans, J.H. (1956) Premature ejaculation: a new approach, *Southern Medical Journal*, Vol. 49, pp. 353–7.
Singer, I. (1973) *The Goals of Human Sexuality*, Wildwood House, London.
Stanley, E. (1981a) Non-organic causes of sexual problems, *British Medical Journal*, Vol. 282, pp. 1042–8.
Stanley, E. (1981b) Principles of managing sexual problems, *British Medical Journal*, Vol. 282, pp. 1200–5.
Stanley, E. (1981c) Dealing with fear of failure, *British Medical Journal*, Vol. 282, pp. 1281–3.
Stanley, E. (1981d) Vaginismus, *British Medical Journal*, Vol. 282, pp. 1435–7.
Truax, C.B. and Carkhuff, R.R. (1967) *Toward Effective Counseling and Psychotherapy*, Aldine Publishing Company, Chicago.
Tunnadine, L.P. (1970) *Contraception and Sexual Life: A Therapeutic Approach*, Tavistock, London (republished Institute of Psychosexual Medicine).
Ward, B. (1976) *Sex and Life*, Macdonald Educational, London.
Wolpe, J. (1958) *Psychotherapy by Reciprocal Inhibition*, Stanford University Press, Palo Alto CA.
Wolpe, J. (1969) *The Practice of Behavior Therapy*, Pergamon, New York.
Worden, J.W. (1983) *Grief Counselling and Grief Therapy*, Tavistock Publications, London.
Yalom, I.D. (1980) *Existential Psychotherapy*, Basic Books, New York.
Zilbergeld, B. (1980) *Men and Sex*, Collins, Glasgow.

CHAPTER 8

DRUGS AND THE TREATMENT OF SEXUAL DYSFUNCTION

Alan J. Riley

Many commonly used drugs carry a burden of sexual side effects. In a series of 1,180 middle-aged men attending a medical outpatient clinic 401 (34 per cent) were found to complain of difficulties with erection. The largest single cause (25 per cent) of erection failure in these patients was medication (Slag *et al.*, 1983). It is therefore important for sex therapists to know which drugs have the potential for impairing sexual functioning. Most textbooks on sexual problems have lists of drugs that can affect sexual responses (e.g. Kaplan, 1983) and an excellent review of this subject is presented by Buffen (1982).

Understanding how drugs can affect sexual function may help to elucidate the physiological mechanisms involved in the sexual responses and more importantly may identify pharmacotherapeutic approaches to the management of sexual dysfunction. It is this latter aspect that is presented in this chapter. Hormonal treatments are not included as they are covered in Chapter 4.

Much of the available information about drug-induced changes in sexual functioning has been obtained from anecdotal case reports or from incidental findings in studies that were not originally designed to investigate such effects. Frequently the data are based on observations that lack adequate control. Very few published reports on alleged drug-induced changes in sexual functioning contain confirmatory evidence. The usually accepted method of confirming drug-induced symptoms is to study what happens to the side effect when the drug is withdrawn (*dechallenge*) and when it is reintroduced (*rechallenge*). If the symptom disappears on dechallenge and reappears on rechallenge the likelihood that it is drug-induced is greatly increased. In the case of suspected sexual side effects this standard approach may be complicated by psychological factors. Improvement in sexual function may not readily follow dechallenge because a secondary psychogenic dysfunction may be superimposed on the primary drug-induced dysfunction causing the sexual symptoms to persist after withdrawal of the drug. If the patient agrees to rechallenge it should be undertaken under double-blind placebo-controlled conditions to reduce the psychological effect resulting from the patient taking a tablet already associated in his or her mind with causing a sexual difficulty.

There are many different mechanisms by which drugs can affect sexual function. One important mechanism is by influencing the activities of chemical messengers (*neurotransmitters*) in the brain or in the autonomic nervous system supplying the genital organs. In the brain the principle neurotransmitters are acetylcholine, dopamine, noradrenaline and serotonin (5-hydroxytryptamine). Studies in animals have shown that dopamine and serotonin exert reciprocal control over sexual behaviour, with dopamine causing excitation and serotonin being inhibitory. The relevance of this model to humans is not definitely known but there are limited observations to suggest that it may be applicable, in part at least. Drugs, therefore, that increase serotonin activity or block the effects of dopamine may impair sexual function. Conversely, drugs which block serotonin activity or increase dopamine may enhance sexual function. The two main neurotransmitters in the autonomic nervous system are noradrenaline and acetylcholine but there are many other neurotransmitters involved, one of which, vasoactive intestinal polypeptide (VIP) is described later. When the neurotransmitter is released from the nerve it combines with a specific receptor on the cell that the nerve controls.

In general receptors can be classified in terms of their specificity for a particular neurotransmitter or response. Thus acetylcholine acts on cholinergic receptors and noradrenaline acts on adrenergic receptors (also known as *adrenoceptors*). Cholinergic receptors are subdivided into nicotinic and muscarinic receptors. In general the former occur at junctions between nerve fibres and the latter at junctions between nerve and other cells. Adrenoceptors are classified as alpha or beta of each of which there are two types designated 1 and 2. $Alpha_2$ receptors are situated on the nerve ending and when stimulated they reduce the output of noradrenaline therefore acting as a negative feedback. $Alpha_1$ receptors occur in smooth muscles in the walls of arterioles (and in other places) and when stimulated cause vasoconstriction. $Beta_1$ receptors are present in heart muscle and when stimulated increase heart rate. $Beta_2$ receptors are found in many different tissues including blood vessels which dilate when they are stimulated.

Drugs that stimulate receptors are known as *agonists*. There are drugs which can bind with a receptor without stimulating it and which by being bound to the receptor stop agonists from stimulating the receptor. These drugs are known as *antagonists*. Thus a drug that binds with a beta receptor without stimulating it is known as a *beta adrenoceptor antagonist* (sometimes referred to as a 'beta blocker').

DRUGS IN THE TREATMENT OF EJACULATORY DISTURBANCES

It cannot be emphasized strongly enough that, with a few exceptions such as retrograde ejaculation, painful ejaculation and perhaps spontaneous ejaculation, the first line of management of ejaculatory disturbances should be a behavioural approach, the results of which are in general very good. Pharmacotherapy should be reserved for those cases which fail to respond to the behavioural approach or where there are factors that make it undesirable or difficult to use behavioural approaches.

Premature ejaculation

Local anaesthetics

By the time the patient presents for treatment of premature ejaculation he may well have already tried one or more of the proprietary local anaesthetic preparations applied to the glans of the penis before intercourse. It is difficult to judge the effectiveness of these preparations because only the patients in whom this management fails will present to the therapist. There have been no controlled clinical trials. Anaesthetic preparations can cause local sensitization reactions which may cause considerable discomfort for the patient or sexual partner. They may also be transferred to the female partner during intercourse resulting in genital anaesthesia. This in turn may cause difficulty and delay in her attaining orgasm.

Psychotropic agents

Many frequently used psychotropic agents have been used in the treatment of premature ejaculation. The monoamine oxidase inhibitors appear to be effective (Bennett, 1961) but the dietary restrictions imposed by these drugs and their side effects do not make them the first choice. Thioridazine is also effective (Mellgren, 1967). Eaton (1973) reported that clomipramine is a very positive help in the treatment of premature ejaculation, producing an almost 100 per cent successful outcome rate. He found that the dose required by most patients ranged from 30–40 mg daily. This higher dose

Figure 8.1 Effect of treatment on control of ejaculation.
(Reproduced by the kind permission of the Editor, *Journal of Pharmacotherapy*.)

Reported by male partner

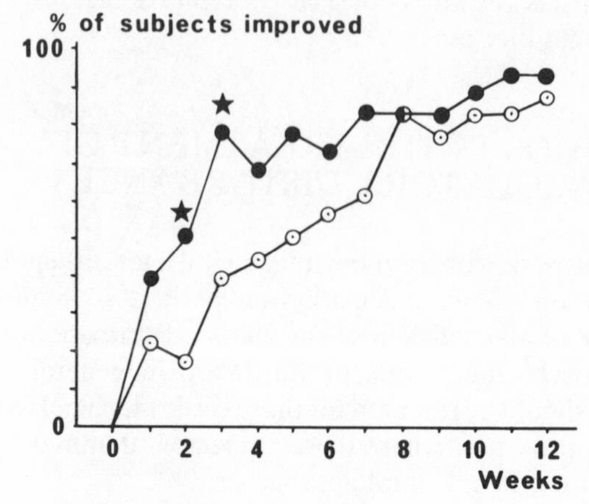

Reported by female partner

% of subjects improved

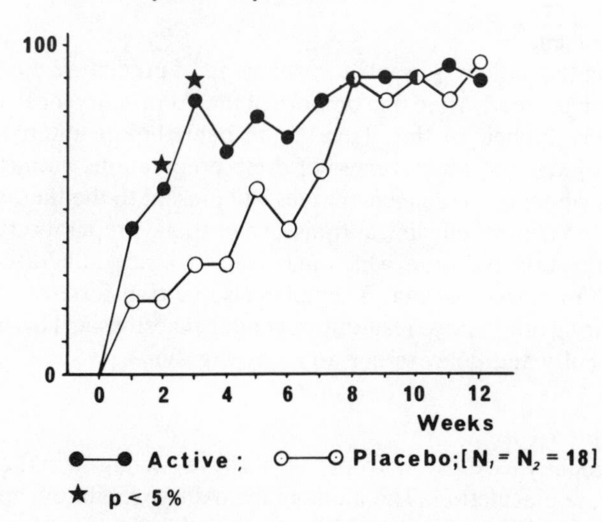

sometimes inhibits ejaculation altogether and may cause side effects.

Goodman (1986) describes a therapeutic regimen using clomipramine. He recommends that the patient takes 10 mg clomipramine at 18:00 hours daily for one week. If control of ejaculation is attained the patient exper-

Figure 8.2 Effect of treatment on male's interest in sex.
(Reproduced by the kind permission of the Editor, *Journal of Pharmacotherapy*.)

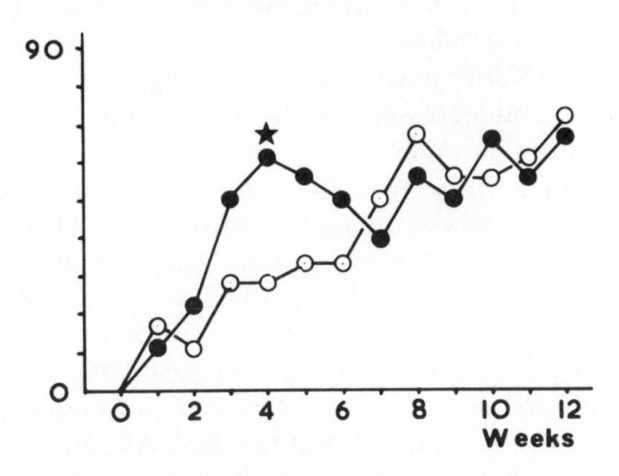

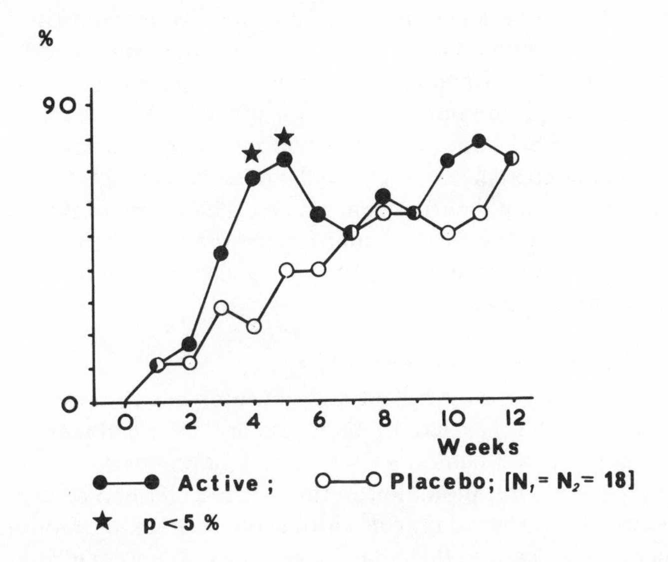

iments by missing doses. If this dose does not control his ejaculation, the dose is progressively increased at weekly intervals to a total single evening dose of no more than 50 mg. If higher doses are required, it is best given in divided doses. When I prescribe clomipramine in this indication my usual routine is to increase the dose from 10 mg at night to 30 mg at night over the course of a week and remain at this dose until ejaculatory control is attained. If it is not controlled within six weeks the dose is increased further. The patient then reduces the dose to the minimum that will control his ejaculation; frequently the drug can be withdrawn at this stage. If clomipramine is still required the patient remains on the minimum effective dose for a month and then again tries to withdraw the drug by back titration against response. Very rarely does the dose need to exceed 50 mg. It is probable that the beneficial effect of antidepressants in the treatment of premature ejaculation is mediated through changes in central serotonin activity.

A combination of amitriptyline and perphenazine (Triptafen DA® Allen & Hanbury's) as an adjunct to the squeeze technique has been evaluated in the management of premature ejaculation by means of a double-blind, placebo-controlled study (Riley & Riley, 1979). Only married subjects were studied and the criterion for entry was failure to control ejaculation for as long as the marital partners would desire on at least 75 per cent of coitus and only patients who habitually ejaculated within three minutes of penetration were included. A total of 36 patients were studied. All patients were instructed in the squeeze technique. The patients and their spouses kept separate diary cards on which they reported on ability to control ejaculation, the male's interest in sex and quality of erection. Treatment with Triptafen or placebo was continued for 6 weeks and the study continued for 12 weeks.

Triptafen DA® promoted the attainment of ejaculatory control early in the treatment programme but did not influence the overall results at 12 weeks (Figure 8.1). Improved ejaculatory control was associated with an increase in interest in sex (Figure 8.2), but again by 12 weeks there was no difference between the treatment groups. The results of this study demonstrate that a combination of amitriptyline and perphenazine can aid the treatment of premature ejaculation. They also confirm the effectiveness of the squeeze technique.

Beta adrenoceptor antagonists

Some studies have shown beta adrenoceptor blockers to have anxiolytic activity, and this has led to their use in the treatment of premature ejaculation. In my clinical experience, I have not found beta blockers helpful in this indication. Furthermore, in a placebo-controlled trial of propranolol (120 mg daily) in chronically anxious men presenting with premature ejaculation, the beta blocker failed to improve either the sexual problem or the signs and symptoms of anxiety (Cooper and Magnus, 1984).

Alpha adrenoceptor antagonists

The ejaculatory process is dependent on alpha adrenoceptor stimulation and can be impaired by alpha blocking drugs. A recent study (Shilon *et al.*,

1984) suggests good results from the use of phenoxybenzamine, an alpha adrenoceptor antagonist, in the treatment of nine cases of premature ejaculation. However, the study was not controlled which makes the results less convincing. Failure of ejaculation was a noted side effect. Good improvement in penile erection was reported by three of the nine men which is in keeping with our observations that oral phenoxybenzamine can facilitate the treatment of erection inadequacy in some men (Riley and Riley, 1984).

Combined alpha and beta adrenoceptor antagonism

In a laboratory study in normal volunteers the antihypertensive agent labetalol, a drug that possesses antagonist activity at both alpha and beta adrenoceptors, delayed ejaculation in a dose-related manner (Riley *et al.*, 1982). We have not found labetalol of benefit in the treatment of premature ejaculation.

Retrograde ejaculation

Retrograde ejaculation, in which the semen passes into the bladder during the ejaculatory process, instead of being emitted to the exterior, results from failure of closure of the internal sphincter of the bladder. It can occur as a complication of diabetes or following operations on the prostate gland or surgical procedures and trauma in which damage occurs to the nerves supplying the sphincter. Since closure of the internal sphincter of the bladder occurs in response to alpha adrenoceptor stimulation, drugs that act as antagonists at alpha adrenoceptors and those that block adrenergic neuronal transmission can cause retrograde ejaculation. Drugs possessing these activities can also inhibit the emission phase of the ejaculatory process.

Drugs exhibiting alpha adrenoceptor agonist activity have been found to be useful in the treatment of retrograde ejaculation in some patients. The first drug that appears to have been used for this purpose is ephedrine (50 mg orally) taken between one and two hours before intercourse (Stewart and Bergant, 1974). Good results have also been claimed with phenylpropanolamine; in a series of six patients, four responded favourably (Sandler, 1979). The two patients who failed to respond had organic disease; whereas in the four successes, the cause of the retrograde ejaculation was said to be idiopathic (i.e. no organic cause found).

Another alpha adrenoceptor agonist which has been found useful in the treatment of retrograde ejaculation is midodrine (Jonas *et al.*, 1979; Schwale *et al.*, 1980). We have used this drug with success in the management of diabetes-induced retrograde ejaculation. Since alpha adrenoceptor agonists can increase blood pressure, careful monitoring of their effect on the cardiovascular system is essential.

Anejaculation

Anejaculation results from failure of the emission phase of the ejaculatory process. Drug treatment by means of an alpha adrenoceptor agonist is sometimes effective in restoring ejaculation in cases where anejaculation has resulted from organic disease affecting the nerve supply to the internal genital organs. For example, Jonas *et al.* (1979) showed that normal ejaculation could be restored with midodrine in patients with anejaculation following extensive abdominal surgery which caused extensive damage to the nerve supply of the internal genital organs.

Schwale *et al.* (1980) reported the case of a 22-year-old man who suffered from anejaculation and anorgasmia for four years. The patient had spermatozoa in urinary sediment. After one week's treatment with midodrine the patient was able to ejaculate and to experience orgasm. Following this course of treatment he continued to experience ejaculation and orgasm. Although this response to treatment was substantiated by the patient's partner, the lack of placebo-control makes it difficult to draw definite conclusions about the effect of midodrine in this case. In view of the continued alleviation of his sexual symptoms following withdrawal of midodrine, it is probable that the patient's problems were largely psychogenic.

Partial ejaculatory incompetence

Partial ejaculatory incompetence is an interesting form of ejaculatory dysfunction in which the patient's principle complaint is lack of orgasmic sensation associated with a dribble of semen from the urethra instead of a forcible ejaculate. Although Kaplan (1974) states that the condition usually responds favourably to psychotherapy, I have found that only about 50 per cent of patients respond to this approach suggesting the existence of an organic aetiology. Masters (cited by Kaplan, 1974) also considers that partial ejaculatory incompetence often results from organic factors which interfere with the filling of the posterior urethral bulb with semen during the emission phase of the ejaculatory process.

I have found midodrine effective in this condition when psychotherapy has failed. Treatment with midodrine improves both orgasmic sensation and ejaculatory efficacy (Riley and Riley, 1982; 1983).

Drug treatment for spontaneous orgasm and ejaculation

Frequent spontaneous orgasms and/or ejaculations can be troublesome and distressing but fortunately is a rare situation. It can occur in association with severe anxiety states in the absence of sexual precipitation (Redmond *et al.*, 1983) and is also a recognized feature during opiate withdrawal. Spontaneous ejaculations can also occur during treatment with centrally acting alpha$_2$ adrenoceptor antagonists such as piperoxan and yohimbine (Holmberg and Gershon, 1961).

Thioridazine is effective in the management of spontaneous ejaculation (Redmond *et al.*, 1983; Riley, 1986). The alpha$_2$ adrenoceptor agonist, clonidine has been reported to be helpful in controlling the symptoms of opiate withdrawal including spontaneous ejaculations (Gold *et al.*, 1978). Clonidine has been used successfully also in the treatment of two women who were troubled by frequent spontaneous orgasms in the absence of sexual stimulation or sexual thoughts (Riley, in press).

Drugs in the treatment of erection inadequacy

Since erection inadequacy has multifactorial aetiology, no single treatment is universally successful. At the present time pharmacotherapy has little to offer in the routine management of erection inadequacy, although some encouraging observations have been made on the erection-promoting potential of some drugs.

Peripherally acting alpha adrenoceptor antagonists appear to promote erection or delay loss of erection (*detumescence*) in some situations. Labetalol, a combined alpha and beta adrenoceptor blocking drug, in a laboratory study, has been found to delay detumescence in a dose-related manner (Riley *et al.*, 1982). As I have observed, this effect has not been seen with beta blocking drugs which do not concurrently block alpha adrenoceptors.

It is possible that in some men erection inadequacy results from excessive alpha adrenoceptor stimulation, resulting from either increased sensitivity of the receptors, to excessive circulating noradrenaline levels or the administration of beta blocking drugs which 'unmask' alpha adrenoceptor activity. The use of an alpha adrenoceptor antagonist in such patients may be expected to facilitate erection. I have found, in clinical experience, that oral phenoxybenzamine, a long-acting alpha adrenoceptor antagonist, is sometimes helpful as an adjunct to behavioural approaches in the management of men with erection inadequacy (Riley and Riley, 1984). Other workers have also reported improved erection during treatment with oral phenoxybenzamine (Shilon *et al.*, 1984).

Intracavernous drug administration

The dose of alpha adrenoceptor blocking drugs that can be administered orally is limited by systemic effects which include peripheral vasodilation resulting in increased heart rate and lowering of blood pressure, particularly on changing from the lying or sitting position to standing. To overcome this problem drugs can be given directly into the erectile tissue of the penis, the route of administration being described as 'intracavernous'. Brindley (1983) has shown that phenoxybenzamine injected directly into the corpus cavernosum induces erection usually within 30 minutes from the injection.

The technique of intracavernous administration of phenoxybenzamine described by Brindley involves the slow injection into one corpus cavernosum of 10 ml of a diluted solution of the drug through a 16 mm × 0.5 mm needle. The injection is made within 2 cm of the corona to reduce the risk of injuring the deep penile artery. As soon as the injection has been made, the corpus cavernosum into which it was made is squeezed once briefly to ensure transfer of the drug to the other side. The distribution of the drug within the cavernosa is then facilitated by pinching both corpora cavernosa at several places in succession.

Brindley regards this as a safe procedure which the patient can undertake at home, the injection being given by his partner. The injection may cause pain which is usually of short duration. The duration of erection produced by this procedure is unpredictable and prolonged painful erections have occurred which have required treatment with intracavernosal injection of metaraminol, and alpha adrenoceptor agonist (Brindley, 1984).

Intracavernosally administered papaverine is now being used in place of phenoxybenzamine. Papaverine, a powerful smooth muscle relaxant, is an opium alkaloid. Of a group of 227 impotent men given a single intracavernosal injection of papaverine (80 mg), 26 per cent achieved a full erection within ten minutes of drug administration (Virag, 1985). In only 20 per cent of the men in whom erection occurred did detumescence occur spontaneously within two hours. The other patients required treatment for their prolonged and sometimes painful erections. The treatment involved aspiration of blood from the corpora cavernosa and in some cases, intracavernosal injection of adrenaline. Virag (1985) believes that the high incidence of prolonged erections following intracavernosal injection of phenoxybenzamine or papaverine may limit the potential value of this method of treatment of erection inadequacy. He proposes that when self-administration is contemplated the dose required to produce an erection lasting long enough but with a spontaneous detumescence should be carefully evaluated and that pharmacologically induced erections should never exceed four hours. Furthermore, Virag proposes that this form of management should be restricted to the diagnosis and treatment of erection failure and should not be used to 'satisfy the unrealistic dreams of already potent men'.

Yohimbine

Yohimbine is an indole alkaloid which is present in a variety of plants including the Rauwolfia root. The most significant source is the bark of *Pausinystalia*, the yohimbe tree. It has several pharmacological actions of which antagonism at presynaptic $alpha_2$ adrenoceptors is probably the most important at therapeutic doses. It may also interact at serotonin and dopamine receptors.

Yohimbine has long enjoyed the reputation of being an aphrodisiac. In recent years there has been renewed interest in the therapeutic potential of this drug in the treatment of erection inadequacy. Beneficial effects of yohimbine in four of six patients with diabetic neuropathy and erection failure have been reported (Morales *et al.*, 1981). The same workers are conducting a placebo-controlled study of oral yohimbine 6 mg three times daily in patients with clearly defined organic erection inadequacy. Preliminary results show a statistically significant benefit of yohimbine compared with placebo with 30 per cent of patients on yohimbine hydrochloride having a complete return of sexual function and a further 30 per cent showing improvement (Morales *et al.*, 1984). At this dose level yohimbine appears to be generally well tolerated.

At the present time, yohimbine is not available in Britain but it is available in many European countries and the United States of America. A large scale clinical trial of yohimbine in the management of erection inadequacy is currently in progress in England.

Nitrites and Nitrates

Mudd (1977) describes a 56-year-old patient with a history of psychiatric illness and erection inadequacy whose erection was improved by sublingual glyceryl trinitrate prescribed for the presumptive diagnosis of angina. Two days after starting this treatment and six hours after dosing the patient awoke with an erection, the first for 2½ years. He subsequently reported that erection lasting for about ten minutes occurred within seconds of taking glyceryl trinitrate. Waking erections resumed and were sometimes unusually painful. He was able to masturbate and have intercourse with orgasm. He also experienced erections during treatment with pentaerythritol tetranitrate. The patient also suffered claudication (pain in the calf muscles due to poor circulation) which was relieved by nitrates. The history suggests that the erection inadequacy in this patient resulted from spasm of the pelvic arteries which was relieved by the nitrates. The nitrates also relieved his angina and claudication which presumably were also of arteriospastic aetiology.

In contrast to this case amyl or isobutyl nitrites (poppers), which are taken to enhance sexual pleasure, cause temporary loss of erection in about 10 per cent of users (Lowry, 1979). They may also cause severe headache.

Priapism

Priapism is prolonged painful erection. It has been reported to occur during treatment with drugs that exhibit alpha adrenoceptor blocking or vasodilating activity (e.g. prazosin, chlorpromazine, hydralazine). Priapism has recently been treated successfully by the intracavernous injection of alpha adrenoceptor stimulant drugs. The drugs used have been metaraminol (Brindley, 1984; Stanners and Colin-Jones, 1984) and adrenaline (Virag, 1985).

Men with sickle-cell disease sometimes suffer night-time attacks of painful erections lasting two to six hours. This condition has been called 'stuttering priapism' and it may herald a major attack of priapism. A double-blind placebo-controlled trial has recently confirmed that stilboestrol, a synthetic oestrogen, is effective in preventing such attacks (Serjeant *et al.*, 1985).

DRUGS IN THE TREATMENT OF SEX DESIRE PROBLEMS

Little is known about the neuroendocrine control of human sexual desire. In both sexes desire is probably dependent on androgen stimulation and it can be inhibited, to some extent, by antiandrogenic preparations (see Chapter 4).

Enhancing sexual desire

There has always been an interest in finding drugs that will increase sexual desire and performance but the ideal aphrodisiac has yet to be discovered. There are reports that L-dopa increases sexual desire or sexual thoughts in patients with Parkinson's disease (Brown *et al.*, 1978) and schizophrenia (Angrist and Gershon, 1976). Any enhancing effect that L-dopa may have on sexual desire has yet to be confirmed in a well-controlled study. Inability to ejaculate has been reported during L-dopa treatment (Hallstrom and Persson, 1970).

Loss of sexual desire occurs in depression and most depressed patients report an increase in sexual activity as a consequence of effective antidepressant therapy (Beaumont, 1973) although recovery from the sexual dysfunction is relatively slow compared to that from other depressive symptoms (Hamilton, 1982). The improvement in sexual functioning is almost certainly related to amelioration of the depression rather than to a direct sexual desire enhancing property of the antidepressant. However, Freed (1983) on the basis of observation in two depressed patients suggested that nomifensine might enhance sexual desire by a direct effect because in these patients improvement in sexual function preceded improvement in other symptoms of depression.

Inhibiting sexual desire

Interest in drugs that will inhibit sexual desire originated in the management of patients with antisocial behaviour. Two antipsychotic agents, fluphenazine enanthate, a long-acting phenothiazine, and benperidol, a butyrophenone, are claimed to be useful for controlling unwanted sexual behaviour (Bartholomew, 1968; Tennent *et al.*, 1974). In a controlled study, benperidol was more effective than either chlorpromazine or placebo in reducing self-rated sexual interest, but it did not reduce the psychophysiological responses to erotic stimuli (Tennent *et al.*, 1974).

USE OF ANTIANXIETY DRUGS IN SEX THERAPY

Performance anxiety is an important cause of sexual difficulties in both sexes. Many non-specialists succumb to the temptation to prescribe tranquillizers, usually benzodiazepines such as diazepam and lorazepam, for patients complaining of sexual difficulties in the hope that they will resolve the problem. There have been very few trials to evaluate the value of tranquillizing drugs in the treatment of sexual difficulties. In a brief report, in which only sparse data were presented, lorazepam was claimed to be significantly superior to placebo as an adjunct to supportive psychotherapy in patients with unspecified sexual difficulties (Maneksha and Harry, 1975). Carney *et al.* (1978) found that diazepam was inferior to testosterone in the management of sexual unresponsiveness in women, when used as an adjunct to behavioural therapy.

In view of the extensive use of minor tranquillizers it is surprising that very few sexual adverse effects have been reported. Hughes (1964) reported a single case of ejaculatory failure caused by chlordiazepoxide. Female anorgasmia has occurred with alprazolam (Sangal, 1985), a modified benzodiazepine which also has antidepressant properties. Riley and Riley (1986a) conducted a volunteer controlled study to evaluate the effects of oral diazepam on female sexual response induced by masturbation. The results show diazepam significantly to impair subjective features of the sexual response in a dose-related manner. Specifically, it decreased the self-assessment of arousability, delayed orgasm and reduced the sensation of orgasm. One of the eight subjects studied experienced anorgasmia after 10 mg diazepam on two out of four occasions. The volunteers who participated in this study were not anxious and the responses seen may not be those that occur in the anxious patient.

Patients may themselves resort to alcohol to reduce anxiety levels before sex. The effects of acute ingestion of alcohol on sexual responses in men and women have been the subject of several well-controlled studies. Sexual arousal was monitored by vaginal photoplethysmography in a group of women who viewed erotic films and were given alcohol (Wilson and Lawson, 1976). Alcohol reduced the vaginal response of sexual arousal whilst it increased the subjective perception of sexual arousal. In another study alcohol has been shown to delay orgasm and to increase orgasmic pleasure, depending on the dose taken (Malatesta *et al.*, 1982).

Farkas and Rosen (1976) found a slight but non-significant enhancement of erection in men after a dose of alcohol that achieved blood-alcohol concentration of 25 mg per cent but at higher blood-alcohol concentrations there was a progressive impairment of erection. Long-term alcohol abuse can lead to endocrine changes including testicular and ovarian atrophy.

TREATMENT OF DRUG-INDUCED SEXUAL DYSFUNCTION

It is evident that the best way to treat drug-induced sexual dysfunction is to withdraw the offending drug. Not all drugs of the same class carry the same burden of sexual side effects, and it is sometimes possible to find a substitute for the offending drug that does not impair sexual function. Riley (1980a), for example, reported a man who experienced loss of erection within two days of starting propranolol, 40 mg three times a day. Within two days of stopping propranolol erections returned. Rechallenge with the same dose of propranolol again induced erection inadequacy. The treatment was then changed to acebutolol 200 mg three times daily which did not cause erection failure. This finding may suggest that propranolol inhibits erection by a central mechanism since propranolol but not acebutolol crosses the blood-brain barrier.

With some drugs, sexual side effects are dose-related so that even if it is not possible to withdraw the drug totally it may be possible to abolish the sexual dysfunction by reducing the dose of the offending drug. For example, anorgasmia occurred in a female patient when she was receiving 45 mg daily of the monoamine oxidase inhibitor phenelzine, but she was able to experience orgasm when the dose was reduced to 30 mg daily (Lesko *et al.*, 1982).

Erection inadequacy occurring during treatment with antihypertensive drugs is sometimes due to the reduced blood pressure rather than a direct pharmacological effect of the drugs use. Riley (1980b) described the case of a hypertensive man who complained of erection inadequacy only at times when his blood pressure was lowered. When there is narrowing of the pelvic arteries in the hypertensive patient caused by atherosclerosis there may be sufficient flow through these vessels before the hypertension is treated to allow erection to occur. When the blood pressure is reduced, there is insufficient 'head of pressure' to force sufficient blood through these narrowed vessels and erection inadequacy results.

Sometimes the patient's primary medical condition makes it impossible either to withdraw or to reduce the dose of a drug that is causing sexual side effects. In such situations it may be possible to relieve the sexual side effect by the concurrent administration of another drug. Sexual dysfunction caused by anticholinergic antidepressants has been reported to be reversed by bethanechol chloride (Gross, 1982). Bethanechol chloride is a cholinergic agonist which has selectivity for muscarinic receptors. In this report bethanechol chloride was used to treat erection inadequacy occurring on tranylcypromine (40 mg/day) in one man, during treatment with isocarboxazid (60 mg/day) in another man and amoxapine-induced anorgasmia in a woman. The effective dose of bethanechol chloride was 12.5 mg in the woman, 30 mg in the patient on isocarboxazid and 40 mg in the man on tranylcypromine. These observations are interesting because the exact role of cholinergic stimulation in human sexual response is uncertain. Atropine in doses sufficient to cause muscarinic receptor blockade does not impair sexual arousal or orgasm in normal men or women (Riley and Riley, 1983; Wagner and Brindley, 1980; Wagner and Levine, 1980) and bethanechol chloride had no effect on the sexual response induced by masturbation in female volunteers (Riley and Riley, 1983).

The sexual side effects of some antidepressants might be related to changes in serotoninergic activity. Animal studies have suggested serotoninergic to have an inhibitory role in the control of sexual behaviour. Decastro (1985) describes a man who experienced anorgasmia during treatment with phenelzine which was successfully treated by the addition of cyproheptadine (12 mg) one hour before intercourse. On occasions when he did not take the cyproheptadine before intercourse, orgasm did not occur. Cyproheptadine is a serotonin antagonist. Female anorgasmia occurring during treatment with nortriptyline has also been successfully reversed with cyproheptadine (Sovner, 1984). In a placebo-controlled study, cyproheptadine successfully treated female anorgasmia induced by clomipramine (one patient) and imipramine (one patient) but it was ineffective in a woman whose anorgasmia was induced by desipramine (Riley and Riley, 1986b).

CONCLUSION

There is now a renewed interest in non-psychological approaches to the treatment of sexual difficulties. This has arisen because of our greater understanding about the organic causes of sexual dysfunction and the realization that not all sexual difficulties respond favourably to psychotherapeutic approaches in a reasonable period of time. There can be no doubt that behaviourally orientated psychotherapy will remain the mainstay of management but at the same time there is the need to explore adjunct treatments that will facilitate the early resolution of the sexual difficulties. There are now increasing observations to support the role of drugs in the management of some forms of sexual dysfunction. It should be possible to identify more therapeutic targets for drug intervention. This will be aided by the development of more selective drugs and greater resources for research into the pharmacology of human sexuality.

ACKNOWLEDGEMENT

The author is grateful to Wendy Phillips for the preparation of the manuscript.

REFERENCES

Angrist, B. and Gershon, S. (1976) Clinical effects of amphetamine and L-dopa on sexuality and aggression, *Comprehensive Psychiatry*, Vol. 17, pp. 715–22.

Bartholomew, A.A. (1968) A long acting phenothiazine as a possible agent to control deviant sexual behaviour, *American Journal of Psychiatry*, Vol. 124, pp. 917–23.

Beaumont, G. (1973) Sexual side effects of clomipramine (Anafranil), *Journal of International Medical Research*, Vol. 1, pp. 469–72.

Bennett, D. (1961) MAOI, for premature ejaculation, *Lancet*, ii, pp. 1309.

Brindley, G.S. (1983) Cavernousal alpha-blockade: a new technique for investigating and treating erectile impotence, *British Journal of Psychiatry*, Vol. 143, pp. 332–7.

Brindley, G.S. (1984) New treatment for priapism, *Lancet*, ii, pp. 220–1.

Brown, E., Brown, G.M., Kopman, O. and Quarrington, B. (1978) Sexual function and affect in Parkinsonian men treated with L-dopa, *American Journal of Psychiatry*, Vol. 135, pp. 1522–5.

Buffen, J. (1982) Pharmacosexology: The effects of drugs on sexual function. A review, *Journal of Psychoactive Drugs*, Vol. 14, pp. 5–44.

Carney, A., Bancroft, J. and Mathews, A. (1978) Combination of hormonal and psychological treatment for female sexual unresponsiveness in a comparative study, *British Journal of Psychiatry*, Vol. 132, pp. 339–46.

Cooper, A.J. and Magnus, R.V. (1984) A clinical trial of the beta blocker propranolol in premature ejaculation, *Journal of Psychosomatic Research*, Vol. 28, No. 4, pp. 331–6.

Decastro, R.M. (1985) Reversal of MAOI-induced anorgasmia with cyproheptadine, *American Journal of Psychiatry*, Vol. 142, No. 6, p. 783.

Eaton, H. (1973) Clomipramine (Anafranil) in the treatment of premature ejaculation, *Journal of International Medical Research*, Vol. 1, pp. 432–4.

Farkas, G.M. and Rosen, R.C. (1976) The effect of alcohol on elicited male sexual response, *Journal of Studies of Alcohol*, Vol. 37, pp. 265–72.

Freed, E. (1983) Increased sexual function with nomifensine, *The Medical Journal of Australia*, Vol. 24, p. 551.

Gold, M.S., Redmond, D.E., Jr. and Kleber, H.D. (1978) Clonidine blocks acute opiate – withdrawal symptoms, *Lancet*, ii, pp. 599–602.
Goodman, R.E. (1986) How to treat premature ejaculation, *British Journal of Sexual Medicine*, Vol. 13, pp. 178–9.
Gross, M.D. (1982) Reversal by bethanechol of sexual dysfunction caused by anticholinergic antidepressants, *American Journal of Psychiatry*, Vol. 139, No. 9, pp. 1193–4.
Hallstrom, T. and Persson, T. (1970) L-dopa and non-emission of semen, *Lancet*, Vol. i, pp. 1231–2.
Hamilton, M. (1982) Symptoms and assessment of depression, in E.S. Paykel (ed.) *Handbook of Affective Disorders*, Churchill-Livingstone, Edinburgh.
Holmberg, G. and Gershon, S. (1961) Autonomic and psychic effects of yohimbine hydrochloride, *Psychopharmacologia*, Vol. 2, pp. 93–106.
Hughes, J.M. (1964) Failure to ejaculate with chlordialepoxide, *American Journal of Psychiatry*, Vol. 121, pp. 610–11.
Jonas, D., Linzbach, P. and Weber, W. (1979) The use of midodrine in the treatment of ejaculation disorders following retroperitoneal lymphadenectomy, *European Urology*, Vol. 5, pp. 184–7.
Kaplan, H.S. (1974) *The New Sex Therapy*, Baillière Tindall, London.
Kaplan, H.S. (1983) *The Evaluation of Sexual Disorders*, Brunner/Mazel, New York.
Lesko, L.M., Stotland, N.L. and Taylor-Segraves, R. (1982) Three cases of female anorgasmia associated with MAOIs, *American Journal of Psychiatry*, Vol. 139, pp. 1353–4.
Lowry, T.P. (1979) The volatile nitrites as sexual drugs: a user survey, *Journal of Sex Education and Therapy*, Vol. 1, No. 5, pp. 8–10.
Malatesta, V., Pollack, R., Crotley, T. and Peacock, L. (1982) Acute alcohol intoxication and female orgasmic response, *Journal of Sex Research*, Vol. 18, pp. 1–17.
Maneksha, S. and Harry, T.U.A. (1975) Lorazepam in sexual disorders, *British Journal of Clinical Practice*, Vol. 22, pp. 175–6.
Mellgren, A. (1967) Treatment of ejaculation praecox with thioridazine, *Psychotherapy and Psychosomatics*, Vol. 15, pp. 454–8.
Morales, A., Surridge, D.H. and Marshall, P.G. (1981) Yohimbine for treatment of impotence in diabetics, *New England Journal of Medicine*, Vol. 305, p. 1221.
Morales, A., Condra, M., Surridge, D.S.H., Fenemore, J. and Owen, J.A. (1984) The effectiveness of yohimbine in the treatment of impotence: results of a controlled trial, *American Urological Association Meeting Abstracts*, A 391.
Mudd, J.W. (1977) Impotence responsive to glyceryl trinitrate, *American Journal of Psychiatry*, Vol. 134, pp. 922–5.
Redmond, D.E., Kosten, T.R. and Reiser, M.F. (1983) Spontaneous ejaculation associated with anxiety: psychophysiological considerations, *American Journal of Psychiatry*, Vol. 140, pp. 1163–6.
Riley, A.J. (1980a) Antihypertensive therapy and sexual function, *British Journal of Sexual Medicine*, Vol. 7, No. 62, pp. 23–7.
Riley, A.J. (1980b) Case report: erectile problems of vascular disease, *British Journal of Sexual Medicine*, Vol. 7, No. 61, pp. 46–7.
Riley, A.J. (1986) Spontaneous ejaculations, *British Journal of Sexual Medicine*, Vol. 13, p. 66.
Riley, A.J. (in press) Spontaneous orgasm, *British Journal of Sexual Medicine*.

Riley, A.J. and Riley, E.J. (1979) Amitriptyline-perphenazine and the squeeze technique in premature ejaculation, *Journal of Pharmacotherapy*, Vol. 2, No. 3, pp. 136–40.
Riley, A.J. and Riley, E.J. (1982) Partial ejaculatory incompetence: The therapeutic effect of midodrine. An orally active selective alpha adrenoceptor agonist, *European Urology*, Vol. 8, pp. 155–60.
Riley, A.J. and Riley, E.J. (1983) Cholinergic and adrenergic control of human sexual responses, in D. Wheatley (ed.) *Psychopharmacology and Sexual Disorders*, pp. 125–37, Oxford University Press, Oxford.
Riley, A.J. and Riley, E.J. (1984) Alpha-blockade and impotence, *British Journal of Psychiatry*, Vol. 144, pp. 215–6.
Riley, A.J. and Riley, E.J. (1986a) The effect of single dose diazepam on female sexual response induced by masturbation, *Sexual and Marital Therapy*, Vol. 1, pp. 49–53.
Riley, A.J. and Riley, E.J. (1986b) Cyproheptadine and antidepressant-induced anorgasmia, *British Journal of Psychiatry*, Vol. 148, pp. 127–8.
Riley, A.J., Riley, E.J. and Davies, H.J. (1982) A method for monitoring drug effects on male sexual response. The effect of single dose labetalol, *British Journal of Clinical Pharmacology*, Vol. 14, pp. 695–700.
Sandler, B. (1979) Idiopathic retrograde ejaculation, *Fertility and Sterility*, Vol. 32, pp. 474–5.
Sangal, R. (1985) Inhibited female orgasm as a side effect of alprazolam, *American Journal of Psychiatry*, Vol. 142, No. 10, pp. 1223–4.
Schwale, M., Frosch, P., Tölle, E. and Niermann, H. (1980) Treatment of retrograde ejaculation and anorgasmy with an alpha-sympathomimetic drug (Midodrine), *Zeitschrift für Hautkrankheiten*, Vol. 55, pp. 756–9.
Serjeant, G.R., DeCeulaer, K. and Maude, G.H. (1985) Stilboestrol and stuttering priapism in homozygous sickle-cell disease, *Lancet*, ii, pp. 1274–6.
Shilon, M., Paz, G.F. and Homonnai, Z.T. (1984) The use of phenoxybenzamine treatment in premature ejaculation, *Fertility and Sterility*, Vol. 42, No. 4, pp. 659–61.
Slag, M.F., Morley, J.E. and Elson, M.K. (1983) Impotence in medical clinic outpatients, *Journal of the American Medical Association*, Vol. 249, pp. 1736–40.
Sovner, R. (1984) Treatment of tricyclic antidepressant-induced orgasmic inhibition with cyproheptadine, *Journal of Clinical Psychopharmacology*, Vol. 4, p. 169.
Stanners, A. and Colin-Jones, D. (1984) Metaraminol for priapism, *Lancet*, ii, p. 978.
Stewart, B.H. and Bergant, J.A. (1974) Correction of retrograde ejaculation by sympathomimetic medication: Preliminary report, *Fertility and Sterility*, Vol. 25, pp. 1073–4.
Tennent, G., Bancroft, J. and Cass, T. (1974) The control of deviant sexual behavior by drugs: A double blind controlled study of benperidoc chlorpromazine and placebo, *Archives of Sexual Behavior*, Vol. 3, pp. 261–71.
Virag, R. (1985) About pharmacologically induced prolonged erection, *Lancet*, i, pp. 519–20.
Wagner, G. and Brindley, G.S. (1980) The effect of atropine alpha and beta blockers on human penile erection: a controlled pilot study, in A. Zorgniotti and G. Rossi (eds) *Vasculogenic Impotence*, pp. 77–81, Charles C. Thomas, Springfield IL.
Wagner, G. and Levine, R.J. (1980) Effect of atropine and methylatropine on human vaginal blood flow, sexual arousal and climax, *Acta Pharmacologica et Toxicologica*, Vol. 46, pp. 321–5.

Wilson, G.T. and Lawson, D. (1976) Effects of alcohol on sexual arousal in women, *Journal of Abnormal Psychology*, Vol. 85, pp. 489–97.

CHAPTER 9

SEX THERAPY IN GROUPS

Lisa Kayata and David Szydlo

Since the pioneering work of Masters and Johnson (1970), the majority of the treatment of psychosexual dysfunction has been conducted on an individual basis, with the therapeutic process evolving between the individual client or couple and the therapist(s). As far back as the early 1970s however, group therapy has been researched and proven successful as an alternative modality in the treatment of sexual disorders. Most of this research and treatment has been carried out in the United States and only relatively recently has group sex therapy been practised in Britain. Indeed, group treatment of sexual problems in Britain utilizes techniques that have been developed in America and with few exceptions (Kayata and Szydlo, 1986; Gillan *et al.*, 1980), there has been little British research published in this area.

The primary strengths of the sex therapy group are twofold. First, the group provides a strong support structure for the patient who feels anxious, guilty, isolated, and ashamed about the sexual problem. Second, the scope of treatment is broadened as the therapy group is a forum in which the dysfunctional patient is educated about sexual anatomy and physiology, strategies of social behaviour are adapted, sexual myths are nullified and sexual attitudes are restructured. While different theoretical orientations may underpin the running of sex therapy groups, group treatment of sexual disorders tends to be conducted in behaviourally oriented groups, although psychodynamic approaches have also been used (Obler, 1973). Group composition also varies and group members might be couples (Leiblum and Rosen, 1979; McGovern *et al.*, 1976), women (Barbach, 1974; Schneidman and McGuire, 1976), men (Zilbergeld, 1975; Lobitz and Baker, 1979), or women and men without partners (Kayata and Szydlo, 1986).

Groups may be homogeneous with regard to the sexual dysfunction being treated (Kaplan *et al.*, 1974; Barbach and Flaherty, 1980) with the view that this is an efficient method of dealing with common problems and reaching common goals. Heterogeneous groups have also been conducted (Leiblum *et al.*, 1976) with the view that these groups provide a greater opportunity for learning from others with a variety of problems and experiences. Overall, groups of couples and mixed sex groups tend to be treated by a dual-sex therapist team and same sex groups are led by one or two therapists of the same sex as the group members, although this is not always the case. Theoretical and methodological issues are considered in this chapter as related to the group treatment of sexual dysfunction within the context of heterosexual relationships.

GROUP PROCESS

Group therapy has long been an established form of treatment in psychiatry, and the diversity of approaches of the theory and technique of group treatment emphasize its popularity. There are, however, fundamental questions that remain unclear. For example, How does it work? What about this form of treatment is important and/or effective? and What is the therapeutic process?

Attempts have been made to look for a basic set of therapeutic components that constitute the therapeutic process and that highlight the theoretical differences intrinsic to alternative models. Yalom (1975) identifies ten curative factors which, based on his own research, are general enough to try to explain therapeutic changes in groups of every theoretical orientation. Sansbury (1977), based on Corsini & Rosenberg (1955) and departing from Yalom's ten curative factors, develops a model of a sequential emergence of factors and proposes a way in which these factors could be furthered by the therapist's intervention. Universality, followed by cohesiveness, are the basic elements allowing for the development of group norms and setting the arena for change to occur. Through these elements which encompass concepts such as group pressure, uniformity of opinion, sharing of information and goals, etc., Sansbury tried to demonstrate that behaviourally oriented interventions foster group process and individual change.

Bloch and Crouch (1985) define a therapeutic factor as 'an element of group therapy that contributes to improvement in a patient's condition and is a function of the action of the group therapist, the other group members, and the patient him/herself' (p. 4). Also based on Yalom's description, Bloch and Crouch develop their own classification which includes ten therapeutic factors: insight, learning from interpersonal action, acceptance (cohesiveness), self-disclosure, catharsis, guidance, universality, altruism, vicarious learning, and instillation of hope. They insist that the concept of a 'therapeutic factor' must be distinguished from technique, a closely related phenomenon. That is to say, although technique does not exert therapeutic effects, it is the tool by which the operation of therapeutic factor is promoted. As we describe the different types of group that have been used in the management of sexual disorders in an attempt to determine their relative effect and the weight of their methods on outcome, it would be of great help to keep the aforementioned concepts in mind, so as to avoid confusing therapeutic factors with variables associated with outcome.

Important changes in sexual attitudes have taken place in society over the past several decades, as a result of many different factors and events (better education, improved contraceptive methods, changes in the abortion legislation, less rigorous pornographic controls, etc.). The effect of these changes can be seen not only in the fact that a more open discussion of sexuality in society has been encouraged but in the fostering of more research in the field of sexual physiology and sexual dysfunction. The investigation of the functional psychological causes of sexual dysfunction has followed a diversity of routes. Group therapy is one of the modalities that has tried to examine the intrapsychic conflict as well as the interpersonal problems in patients. Group treatment of sexual disorders has had, like most other approaches, its fair share of speculation regarding the elements in the group process that bring satisfactory results and the effectiveness of the techniques used. The extent to which each therapeutic factor will be found helpful or unhelpful by the group members will depend on the theoretical orientation of the group (psychodynamic, behavioural, or educational), on the group's composition (single male, single female, couples, single mixed sexes), and other relevant variables (age of members, duration of the group, group goals, group size). There are not enough studies which are specific to process in groups that are focused on sexual disorders for conclusions to be drawn, but some general premises are applicable. Bloch and Crouch suggest that some form of self-understanding (insight) is linked with improvement and say that 'acceptance and self-disclosure are also relevant though to a lesser degree and, the weakest correlation with outcome are vicarious learning and guidance' (p. 247).

Different programmes use different techniques and therefore, promote different therapeutic factors. The literature is filled with descriptions of such programmes applied and developed in both America and Britain. We have found that the majority of these programmes have the following elements in common: educational input, social skills training, specific interventions for the treatment of the sexual dysfunction, and sessions open to 'spontaneous' participation (self-disclosure, group interaction, group support, etc.).

Finally, we would like to point out that the two main sources of knowledge in the area of group therapy are the clinician and the researcher. The questions that will have to be taken up by both in the coming years are those referring to the relationship between therapeutic factors and outcome, the relationship between curative factors and both group differences and individual differences, and the effect of specific techniques on the promotion of these factors.

A perplexing issue concerns whether the group or group process is the predominant force influencing growth and change, rather than a new, healthier marital relationship or the development of independent self-realization. This could imply either of the following: that once the group stimulus is removed and treatment is terminated, the significant source of reinforcement and support is removed and group members are inclined to regress, re-adopting the dysfunctional behaviour; or, more positively, that group process has a catalytic effect on the group members which is a necessary concomitant of their individual behaviour change.

It is hoped that new studies will emerge that will shed light on the nature and impact of this form of treatment.

TOWARDS A BEHAVIOURAL-PSYCHOANALYTIC APPROACH

Generally speaking, groups that attempt to treat psychosexual dysfunction are behavioural in approach. This can be said about the techniques used for social skills training (role-play, modelling, successive approximation), for the treatment of the sexual dysfunction through exercises and couples' programmes, and for some of the assessment procedures (target-problem evaluation), many of which are incorporated into the group process itself. Some of the therapeutic tools available to the therapist during open discussion will also include verbal reinforcement, guided participation, and so forth.

Given that group psychoanalysis is not only a therapeutic technique but also a method of studying problems arising from human interaction, its contribution to the understanding and treatment of sexual disorders is undeniable. In the context of group sex therapy however, the psychoanalytic techniques of free association, transference, and interpretation, rather than directive structured intervention, would be deemed the essential features that facilitate change. If group therapy polarizes between open-ended, non-directive discussion methods using psychodynamic concepts, and a goal-oriented, behavioural, therapist-directed method, which type of group provides patients with what they expect, with what they need or with what will help them?

Yates (1983) discusses the possible relationship between behaviour therapy and psychoanalytically oriented psychotherapy and explores the grounds for reconciliation and integration as opposed to basic conflict. He states that some behaviour therapists believe that psychotherapy can be reduced to behavioural technique, arguing that psychodynamically oriented therapists unwittingly make use of behavioural techniques (selective reinforcement) and that it is this aspect of intervention that results in successful outcome. Likewise, some psychoanalytical oriented therapists argue that it is the unwitting use that behavioural therapists make of psychodynamic techniques (interpretation or resolution of transference problems) that results in successful therapy. These positions point to a very complex theoretical and technical discourse, and many of the questions that arise from it remain unanswered. Several studies have been reported in the literature concerning the combined use of these techniques in the treatment of sexual dysfunction in groups. Unfortunately, most of them lack adequate methodological controls. Interestingly though, there has been no attempt to demonstrate that the combined behavioural/psychoanalytic approach is better than the use of either approach alone.

Some authors (Woody, 1973; Kaplan, 1974; Levay and Kagle, 1977) have reported the use of a combined approach in the practice of sex therapy, incorporating behavioural techniques for specific sexual problems and analytic therapy for more general problems in the treatment of the individual. Others consider it totally inappropriate for a person to be in both psychotherapy and sex therapy at the same time. Intensive group therapy has been suggested as the treatment of choice when one wants to explore the deeper layers of the mind and the underlying psychodynamics and psychopathology of patients. Through the synthesis of intellect and emotion, patients in a group are helped to understand those aspects of themselves which will enable them to confront new situations with more awareness and skill.

It is common to come across patients who do not seem to benefit from behavioural treatment and whose sexual difficulties are the symptom, or the expression, of the intrapsychic conflict, a process not always available to conscious thought. For these patients, as well as for those who expect a deeper understanding of their problems, psychodynamically oriented psychotherapy in groups may be the treatment of choice, whether in combination with or at the exclusion of other approaches. We have mentioned a few studies in this section that describe the attempts that have been made to use this pioneering form of group interaction to study the disturbances that occur in relationships. The idea that the group itself is the instrument used to work towards a solution of general problems is certainly one of the motivations to use group therapy as a mode of treatment for specific problems, among them, sexual dysfunction.

One problem that merits a special note is that of research into an integrated behavioural-psychoanalytic approach to sex therapy. On the one hand, most psychodynamic understanding emerges from personal experience and single case reports (with individuals and groups) and is structured around a specific theoretical framework which is not empirically based. On the other hand, empirical support for the efficacy of behavioural techniques in group treatment is available but it is neither methodologically problem-free nor conclusive. Therefore, the development of studies which could evaluate the value of the combined approach or the relative weight of each individual approach would be extremely difficult.

Let us now proceed to some of the studies that have been recorded in the treatment of couples, single women, single men, and mixed groups, most of them behavioural in approach.

COUPLES' GROUPS

Group therapy is one approach used to treat sexually dysfunctional married (or unmarried) couples, and is the predecessor of the treatment of men and women in single-sex groups. Some clinicians advocate the efficacy of groups as a form of follow-up for couples who have already been through individual sex therapy, but the main application of couples' groups has been the development of treatment situations that can offer more economical and long-lasting help for patients.

There are three main goals incorporated within the behavioural programme for couples' group sex therapy. The first goal is to provide a progressive, structured format for the therapy which allows couples to rebuild their sexual relationships gradually. This involves a step-by-step procedure whereby each couple can satisfactorily complete one stage of treatment (i.e. non-genital sensate focus), before moving on to the next (i.e. genital sensate focus). In the group situation, this serves to highlight the differences between individual couples' goals, expectations, and levels of sexual functioning, and to dispel the notion of striving for idealized societal norms of sexual behaviour.

The second goal is to help both couples and therapist(s) identify the specific factors which may be maintaining the sexual problem. This would involve an exploration of individual partners' sexuality and of associated relationship difficulties. It is often the case that difficulties with or reactions to homework assignments may help to elucidate couples' interactional dynamics and, thus, contribute to their understanding of a problem. Similarly, the group technique of role-play facilitates the processes of modelling and observational learning among couples.

The third goal of the behavioural programme is to provide couples with specific techniques to tackle specific dysfunctional and associated relationship problems (i.e. the stop-start technique and communication skills) both during treatment and in the future. A group can provide a constructive framework with which to achieve this goal.

There have been two primary modalities of treatment for couples' groups. The first involves intensive programmes over short periods of time in which couples receive an important educational package and general discussion regarding worries, fears, myths and attitudes is fostered. Leiblum and Rosen (1979) view this approach as a synthesis of group sexual treatment and self-help methods. Blakeney *et al.* (1976) reported on the outcome of 59 couples who followed short, intensive programmes. Seventy-four of 118 individuals still had some form of sexual dysfunction at the end of the workshop with a symptom reversal of 36 per cent. At a follow-up several months later, the symptom reversal was 63 per cent in the same population. Chesney *et al.* (1981) in a better controlled study found that the symptom reversal in a sample of 106 individuals was 57 per cent. The second more commonly used form of group involvement is group therapy for couples over a period ranging from 15 to 20 sessions.

A couples' group will consist of two or more committed relationships and one or two therapists. Various technical considerations are brought to our awareness by different authors who ask questions such as: Is it likely that two therapists will bring about better results than one? Is it important that the therapists should be of different sexes? Is it more likely to achieve the desired result if the couples present with the same dysfunction? Is age an important factor for outcome? and Is group therapy the most effective approach?

Unfortunately, there are no valid outcome studies in the literature or empirical bases to answer these questions or to evaluate the appropriateness of group therapy for couples. Having said that, we mention some studies that give a relatively useful indication of the trend that couples' treatment in groups is following.

A report by Kirkpatrick *et al.* (1977) suggests that group therapy is a more effective mode of treatment for couples and they hint that it offers advantages over individual treatment. Couples seem to feel less inhibited and more stimulated by the presence of other couples when sharing their problems. Members of couples' groups reported feeling less pressured in a group setting than sitting with an individual therapist and a powerful modelling effect was considered to be an important asset of these groups. Duddle and Ingram (1980), on the other hand, reported that many couples refused group treatment, presumably because they did not wish to discuss their sexual relationships with other couples. While the first study concludes that the group treatment programme seems to have afforded some distinct advantages over individual treatment, the second study saw it as a useful therapeutic tool but by no means superior to individual couple treatment.

There have been several attempts to evaluate factors which predispose couples to benefit from treatment in a group situation. Martin (1983) produced a list of indications and contraindications for group therapy for couples based on the quality of the relationship, the individual characteristics of the partners, the financial situation of the couple, the results of previous attempts to treat the problem, and the degree of commitment. Other classifications try to organize these issues based on the types of problem and the type of people for whom this mode of treatment would be the first choice. It is important to indicate that there are opposite views regarding which personality types or interactional styles would represent an indication or a contraindication for group treatment. Birk (1984) proposes a combined concurrent-conjoint psychotherapy approach for couples which involves individual therapy for the couple, group therapy for couples, and group therapy for individual partners. This study, as well as most of the ones described, is particularly deficient in terms of methodological controls.

WOMEN'S GROUPS

Group sex therapy for women has been used extensively for the treatment of anorgasmia. The primary goal of these groups is to help the woman achieve an orgasm on her own, and then with her partner. The general format involves a progressive series of exercises focusing first on exploration and arousal, and then on 'letting go' and reaching a climax. Concurrent with behavioural exercises are group discussions about sexuality in general and about sexual issues specific to women. Through these discussions, sexual myths about women such as 'Only through intercourse can a woman experience a genuine orgasm' and 'I do not fit the media's current profile of the sexually liberated woman, therefore I am inadequate' can be dispelled. Often, attitudes towards masturbation must be changed as women learn to acknowledge their rights to sexual pleasure. A woman's realization that she is not alone in feeling defective or incomplete because she cannot have an orgasm is often a great source of relief and is a major contributor to group cohesion. The most powerful aspect of these groups is that women share with other women their sex histories, feelings of anxiety, low self-esteem, conflicts about men and concerns about body image.

Barbach (1974) pioneered the approach of group treatment for women suffering from orgasmic dysfunction. She introduced the term *pre-orgasmic* to promote an optimistic attitude towards the outcome of treatment and to avoid the stigmatic effect of the term *non-orgasmic*. Her programme incorporates the masturbation training programme of LoPiccolo and Lobitz (1972) with progressive homework exercises, attitude exploration, and sex education.

Barbach's groups include between five and ten women and are usually led by two women, although a man may be involved at some stage to offer male attitudes about male and female sexuality. Partners are not included in women's group treatment sessions because the exclusive interaction between women is seen as a powerful therapeutic tool, although some therapists introduce partners in later stages of the programme as a means of facilitating the generalization of orgasm by self-stimulation to orgasm by partner stimulation. The treatment schedule consists of ten sessions with one follow-up group held approximately three months after the end of treatment.

Treatment begins with work on body image and women are asked to spend time at home looking at themselves dressed and undressed in a full-length mirror. Many women successfully avoid visual contact with their own bodies and/or magnify in their minds those aspects of themselves that they consider physically unattractive. This homework assignment is intended to help diminish such distortions, and to help women to become comfortable with their bodies, and to learn to criticize themselves rationally and constructively. Kegel (1952) exercises and literature about the health and sexuality of women are also introduced at this stage.

At the next stage, there is a specific educational input to enhance what the women have been reading. Specifically, female sexual anatomy and response are described. Homework progresses, self-focusing is introduced, and women are asked to examine their genitals visually and manually.

Women are shown a film about masturbation during the next stage. Feelings and attitudes are discussed in the group, and the homework for the women is to begin to masturbate. It may be stressed at this stage that women should not attempt to proceed to orgasm, in order to avoid any performance pressure and to avoid a repetition of experiences that have made them feel inadequate in the past.

The remaining treatment sessions are tailored to the individual progress of each group member and women are encouraged to try to reach orgasm. Erotic literature, sexual fantasies, and vibrators are discussed and suggested when appropriate. Many women may have never allowed themselves to have conscious sexual fantasies and are able to do so for the first time with the encouragement of the group. Finally, the women discuss how they will transfer what they have learned and experienced during the group to a sexual relationship with a partner. For example, it is suggested that if her partner is willing, she may show him how she stimulates herself and guide him through non-genital and genital caressing. Advice may be offered concerning how the woman might stimulate herself during intercourse and how her partner might do the same.

Overall, the results of pre-orgasmic groups are good, Barbach reported a 92 per cent success rate for the first 83 women who completed the programme. The achievement of orgasm via any mode of stimulation (typically masturbation) was the criterion for success. In an analysis of 17 women from three separate groups in an eight-month follow-up, orgasmic ability was maintained and 87 per cent of these women had achieved orgasm via partner stimulation at the follow-up assessment. Reports of improvement in sexual satisfaction, level of relaxation and enjoyment, communication with partner, and general level of functioning were also found. Since the introduction of Barbach's pre-orgasmic groups, the group treatment of women has been widely utilized in America and will, we hope, become a more popular intervention in Britain.

Leiblum and Ersner-Hershfield (1977) found that the generalization of orgasm via self-stimulation to orgasm via partner stimulation or intercourse was less apparent in a study of 16 women, 14 of whom became orgasmic by the end of group treatment. In a later study, results indicated that orgasm with a partner was equally likely for women treated in women-only groups and for women treated in groups with their partners. Of the 22 women treated, 91 per cent became orgasmic through masturbation by the end of treatment and 82 per cent became orgasmic with their partners by the ten-week follow-up (Ersner-Hershfield and Kopel, 1979). Schneidman and McGuire (1976) found that pre-orgasmic groups were more successful for women under 35, and suggest that individual therapy may be more appropriate and effective for older women.

Barbach and Flaherty (1980) have adapted pre-orgasmic women's groups for situationally orgasmic women with a two-thirds success rate on 26 women treated.

MEN'S GROUPS

The group treatment of men with sexual difficulties has been explored to a lesser degree than that of women. The reasons for this are open to speculation. Although it could be partly due to sexual myths and the stigma that men attach to an acknowledgement of their sexual problems (which has increased the difficulty of engaging them in groups), it could also be explained in terms of other mechanisms such as denial and avoidance and certainly the inferior results of men's groups as compared with women's groups.

Group therapy for men exists in two modalities, for patients who do not have available partners or as part of a programme in combination with couples' therapy. This type of treatment was pioneered by Zilbergeld in 1975 when he treated a group of men with erectile and ejaculatory problems in the United States. The format included homework exercises, sexual education, and discussion of individual problems. The results of the trial, based on clinical observation and self-reports, showed success in two thirds of the subjects. All patients also reported improvement in non-sexual areas such as assertiveness or increased self-esteem.

Group therapy for men shares with other types of groups, the diversity and the variations that can occur in terms of group constitution or treatment programmes. Hence, the few reports that we find in the literature describe groups where patients suffer from the same or different dysfunctions, where the age range is wide or narrow, and where the patient was single or involved in a committed relationship, although the majority of groups treat single, unattached men.

The behaviourally oriented homework assignments for men's groups involve two basic techniques: self-exploratory exercises, and techniques specific to ejaculatory control and erectile difficulties (the stop-start and squeeze techniques). Many groups report the use of relaxation training as well, although controversy exists around the validity of its usefulness. One of the techniques originated in men's groups and subsequently used in other sex therapy groups is the discussion of sexual myths introduced by Zilbergeld (1978) as a way of dismantling damaging sexual attitudes.

Most reports claim a reasonable gain for treatment. Zilbergeld (1978) claims that two thirds of the men in his group achieve their goals by the end of treatment. Lobitz and Baker (1979) in a group of nine men with erectile dysfunction, reported significant improvement in all of them, although those with primary erectile dysfunction did not do as well as those with secondary erectile problems.

There have been attempts to treat men in a group without partners even if they have been involved in a steady relationship. Zeiss and his colleagues (1978) report on a group for men with premature ejaculation in which two groups of three men were seen in six weekly sessions plus a follow-up session. Their female partners did not participate in the treatment sessions, but were expected to co-operate with the sexual and communication exercises between the meetings. Four of the six couples were successful at the end of the group, and three men maintained improvement at an eight-month follow-up.

Two interesting reports compared treatment of patients in groups with patients allocated to a waiting list. Price *et al.* (1981) report on such a group in which the progamme did not include social-skills training, and there was no difference in outcome between the groups. On the other hand, Reynolds *et al.* (1981), modifying Price's model, found that men with erectile difficulties improved significantly more when treated in a group that included social-skills training, as compared with those on a waiting list.

It seems clear that there is a need for further research and development of group treatment for men with sexual problems, not only because it has received so little attention until now but because of the changing attitudes relating to the way in which sexual problems in men are perceived. This can be observed in that there is an increasing demand for general practitioners and psychosexual dysfunction clinics to treat single men's sexual problems.

MIXED SEX GROUPS

The group treatment of psychosexual dysfunction has usually involved the participation of couples, women, or men in the group situation. It is our belief however, that when an individual who is sexually active but not involved in a committed relationship presents with sexual dysfunction, his or her treatment in a group containing members of the opposite sex is a viable and effective approach. This belief is based on the limitations of individual treatment techniques as compared with those used for couples individually and in groups, and on the crucial aspect of heterosexual interaction inherent in the development and maintenance of most sexual dysfunction.

Much of the work done in the area of sex therapy has been proven most successful when carried out within the context of an ongoing relationship. Here, the interaction between partners is the primary therapeutic tool, and the valuable marital therapy techniques of communication training, negotiation, and contracting can be utilized. The notion that a sexual problem is shared by both partners in a relationship contributes to their ability to share the responsibility of its resolution. The reciprocal nature of Masters and Johnson's (1970) sensate focus exercises, for example, allows the couple slowly and gradually to explore their difficulties without the pressure and fear often associated with intercourse.

The approach and progression of treatment for the single woman or man has very much stricter limitations. The scope of individual therapy techniques is confined to relaxation training, self-exploration, and masturbatory exercises. When one considers the numerous and complex factors contributing to the onset and maintenance of sexual problems, the importance of group treatment is apparent. The prevalence of anxiety may be associated with limited sexual activity, combined with an ignorance of the intricacies of male and female sexual anatomy. A process highlighting the plight of the dysfunctional individual is the fear or avoidance of performance with a new partner, as this might lead to exposure of the sexual problem. No sex, and therefore, an avoidance of any close heterosexual contact may seem the only 'safe' alternative. Deficits in social skills are common and often preempt successful sexual activity many stages before arousal and intercourse. A poor or misguided education, restrictive cultural or religious upbringing, poor self-image, feelings of inadequacy and hopelessness, belief in sexual myths, and the inability to share the problem with friends or family are other contributing agents.

In light of these factors, we have attempted to treat single men and women in a group situation in the first reported group of its kind in Britain (Kayata and Szydlo, 1986). While the prognosis for primarily anorgasmic women participating in pre-orgasmic groups is generally quite good (Barbach, 1974) the level of improvement of men suffering from primary erectile dysfunction who are treated in men's groups is less clear (Lobitz and Baker, 1979). From the experience of colleagues who have run single sex groups, we understand that while women's groups often focus on female sexual functioning and attitudes and may adopt a feminist or even an anti-male approach, men's groups often produce a high drop-out rate as well as a limited scope of discussion of female sexual attitudes. We feel that a combined sex group provides a forum for a healthier, more realistic balance of ideas, an awareness of opposite sex difficulties, and a greater motivation for input and attendance. Further, the concepts of sexual dysfunction and sexual fulfilment are more easily connected to the establishment and dynamics of the heterosexual relationship, if aided by the process of male/female interaction in the group.

Our mixed sex group incorporated sex education, the treatment of sexual dysfunction, social-skills training, and an exploration of sexual myths and attitudes. It was a structured behavioural group consisting of 15 1–2-hour sessions and a 4-month follow-up and we tried to balance the membership as much as possible as an aid to integration. The main criteria for selection were that members were sexually active but not married, or involved in a long-term committed relationship, and that they were between 18 and 45 years old. There were 5 men and 3 women in the group and their presenting problems included primary and secondary impotence, premature ejaculation, inhibited sexual arousal, vaginismus, and primary anorgasmia.

The treatment period involved two distinct but progressive stages. First, each patient was seen individually by both therapists for three sessions during which treatment was initiated in the form of relaxation and self-focusing exercises. These sessions enabled us more thoroughly to diagnose each patient's unique problem and its associated factors and to facilitate the process of group self-disclosure for each member with the prior development of a relationship with the male and female therapists.

The second stage of treatment consisted of 15 group sessions in which a structured programme was applied. The first session was introductory and group members got to know each other and became acquainted in a very general way with each other's problems. An exercise followed in which they anonymously expressed their hopes and fears about the group, followed by a general discussion. The rest of the meetings were divided in the following way:

There were four educational sessions including the use of slides depicting the male and female sexual anatomy and the Masters and Johnson stages of arousal, and films explaining the aetiology and treatment of sexual dysfunction and depicting a couple moving from foreplay and arousal to intercourse. These sessions triggered discussions of members' confusion or anxiety about the appearance and functioning of their own bodies. The films were unanimously perceived as clinical and off-putting, but fostered discussions of the necessity of tenderness and communication during love-making as opposed to the somewhat mechanistic display of sex on the screen. This exposure facilitated the process of desensitization and permission-giving, which we saw as integral parts of the educational phase of treatment. Four social skills training sessions focused on non-verbal and verbal communication, assertiveness, and heterosexual interaction and involved warm-up exercises in the sessions, role-plays, and homework tasks. Members reported that role-playing difficult social situations with members of the opposite sex was invaluable to them. In addition, during these sessions opposite sex feedback offered members useful insight about the incongruity between their feelings and behaviour during heterosexual interactions. Six sessions were devoted to general discussion of individual problems and of issues associated with them. Members were asked to read Zilbergeld's *Men and Sex* (1978) and Barbach's *For Yourself* (1976) in preparation for discussions about sexual myths, incorporated into these sessions.

The results of this group were good in terms of improvement in the level of sexual functioning, associated factors (performance anxiety, poor self-image), and social and sexual satisfaction. At the four-month follow-up assessment, 75 per cent of the group as a whole had improved on the basis of our objective measure (Golombok and Rust, 1983) and 88 per cent had improved on the basis of subjective self-reports.

The application of sex therapy in mixed-sex groups has been only minimally explored and we strongly feel that it holds great potential for future research and treatment.

INDICATIONS FOR SEX THERAPY IN GROUPS

The group treatment of sexual problems appears to have certain advantages over individual treatment for couples and for men and women who are single or whose partners refuse to participate in therapy. First, the scope of treatment is broadened with the ability to incorporate methods such as sex education, social-skills training, sex therapy, role-playing, and self-disclosure into a group situation which, in turn, provides a sense of support and encouragement for its members. The discovery that a problem is shared and that one's difficulties have been experienced by others helps to normalize an individual's self-perception and reduce feelings of inadequacy. Comfort and confidence are gained from the knowledge that a problem is acceptable to other group members. Advice, information, and feedback come from peers as well as from therapists, offering a wider frame of reference for individual growth and change. Same and opposite-sex peer interpretations can be very powerful, as can same-sex identification.

The presence of other couples or individuals can also promote a modelling effect. Some group members are likely to follow the lead of others to embark on new techniques of self-stimulation or perhaps, to disclose information which may be particularly painful or embarrassing to recall. One member's reluctance to carry out weekly exercises, for example, may be influenced by another's enthusiasm and determination to do them in an effort to learn, improve, and experience positive sexual feelings. The effect of modelling is particularly apparent during role-playing and behaviour rehearsal. Therapists can initially act-out specific role-plays for the group to introduce the behaviours involved and set an example for members of how to approach this, often very frightening task. Couples can model alternative interactions for other couples. Dysfunctional and constructive behaviours of group members can be alternately mirrored or reproduced by other members as a means of clarifying and identifying the different behaviour types and developing new interactive strategies.

Another advantage of a group is that the presence of other members can act as an anxiety reducer, rather than a stimulus for anxiety. Couples or individuals may feel less pressured since the therapists cannot focus solely on them. The group situation may be comparable to a classroom experience, participation in a club or organization or some other group experience in which the individual could integrate into an existing structure without submitting to direct, constant attention. The process of desensitization is greatly facilitated, as the exposure to threatening sexual material (films, slides) is more acceptable when the individual's feelings and reactions are not being singularly monitored and anxiety can be diffused throughout the group.

Structured group discussion can provide a forum in which long-held beliefs in sexual myths are explored and perhaps rejected and substituted with healthier views about sexuality. The presence of group members also tends to promote rapid attitude change.

An advantage of group treatment specific to couples is that group members may help to reconcile initially divergent accounts of crisis situations. If a husband reports his version of an event, his wife's account of the very same event may be quite different, leading to applied pressure on the couple from the group to establish one realistic and cohesive shared view to which all can subscribe.

The opportunity to offer social-skills training as part of a sex therapy group is invaluable for the treatment of individuals. The therapist can actually sit back and observe the individual functioning within a dynamic social system. In addition to the therapists' support, empathy and endorsement of the socially dysfunctional individual, they are able to make a more considered behavioural diagnosis and establish which behaviours preclude him or her from forming relationships.

In our experience with sex therapy groups in which single men and women are treated together, we observed two further advantages of this type of group treatment. For women and men without partners, the group offers a safe and structured forum for an exchange of ideas about sexuality in general and about particular sexual problems. The balance of male/female ideas offers a realistic model as a guide to heterosexual communication and this type of group can build a foundation from which the individual can learn to develop a healthy sexual relationship with a partner. An additional outcome is that the group seems to mobilize its members to identify and act on sources of dissatisfaction in their lives. Taking advantage of the support structure available to them, group members risk making changes in their social, sexual, or personal lifestyles which were formerly inconceivable to them.

Finally, the view that group treatment of sexual dysfunction is an economical approach has been suggested, in that it can be less expensive for the client and less time-consuming for the therapist, although this view has not been empirically supported. While this may be the case, it is also true in our experience that the preparation and management of groups is, overall, more energy-consuming for the therapists.

CONTRAINDICATIONS FOR SEX THERAPY IN GROUPS

Although the group treatment of sexual problems is a powerful and effective mode of treatment, there are some problem issues which must be considered in association with it.

The process of self-disclosure can be frightening and difficult for most and there is often reluctance on the part of group members to expose themselves in this way. Many individuals have not discussed their sexual problems with family or close friends and feel isolated and alone in their efforts to disguise, deny, or avoid it. They may fear a breach of confidentiality from within the group, embarrassment, humiliation, or rejection.

The element of competition is an unavoidable aspect of group interaction. One member's goal may be to reach an orgasm. Another's may be to learn to enjoy sexual contact with a partner, and yet another's may be the reduction of anxiety associated with any heterosexual contact and the desire to begin to learn to experience sexual feelings. These qualitative differences can promote fears about the individual expectations of the group's members and their subsequent ability to meet those expectations. Competitive instincts also come into play when the rate of progress differs between group members, as it inevitably will. The fear of failure is prevalent in any form of sex therapy, but within the context of group treatment it is intensified. If an individual or couple 'fail' or do not achieve the goals that they aspire to achieve, they often perceive themselves as letting down not only spouse and/or therapist, but the entire group.

Because the therapists' focus is removed from the individual and diffused throughout the group, there is an increased likelihood of the problems of irregular attendance and dropping-out which can be very disruptive to the dynamics of the group.

A drawback of single sex group treatment is the lack of involvement of a group member's partner, if he or she has refused to attend sessions as part of the couple. This is especially true of the husbands of women attending a sex therapy group for women. Men may feel threatened or alienated by this approach and may consciously or unconsciously try to sabotage its effect or simply remain detached and unsupportive. A drawback of couples' group treatment is that there tends to be an emphasis on dyadic issues and entanglements resulting in a neglect of the problems of the individual as a unique and independent component of the pair. A spouse may use dyadic disputes as a defence against disclosing his or her own feelings, desires, and difficulties. Finally, a potential problem in mixed sex and couples' groups is the sexual attraction which may develop between group members as a result of the often erotic and intimate nature of the therapeutic situation.

FACTORS ASSOCIATED WITH OUTCOME

In a thorough review of the outcome literature of the group treatment of sexual dysfunction, Mills and Kilmann (1982) tentatively outline various relevant factors, noting the many methodological deficiencies in the existing data and suggesting the need for further controlled, empirical research.

In summary, the treatment of primary and secondary anorgasmia and secondary erectile dysfunction offers the most support for the group format. Couples' groups and same-sex groups generally promote comparable improvements. Although the efficacy of different treatment methods have not been sufficiently evaluated, we speculate that sex education and specific skills training may be more easily and efficiently accomplished in groups. By contrast, individual or conjoint formats may be more appropriate for the treatment of relationship or intrapersonal conflicts.

In studies comparing the therapeutic outcome of groups and individual sessions, the group treatment of sexual dysfunction appears more successful (Nemetz *et al.*, 1978; Golden *et al.*, 1978), although the identification of which patients will benefit from one or the other approach is not clear. Research suggests that younger women will derive greater treatment benefits from groups (Schneidman and McGuire, 1976) as will couples with a more positive marital adjustment (Leiblum *et al.*, 1976).

Self-disclosure, shared experience and group support and acceptance have been identified as therapeutic factors which contribute to group members' improvements in social and sexual functioning and in their positive evaluation of the group experience. Group process variables operative in general group psychotherapy (Bloch *et al.*, 1981) are consistent with these self-reports of group sex therapy.

CONCLUSION

There seems to be a general agreement amongst clinicians regarding the immense value that group therapy offers to the treatment of sexual disorders. In an area of knowledge in which scientific research seems to pose particularly difficult methodological problems, the objective assessment by field workers as well as objective empirical evaluation available, however limited, take paramount importance. Nevertheless, the search for new and more effective measurement instruments should remain in the forefront of the work done by both researchers and clinicians. As we have frequently indicated in this chapter, there are many questions that need careful consideration. Given that the investigation of these paradigms is both a lengthy and expensive business, attention must be drawn to the more relevant lines of inquiry. We believe that such lines are those related to therapeutic factors, and those trying to establish the technical elements which bring about better and more permanent therapeutic results.

REFERENCES

Barbach, L.G. (1974) Group treatment of pre-orgasmic women, *Journal of Sex and Marital Therapy*, Vol. 1, pp. 139–45.

Barbach, L.G. (1976) *For Yourself: The Fulfillment of Female Sexuality*, Signet, New York.

Barbach, L.G. and Flaherty, M. (1980) Group treatment of situationally orgasmic women, *Journal of Sex and Marital Therapy*, Vol. 6, pp. 19–29.

Birk, L. (1984) Combined concurrent-conjoint psychotherapy for couples: rationale and efficient new strategies, in C.C. Nadelson and D.C. Polonsky (eds) *Marriage and Divorce*, Guilford Press, New York.

Blakeney, P., Kinder, B.N., Creson, D., Powell, L.C. and Sutton, C. (1976) A short-term, intensive workshop approach for the treatment of human sexual inadequacy, *Journal of Sex and Marital Therapy*, Vol. 2, pp. 124–9.

Bloch, S. and Crouch, E. (1985) *Therapeutic Factors in Group Psychotherapy*, Oxford University Press, Oxford.

Bloch, S., Crouch, E. and Reibstein, J. (1981) Therapeutic factors in group psychotherapy, *Archives of General Psychiatry*, Vol. 38, pp. 519–26.

Chesney, A.P., Blakeney, P.E., Chan, F.A. and Coley, C.M. (1981) The impact of sex therapy on sexual behaviors and marital communication, *Journal of Sex and Marital Therapy*, Vol. 7, pp. 70–9.

Corsini, R. and Rosenberg, B. (1955) Mechanisms of group psychotherapy: process and dynamics, *Journal of Abnormal and Social Psychology*, Vol. 51, pp. 406–11.

Duddle, C.M. and Ingram, A. (1980) Treating sexual dysfunction in couples' groups, in R. Forleo and W. Pasini (eds) *Medical Sexology*, Elsevier, North Holland.

Ersner-Hershfield, R. and Kopel, S. (1979) Group treatment of pre-orgasmic women: evaluation of partner involvement and spacing of sessions, *Journal of Consulting and Clinical Psychology*, Vol. 47, pp. 750–9.

Gillan, P., Golombok, S. and Becker, P. (1980) NHS sex therapy groups for women, *British Journal of Sexual Medicine*, Vol. 11, pp. 210–2.

Golden, J.S., Price, S., Heinrich, A.G. and Lobitz, W.C. (1978) Group vs couple treatment of sexual dysfunctions, *Archives of Sexual Behavior*, Vol. 7, pp. 593–602.

Golombok, S. and Rust, J. (1983) *Golombok Rust Inventory of Sexual Satisfaction*, City Press, Glasgow.

Kaplan, H.S. (1974) *The New Sex Therapy*, Brunner/Mazel, New York.

Kaplan, H.S., Kohl, R.N., Pomeroy, W.B., Offit, A.K. and Hogan, B. (1974) Group treatment of premature ejaculation, *Archives of Sexual Behavior*, Vol. 3, pp. 443–52.

Kayata, L. and Szydlo, D. (1986) The treatment of psychosexual dysfunction in a mixed sex group: a new approach, *Sexual and Marital Therapy*, Vol. 1, pp. 7–17.

Kegel, A.H. (1952) Sexual function of the pubococcygeus muscle, *Western Journal of Surgery, Obstetrics and Gynaecology*, Vol. 60, pp. 521–4.

Kirkpatrick, C., McGovern, K. and LoPiccolo, J. (1977) Treatment of sexual dysfunction, in G. Harris (ed.) *The Group Treatment of Human Problems*, Grune & Stratton, New York.

Leiblum, S.R. and Ersner-Hershfield, R. (1977) Sexual enhancement groups for dysfunctional women: an evaluation, *Journal of Sex and Marital Therapy*, Vol. 3, pp. 139–52.

Leiblum, S.R. and Rosen, R.C. (1979) The weekend workshop for dysfunctional couples: assets and limitations, *Journal of Sex and Marital Therapy*, Vol. 5, pp. 57–69.

Leiblum, S.R., Rosen, R.C. and Pierce, D. (1976) Group treatment format: mixed sexual dysfunctions, *Archives of Sexual Behavior*, Vol. 5, pp. 313–22.

Levay, A.N. and Kagle, A. (1977) A study of treatment needs following sex therapy, *American Journal of Psychiatry*, Vol. 134, pp. 970–3.

Lobitz, W.C. and Baker, E.L. (1979) Group treatment of single males with erectile dysfunction, *Archives of Sexual Behavior*, Vol. 8, pp. 127–38.

LoPiccolo, J. and Lobitz, W.C. (1972) The role of masturbation in the treatment of orgasmic dysfunction, *Archives of Sexual Behavior*, Vol. 2, pp. 163–71.

Martin, P.A. (1983) Group psychotherapy with couples, in H. Kaplan and B. Sadock (eds) *Comprehensive Group Psychotherapy*, Williams and Wilkins, Baltimore.

Masters, N.H. and Johnson, V.E. (1970) *Human Sexual Inadequacy*, Churchill, London.

McGovern, K.P., Kirkpatrick, C.C. and LoPiccolo, J. (1976) A behavioral group treatment program for sexually dysfunctional couples, *Journal of Marital and Family Counseling*, Vol. 2, pp. 397–404.

Mills, K.H. and Kilmann, P.R. (1982) Group treatment of sexual dysfunctions: a methodological review of the outcome literature, *Journal of Sex and Marital Therapy*, Vol. 8, pp. 259–80.

Nemetz, G.H., Craig, K.D. and Reith, G. (1978) Treatment of female sexual dysfunction through symbolic modeling, *Journal of Consulting and Clinical Psychology*, Vol. 46, pp. 62–73.

Obler, M. (1973) Systematic desensitization in sexual disorders, *Journal of Behavior Therapy and Experimental Psychology*, Vol. 4, pp. 93–101.

Price, S., Reynolds, B.S., Cohen, B.D., Anderson, A.J. and Schochet, B.V. (1981) Group treatment of erectile dysfunction for men without partners: a controlled evaluation, *Archives of Sexual Behavior*, Vol. 10, pp. 253–68.

Reynolds, B.S., Cohen, B.D., Schochet, B.V., Price, S.C. and Anderson, A.J. (1981) Dating skills training in the group treatment of erectile dysfunction for men without partners, *Journal of Sex and Marital Therapy*, Vol. 7, pp. 184–94.

Sansbury, D.L. (1977) Behavioral group techniques and group process issues, in G. Harris (ed.) *The Group Treatment of Human Problems*, Grune & Stratton, New York.

Schneidman, B. and McGuire, L. (1976) Group therapy for nonorgasmic women: two age levels, *Archives of Sexual Behavior*, Vol. 5, pp. 239–48.

Woody, R. (1973) Integrated aversion therapy and psychotherapy, two sexual deviation case studies, *Journal of Sex Research*, Vol. 9, pp. 313–24.

Yalom, I.D. (1975) *The Theory and Practice of Group Psychotherapy*, Basic Books, New York.

Yates, A.J. (1983) Behaviour therapy and psychodynamic psychotherapy: basic conflict or reconciliation and integration, *British Journal of Clinical Psychology*, Vol. 22, pp. 107–25.

Zeiss, R.A., Christensen, A. and Levine, A.G. (1978) Treatment for premature ejaculation through male-only groups, *Journal of Sex and Marital Therapy*, Vol. 4, pp. 139–43.

Zilbergeld, B. (1975) Group treatment of sexual dysfunction in men without partners, *Journal of Sex and Marital Therapy*, Vol. 1, pp. 204–14.

Zilbergeld, B. (1978) *Men and Sex*, Little, Brown & Co., Boston.

CHAPTER 10

FROM SEXUAL PROBLEMS TO MARITAL ISSUES

Eddy Street and Jean Smith

It is perhaps surprising that something so central to marriage as sexual activity should warrant its own 'therapy' distinct from marital therapy. In the early years of psychotherapeutic endeavour marital and sexual dysfunction were both treated within the sphere of the then traditional psychodynamic approach. However, the theories of Freud and his contemporaries were developed at a time when knowledge of the physiology of the sexual response was exceptionally scant; therefore these theories have been found wanting in several respects. The important breakthrough in the treatment of sexual dysfunction marked by Masters and Johnson's work (1970) was heralded by a growing understanding of the physiology of the sexual response. This 'sex therapy' in opposition to psychodynamic formulations was heavily based on behavioural treatment principles.

Since the pioneering work of Masters and Johnson other authors, notably Kaplan (1974), have developed a model for sex therapy. Heiman *et al.* (1981) noted that whereas these models differ in the degree to which behavioural terminology is used they all include similar broad-based behavioural programmes which involve the reduction of performance anxiety, sex education, and skills training in both sexual techniques and communication. Heiman and her colleagues state that what is regarded as sex therapy can be 'conceptualized as a type of cognitive behavioral therapy applied to couples with sexual problems'. That such a definition is offered illustrates the extent to which 'sex therapy' is separated from the range of models and techniques that are applied to marital problems (see Dryden, 1985). Thus an arbitrary divide continues between the treatment of sexual and marital problems which reflects the development of knowledge rather than the actuality of the problems themselves.

Clinical experience strongly suggests that the division between marital and sexual problems is not straightforward and that there is an interrelationship between sexual and marital needs to which the therapist must attend. As Polonsky and Nadelson (1982) comment, couples often present with a sexual problem only for a marital difficulty to emerge; similarly couples who present with marital problems often have associated sexual difficulties which require attention. As couples can and do present with several difficulties, the therapist needs to be able to adopt a flexible multifocal approach. In this chapter we intend to present a model which attempts to integrate the marital and sexual dimensions into an overall framework based on the view of marriage as an open system. In our work we find this model based as it is on how the couple relate to each other interactionally allows us to deal with a variety of problems simultaneously. It is a model which stresses the way in which a couple construct their intimate relationship and deals with the manner in which sexual activity is incorporated into this relationship. It is a framework which allows us to move from the sexual dysfunction as presented to the core issues that affect the relationship at a particular point in time.

INTIMACY IN MARRIAGE

Given the multitude of problems that beset any marriage one wonders why individuals are attracted to such relationships which they hope will be permanent and stable. Clearly there is something about a marriage, whether legal or otherwise, that satisfies a fundamental need for people. It is simple to catalogue the types of need that can be met in a marriage, such as the need for love and security, the need for care and support, the need to offer these things to someone else and the need for parenthood.

However, it soon becomes apparent that each of us has a different definition of what constitutes love, security, care. Therefore the giving and receiving of these emotional commodities becomes dependent on our own particular definition of them, definitions which are part and parcel of our definition of ourselves, that is, our identity. The process of building and maintaining our identity leads us to form permanent relationships. Thus a substantial part of who we are is interpersonally based.

Psychologically, life can be viewed as the discovery and unfolding of our identity through the developmental cycle. It is as if we live whilst we ask the question 'Who am I?' The activities we undertake are used both to answer this question and to validate the answer we wish to adopt. Indeed, there is a continual shifting balance between the way we use our life's activity to demonstrate the identity we believe we have and the way we allow elements of our identity to be formed by the manner in which we deal with life's tasks. Paradoxically we require some sense of continuity and stability in our identity whilst dealing with new experiences and the changes that these tasks might entail. Issues which lie at the centre of this paradox and hence at the core of our identity are issues which are labelled as intimate – the way we view the love we offer and receive; how we arrange for ourselves to be cared for and comforted; the type of sexual person we feel ourselves to be. These are issues which we can only deal with adequately within the ongoing tasks of a relationship. Thus the idiosyncratic way in which we ask and answer the identity questions determines the type of intimate relationships that we construct. Intimacy and identity are therefore closely intertwined.

Individuals in a marriage behave in a way which feels comfortable for themselves and they hope and expect that their behaviour will mesh in with a comfortable identity for their partner. Thus, marriages are therefore reciprocally constructed for the benefit of each partner. It frequently happens however that the behaviour of one person does not fully synchronize with that of the partner and it is at these moments, when conflict potentially exists, that the partners need to be able to negotiate whether any changes should be made by either or both of them. Some changes may be quite easily accommodated within an individual sense of self but some may indeed be quite threatening to a person's identity and view of intimacy. Conflict concerning these issues is inherent in all relationships and a satisfactory outcome would be for the couple to negotiate, mutually agree and adopt a solution that was acceptable to them both. In this way the couple will have successfully dealt with the conflict that their intimacy brings. They will have tolerated some ambiguity in their own identity and willingly accepted some changes as a consequence of being in a relationship with a particular person. Less helpful solutions would be for the couple to tolerate unhappily the conflict area without any negotiation, to 'agree' to avoid the issue that was causing conflict or to argue permanently about the issue without any resolution. Whatever strategy the couple employ, their intimacy is affected for the nature of their interaction will change. Non-negotiation leads to the couple disengaging from each other in various areas of life, conflict-avoidance leads to a false closeness in which only 'positive' views are allowed and non-resolution of conflict leads to intimacy that is dominated by anger and hostility. This type of situation has been well described by Feldman (1976) in relation to depression in marriage.

The strategies a couple adopt in dealing with their conflict have an important message for each individual in their search for identity. The 'answers' to the identity questions that are provided in the relationship may not immediately correspond with the view that an individual has of himself or herself. 'You are someone who does not care for people,' 'You are someone who looks for problems – aren't you happy?' 'You are someone who gets angry about the wrong things' are the kinds of statements which arise from conflict and which can threaten the sense of wholeness and security that the self requires. If such statements were 'not true', the individual would confidently dismiss them as being irrelevant to the question 'Who am I?' However, usually in our intimate relationships our partner has the ability to make statements about ourselves which we hope are not accurate but which we fear just might be. As the issue of 'Who am I?' is never satisfactorily resolved there always remains a grey area, where we are uncertain of what we are truly like and of how we behave.

It is in this area that we suffer the human anguish of fearing the worst about ourselves. These areas constitute just as much a part of who we are as those of which we are quite certain. Consequently we do not just select partners who validate that bit of ourselves of which we are certain, we select partners who at the same time validate that bit of which we are uncertain. It is this uncertain area of our identity in which it feels risky to take a chance to discover our 'true selves'; therefore we all regulate the type of intimacy that we allow in order to prevent ourselves from entering this 'risky' area too often. An example of this distance regulation would be someone who fears that his or her answer is not acceptable, choosing to relate to a partner who blocks off every time anger is expressed. We regulate distance in this way so that we need not interactively confront a potentially difficult issue about ourselves.

To cope with the natural stresses inherent in reciprocal relationship all couples develop their own repertoire of distance regulators. There are three basic ways of regulating this intimate distance: first, the establishment of emotional 'no go' areas in which the messages not to enter are very clearly specified and which if broken lead to periods of virtual non-interaction; second, limiting the amount of time during which intimacy can occur, for example, by working long hours; finally, by involving a third person in their interactions: this is known as *triangulation* and serves the purpose of limiting the potential intimate reaction of a dyad. On some occasions one or the other partner will attempt to ignore the distance regulator as an attempt to reach some solution to a problem that the relationship brings. It is at this time that we as part of a couple can enter into the 'grey' area of identity and allow for a development and a growth of ourselves and our relationship to occur.

It is clear that even though distance regulators are used it does not mean that the difficult issues disappear for the areas of concern we have about ourselves and our partners are always operating as undercurrents. The practical tasks of life, by their continual nature are constantly available as distance regulators. These tasks and their attendant problems can therefore become areas in which intimacy and hence identity issues are played out. For example, how we set about the task of feeding ourselves is at some level a statement about how we wish to give and receive nurturance: any argument between a couple about who should prepare the meal at the end of the day is just as much about how two individuals will care for each other as it is about cooking. If one person is feeling uncared for he or she may well, in these circumstances, 'choose' to solve the problem by arguing about the cooking arrangements. There is therefore a continuing interaction between the ordinary tasks of married life and fundamental intimacy issues.

When ongoing these intimacy issues most easily find expression in and interfere with the meeting of sexual needs, for the uncertainties of simply discovering one's identity as a man or woman are often masked by the ambiguities of fulfilling oneself sexually. Kopp (1972) addressed himself to several reasons as to why sex becomes the arena that attracts other problems more readily to it:

1. Sexual longings are to some extent instinctual and therefore dependable. Since they can be reliably expected to occur in everyone, this makes it an area which everyone knows exists and which hence can be exploited for whatever ends.
2. Although instinctual, sexuality is unlike hunger and thirst as it is not a life-dependent need and as such is capable of being turned 'on' and 'off'. Sexual needs do not necessitate satiation for life to continue and are therefore more manipulable than other needs.
3. Sexuality is the only instinctually based need that is interpersonal, therefore issues to do with personal relationships are easily attracted to it. This is particularly so about struggles to do with the polarities of relationships, dominance and submission, parenting and dependency, power and helplessness, persecuting and playing victim.
4. An individual's sexuality is very vulnerable to shifts of mood, attitude and behaviour in either partner. Men and women are so easily 'turned on' and 'turned off' by a gesture, a word, a facial expression that sexual interplay becomes a most tempting battleground on which to carry on the nuances of unresolved longings and resentments.

The conduct of the sexual relationship therefore readily reflects the way a couple deal with their intimacy and identity issues. Throughout marriage however the sexual relationship has to be placed in context of the developmental issues that face the couple.

Developmental stages of marriage

Within the marital relationship, as indeed within all relationships, there is an ongoing process of development, that is, a marital life cycle. In the normal cycle of a couple's development it is therefore possible to identify particular developmental stages and their respective marital tasks to which the couple will have to attend.

Table 10.1 Developmental phases and tasks in marriage

Developmental phase	*Marital task*	*Sexual task*
Courtship and marriage		
Balancing the merging process of loving with the maintenance of separate identity	Begin to negotiate life together	Honeymoon period Exploratory phase gaining knowledge of partner's sexuality
Young adulthood parenting		
Accept dependency of self and others Accept roles that family life brings Rely on help of others including extended family	Redefinition of closeness Acceptance of third individual Support for carer	Recognition of dual role of sex: 1. reproduction 2. expression of feelings Finding 'a place' for sexuality within a family context
Early mid-life		
Reappraisal of own power and status Creating self roles other than sex and work roles Awareness of mortality	Negotiate end of child-rearing Deal with change in maternal role Renegotiate separateness and togetherness Support during periods of crisis and doubt that mid-life brings Review notion of marriage	Dealing with reverberations of children's emerging sexuality End of reproduction function of sex Maintain sexuality within the context of the re-establishment of the couple relationship
Late mid-life		
Acceptance of achievements and plateau of achievements Continuing development of spiritual and cultural interests	Preparation for closeness that retirement will bring	Continuing sexual intimacy
Retirement		
Acceptance of loss of work roles Evaluation of life successes and failures	Accept changing nature of dependency Accept new roles that retirement brings	Accepting changing nature of sexual relationship in response to physical changes
Old age		
Acceptance of dependency Acceptance of infirmity and death	Accept future loss of partner	

Source Adapted from Street, 1985.

In Table 10.1 (adapted from Street, 1985), six developmental phases with their specific sexual elements are identified in the life cycle of a couple: courtship and marriage, young adulthood and parenting, early mid-life, late mid-life, retirement, and old age. The central marital tasks relating to each of these phases are also identified. These tasks are not problems to the couple, but are rather experiences to be enjoyed.

Most couples will pass through such a six-stage life cycle with the attendant marital tasks but for a substantial number the marital tasks may be atypical due to a variety of life events, i.e. the absence of children, second marriages or the early death of a partner.

Of particular interest to us is the nature of the development and growth that takes place between a married couple and also the difficulties they experience. Pursuing a developmental perspective, we should be able to identify how certain problems are relative to different aspects of the life cycle and have the potential to become the focus for conflict.

Problems confronting couples in their marital relations are mirrored in their sexual interactions and vice versa. It is therefore essential that any presenting sexual problem is placed within the appropriate developmental phase of the relationship in order to identify the issues that are currently important for the couple.

INTERACTION IN MARRIAGE

As the tasks of marriage change within the context of daily life, every couple is faced with organizing themselves so that their emotional and physical needs are met. Couples therefore require rules of behaviour so that this organizing task can be met and hence their identities mutually reinforced. These rules prescribe certain sequences of interaction and every couple rapidly acquires a set of interactional sequences that describes their intimacy and which will include the distance regulators that they use. It is usually found that particular repeated tasks have particular repeated sequences, so the way the pair set about making the gravy, cleaning the car, deciding where to go on holiday, talking about the in-laws will be characterized by similar interactional patterns. In each of these situations, the rules will be quite specific, so that the couple will know who is to perform what task, and who is to behave in a certain way, one element of interaction leads naturally to another.

Typically each sequence is circular in terms of its overall pattern and the couple form a human system in which the interactions are quite prescribed, and the degree of permissible intimacy clearly stated. 'I am the person who takes domestic responsibility.' 'I am the person who it is dangerous to make angry.' 'I am the person who becomes depressed.' One partner makes these statements and the other, by virtue of his or her behaviour, agrees: 'Yes, you are the person who it is dangerous to make angry,' resulting in a mutual reinforcement of identities. Hence, as Haley (1976) has noted, behaviour means more than just itself for there is always a metaphorical meaning embedded in any interaction, a meaning about identity as well as about the relationship. Each marriage is therefore an amalgam of particular interactions and the specific meanings they contain.

As the 'couple' interact in their characteristic styles and offer consistent support for notions about themselves, life events can easily unbalance the desired equilibrium; for example, sometimes the dinner-maker cannot get home early enough, a sickness in an in-law requires a different visiting pattern, or a change in financial circumstances requires an adjustment. In these circumstances the couple will have to be flexible about their rules of interaction for some changes of behaviour will be required. A couple demonstrating this flexibility indicate that their respective ideas about their identities are not so fixed or uncertain that they lose some sense of who they are in changing their behaviour. Indeed, as previously noted, it is in meeting these difficulties that face any relationship that our sense of self is enhanced.

For example, a man might discover that he can take on part of the home-maker role without losing any masculinity and reciprocally the woman can encompass that part of her potential which can be met when not being the home-maker. On such occasions the partners need to be willing to allow the development of new aspects of their identities to seek a solution. This may feel to the individual to be something of a risk. The nature of their intimacy therefore needs to be such that they can tolerate uncertainty and ambiguity in themselves and their partner whilst the change of behaviour is occurring.

Couples encountering difficulties face problems in another way for research has demonstrated that they do not interact with flexibility. Gottman (1979) shows that distressed couples demonstrate more structure and patterning in their interactions than non-distressed couples do. With marital distress therefore there are likely to be fewer interactive patterns over a variety of tasks. Clearly this is because the rules of interaction become rigid as there is fear of entering into an intimacy area that potentially provides messages that a partner is unable or unwilling to cope with. Couples consequently protect themselves and each other by limiting the area of ambiguity in their intimacy. Paradoxically, not only do they protect each other but, because of the overly repeated nature of the interaction, they distress each other by overemphasizing the negative views that they secretly hold about their own individuality. Each relationship must deal interactively with this type of distress, for growth only develops through confronting negative self-images we hold; however, in relationships which have a great deal of distress, it would seem as if the couple are locked into a set of interactions which constantly reinforce the negative elements of identity. Consequently, gravy-making, car-cleaning and holiday decision-making all follow similar patterns which were designed to protect but which ultimately distress both partners.

SEXUAL INTERACTION

The sexual context is no different from any other context found within marriage. The healthier the relationship is the more likely the interactive pattern will be specific to the couple's sexuality. The interaction around sex can however be conceived at two levels. First, there is the interaction that is to do with the sex act itself. This will be different for each couple and will tend to follow a prescribed pattern from the initiation to the preliminaries, to the act of intercourse and to the immediate postcoital period. Each couple will also have its rules allowing for this pattern to be changed. Consequently there will be important behavioural signals which allow for a change of initiator, of the location and time of the intercourse and of other elements in the behavioural chain.

The second level of sexual interaction involves the way in which the sex act is embedded in other elements of a couple's behaviour. For example, sexual activity is dependent on certain mood states and the couple may have sequences of interaction which either increase or decrease the likelihood of intercourse occurring.

Following an argument some couples may typically only have sex as part of the 'making up' process. While one couple may avoid arguments to maintain their sexual activity, another couple may have an argument in order to get near to the intimate situation that brings sex with it. This level of interactional sequences also includes those interactions that revolve around the saying of 'no'. The way the couple deal with the sexual refusal will be habitual. So returning to the preceding example, 'no' by the first couple may indicate that not enough time has lapsed or distance maintained before sex is initiated – the 'no' being part of the negotiating process of how close the couple are. With the second couple 'no' could in fact start a process of resentment and punishment that leads to argument elsewhere, which then has sex as a consequence. Here 'no' becomes a necessary preliminary to the sexual 'yes'. For many couples the 'no' may indicate that another type of intimate behaviour can and should occur and the individuals will respond accordingly. A couple's sexual behaviour is therefore composed interactively of more than merely the elements of the sex act and it needs to be viewed as such.

As sexuality can easily attract to it problems from other areas of the relationship, the interactive pattern of the couple's sexual behaviour can

Figure 10.1 A circular pattern of interaction in marriage

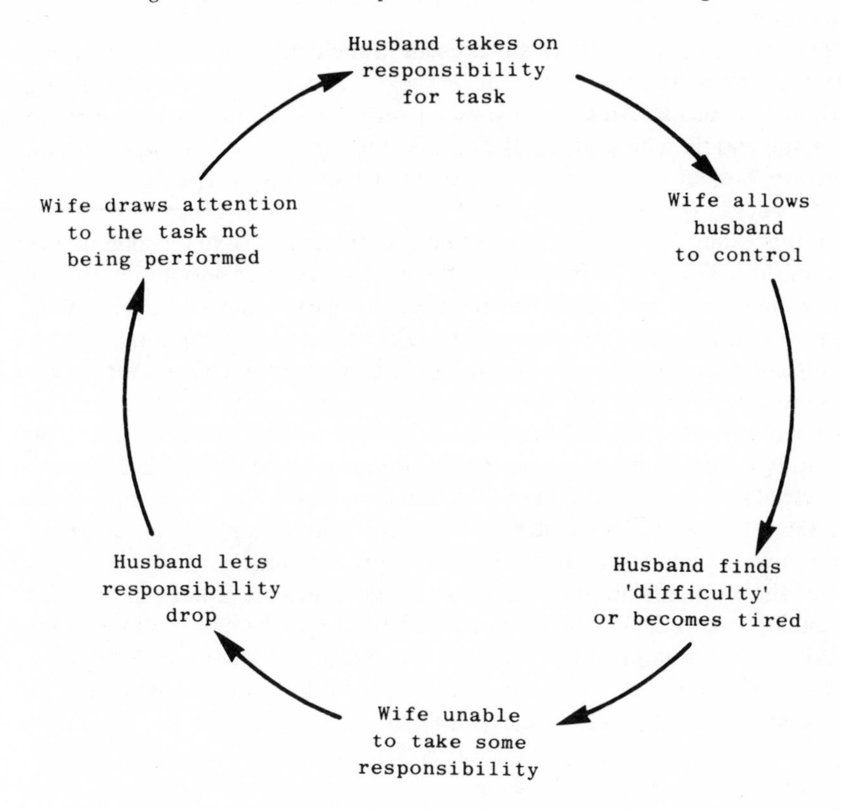

very easily mirror a pattern from an area in which the couple experience some distress. Such a mirroring can occur either in the couple's general way of dealing with sexuality or in their sexual activity. Typically these patterns are communications which have core implications for how the couple view themselves both as individuals and in terms of the relationship. This is due to the strength that sexuality has in the construction of identity and relationships. For distressed couples sexual problems are therefore linked to other areas in which there are problems of intimacy and hence identity. For example, in a couple whose sexual activity is variable and always dependent on the man's initiative, a similar circular pattern of intensity and lethargy may be identified in their dealings with social contacts or in the way they attempt to solve financial problems. In such an interactive pattern the woman typically views herself as someone who has no right or ability to initiate something successfully while the man views himself as someone who is in charge but who cannot sustain this role. Paradoxically therefore both behave towards each other in a way that reinforces the negative aspects of their identities.

This pattern (Figure 10.1) was present in the couple's sexual behaviour. The man would lose his erection during sexual activity and would stop being involved in the activity, the woman would indicate that she wished to continue and then he would make an effort to try to 'make himself' have an erection. Similarly this pattern was repeated in the way the couple dealt with the frequency of their sexual activity.

In this example it is no surprise that the presenting sexual problem was that of difficulties with erection; for the man's statement about himself was 'I'm a man, but I can't sustain it.' It is here that we see that a sexual problem carries with it typical messages that make important metaphorical statements about how the couple view their identity. As interaction is reciprocal and circular each message carried by it is guaranteed by the behaviour of both partners and so for the man his behaviour implied the statement 'I'm not fully a man,' and his wife's contribution to the difficulty implied the message 'You're not fully a man.' Similarly the man's behaviour implied the message 'You won't let me be a man' and the woman implied the statement 'I don't want you to be a man.' Similarly there are messages and statements about the woman's ability to initiate, support and assist her partner, for example, 'I am unable to take control.' Therefore each element of the interaction is both a statement by each partner and a message to each partner.

In psychological terms the typical messages/statements associated with the usual sexual difficulties are as follows:

Premature Ejaculation
Male: 'I want this (intimacy) over as quickly as possible.'
'I want to be strong – but not for too long.'
'I'm not in control.'
Female: 'You're okay and then things go suddenly wrong.'
'I want this over as quickly as possible.'

Retarded Ejaculation
Male: 'I'm not going to give you all of me.'
'You're not allowing me to really let myself go.'
'I'm afraid of enjoying myself.'
Female: 'Keep trying – but you'll never make it.'
'I don't want the bit that can become messy.'

Erectile Difficulties
Male: 'I'm not man enough.'
'You don't interest me.'
'Strength and control frighten me.'

Female: 'I'm the strong one.'
'Strength and control frighten me.'
'You can't be man enough.'

Vaginismus
Female: 'I don't want to be intimate with you.'
'You hurt me.'
'Perhaps just a little – not too much.'
Male: 'You're too fragile to touch.'
'You don't want to be intimate with me.'

Non-Orgasmic
Female: 'You don't do things right – try harder.'
'I'm not going to let go with you.'
'Come and get me – you missed.'
Male: 'I can't get it right.'
'You won't let go with me.'

Lack of Desire
Female and Male: 'Keep your distance.'
'You don't interest me.'
'I've given up.'

Typically the couple focus psychologically on the messages about the partner who is labelled as possessing the problems. Thus within the terms of the preceding examples the message and statement reported were 'You're not fully a man' and 'I'm not fully a man.' This couple were struggling with the sharing of responsibility and control and both privately fearing that they did not possess the necessary characteristics to allow for this sharing without losing some sense of self. Even though this was the difficulty for both they 'agree' that one partner would experience the identity issue more openly than the other, in this case the male. Bowen (1978) has noted that couples share between them the strength of self that they jointly possess. They do this to allow one of them to function more ably in the world than the other would alone, whilst the other experiences some distress. This unbalanced view of themselves is the one that is presented clinically with the focus on the sexual issue.

The therapeutic task

If, as has been argued, sexual problems provide the representation of other marital problems, the central therapeutic task therefore is to cast the presenting sexual difficulty into the context of problem-solving as a marital issue, thereby providing a link between the sexual problems and the ways in which the couple attempt to solve the intimacy problems that confront them. This will be linked to the couple's construction of their intimacy.

To begin this therapeutic task therefore three aspects of the couple's relationship require assessment:

To assess the nature of the developmental issues for the couple. This will require an awareness of the stage of the pair in their marital life cycle. Some couples will fit very well into the typical cycle, in that they will be of the appropriate age and have passed through earlier stages. However, many couples will be atypical, in that there may have been loss of previous partners, in-laws may live with them, illness may have caused some changes. The serendipitous ways that alter people's lives are numerous, and such events can and will have a major effect on the nature of the developmental task that faces a couple. This assessment then will provide the therapist with the general context in which the couple's problem exists.

To assess the typical marital interactive patterns. For this the therapist needs to question the couple about the way that they solve the ordinary problems of life. The way that a couple interact when one or the other of them is upset or angry will be particularly relevant. It is surprising how well couples are able to describe in minute detail the various steps that they go through concerning a particular issue. As one might expect, however, the meanings that the couples have ascribed to their interactions will not be adequate for them to solve their difficulty.

To assess the nature of the intimacy problem for the couple. Here the therapist is looking for the emotional issue – nurturance, control, anger – that the couple have difficulty in dealing with in the context of their intimacy and the therapist will be keen to establish the means by which the couple regulate this intimacy. Time, distance, busy-ness, triangulation, all could be possible distance maintainers. Thus, it is in assessing the intimacy problem, that the first links between this and the sexual problem will be made.

This model of acquiring information about marital/sexual dysfunction does not prescribe a certain method of work with the marital pair. If the links are made between the sexual problem and the general marital interaction then it is possible to follow a number of schools of marital therapy (cf. Dryden, 1985). Neither does this model preclude the use of the usual techniques for dealing with specific sexual problems; indeed it is an integral part of the approach. In our own work we rest very heavily on the behavioural techniques established by Masters and Johnson (1970). In using these techniques we are then able to offer a secure base from which the couple can deal with their sexual intimacy and from which they can develop problem-solving strategies that may be appropriate elsewhere. The means by which this is established is by linking the message from the intervention technique to other areas of the couple's intimacy. As this approach does depend on this continual linkage, typical problems with couples do tend to emerge and these will be dealt with in the next section.

Triangulation as a therapeutic issue

As has already been noted, triangulation is a common means by which a couple regulate their intimacy. In marital therapy, the couple, for healthy reasons, enter into a triadic relationship with the therapist because of the difficulties they are encountering dyadically. Marital therapy can, in fact, be characterized as the efforts of therapists to de-triangulate themselves so that the couple can enjoy their dyadic intimacy. Not uncommonly it is found that the couple have triangulated with another family member; usually one of their parents but sometimes with a child or even a pet. Indeed, some theorists would argue that a couple experiencing intimacy problems are always triangulated with their family of origin as they have not separated at a psychological level (Bowen, 1978) and the therapist with leanings towards family and historical ways of dealing with individuals will take cognizance of this. Under these circumstances the therapist will attempt to move to the marital issues through the family issue. With regard to the triangulated child the necessary therapeutic strategy has been described elsewhere (Street, 1985).

Regardless of the nature of the intrafamilial triangulation, the couple who present with a sexual difficulty will often attempt to triangulate with the therapist in order to diminish the potency of therapy. The unconscious aim of the couple is to undermine the therapist's strategies so that they do not have to enter into areas that they perceive as threatening. There are two broad ways that this issue can be tackled. First, the therapist by displaying genuineness and empathy with perhaps some interpretation can attempt to lessen the perceived threat. Second, by creating a safe environment the therapist can begin to explore the fears that led the couple into triangulation strategically. The latter is the approach favoured by ourselves as it tackles the issue immediately as an interactive one, and thus leads all individuals to an appropriate context for change.

There would seem to be two typical ways that couples set about triangulating the therapist. In the first, the couple agree that one of them is the problem and then, when the marital issue arises, both partners indicate that they believe the therapist is dealing with the wrong issue. 'It's nothing to do with our marriage, I'm the problem, just help me have sex properly,' are the usual comments made under these circumstances. More often than not the partner 'with the problem' attempts to enter into conflict with the therapist about the course of therapy and he or she is quietly but nevertheless ably supported by the other partner. The nature of this triangulation is that the couple would prefer to have one member in open conflict with the therapist, rather than deal with the potential conflict between themselves.

In the other type of triangulation the couple tentatively agree about the links that have been made but then jointly criticize the therapist for going either too fast or too slow. Here the couple construct an agreement in order that they can form a coalition against the therapist; in both of these manoeuvres the aim is to transfer the focus of conflict from the couple onto a relationship that involves the therapist. When the therapist is offered either of these triangulations, the 'logical' solution would appear to be to explain to the couple the 'therapist's view'. All too easily therapists can then find themselves justifying everything that is being done to such an extent that nothing gets done! Naturally this course of 'logical' action does nothing but delay the implementation of therapeutic strategies.

The manner of dealing with these problems is to keep the interactive nature of the marriage firmly in the foreground, for the interactive framework ultimately is the context for dealing with all issues between the couple. This is primarily done by utilizing simple behavioural tasks linked to a general contract. Prior to using any tasks the therapist should agree with the couple that no task will be given without prior agreement of all parties. These tasks may vary depending upon the nature of a couple's difficulty and the stage of therapy. They may, for example, involve the keeping of private diaries of sexual activity or may involve the agreeing of a couple to pursue a behavioural, Masters and Johnson task, such as sensate focus. In some cases the tasks set may not be sexual in nature, for example, going out for an evening together, or even spending time apart. By this means the therapist attempts to set an actual problem for them to solve, and one that should just encompass their notions of safety.

The interactive way that the couple either completes, fails or agrees to postpone a task then becomes grist to the therapeutic mill. So, for example, should a couple agree to embark on sensate focus and then at the following appointment report that they have not done it because therapy is 'going too fast', the therapist can remind them of the contract and investigate how the task broke down, and how they agreed things were going too fast. Additionally they can then be asked to discuss between themselves what the appropriate speed should be. Consequently, the therapist then has further information about their interaction as well as a theme which they can then discuss in therapy. Now they have been given an intimate problem to solve rather than them being allowed to focus on how therapy can be better. It is under these conditions that the couple are likely to produce interactive sequences typical for themselves.

By encouraging their dyadic discussion the therapist can then make whatever intervention seems appropriate to their dysfunctional sequences. Our own approach is to point out the nature of the interaction and then relate this metaphorically to the dysfunction around the sexual interaction. Thus there is a constant oscillation between sexual and general themes which the interactive framework allows, and which it is hoped leads to change.

CASE STUDY

Mr and Mrs S were referred by their general practitioner with a request for help with sexual problems within their marriage. For both partners this was their second marriage. Their family comprised two adolescent children from Mrs S's first marriage, and two young children from this second marriage. Mr S had an adolescent daughter who lived with his first wife.

In terms of their age this couple developmentally should be in the Early Mid-Life Phase (see Table 10.1), but in marital terms they were in the Young Adulthood Parenting Phase. It was possible therefore to hypothesize that Mr and Mrs S would be experiencing problems in balancing the different tasks of these two stages. Indeed these were topics during therapy, particularly relating to how the couple wished to spend their intimate time.

With respect to their sexual difficulties, Mrs S presented saying that she had never achieved orgasm, and that she was no longer interested in sex. This lack of libido was reported by both partners to have begun when they had re-entered into the Young Adult Phase with the birth of their two youngest children. Mrs S described herself as sexually ignorant, whereas her husband was portrayed as being very knowledgeable sexually.

In terms of the arguments put forward in this chapter it was possible therefore to consider the metaphorical statements that both partners were making, and to see how these related to the basic intimacy issue for them. The statement being made by Mrs S was 'I am in control, I am not going to let go.' While Mr S was saying 'I know how to do it – if you'll let me.' Therefore the basic intimacy issue seemed to hinge on 'control'. They both believed that only one person could be in control at any one time and they both agreed that it was Mrs S. Their sexual behaviour never got very far for Mrs S would say 'I am in control.' At the same time, in marital terms, she took or made decisions concerning the family and was responsible for the purse strings. Mr S had become depressed after he was unemployed and viewed himself as a 'capable worker, but nobody would give me the chance'. This statement was mirrored in the couple's sexual functioning. Mrs S's way of supporting her husband reinforced this view as she frequently took responsibility away from him.

In therapy the couple at the outset triangulated with the therapist by identifying Mrs S as the problem. Initially attempts were made to increase Mrs S's sexual knowledge and awareness. This was thwarted as she refused to engage in any self-examination and rejected the opportunity to increase her sexual knowledge. Therefore the system was being maintained. We changed this approach and attempted to redefine the problem in terms of their mutual responsibility to their interaction. This had been avoided initially as it might undermine Mr S's confidence. This was dealt with successfully by stressing the inadequacies of both. The intimacy issue then became 'If you feel inadequate, how can you help someone who feels the same?' For Mr S this meant a focus on the problems of unemployment, for Mrs S upon her sexuality. As we pursued the common inadequacy theme it became apparent that Mr S's 'expertise' was proved to be a myth. In this way then it was possible to redefine the sexual problem from the focus being Mrs S to a problem that the couple were experiencing.

This redefinition then enabled us to set the couple joint tasks and we moved on to sensate focus. Initially both refused complaining that we were going too fast, and the emphasis was again upon Mrs S having difficulties. The issue returned to control and letting go. At this stage they were given a marital task designed to give Mr S control over some aspects of their life and he set about sorting out the family's problems of rent arrears. Mrs S found it initially difficult to accept his taking responsibility for this activity but the task was successfully completed. Having completed this task which allowed for a rebalance of control, the couple began to have sexual intercourse once again. Shortly after this they left therapy, the orgasm issue not having been resolved. The therapist took this outcome as indicating that although some success had been achieved some intimacy issues remain unresolved between the couple.

CONCLUSION

In the introduction to this chapter we commented on the division that developed historically between sex therapy and marital therapy. Unfortunately this division has fostered an inappropriate separation of sexual difficulties from other aspects of the marital relationship. We have attempted to outline an approach not just to marriage but to relationships in general that incorporates sexual activity as a control element. This approach does deal not just with the problems identified by the relationship but with the relationship *per se*. As more couples seek help to resolve the dilemmas of their relationships and lives, therapists and counsellors will have need of a flexible approach to the difficulties presented to them. This chapter has presented a model which can provide a framework on which such flexibility can be based.

REFERENCES

Bowen, M. (1978) *Family Therapy in Clinical Practice*, Jason Aronson, New York.

Dryden, W. (ed.) (1985) *Marital Therapy in Britain, Vol. 1: Context and Therapeutic Approaches*, Harper & Row, London.

Feldman, L.B. (1976) Depression and marital interaction, *Family Process*, Vol. 15, pp. 389–95.

Gottman, J.M. (1979) *Marital Interaction: Experimental Investigations*, Academic Press, New York.

Haley, J. (1976) *Problem Solving Therapy*, Jossey-Bass, San Francisco.

Heiman, J., LoPiccolo, L. and LoPiccolo, J. (1981) The treatment of sexual dysfunction, in A.S. Gurman and D.P. Kniskern (eds) *Handbook of Family Therapy*, Brunner/Mazel, New York.

Kaplan, H. (1974) *The New Sex Therapy*, Brunner/Mazel, New York.

Kopp, S. (1972) *If You Meet the Buddha on the Road, Kill Him!* Science and Behavior Books, Palo Alto CA.

Masters, W.H. and Johnson, V.E. (1970) *Human Sexual Inadequacy*, Little, Brown & Co, Boston.

Polonsky, D.C. and Nadelson, C.C. (1982) Marital discord and the wish for sex therapy, *Psychiatric Annals*, Vol. 12, pp. 685–95.

Street, E. (1985) From child focused problems to marital issues, in W. Dryden (ed.) *Marital therapy in Britain, Vol. 2: Special Areas*, Harper & Row, London.

CHAPTER 11

SEXUAL DYSFUNCTION IN A TRANSCULTURAL SETTING*

Patricia d'Ardenne

In this chapter, I consider the effects of transcultural settings on human sexuality and sexual dysfunction. Also I suggest a more appropriate model for future clinical assessment, treatment and research, that would make the investigation of sexual dysfunction in any black community more workable.

The caring professions have taken a long time to recognize the emerging multiethnic nature of our post-war society and the particular demands this has made of current practice. But our growing awareness of health and illness as evaluative, culturally bound concepts has meant that we have had to redefine these notions within the broader framework of who is ill, under what circumstances, and by whose criteria. Traditional health care practice is no longer flexible enough for the many different cultures in society (Helman, 1985; Henley, 1980; Henley and Taylor, 1980; Kiev, 1972; King's Fund Centre, 1982; and THIRCC Health Campaign, 1982).

This is particularly true in the case of psychological dysfunction or illness, where our white culture and its system of beliefs and values provide us with the framework for judging what is adaptive or non-adaptive, and what is sick or sane (Littlewood and Lipsedge, 1982). The topic of sexual dysfunction provides an even less certain frame of reference for the diagnosis and treatment of disorders. The politics of race and sex cannot be dismissed as uncomfortable distractions to our thinking; they are an intrinsic part of it and need to be fully acknowledged as we struggle for a clearer understanding of all the issues involved.

* Based on an original paper submitted to *Sexual and Marital Therapy*, Vol. 1, No. 1, (1986), pp. 23–34.

EXISTING MODELS IN ETHNIC HEALTH CARE

Before considering models of psychological and psychosexual disorders in other cultures, it may be valuable to examine the attempts that have been made already by health workers, aware of the inadequacies of our present practice. The elegant work of Alix Henley (Henley, 1979; Henley and Taylor, 1980) tackled the very particular issues of various Asian cultures in all health-care settings. She attempted to incorporate the existing system of beliefs held by the 'aliens' within the traditional assumptions maintained by those responsible for their care, that is, the 'alienists'. Her work began with the very simple but important task of getting people's names correct, and then progressed to the way alternative diets, religious practices and habits impinged upon health care. Her work did much to raise the consciousness of health workers and health planners and she demonstrated that their global assumptions about good health-care practice were limited, subjective and relative.

Psychosexual disorders are often seen in a psychiatric setting, and Lipsedge and Littlewood (1982) give numerous examples of how insane behaviour is expected to invert the basic rules of any culture. They argue that every society has its characteristic mental illness, and that this serves as both a social control and a convenient peg on which that society may hang its most feared preoccupations. When patients from another culture are involved, they may react by distancing themselves further from their own alienation. It is argued that most people seek economic security, a satisfactory personal, family and occupational life, and the need to make sense of his or her own world. But the outsider has the further task of achieving all these tasks in a strange, hostile and often racist environment.

Lipsedge and Littlewood (1982) describe the active role of alienation achieved by the host culture, and they conclude that mental illness can be an intelligible, and sometimes adaptive response to racism and social disadvantage. It is not so much that psychopathology determines society but that society limits and directs pathology for its own purpose. Such an idea enables, indeed obliges, us to ask what purpose a dysfunction serves, as well as to understand the prevailing conditions which sustain it.

COUNSELLING AND ETHNIC GROUPS

Psychosexual difficulties that present in counselling and psychotherapy need also to be assessed in terms of their relevance to ethnic groups. Triseliotis (1986) argues that Western approaches would require considerable modification if they are to be of any relevance to black and Asian communities.

Since the days of Freud, Europeans expect to attribute personal problems to early childhood experiences; this is not necessarily a familiar idea in other cultures. For them, their concerns about their present circumstances and the future may be far more meaningful. Related to this is the belief among many ethnic minorities in a philosophy that accepts fate and the considerable influence of outside factors in shaping our destiny. On the other hand, white culture and therapies place much greater emphasis on individual responsibility, on self-examination and introspection, requiring a detailed examination of one's attitudes and behaviour.

In addition, Triseliotis quotes the work of Atkinson *et al.* (1978), who comment that people of different cultural backgrounds respond differently to the use of different counselling skills: 'Asians prefer a logical, rational, structured counselling approach over an affective, reflective, ambiguous one.' He also quotes Sue (1981), who similarly argues that the unstructured nature of counselling 'may generate anxiety among minorities who have been reared in an environment that actively structures social relationships and patterns of interaction'.

SEXUAL PROBLEMS IN ETHNIC GROUPS

Nowhere is there stronger feeling and apparent contradiction than in the realm of sexual beliefs and behaviour. Masters and Johnson's (1970) original work is based on a culturally homogeneous population and many of our precepts about the nature of dysfunction are ethnocentric and stereotyped.

Furthermore, the existing nomenclature of sexual dysfunction is phenomenological. The diagnostic categories do no more than describe observed levels of arousal and activity, and may themselves be incorporated into a larger system of behaviours or beliefs, both culturally and biologically determined.

Bancroft (1983) examines patterns of heterosexual behaviour between cultures and, in particular, the differences between Oriental and Occidental attitudes to intercourse within marriage. He refers to the Hindu and, to some extent, the Muslim belief that semen is a source of strength and should not be wasted, together with the implications for this when assessing reasons for intercourse not occurring, for example, during an infertile period. He also considers the widespread avoidance of intercourse during menstruation in Hindu, Muslim, Jewish and Judeo-Christian cultures and wonders whether this explains our virtual ignorance about this sexual activity in the Western world.

Hawton (1985) refers to the increasing problems that are now presenting in clinics, when partners are of a culture different from that of the therapist. He stresses the importance of understanding the cultural framework within which the couple are functioning, and the desirability of therapists of the same culture being trained to help their own communities.

Both Hawton (1985) and Rack (1982) extensively quote the work of Aslam (Aslam and Davis, 1979) who describes the role of the folk healer, called a *hakim*, and his role in the immigrant Asian community. The most common presenting problems to him are psychosexual ones, but they are inevitably perceived as part of a larger index of general health, and could not be compared to the more specific complaints met at a Western sex-problems clinic.

Bourne (1985) makes the observation that both Muslim hakims and the Hindu equivalents, called *vaids*, have the time and patience to listen to the patient in a way that no busy GP could hope to, and suggests that this may be an important part of their therapeutic efficacy.

Rack (1982) describes in some detail two psychosexual disorders which he includes in his chapter on culture-bound syndromes. They do not fit into any Western classification system, and are considered to be specific to a culture. The first of these is *koro*, when patients have a delusional fear that their penis will retract into the abdomen and thereby cause death, and is found among the Chinese in Britain. The second is the *jiryan*, or *dhat*, syndrome, which is a fixed belief that the sperm is leaking from the body through the urine, and which is causing general debility and weakness. This syndrome is found throughout the Indian subcontinent, in both Hindu and Muslim society.

Ballard (1982) reports that sexual potency here is seen as the desirable consequence of healthy manhood, but that there is the ever-present threat to such potency through masturbation – whether past or present. He recounts a saying that it takes 40 drops of blood to make one drop of semen, and 40 drops of semen to make one drop of brain fluid. Masturbation therefore saps the mind as well as the body. Intercourse does the same, but the energy can be replaced without too much difficulty in a healthy man.

Ballard (1982) observes that in Asian men, sexual potency is part of a much larger cosmology, which gives them a framework within which to view their whole existence. Secondly, these men expect to exercise a much greater degree of personal dominance over their wives and are consequently more concerned about their ability to fulfil the demands of that role. He argues that any Western therapy that attempts to demythologize these beliefs and to impose another set is erroneous. He believes that the therapist's constructs are no more valid than the patient's, and that any methodology must incorporate, rather than undermine, the existing system of beliefs pertinent to any culture.

In a brief survey of GPs seeing Asian families in East London (d'Ardenne, 1984), both men and women report premature ejaculation as a common problem, and one which is frequently severe enough to prevent intercourse from occurring. The GPs interviewed remarked that the women complain about painful intercourse much less frequently. Their most common complaint is also one of discharge. Even normal vaginal discharge is seen as dirty and unhealthy – and something requiring treatment. Many GPs of Asian origin adopted a Western medical approach and tended to treat any symptom with prescriptions rather than counselling. The exception to this was when referrals were made to the psychosexual clinic, after all physical examinations had been exhausted. To illustrate the issues faced by his patients, one of the practitioners seen offered the following example of a typical case that had come to his attention:

> A young Bangladeshi man has just arrived in this country without his wife to establish himself in East London. He has no legitimate sexual outlet. He is a devout Muslim and would consider sexual relations with another woman as unthinkable. He is advised not to use white prostitutes, and masturbation would be seen as a waste of his own life forces. All his energies are expected to be used in securing financial security for a woman he very rarely sees, but with whom he is expected to establish a family as soon as she arrives in England. All around him, this young man is bombarded by a strange world that is sexually permissive, and offers romantic images of sexual love that have no bearing on the arranged partnership that his parents have lovingly chosen for him through the family of his bride. She arrives in London, and the first few sexual encounters are disastrous. He ejaculates long before he is able to penetrate his bride, and his semen is wasted. He tries to satisfy his wife with increasing ardour and his efforts reap even fewer rewards. He becomes increasingly distressed and anxious. This aggravates the problem. His family in this country are surprised and disappointed. Many members of the family who might have been available for support or advice are not actually here. The longed-for baby does not appear. The doctor or the hakim is sought and the consultations begin.

What is surprising about this example is not that anyone should be dysfunctional under these circumstances, but that young couples function as well as they do under stressful and alienating conditions. Research in any area of behavioural dysfunction should focus as much on the resourcefulness of individuals and present coping patterns, as on what the individual or couple is not able to do.

CLINICAL REPORTS

Ghosh *et al.* (1985) recently reported their treatment of patients of Asian origin living in the Greater Manchester region, and concluded that the usual types of therapy offered at psychosexual clinics in the United Kingdom would have to be modified considerably to be acceptable to these patients. When compared with a group of non-Asian patients, they were distinguished by the frequent presentation of male problems (93 per cent of the Asian group had a male presenting, compared with 50 per cent of the non-Asian group) and by their preference for medical or surgical methods of treatment (89 per cent of Asians compared with 6 per cent of the non-Asian controls). Though this is a preliminary study, it well highlights the notion of a culture-bound sexual neurosis, and indicates that our present approach may be poorly adapted to the needs of those whose values are derived elsewhere.

Christopher (1984) has offered a very graphic account of her experiences of helping over a thousand sexually dysfunctional patients from a wide variety of cultures in her family-planning clinic. She describes the ethnic and sexual differences, both in the presentation of sexual dysfunction and in the perceived mode of therapy by the client. She also refers to the transcultural effects, as yet unmeasured, as first and second generation immigrants begin themselves to be influenced by the dominant culture.

Her work serves to pose some of the important and complex questions that need to be raised in transcultural sexual research. In particular, she emphasizes the enormous range of beliefs, constructs, and prejudices that exist within cultures – between the sexes, between social classes, and between the helping professions – and argues that these may be as great as those presumed to exist between cultures.

Bhugra and Cordle (1986) report briefly on their clinical experiences with 32 Asian patients who presented with sexual dysfunction between 1977 and 1983 and found that their results compared poorly with their white patients. Of the 18 couples who were taken on for treatment, only 5 (27.7 per cent) reported an improvement. The authors offered many explanations about their lack of success, including at least one reference to the passivity of the women, and the general lack of motivation in Asian couples undergoing sex therapy. The argument is tautological; patients cannot expect to be motivated to change within a therapy mode that is inappropriate to their expressed needs and cultural expectations. The authors intend to make a larger prospective study, but give no indications as to the changes that might be required from the therapists to achieve a better clinical result.

In response to this, d'Ardenne and Crown (1986) reported a rather different experience with 29 first generation Bangladeshi couples using Masters and Johnson therapy with some modifications. Eighteen cases presented with premature ejaculation, which was severe enough in most cases to cause infertility. The remaining eleven included six cases of secondary impotence, three cases of general sexual unresponsiveness, and one case of vaginismus.

A modified Masters and Johnson approach was offered to these patients in the absence of any other help known to the clinic, and the immediate outcome compares very favourably with those achieved in the psychosexual clinic, and for a white population (Crown and d'Ardenne, 1982; for a more detailed account, d'Ardenne, 1986b).

Seventy-six per cent of these improved substantially or in some part. The only measure of change was the couples' self report, usually given by the man, though the advent of births in four couples at least confirmed fertility.

A Bengali form of the Golombok-Rust inventory of sexual satisfaction (Rust and Golombok 1985) was offered to seven couples seen since its publication. A written questionnaire proved less than satisfactory, and there are no reliable results presently available.

Female disorders responded less well to a Western approach; only 50 per cent of cases resulted in partial or complete cure and reflected a more complex social and interpersonal picture than that for the men. The wives had fewer contacts with English culture and their mastery of English was less. None of the female disorders resulted in infertility, and this may well have had some bearing on the couples' motivation for therapy. It is clear that those couples who wished to conceive were the most motivated, and the usual practice of requesting that couples use contraception during the period of specific therapy was not observed.

The modifications to the basic Masters and Johnson therapy may be listed as follows:

1. Therapy was conducted in English, with the man speaking for both himself and his wife. He spoke enough English in all but three cases where an official interpreter was used.
2. Separate interviews for each spouse were offered in only four cases, where either one or both partners actually requested this.
3. Access to time and privacy had to be anticipated and organized. Other members of the family were involved in baby-sitting or giving the couple a quiet, uninterrupted evening together.
4. In three cases, a senior male family member was also involved in the initial assessment procedure. In two cases, this was the father of the husband, and in the third, the older brother of the wife.
5. Drawings and diagrams were used extensively to assist communication. Kaplan's (1976) *Illustrated Manual of Sex Therapy* was of considerable use here as the couples found the drawings both aesthetic and acceptable.
6. The 'stop-start' technique was used in all but one case of premature ejaculation. It was carefully explained that the purpose of this was to acquire ejaculatory control. Any masturbatory loss of semen was thus construed as the necessary means to achieving fruitful intercourse. The one exception was where one of the wives did not agree to participate in this procedure, and her husband used the technique himself, with some success.
7. As far as possible, the therapist avoided the use of medical terms, and the language of sickness, although every couple had already seen their General Practitioner and/or a psychiatrist. Therapy was offered as new

learning. Home assignments were called 'practice'. Specific techniques were called 'exercises'. Special emphasis was placed on the family and its resources and aspirations.

8. Instructions were given repeatedly and authoritatively, and were executed to the letter.
9. The attendances at the clinic were characterized by considerable motivation and complete compliance with home assignments. There were, for example, no difficulties concerning the initial ban on intercourse.
10. For both cultural and linguistic reasons, there was a minimum of discussion, and very few questions were asked by either the couple or the therapist. There was greater emphasis placed on performance indicators than on experiential ones – and there were no difficulties in keeping personal records of assignments.

THE DEVELOPMENT OF FUTURE SERVICES

Recent literature (Helman, 1985) on the provision of health care in a multiracial society stresses the importance of recruiting and training staff from ethnic minorities, as well as educating existing staff about the cultures, backgrounds and experiences of black and ethnic minority patients and their families. In the current political climate, it seems unlikely that there will be much funding available for professional training in sexual dysfunction.

Nevertheless, the untested assumption that sex therapists from one's own culture are better than those from another needs closer comparison and examination. In order to do this, it is essential to consider the primary-care workers in close contact with local communities and the role of volunteers from within the ethnic groups themselves. There is evidence (Brown and Bollinger, 1985) to show that volunteers can be trained to produce results similar to those of professional therapists. There are the similarly untested support groups in each community, as well as specific liaison schemes between statutory bodies and the community (Maternity Services Liaison Scheme, 1984), all of which might be usefully linked to the provision of help with sexual disorders.

The value of training therapists of a similar culture in specific techniques has already been considered. There may be, however, qualities inherent in the treatment itself that make it a flexible instrument for transcultural practice. Behaviour modification offers a symptom-orientated approach that uses few verbal mediators, that is brief and demonstrably effective and that can be implemented by family or members of the patient's community in an immediate and practical way.

In Masters and Johnson therapy, any sexual problem can be seen as faulty learning that can be corrected by structuring new learning between the couple. Home assignments can be carried out in the couples' own cultural and family setting, with adjustments made for the requirements of that culture. It may not be essential to good outcome that therapist and patient share the same set of values and beliefs. Treatment outcome is measured by easily defined therapy goals and is much less likely to be affected by the quality of interaction between therapist and patient than other more dynamic therapies (d'Ardenne, 1986a).

FUTURE RESEARCH METHODOLOGY

We need to address ourselves to some of the clinical and research issues raised by black couples who experience specific sexual dysfunction, and whose difficulties might be attributable to the stress of their transcultural status. It may seem that these issues are too varied and complex to fall within the confines of a single research undertaking, and experiments set up to look at these questions have already raised even more questions. But it is clear that a transcultural methodology must be evolved if any progress is to be made in this rapidly changing field.

If we were to examine sexual dysfunction in a transcultural setting, our methodology would have to enable us to pose and begin to answer the following questions:

What is the incidence and the prevalence of sexual dysfunction in the entire population of the area in question?

What is the incidence and the prevalence of sexual dysfunction in the identified ethnic minorities?

In what ways are sexual dysfunctions of any specified community made public?

How does the identified community see its difficulties, their causes and possible solutions?

What present resources are available to this group?

Which resources are being used by this group?

Are these issues perceived by the ethnic community as originating from within their own culture?

Are these issues perceived by the ethnic community as the result of being placed within an alien culture?

Are there differences between what is perceived as cultural and what is perceived as transcultural in origin, that is, within or between cultures?

How might these differences be assessed?

Are these differences significant?

How might these identified difficulties be tackled most appropriately and most effectively?
Is this approach flexible and replicable in any transcultural setting?
What evidence is there that the ethnicity of the therapist (together with his or her associated cultural, social, moral, racial and political values) affects the validity of diagnosis?
What evidence is there that the ethnicity of the therapist has any significant bearing on the willingness of couples to come for therapy, and on the effectiveness of outcome?
What are the implications for training staff and for the development of a clinical service?
What evidence is there that the availability and proximity of treatment has any significant bearing on the willingness of couples to come for therapy, or on the effectiveness of outcome?
Which assessment criteria are reliable and valid for a population of differing ethnic origin?
How might these be involved? And by whom?
Should friends or family be evolved in assessment, treatment or follow-up? In what way?
Should folk healer, priest or hakim, for example, be used in conjúnction with Western therapy, and how?
What help could they offer that would not be available via Western methods alone?

CONCLUSION

A great number of questions have been raised by the fact that sexual dysfunction manifests itself in a transcultural setting, and that few treatment models exist. The most pressing issue is to assess what ethnic groups themselves are presently needing and wanting. Gaining access to this information is a delicate, time-consuming but indispensable task. Any research on transcultural differences must use the most important resource available, the community itself. Any therapy must take into account the backgrounds and expectations of patients from different groups. And future training policy must include the active recruitment of ethnic minority staff who share as similar a culture to their patients as possible.

Good clinical research is not just the pursuit of knowledge but the dissemination and sharing of that knowledge, the improvement of quality of service available, and the provision of impetus for training suitable candidates for continuing work in the field.

REFERENCES

Aslam, M. and Davis, S. (1979) The hakim and his role in the immigrant community. Unpublished report to the Department of Health and Social Security, London.

Atkinson, D.R., Marruyama, M. and Natsui, S. (1978) The effects of counselor race and counseling approach to Asian Americans' perceptions of counselor credibility and utility, *Journal of Counseling Psychology*, Vol. 25, pp. 76–83.

Ballard, R. (1982) Asian men's assumptions about the consequences of sexual activity. Unpublished notes.

Bancroft, J. (1983) *Human Sexuality and Its Problems*, Churchill-Livingstone, Edinburgh.

Bhugra, D. and Cordle, C. (1986) Sexual dysfunction in Asian couples, *British Medical Journal*, Vol. 292 (11 January), pp. 111–2.

Bourne, S. (1985) Traditional remedies or health risks? *The Listener*, 23 November, pp. 8–10.

Brown, P. and Bollinger, C. (1985) Training non-psychologists in the treatment of sexual dysfunction. Symposium on 'Sharing Psychological Skills', *British Journal of Medical Psychology*, Vol. 58, pp. 257–65.

Christopher, E. (1984) Experiences of working with people from different cultural backgrounds. Unpublished paper presented to Association of Sexual and Marital Therapists Conference, September 1984, London.

Crown, S. and d'Ardenne, P. (1982) Symposium on sexual dysfunction, *British Journal of Psychiatry*, Vol. 140, pp. 70–7.

d'Ardenne, P. (1984) Sexual dysfunction in East London; a preliminary report. Unpublished paper presented to the Tower Hamlets District Department of Psychology, London.

d'Ardenne, P. (1986a) Behaviour therapy and ethnic minorities, in R. France, and M. Robson, (eds) *Behaviour Therapy in Primary Care: A Practical Guide*, Croom Helm, London

d'Ardenne, P. (1986b) Sexual dysfunction in a transcultural setting: assessment, treatment and research, *Sexual and Marital Therapy*, Vol. 1, No. 1, pp. 23–34.

d'Ardenne, P. and Crown, S. (1986) Sexual dysfunction in Asian couples, *British Medical Journal*, Vol. 292 (19 April), pp. 1078–9.

Ghosh, G., Duddle, M. and Ingram, A. (1985) Treating patients of Asian origin presenting in the U.K. with sexual dysfunction. Paper presented to the Seventh World Congress of Sexology, New Delhi.

Hawton, K. (1985) *Sex Therapy; A Practical Guide*, Oxford University Press, Oxford.

Helman, C. (1985) *Culture, Health and Illness*, J. Wright and Sons, Bristol.

Henley, A. (1979) *Asian Patients in Hospital and at Home*, King's Fund Publication, London.

Henley, A. (1980) *Asians in Britain; Asian Names and Records*, DHSS/King's Fund, 18, Brooklands Avenue, Cambridge.

Henley, A. and Taylor, C. (1980) *Register of Research Projects Related to Health Care Needs of Ethnic Minorities*, King's Fund Centre, London.

Kaplan, H.S. (1976) *The Illustrated Manual of Sex Therapy*, Souvenir, London.

Kiev, A. (1972) *Transcultural Psychiatry*, Penguin, Harmondsworth.

King's Fund Centre (1982) *Ethnic Minorities and Health Care in London,* King Edwards Hospital Fund for London, London.

Littlewood, R. and Lipsedge, M. (1982) *Aliens and Alienists*, Penguin, Harmondsworth.

Masters, W.H. and Johnson, V.E. (1970) *Human Sexual Inadequacy*, Churchill, London.
Maternity Services Liaison Scheme (1984) *Annual Report*, Montefiore Centre, Deal St, London, E1.
Rack, P. (1982) *Race, Culture, and Mental Disorder*, Tavistock Publications, London and New York.
Rust, J. and Golombok, S. (1985) The Golombok Rust inventory of sexual satisfaction (GRISS), *British Journal of Clinical Psychology*, Vol. 24, pp. 63–4.
Sue, D.W. (ed.) (1981) *Counseling the Culturally Different*, Wiley, New York.
THIRCC Health Campaign (1982) *Taken Bad; The State of Health in Tower Hamlets*, Oxford House, Derbyshire St, London E2.
Triseliotis, J. (1986) Transcultural social work, in J. Cox (ed.) *Transcultural Psychiatry*, Croom Helm, London.

PART 3
SEX THERAPY WITH SPECIFIC GROUPS

CHAPTER 12

SEX THERAPY WITH PEOPLE WITH A PHYSICAL DISABILITY

Mary Davies

THE PROBLEM

People with a physical disability have the same range of emotional and sexual needs as other people and just like anyone else they can sometimes have problems fulfilling these needs. The physical disability can, in some cases, be itself the cause of sexual and emotional problems. This can occur whether the disability is congenital or acquired. In a survey carried out by Stewart (1975), over 72 per cent of a sample of people with physical disabilities experienced sexual problems often over a considerable time period. Nearly half (45 per cent) of the problems were caused by physical factors, 15 per cent were due to psychological factors and 36 per cent were due to both. The physical factors were wide-ranging.

Some disabilities have a direct effect on sexual function so that a man may have difficulties with erection or be unable to ejaculate, and a woman does not get increased vaginal lubrication when sexually aroused. This occurs when the disability affects the spinal cord, as in spinal injury or spina bifida, or when the autonomic nerves passing to the penis are affected, as in multiple sclerosis or diabetes mellitus. Such effects can also occur if these nerves are damaged after surgery, for example, after a colostomy some men develop erectile problems. Other disabilities, although not having such a direct effect on sexual function, can cause problems in more indirect ways as explained below. If sexual intercourse is associated with pain, then sexual contact may soon begin to be avoided and the libido may also be reduced. This often occurs when a woman has arthritic hip joints, which make it painful to lie with her legs spread apart. If sexual intercourse causes pain this may disturb the partner also who then no longer seeks sexual contact. The disabled spouse may then feel rejected.

Many sexual relationships are lost because of fear of dire physical consequences, for example, after a heart attack or a stroke or after cancer and its treatment. Often information on when and how to resume sexual relationships is omitted from the rehabilitation programme.

Some physical disabilities cause incontinence, that is, lack of bladder or bowel control. This can be viewed by the individual and/or the partner with extreme distaste, and he or she may be too ashamed even to admit to the problem. Some people believe that the leakage of urine during sexual intercourse may harm their partner or themselves. Where a catheter is worn there may be fear of it being pulled out during sex, and many people are not even aware that sexual intercourse can be experienced while they are catheterized. Incontinence can lead to feelings of anxiety about personal attractiveness and thus a negative body image. Having a positive body image or feeling good about oneself is essential if a person is to feel happy in personal interactions and in forming relationships. We live in a society in which, according to the media, a high value is placed on physical attractiveness and, in addition these days, physical fitness. Many disabilities cause the individual to look, move or talk in a way which is 'different' from the norm, as in cerebral palsy, after an amputation or a stroke or a colostomy. Sexual problems may well occur in these instances.

An additional problem for the individual with a congenital disability is that he or she may have grown up in an overprotective environment, perhaps treated as an asexual person throughout life. One of the consequences of this is that the individual may have been denied sex education, particularly about the effect of his or her particular disability on sexual function and ways of overcoming problems. He or she may have also been denied opportunities for meeting and interacting with other young people and consequently have a lack of social skills as well as any real understanding about forming relationships.

In such a situation expectations can be unrealistic and on the rare occasions when social and sexual encounters do occur these can end in disappointment and frustration. Frustration can be particularly intense if disabled hands or poor co-ordination make masturbation difficult or impossible. Many people with a mental handicap are also denied sex education and an opportunity to learn social skills. This can put the individual at risk from unwanted sexual advances and lead to inappropriate sexual behaviour such as public masturbation. Other practical difficulties include coping with muscle spasms, or limited limb movements which prevent the individual from adopting certain body positions deemed by some people the 'norm' for sexual intercourse. Table 12.1 summarizes the possible effects of some specific physical disabilities on sexual relationships.

Table 12.1 Possible sexual effects of some physical disabilities

Disability	*Possible effects*	*Practical suggestions*
Arthritis	Pain; stiffness; difficulties in getting into certain positions	Pain killers before sex; different positions helped by cushions and pillows
Cerebral palsy	Lack of control of movement; negative body image	Tranquillizing medication before sexual activity; experiment with sexual positions
Diabetes mellitus	Problems with erection; inflammation of the vulva in women	Alternative to sexual intercourse; sex aids
Multiple Sclerosis	Lack of genital sensation; problems with erection; lack of vaginal lubrication; lack of control of movement; negative body image; incontinence	Try different positions; water-soluble lubricant for women; alternatives to sexual intercourse, e.g. mutual masturbation, orogenital sex, sex aids
Muscular dystrophy	May be atrophy of testes and hormonal disturbance; physical disability; deformity; hand movements may be difficult; heart disorders; negative body image; fear; anxiety	Try different positions; a vibrator where hand movements are difficult; alternatives to sexual intercourse
Poliomyelitis	Paralysis; difficulty with some positions; negative body image	Alternative positions; partner may need to take active role
Spina bifida	May be erectile and ejaculatory difficulties; reduced vaginal lubrication; spasticity; postural difficulties; negative body image; incontinence	Partner may need to take active role; try different positions; alternatives to sexual intercourse
Spinal injury	May be ejaculatory and erectile difficulties; reduced vaginal lubrication; paralysis; spasticity; incontinence; negative body image	Different positions; experiment with self-masturbation to aid erection; alternatives to sexual intercourse; use water-soluble lubricant
Stoma	If a colostomy, may be erectile or ejaculatory difficulties in men and reduced vaginal lubrication in women; negative body image; anxiety	Alternatives to sexual intercourse; different positions; sex aids; choosing sexy clothes to conceal stoma if requred; attention to diet

There is now increasing information (Davies and D'Mello, 1985 and see Chapter 8) that many prescribed drugs can cause sexual problems, for example, beta blockers can cause erectile problems. So the therapist requires information on the client's medication otherwise a great deal of time can be wasted and unnecessary distress caused.

In some instances, becoming disabled can lead to powerful feelings of anger, despair, denial or depression. Each of these feelings can profoundly affect emotional and sexual relationships, and make the job of the sex therapist more difficult. But, it is also important to note that the sexual problems of people with a physical disability may not in any way be related to that disability but to other psychological or physical causes.

SOME SOLUTIONS

Solutions can range from giving reassurance, information, which takes the form of sex education in some instances and practical advice, to more long-term counselling or sex therapy. Fear of having sex because of potentially disastrous consequences, for example, after a heart attack or stroke or hip replacement surgery, is often based on a lack of information. This fear can be reduced when it is appreciated that there are ways of enjoying sex which will not harm either partner. This may involve a change in position for sexual intercourse, or a role-change so that the fitter person plays the more active part. The partner of the person with the disability may also require reassurance.

Information can be helpful when clients have to cope with practical problems such as incontinence. Reducing fluid intake for a few hours prior to sexual intercourse and emptying the bladder can minimize the problem. It can be helpful to reassure the couple that even if there is urine leakage it is not harmful and catheters do not have to be removed before sexual intercourse. If the problem is lack of vaginal lubrication in the woman, such as after a spinal injury, then information on how this can be overcome with a water-soluble lubricant can be helpful.

If information and/or reassurance is not given soon enough, either to young people with a congenital disability or to clients during the rehabilitation programme after an injury or illness, then physical difficulties can be overlaid by emotional difficulties. This can occur when an individual develops multiple sclerosis. One effect that multiple sclerosis can have is to create problems getting an erection. The cause of this can be physical, as the nerves innervating the penis may be affected by the disease. No amount of sex therapy will alter this, and if the physical component is not appreciated by the therapist then a great deal of extra distress can be caused if the client feels that he or she also has psychological problems, or if the partner feels that she or he is no longer loved and wanted.

Many clients find it easier to find ways around the problems when they know that the problems are due to the disability, rather than psychological in origin. For many people who have a congenital disability, their overprotective upbringing and special schooling has meant that they have been denied sex education. They may well need not just sex education but individual counselling, particularly when learning the effect of their physical disability on sexual and reproductive functioning. In some cases the sexual problem is due to very intense feelings such as anger or resentment which may or may not be related to the physical disability.

WHEN IS SEX THERAPY APPROPRIATE?

There are various forms of sex therapy which can be helpful, such as anxiety-reduction, non-genital sensate focusing and group therapy. During sex therapy it is useful to discuss what having a sexual relationship can mean in physical terms. Many people equate sex with sexual intercourse and have never explored other possibilities. For some sexual intercourse will not be physically possible. The couple may not be able to position themselves. There may be impotence of physical origin, or the woman may be unable to experience penetration, as after surgical removal of the vagina. Learning about enjoying other parts of the body, through massage and exploring touch, can be a positive way of optimizing sexual and sensual possibilities. It is important that they are seen as a source of pleasure in themselves rather than the 'means to an end'. Enjoying one's own and a partner's body in this way can help create a positive body image.

Learning to masturbate can be a source of pleasure, as a woman with a physical disability said, 'It seems that a disabled body is so often a source of such negatives – pain, bladder and bowel hassles – that masturbation can become one really positive pleasuring experience making you feel a lot better about your body in general.' According to Hite (1976) many women find that it is difficult to experience an orgasm during sexual intercourse. Many are able to gain great enjoyment from mutual masturbation or orogenital sex. Clients can be 'given permission' and encouraged to rediscover their body, which is now different as a result of their injury or physical disability. After a spinal injury some men find the easiest way to have an erection is by masturbation so that although there is no sensation in their penis, they get the sensation of their erection via their hands. Even when ejaculation is not possible some men have described experiences of orgasm as a diffuse sensation not focused on the penis.

For some clients using a sex aid may be a way of enhancing a sexual relationship. When the man finds it difficult to get an erection, an energizing ring (the Blakoe ring) may be tried. This is a ring made of ebonite with copper and zinc electrodes in either end. It is worn around the base of the penis and scrotum next to the body and is thought to encourage an erection by a constrictive effect on penile veins. For some people an artificial erect penis which can be worn over the man's own flaccid penis is preferable. To enhance both the sensation and physical comfort, lubrication can be assisted by various commercial jellies, etc.

In some situations where vaginal penetration is not possible, for example, after radical surgery due to cancer, an artificial vagina may be a useful aid. This can be held between the woman's thighs. Lubrication using a water-soluble jelly is necessary. There are other sex aids which can be helpful, such as a vibrator. This can help a woman with reduced genital sensation experience an orgasm, since it can provide a powerful stimulus. A vibrator can also be used by a couple to stroke each other, and this can be particularly helpful if either partner has reduced hand movement or co-ordination.

Many people obtain a great deal of pleasure from masturbation. If hands are too disabled to allow this, a vibrator can be used by a woman and a man can obtain sexual pleasure from the use of the artificial vagina, which contains a vibrator. If the penis is put in the artificial vagina lubricated by a water-soluble jelly, when the vibrator is switched on a masturbatory effect takes place.

Introducing the client to sex aids can be a useful role for the therapist. However, it is most important that the therapist feels comfortable about the use of the aids or mixed messages may be given to the client and a potentially useful way for sexual fulfilment will be missed. It can be useful if the client's partner is also included in the therapy. The occurrence of the disability may have necessitated role-changes within the family, and for some partners the roles of nurse and lover are not compatible. Some partners are afraid to resume a sexual relationship because of fear of 'damaging' or 'making the problem worse'. They need reassurance and appropriate information.

In some countries discussion groups have been set up to help clients explore their feelings and attitudes about sexuality and disability, as well as to provide opportunities to work on developing a positive body-image and raised self-esteem. Vrancken (1985) in his review of this work reported that the content of most programmes includes (a) providing anatomical and physiological information, (b) explaining and redefining attitudes and (c) group discussion on topics such as social skills, sexual assertiveness, fertility and others initiated by members of the group. Much work still needs to be done in this area since unanswered questions include whether any partners should be included in the group, whether the group should be composed of clients with one particular disability, and what age and experience range of clients is appropriate.

WAYS FORWARD

At present in Britain, there is only one organization, *viz*. SPOD (The Association to Aid the Sexual and Personal Relationships of People with a Disability) whose primary role is to provide information, advice and counselling for people with disabilities, who have emotional and/or sexual problems. (SPOD also has an educational role providing information and training for professionals.) Since about 10 per cent of the population in Britain are physically disabled, one small voluntary organization cannot meet the needs of so many people. So how can these needs be met?

As pointed out in a recent report by The Royal College of Physicians (1986), the doctor is frequently in a position to offer helpful advice to patients who have a physical disability, for example, after surgery. Often doctors have had little or no training in the subject of human sexuality and opt out of this role. Where more than reassurance and straightforward information is required, the doctor may not have sufficient time and appropriate skills to provide the counselling or therapy required. So doctors and other allied health professionals, including nurses, social workers and occupational therapists, need to be aware of the services offered by sex therapists and ways of referring clients to them. This should be a service *offered* to the patient who should not themselves have to go through the trauma of asking.

SEX THERAPISTS FOR PEOPLE WITH DISABILITIES

At present some counsellors and sex therapists are reluctant to take on people with a physical disability as clients. This may be due to a lack of knowledge on their part about the effect of physical disability on sexual functioning which can make them doubt their ability to help the client. This lack of knowledge can be overcome and relevant information is available.*

A further inhibition for some therapists is their lack of experience of working with people with a physical disability. They may not be used to and/or comfortable working with people who look physically different or who have a speech impediment. As pointed out by Brearley and Birchley (1986), for counselling persons with speech or other communication difficulties, 'It is always preferable to assume that anyone you may contact is an intelligent, sensitive and feeling fellow human, and to speak to him or her accordingly. You will more often than not be correct in your assumption and to be wrong does not harm' (p. 113).

* Further information is available from SPOD, 286 Camden Road, London N7 0BJ.

Therapists may also have unexplored feelings and fears about sexuality and physical disability. Opportunities should be provided, during the training of all sex therapists, to obtain this relevant information about the problems caused by physical disability and how to cope with them. Even more important, the therapist should be given the opportunity to explore his or her own feelings about physical disability and sexuality and hear from people with physical disabilities themselves what sexuality means for them. They are the experts and therapists can only work *with* them not for them.

REFERENCES

Brearley, G. and Birchley, P. (1986) *Introducing Counselling Skills and Techniques: With Particular Reference for the Paramedical Professions*, Faber and Faber, London.

Davies, M. and D'Mello, A. (1985) The effect of drugs on sexual function, *British Journal of Pharmacology*, Vol. 84, p. 126.

Hite, S. (1976) *The Hite Report*, Macmillan, New York.

Royal College of Physicians (1986) *Physical Disability in 1986 and Beyond*, a report, 11 St Andrews Place, London NW1 4LE.

Stewart, W.F.R. (1975) *Sex and the Physically Handicapped*, The National Fund for Research into Crippling Diseases, Horsham.

Vrancken, P.H. (1985) Rehabilitation and sexuality, in B.H.H. Dechesne, C. Pons, and A.M.C.M. Schellen, *Sexuality and Handicap: Problems of Motor-Handicapped People*, Woodhead-Faulkner, Cambridge.

CHAPTER 13

SEX THERAPY WITH GAY MEN

Peter Gordon

In this chapter I discuss some of the issues encountered in conducting sex therapy with gay men. Lesbians will not be included as I have not worked with lesbian clients and it appears that they rarely seek help (at least from non-lesbian agencies) with sexual problems. Also, like gay men, they may be distrustful of the medical profession and may encounter difficulties in obtaining such help. I will look briefly at each of the following areas: heterosexism and homophobia and how they affect gay men; the inadequacies of the 'psychosomatic model' for treating gay men's sexual dysfunction; the nature and causes of gay men's sexual problems; the issue of conversion; some training issues, and a brief mention of some issues raised by HIV (Human Immunodeficiency Virus) and AIDS for therapists.

HETEROSEXISM AND HOMOPHOBIA

The word *heterosexism* refers to the set of attitudes and beliefs, institutionalized in our culture through language, religion, law, family and the media, which maintain that only heterosexuality is 'natural' and 'normal'. These attitudes dismiss other sexual orientations as 'inferior' or 'deviant'. Heterosexuality is energetically encouraged while

> A heterosexist society stifles any information to the contrary and makes scapegoats of lesbians and gay men for rejecting this. Such a society uses threats of violence . . . and withdraws benefits . . . to make clear its disapproval. (GLC, 1985, p. 9)

Homophobia, the irrational fear of the homoerotic, encourages the maintenance of heterosexism. Anthropology has taught us to be wary of generalizing from our own cultural experience since it is by no means true that all societies have responded in as negative a fashion towards homosexuality as has our own.

Homophobia is implicit in the attitudes of our society towards sex, and it would be very unlikely that any of us, including those of us who are gay, could grow up unaffected by it. Homophobia is internalized by gay men and may be acted out in a variety of ways. Before dealing with gay clients, therapists must have acknowledged and confronted their own homophobia. Rubin (1984) argues that modern Western societies view sex as 'guilty until proven innocent'. Democratic principles simply do not apply to the area of sexuality: a heterosexual chauvinism permeates our thinking about sex. Rubin points out that we are learning to appreciate cultural differences as 'unique expressions of human inventiveness'; she argues the need for a similar willingness to understand different sexual cultures.

The emergence of a specifically gay identity is a relatively recent phenomenon in the Western world (Plummer, 1981; Weeks, 1977). We must bear in mind that those who identify themselves as gay do not have a monopoly on homosexual behaviour. It is perfectly possible to incorporate homosexual thoughts, feelings and/or behaviour into a wide variety of lifestyles and sexual identities. However, the advances that have been made in improving the status of homosexuality have been made possible largely through the efforts of those who identify themselves as gay.

This said, the position of gay people today is far from satisfactory. Discrimination in almost every aspect of life is an everyday reality for all but a minority. Many are unable to 'come out' (acknowledge and declare their sexual identity to themselves and others), fear of prejudice or discrimination, and are consequently socially isolated and emotionally vulnerable. The threat of violence is a fact of life, and the issues raised by HIV/AIDS and the associated hysteria have done nothing to improve this state of affairs. Sexism, heterosexism and homophobia perpetuate and justify this situation.

THE PSYCHOSOMATIC MODEL REVISITED

Bancroft (1983) proposes that sexual function is a prime example of a psychosomatic process which he depicts diagrammatically as a circle comprising: the limbic system, genital responses, non-genital peripheral arousal, tactile stimulation, orgasm and ejaculation, and psychological factors and associated emotional states. Sexual dysfunction arises when negative factors operate at some point in this circle. While biological capacities are prerequisites for our sexuality, we cannot understand human sexuality in purely biological terms. As Rubin (1984) says: 'The belly's hunger gives no clues as to the complexities of cuisine' (p. 276).

What may be unclear in such a model is a framework which allows us to understand that in addition to being a profoundly personal experience, sexuality is also a social, cultural and historical experience. The beginnings of such a framework are the result of recent gay and feminist scholarship (e.g. Rubin, 1984; Weeks, 1977; 1985) which stress the crucial role played by social forces in the ways in which we experience ourselves as sexual beings:

> Sexuality is as much about words, images, ritual and fantasy as it is about the body: the way we think about sex fashions the way we live it. We give a supreme importance to sex in our individual and social lives today because of a history that has assigned a central significance to the sexual. (Weeks, 1985, p. 3)

Sex therapy with gay men brings us into the realm of sexual politics: our own attitudes towards, experience of, and assumptions about homosexuality will influence our therapy. Since it is unlikely that non-gay therapists will have had an opportunity to deal with their own heterosexism and homophobia, it could be argued that wherever possible those who work with gay people should be gay themselves. However being gay is no guarantee of unresolved homophobia, and since this may be the most important factor in treating gay people (McWhirter and Mattison, 1980), it is essential that all therapists intending to work with gay clients have an opportunity to recognize and deal with their own homophobia.

Working with gay men requires an understanding of the psychosomatic process but also an awareness of the role played by social factors in creating both our own and our clients' perceptions of sexuality. Therapists are often required to perform a consciousness-raising role (McWhirter and Mattison, 1980), and a therapist who is not gay himself or herself and who is unfamiliar with the issues which face gay men may find this difficult to do.

Therapists need to recognize the limitations of their treatment models and should not be too ready to blame treatment failure on poor motivation on the part of the client. Therapists should be sensitized to their clients' experience and perception of discrimination (actual or threatened), their lifestyles, relationships and sexual behaviour. Most available information regarding the latter is based on anecdotal accounts or else extrapolated from US studes. It is unfortunate that it has taken the threatened spread of HIV in Britain to stimulate research into these areas.

One example of how heterosexist assumptions might interfere with therapy concerns the issue of monogamy or sexual exclusivity. From personal and professional experience, it is evident that it is relatively common for gay men to have a primary relationship with one partner which does not preclude their sexual or emotional involvement with others. Bancroft (1983) believes that single homosexuals are the rule, but it simply is not possible to estimate the numbers of gay men who are married or are involved in long-term gay relationships. Sexual activity with multiple partners does not in itself indicate the absence of a committed relationship, or that such activity is impersonal.

Gay men are reared as heterosexual and usually exposed only to heterosexual models of relationships as they grow up. Clients may present for help with difficulties in establishing or maintaining rewarding relationships. In such instances co-therapy teams comprising two gay therapists may provide useful role-models and in the process dispel the myth that all gay relationships are based on rigid sex and gender role stereotypes.

GAY MEN'S SEXUAL PROBLEMS

In view of the largely invisible nature of the gay population it is impossible to estimate the incidence of sexual problems which affect gay men. Like other males, gay men may experience problems with desire, arousal or ejaculation; additionally they may experience problems with anal sex. Both Masters and Johnson (1979) and Silverstein (1979) found that difficulties with erection were the most common presenting problem of their gay clients. They also agreed that premature ejaculation was likely to be the next most common presenting problem. However, the findings of George (1981) and McWhirter and Mattison (1980) indicate that gay men may be more likely than their heterosexual counterparts to present with retarded ejaculation. Additionally in my own clinical experience the issue of sexual exclusivity may arise in the course of therapy with gay clients and merits discussion.

Sexual exclusivity

Sexual exclusivity is potentially a major source of conflict in gay men's relationships although the issue may not arise in a relationship until it is of some duration. Problems of course will only arise when there is conflict. Therapists should remember that monogamy is only one, amongst a variety, of ways of arranging a relationship and one which is no more desirable than any other. Teaching communication and assertion skills can provide the couple with the tools to address this, and most other sources of conflict in their relationship. Fears of intimacy, commitment and abandonment may be themes which need exploring. An unacknowledged battle over sexual exclusivity can lead to sexual problems, as can the fear of commitment which this battle often disguises.

The factors which give rise to sexual problems in heterosexual men can all affect gay men; additionally two other factors specific to gay men should be mentioned: internalized homophobia and stereotyped gender role-behaviour (George, 1981).

Internalized homophobia

Gay men are generally reared to be heterosexual and in the process are exposed to and internalize the all-pervasive negative messages about gay sexuality. Coming to terms with a gay sexual orientation requires that these messages be recognized, challenged and replaced with those which promote and validate a gay identity. It is essential for therapists to realize that the client may have become 'what he has been reared to despise'. It is vital that therapists are familiar with the facilities and resources of the local gay community since gradual, gentle introduction to these will enable the client to dispel the myths he has been brought up to believe.

Stereotyped gender role-behaviour

Two men behaving in stereotyped masculine roles may find that they are unable to experience the intimacy they desire. Gay men are not reared to be gay, but they are socialized as males with the taboos on emotionality, sensuality and intimacy that this implies. While many gay men are able to question and dismiss male stereotypes and discover satisfying ways of relating sexually and emotionally, some are not and may present in the context of sexual dysfunction. Again, gay male therapy teams can provide valuable role-modelling and help overcome the problems caused by male stereotyping. It should be noted that Masters and Johnson (1979) did not offer this facility to their gay clients; the principle of 'therapist as advocate' it seems did not apply to gay people.

Therapists should refrain from thinking or talking with gay clients in terms of heterosexual marriage stereotypes when discussing roles within a relationship. Gay relationships are not marriages and receive none of the support and benefits which marriage can bestow socially and legally. Gay people may resent their relationships being conceptualized in this way. Some gay men have difficulties in making or sustaining relationships. This may be the presenting difficulty or it may be associated with sexual dysfunction.

Problems with anal sex

Problems with anal sex vary from discomfort to a complete inability to be penetrated (Morin, 1981), and a full understanding of the anatomical and physiological aspects of anal intercourse can be very helpful (Agnew, 1985). Two particular themes can often be identified as contributing to such problems: the fear of faeces, and the fear of being 'passive'.

It is common for people to use sex for reasons other than sexual pleasure: clarifying and exploring these issues with the client can allow him the opportunity to discover if he really does want to explore and enjoy anal sex. Problems with anal sex can be treated with a systematic desensitization programme jointly decided by client and therapist.

It is essential that the role of anal sex in transmitting HIV is discussed and that therapists have accurate and up-to-date information at their disposal to share with the client. The role and effective use of condoms should also be discussed. However, clients should understand that where there is any risk of infection anal sex is a very effective mode of transmission of HIV.

Gay men can participate in a wide variety of sexual activities and it has been suggested that being labelled 'deviant' facilitates participation in 'deviant' sexual activities (McWhirter and Mattison, 1980). Whether or not this is the case it is possible that clients may use sexual terms with which the therapist is unfamiliar. To avoid discomfort or resentment on the part of the client, therapists should endeavour to be aware of the range, variety and language of gay men's sexual behaviour. It can be difficult for clients to have the task of educating the therapist.

In my experience it is common for problems to arise in a relationship where one partner is reluctant about or aversive to particular sexual activities. Again, communication and assertion skills, and when appropriate, systematic desensitization can provide useful approaches to this problem.

Where gay men present

The requirement at some centres of a GP referral letter discriminates against gay people who are unable to come out to their GP or whose GP (as is too often the case) is unsympathetic. One man I saw recently was told that the tests requested by his GP were far too expensive to waste on a gay man who would not be marrying and having children. Gay men are more likely to present covertly in Sexually Transmitted Disease (STD) Clinics where sensitive interviewing may uncover a sexual problem, or else they may present to gay support services. My own experience working in an STD Clinic with gay support agencies able to make direct referral to me ensured a variety of referrals. One should not underestimate the suspicion with which some gay people view medical/therapy/counselling services. Aversion therapy may have been simply another treatment to psychiatrists and therapists, but to the gay community it is a reminder of the need for caution in dealing with non-gay professionals.

It is also common for gay men to present without partners and therapists may need to explore alternative ways of working in this context, as to the best of my knowledge, no one in Britain is offering surrogate partners therapeutically to gay men. Sharing ideas with colleagues and those experienced in working with individuals can be productive and valuable.

CONVERSION

The term *conversion* refers to the changing of orientation, in this instance from homosexual to heterosexual. Masters and Johnson (1979) also refer to 'reversion' in the case of those whose histories reveal an amount of prior heterosexual experience. Bancroft (1983) provides a useful summary of the controversy surrounding conversion. He expresses the view that it is arrogant to deny a person the right to choose to conform. The therapist is, he argues, entitled to decline to help the client who wants to change his sexual orientation, but this does not give him the right to criticize those who are willing to offer such help.

Given the extent to which a homosexual orientation is stigmatized in our society, it is not surprising that some individuals may wish to change. It may be possible to extend a client's sexual repertoire to include a degree of heterosexual functioning. However, it seems unlikely that a therapist will be able to achieve what several years of aggressively heterosexual socialization have failed to accomplish. Requests for conversion are inevitably the result of social pressure, overt or covert, and provide evidence of the extent to which oppression is internalized.

Oppression operates at both personal and political levels and effective intervention should address both. Conversion, endorsing as it does the privileged status of heterosexuality, implicitly (even if unintentionally) reinforces definitions of homosexuality as inferior.

In the face of considerable opposition and hostility gay people have gradually succeeded in 'demedicalizing' homosexuality and placing the issue of sexual orientation in the arena of sexual politics. The conversion issue is a symbol of the (often unacknowledged) political implications of what is sometimes done in the name of therapy.

The client may indeed have the right to choose to conform; from my perspective this begs the question. Does he not, more fundamentally have the right to freedom from the pressure and fear which makes conformity appear so attractive?

TRAINING

In planning sex therapy courses trainers should consider the broad range of potential clients who might benefit from sex therapy, including gay men and lesbians, and plan courses accordingly. While it is hoped that by the end of their training therapists will be able to respond to the needs of a wide variety of clients, it should be recognized that gay people are unlikely to seek help from the usual NHS facilities and recruitment from within the gay community will be necessary to demonstrate a truly positive commitment to sexual democracy.

While the presence of gay trainees can provide a valuable learning opportunity for trainees and trainers alike, it should not be assumed that they will provide the course's gay/lesbian perspective. There is a danger that the gay trainee will become a token display of the course's 'tolerance'. The responsibility of challenging each and every manifestation of heterosexism can soon become a burden and lead to the trainee being labelled 'paranoid' or 'having a chip on his (her) shoulder'.

The need and special concerns of gay and lesbian people cannot be confined to one lecture, presentation or workshop. While special events may be necessary, for example, heterosexism awareness training, making use of gay community resources etc., gay and lesbian issues should be considered in relation to every topic covered in the course curriculum.

This may appear a tall order, but if we truly wish to endorse the principles of sexual democracy nothing less will do.

POSTSCRIPT: AIDS – REDRESSING THE BALANCE

The spread of HIV has highlighted and reinforced the oppression of gay men. The increasing awareness of the threat posed by HIV raises serious questions for us as therapists whether or not we work with gay men since *AIDS is an issue for us all* both personally and professionally. However, it is beyond the scope of this brief section to raise these questions and it is hoped that we will raise and explore these issues and their implications for our work in our professional groups and meetings.

However, in working with clients (including but not only gay men) therapists may be called upon to provide accurate information about the transmission of HIV and the role and use of condoms, to help clients learn assertion and communication skills to negotiate safer sex with partners, and to help the client to address the issues of safer sex, thereby creating new ways of being sexual safely.

Recent evidence suggests that gay men have responded in an exemplary fashion to the changes in sexual behaviour made necessary by HIV and have paved the way in demonstrating the possibilities of developing alternative, gratifying ways of being sexual and exploring the erotic potential of safer sex.

REFERENCES

Agnew, J. (1985) Some anatomical and physiological aspects of anal sexual practices, *Journal of Homosexuality*, Vol. 12, No. 1, pp. 75–96.

Bancroft, J. (1983) *Human Sexuality and Its Problems,* Churchill-Livingstone, Edinburgh.
George, K. (1981) Etiology and treatment of sexual dysfunction in gay male patients. Paper presented 5th World Congress of Sexology, Israel.
GLC/GLC Gay Working Party (1985) *Changing the world: A London Charter for Gay and Lesbian Rights,* GLC Public Relations Branch, London.
Masters, W.H. and Johnson, V.E. (1979) *Homosexuality in Perspective*, Little, Brown & Co., Boston.
McWhirter, D.P. and Mattison, A.M. (1980) Treatment of sexual dysfunction in homosexual male couples, in S.R. Leiblum and L.A. Pervin (eds) *Principles and Practice of Sex Therapy*, Guilford Press, New York.
Morin, J. (1981) *Anal Pleasure and Health*, Down There Press, Burlingame CA.
Plummer, K. (ed.) (1981) *The Making of the Modern Homosexual*, Hutchinson, London.
Rubin, G. (1984) Thinking sex, in C.S. Vance (ed.) *Pleasure and Danger,* Routledge & Kegan Paul, Boston.
Silverstein, C. (1979) Sexual problems of gay men, in L. Richmond and G. Noguera (eds) *The New Gay Liberation Book*, Ramparts Press, Palo Alto CA.
Weeks, J. (1977) *Coming Out: Homosexual Politics in Britain, from the Nineteenth Century to the Present*, Quartet Books, London.
Weeks, J. (1985) *Sexuality and Its Discontents*, Routledge & Kegan Paul, London.

CHAPTER 14

SEX THERAPY WITH MALE SEX OFFENDERS

Derek Perkins

Sex offenders* presenting for psychological or medical treatment do so in a number of ways. They may go to their general practitioner or direct to some specialized treatment facility voluntarily (i.e. before their offending is known to the police) but this is rare. More often, sex offenders seek treatment only after they have been apprehended.

Treatment may be discussed with them by, amongst others, forensic psychiatrists, clinical psychologists, probation officers or social workers. When this occurs before a case comes to court, recommendations to the court for treatment might result in the offender being sent to a special hospital (if he is diagnosed as mentally disordered under the terms of the Mental Health Act), but this is rare. Only 154 (2.3 per cent) of the 6,614 convictions for sexual offences in 1983 resulted in special hospital placements (Howard League Working Party, 1985).

More typically, the offender will be sent to prison, where he may or may not receive treatment, or he may be offered treatment in the community, either voluntarily or as a condition of a probation order.

When treatment in the community is being considered, professional opinions differ on whether purely voluntary treatment or treatment linked to a probation order is most likely to be effective therapeutically. Whatever the truth may be, courts may well feel that public safety is better served by making treatment mandatory rather than leaving this responsibility solely with the offender.

Imprisonment of sex offenders will usually follow for the more serious

* Most sex offenders are male and this short chapter focuses on this group.

classes of offence, that is, those which attract the heaviest maximum penalties. Of those convicted in 1982 for rape, for example, 94 per cent received a custodial sentence, and for incest the corresponding figure was 73 per cent. This compares with 21 per cent receiving custodial sentences for indecent assault against females, and 20 per cent for indecent assault against males, both offences which attract lower maximum penalties.

Whilst the Prison Service does not claim to offer treatment to all imprisoned sex offenders, a number of local initiatives have evolved over the years. One of these is a programme of psychological treatment for sex offenders which began at Birmingham Prison in 1974 and which subsequently expanded, in 1980, to encompass outpatient treatment through the adjacent All Saints Hospital, Birmingham. Details of this programme, from which the illustrative case material in this section is drawn, and the productive collaboration between Prison Psychological Services at Birmingham and the Midland Centre for Forensic Psychiatry are reported elsewhere (Perkins, 1980; 1983; in press).

PRESENTING FOR TREATMENT

Sex offenders presenting for treatment often do so with mixed motives. In addition to wanting to tackle their problems, they may also wish to influence courts to allow non-custodial treatment for them (if their cases are still to be heard) or to obtain parole (if they are serving prison sentences). To be seen to be co-operating in treatment is one way of attempting to achieve these ends. Offenders may also be seeking treatment partly in response to pressures on them to do so from their relatives, often wives or, in the case of homosexual men, their male partners. Their partner may have left the offender, or be thinking of doing so, and the offender's request for treatment may be aimed partly at securing a reconciliation with the partner or with his family.

Such pressures operating upon offenders complicate many therapists' ideal of working solely with voluntary clients/patients, and many different paradigms for the ethical resolution of treating sex offenders in prison or other secure environments have been reported. The principles which were applied in the Birmingham programme are reported by Perkins (1980; in press).

ASSESSMENT

A prerequisite to the treatment of sex offenders is as full an assessment as possible of the 'problem behaviours' to be eliminated and the 'target behaviours' which need to be built up in their place. Because of the medicolegal context in which such assessments often take place – impending court cases, forthcoming parole reviews etc. – it is inadvisable to rely solely on information derived from interviews with offenders. As indicated earlier, there will be many pressures operating on offenders which may result in inaccurate self-reporting.

There are two implications in this. First, it is more likely with sex offenders than with other clinical groups that a full picture of their problem behaviours will only emerge over time. The process of treatment, successes and failures, will feed new information into the analysis of the offender's behaviour, which in turn will feed new ideas into the treatment process.

Second, it is important that the widest range of characteristics of the offender which might relate to his offending should be considered, along the lines of the 'multimodal' system of analysis proposed by Lazarus (1976) and the 'broad-based' approach advocated by Crawford (1979).

Specifically, not only do sex offenders' overt behavioural responses need to be set out in any analysis, but so too do related attitudes, emotions, patterns of sexual interest, interpersonal relationships and modes of thinking.

At each of these levels of functioning, particular assessment techniques have been developed, although not always specifically with sex offenders in mind. At the cognitive level the work of Meichenbaum (1976) is relevant. The work of Howells (1978), using the repertory grid technique, and Holmstrom and Burgess (1980) have demonstrated the importance of sex offenders' emotional states in mediating their offending.

Data on offenders' attitudes and interpersonal relationships can be derived partly from collecting information from significant others in the lives of the offenders and partly by direct interviewing or paper and pencil 'attitude' or 'personality' measures. However, the dangers of relying too heavily upon the latter, which rarely correlate with the behaviours they purport to measure at levels higher than 0.3, are highlighted by, for example, Mischel (1968) and Bancroft (1974).

At the level of sexual interests, much work on the psychophysiological (mainly penile erection) responses of sex offenders to different kinds of photographically presented, audio-taped or video-taped, material depicting various sexual scenarios has been carried out (e.g. Freund, 1965; 1967; Abel *et al.*, 1975; Abel and Blanchard, 1976). Whilst evidence exists to suggest that such penile responses to sexually related material can differentiate between different classes of sexual interest, thereby providing useful pre-treatment and post-treatment measures and contributing information concerning sexual interests relevant to therapy, there is also evidence that faking of penile response measures can occur (Freund *et al.*, 1979) in a significant minority of cases. If subjects are motivated to fake assessments, averting eye gaze from visual material and distracting themselves from auditory material (e.g. by engaging in mental arithmetic) can sometimes also achieve this effect.

The possibility of faking is more likely to be an issue when offenders are due to be dealt with by the court or are being reviewed for release from prison by the Parole Board or from special hospital by responsible medical officers or mental health review tribunals.

No single level of assessment – sexual interests, attitudes, emotions, interpersonal relationships etc. – can fully account for a sex offender's behaviour. However, an amalgam of techniques applied creatively with an individual offender can yield a valuable understanding of his offence behaviour. When this is done in the context of a behavioural analysis, in which the antecedents and consequences of the offender's deviant behaviour are systematically assembled, a complex network of interactions and influences can be identified.

Based upon clinical material from the Birmingham treatment programme for sex offenders, the schematic representation of interactions between the various levels of a sex offender's functioning is illustrated in Figure 14.1. The arrows indicate which events, thoughts, feelings etc. precede other such phenomena, and the whole system represents something of a vicious circle of influences, from which a sex offence can be potentially triggered.

The pattern of functioning represented in Figure 14.1 may remain stable for some time, but at some point an event or combination of events (external to the offender or within his own thoughts or feelings) may trigger an offence. For example, if at point A the man and his wife were to separate, he may feel particularly angry, seek out alternative sexual satisfaction and, when rebuffed at point B, after a particularly heavy bout of drinking, he may commit the offence of rape, telling himself that nothing really matters any more.

Alternatively, he may, at point C, lose his job, suffer a further reduction in self-esteem and, following an argument with his wife, experience a particularly high level of anger towards women. After only moderate drinking, he may follow and rape a woman, telling himself that she is typical of her sex and deserves what has happened to her, and even if he is apprehended, that his offending will only serve to prove to his wife how desperate he really was.

The purpose of these examples is to illustrate that a sexual offence cannot be considered the product of any one level of functioning – deviant attitudes, inappropriate emotional responses, deviant sexual interests etc. – nor can it be considered the product in any simple additive way of combinations of these factors. Rather, there is a dynamic interaction between the various levels of the offender's functioning which can periodically trigger an offence. Although the timing and precise nature of a particular offence cannot, even

Figure 14.1 Schematic representation of the interaction between a sex offender's behaviour, attitude, thoughts, feelings and sexual interests

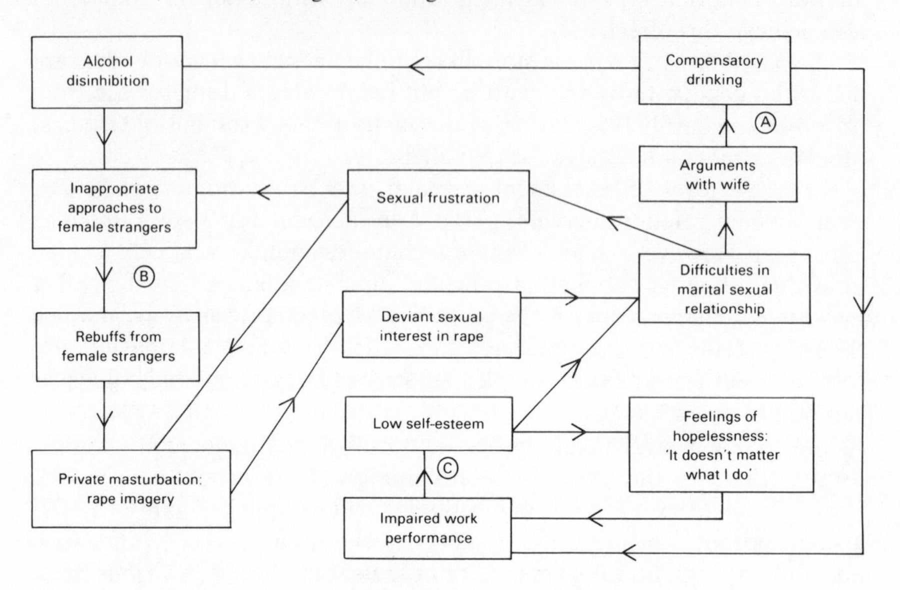

in principle perhaps, be predicted, an analysis of the typical flow of events in the offender's lifestyle can, as illustrated in Figure 14.1, identify 'danger points' with respect to possible future offending and points of difficulty for the offender towards which treatment might most appropriately be directed.

TREATMENT

Often, and particularly within prison, 'treatment' is taken to mean anything from the physical conditions of the establishment to particular interpersonal aspects of the regime which may influence the offender's behaviour. Psychological treatment has a more specific meaning, the essence of which is that offenders wishing to modify their behaviour are helped to do so in a systematic way by the application of psychological principles and procedures.

Unlike the more general use of the word *treatment*, psychological treatment implies the informed consent of the offender. The problems associated with obtaining the informed consent of incarcerated offenders, and indeed some non-incarcerated offenders, are complex and have been set out in the Joint Working Party report on ethical guidelines for the conduct of behaviour modification programmes (Zangwill, 1980), the Council for Science and Society Working Party Report, *Treating the Troublesome* (1981) and the Howard League Working Party on Sex Offenders (1985).

Approaches to the treatment of sex offenders are directed at the same levels of functioning as those outlined earlier in relation to assessment, namely sexual interests, emotional, attitudinal, cognitive and interpersonal functioning. These may be broadly subdivided into treatments dealing with deviant sexual interest and those dealing with sociosexual behaviour.

PROBLEMS OF DEVIANT SEXUAL INTEREST

Some sex offenders, but by no means all, display a greater sexual interest in deviant *objects* (e.g. children) or deviant *acts* (e.g. sadism) associated with their offences than they do in non-offending sexual behaviour. Typically, such offenders report similarly deviant masturbation fantasies which, like self-report and psychophysiological assessments of sexual interest, can also be monitored before, during and after treatment. This information can contribute to an understanding of an offender's pattern of sexual interest and can be used to monitor treatment progress.

One approach to the reduction of deviant sexual interest is aversion therapy, in which deviant material is paired with unpleasant stimulation, for example, electric shocks (e.g. Matthews, 1977), unpleasant imagery, as in covert sensitization (e.g. Barlow *et al.*, 1969) or unpleasant social consequences, as in shame therapy (e.g. Serber, 1970)

Enhancement of non-deviant sexual interest has, in some instances, been achieved by some of the aversive procedures previously referred to as well as by the more direct procedures of masturbatory conditioning (Abel *et al.*, 1973), in which the offender replaces deviant with non-deviant masturbation fantasies.

Systematic desensitization has been used to increase non-deviant sexual behaviour by a process of gradually exposing offenders to the aspects of non-deviant sexual situations which cause them anxiety, for example, certain adult female sexual characteristics (e.g. Perkins, 1983).

Surrogate therapy is a version of desensitization in which sexually anxious or incompetent males are helped to achieve satisfactory sexual intercourse by suitably trained female partners (e.g. Kohlenberg, 1974; and see Chapter 16 in this book). Reports of this approach, which has only been used with non-imprisoned sex offenders, have shown mixed results. Simple exposure to sexual material and sex education are two other procedures which not only serve to increase non-deviant sexual interest but are relevant to the modification of sexual interests and the establishment of appropriate sociosexual behaviour (e.g. Woodward, 1980), other aspects of which are dealt with below.

PROBLEMS OF SOCIOSEXUAL BEHAVIOUR

In addition to problems of sexual interest, sex offenders inevitably display problems of social and sexual behaviour. Many offenders are anxious in adult social situations and frequently do not possess the skills necessary to function adequately in them. It is quite possible for an offender who is not sexually deviant to engage in sexual activity with, for example, children, as a result of social inadequacies or anxieties.

Social-skills training is perhaps the best known treatment for social behaviour problems, and attempts have been made to apply this approach with sex offenders (e.g. Crawford and Allen, 1979). Modelling or coaching, rehearsal and feedback in role-play situations relevant to the offender's problem behaviour are key elements. Whilst the approach shows promise, many workers in the field now comment on the need for adequate data about what constitutes 'appropriate behaviour' for particular client groups.

Cognitive behaviour modification is an increasingly valued approach to the treatment of sexually deviant behaviour. The approach, which involves intervening directly at the level of the offender's thoughts, self-statements and rationalizations, is now beginning to be used as a treatment in its own right rather than as an adjunct to other forms of therapy (e.g. Perkins, 1983).

Empathic therapeutic relationships are recognized to be a common element in many successful treatment programmes, but so too is confrontation between therapists and offenders where denial is a major issue (e.g. Boozer, 1975).

EVALUATION

A fundamental statistic, but one which is not readily available from the literature, is the proportion of sex offenders who might benefit from treatment if this were available. This raises three related questions:

1. How many sex offenders would wish to change their behaviour by psychological or other forms of treatment?
2. For how many of these would their problems be amenable to analysis and treatment?
3. In how many of those treated could lasting changes be brought about?

The disappointing fact is that there is little common ground in the published work on the treatment of sex offenders. Whether carried out in institutions or in the community, treatment programmes draw their candidates from a variety of different sources and treatment procedures differ from programme to programme. Evaluation methodology is also variable. The result of this is that authoritative statements about sex offender treatment are difficult to make. Nevertheless, we are left with a number of promising

Table 14.1 Sex offender treatment research studies

Reference	*Sample*	*Treatment*	*Outcome*
Peters and Roether (1968)	92 sex offenders on probation	Group psychotherapy (Control group design: 75 sex offenders)	2-year follow-up: 8% control group, and 1% treated group re-offended sexually
Wickramasekera (1976)	16 repetitive indecent exposure offenders	Aversion therapy (no control group)	Follow-up 3 months to 7 years: no relapses
Fox (1980)	38 mixed sex offenders	Discussion/social learning group (no control)	Follow-up 6 years: 79% not re-offended
Perkins (in press)	62 mixed sex offenders	Broad based behavioural (Control group design: 12 sex offenders)	Over 4-year follow-up: 64% of control group re-offended (including 5 indecent assaults), and 14% of treated group re-offended (including 1 indecent exposure)

pointers as to which procedures and practices are most likely to be worth pursuing and developing.

Table 14.1 sets out the results of some British and American studies on sex offender treatment which, although suffering difficulties of sample size, research design and variable follow-up lengths, indicate that treatment can be effective with some sex offenders, particularly when broad-based approaches to treatment are applied, continuity of treatment from institution to the community is effected and when treatment attempts are not terminated prematurely.

CONCLUSIONS

Sex offending is a complex matter requiring an understanding of:

1. The particular characteristics of subsets of sexual offending – rape, incest, indecent exposure etc.

2. The nature and effectiveness of different methods of assessment and treatment, and
3. The network of influences operating on any individual offender, including the social and legal context of his circumstances when assessed for treatment, and the ways in which the various levels of his functioning interrelate – emotional, attitudinal etc.

Although public condemnation of sex offending is understandably high, this is not inconsistent with, nor should it detract from, the emerging evidence that effective treatment is possible with some groups of sex offenders both in prison and in the community.

Except for those minority of sex offenders on indeterminate sentences in prison or in special hospitals, most sex offenders will at some point automatically be free of legal or physical controls. To involve such men, wherever possible, in treatment programmes designed to minimize the probability of future sex offending is surely to be encouraged, not only in the interests of the sex offender himself but also, more importantly, in terms of those who would otherwise be victimized in the future.

NOTE

The views expressed are those of the author and are not necessarily those of the DHSS.

REFERENCES

Abel, G.G., Barlow, D.H. and Blanchard, E.B. (1973) Developing heterosexual arousal by altering masturbatory fantasies: a controlled study. Paper presented at the Association for Advancement of Behavior Therapy, Miami.

Abel, G.G. and Blanchard, E.B. (1976) The measurement and generation of sexual arousal in male sexual deviates, in M. Hersen, R.M. Eisler and P.M. Miller (eds) *Progress in Behavior Modification,* Vol. 2, Academic Press, London.

Abel, G.G., Blanchard, E.B., Barlow, D.H. and Mavissakalian, M. (1975) Identifying specific erotic cues in sexual deviations by audio-taped descriptions, *Journal of Applied Behavior Analysis,* Vol. 8, pp. 58–71.

Bancroft, J. (1974) *Deviant Sexual Behaviour: Modification and Assessment,* Clarendon Press, Oxford.

Barlow, D.H., Leitenberg, H. and Agras, W.S. (1969) The experimental control of sexual deviation through manipulation of the noxious scene in covert sensitization, *Journal of Abnormal Psychology*, Vol. 74, pp. 596–601.

Boozer, G. (1975) Offender treatment: programing workshop. Paper presented at the Sixth Alabama Symposium on Justice and the Behavioral Sciences, University of Alabama, Tuscaloosa.

Council for Science and Society (1981) *Treating the Troublesome*, CSS, London.

Crawford, D.A. (1979) Modification of deviant sexual behaviour: the need for a comprehensive approach, *British Journal of Medical Psychology*, Vol. 2, pp. 151–6.

Crawford, D. and Allen, J.V. (1979) A social skills training programme with sex offenders, in M. Cook and G. Wilson (eds) *Love and Attraction: Proceedings of an International Conference,* Pergamon, Oxford.
Fox, C.A. (1980) The non-violent sex offender. Alternatives to present provisions and practices, in D.J. West (ed.) *Sex Offenders in the Criminal Justice System.* Proceedings of the 12th Cropwood Conference, University Institute of Criminology, Cambridge.
Freund, K. (1965) Diagnosing heterosexual paedophilia by means of a test for sexual interest, *Behaviour Research and Therapy*, Vol. 3, pp. 229–34.
Freund, K. (1967) Erotic preferences in paedophilia, *Behaviour Research and Therapy*, Vol. 5, pp. 339–48.
Freund, K., Chan, S.L. and Coulthard, R. (1979) Phallometric diagnosis with non-admitters, *Behaviour Research and Therapy*, Vol. 17, pp. 451–7.
Holmstrom, L.L. and Burgess, A.W. (1980) Sexual behavior of assailants during reported rapes, *Archives of Sexual Behavior*, Vol. 9, pp. 427–39.
Howard League Working Party (1985) *Unlawful Sex*, Waterloo, London.
Howells, K. (1978) Some meanings of children for paedophiles, in M. Cook and G. Wilson (eds) *Love and Attraction*, Pergamon, London.
Kohlenberg, R.J. (1974) Treatment of a homosexual pedophiliac using a vivo desensitization: a case study, *Journal of Abnormal Psychology,* Vol. 83, pp. 192–5.
Lazarus, A.A. (1976) *Multimodal Behavior Therapy*, Springer, New York.
Matthews, R. (1977) Assessment of sexual offenders at Wormword Scrubs. Paper presented at annual conference of the British Psychological Society, Exeter.
Meichenbaum, D. (1976) Cognitive behavior modification, in J.T. Spence, R.C. Carlson and J.W. Thibaut (eds) *Behavioral Approaches to Therapies*, General Learning Press, New York.
Mischel, W. (1968) *Personality and Assessment*, Wiley, New York.
Perkins, D.E. (1980) Psychological treatment of sex offenders, *Prison Service Journal* (July), pp. 15–17.
Perkins, D.E. (1983) The psychological treatment of sex offenders in prison and the community. Unpublished Ph.D. thesis, University of Birmingham.
Perkins, D.E. (in press) A psychological treatment programme for sex offenders, in B.J. McGurk (ed.) *Applying Psychology to Imprisonment*, NFER, Slough, Bucks.
Peters, J.J. and Roether, H.A. (1968) Group psychotherapy for the sex offender, *Federal Probation*, Vol. 32, pp. 41–5.
Serber, M. (1970) Shame aversion therapy, *Journal of Behavior Therapy and Experimental Psychiatry*, Vol. 1, pp. 217–26.
Wickramasekera, I. (1976) Aversive behavioral rehearsal for sexual exhibitionism, *Behavior Therapy*, Vol. 7, pp. 167–76.
Woodward, R. (1980) Brief report on the effects of a sex education course on Borstal trainees. Home Office Prison Department Psychological Services DPS Reports, Series II, No. 78.
Zangwill, O.L. (Chairman) (1980) *Behaviour Modification: Report of a Joint Working Party To Formulate Ethical Guidelines for the Conduct of Behaviour Modification Programmes in the National Health Service*, HMSO, London.

CHAPTER 15

SEX THERAPY IN PATIENTS WITH MEDICAL PROBLEMS

Alan J. Riley and Elizabeth J. Riley

At one time sexual problems were considered to be almost always due to psychological factors. It is now accepted that many disease processes, surgical intervention and drugs are also important causative factors in some forms of sexual dysfunction. Successful sexual activity involves several components each of which can be impaired either selectively or collectively by medical conditions. These components include the generation of sexual desire, the occurrence of genital responses and the psychological and physical capability to convert sexual desire into meaningful activity which may or may not be dependent on the presence of genital sexual responses. Except in the case of masturbation the availability of a partner and the partner's willingness to participate in sexual activity are also obvious necessities.

The actual effect that medical conditions have on sexual activity depends to some extent on the patient's pre-morbid sexual adjustment and also on the attitude of the patient's partner. A study by Abramov (1976) demonstrates this point. Of a group of 100 women aged 40 to 60 years, interviewed shortly after being admitted to hospital with myocardial infarction, 65 per cent reported sexual dissatisfaction before their infarction. In contrast, only 24 per cent of 100 women of similar age admitted to hospital for other reasons reported sexual dissatisfaction.

A patient (or partner) may use the occurrence of an illness as a welcome excuse to avoid sexual activity or he or she may use the illness to seek help with a sexual problem that had been present since before the illness started. It is therefore important to assess the quality of the pre-morbid sexual functioning and relationship. It is also important to review carefully the patient's drug treatment bearing in mind that many commonly prescribed medicines can adversely affect sexual responses (see Chapter 8). Space here does not permit a full description of how different diseases can affect sexual function. It is more useful to review in general terms factors involved in the general management of patients presenting with sexual problems relating to medical conditions.

ALLAYING FEAR

Some patients experience sexual difficulties because they fear that sex will aggravate or complicate their medical condition. Patients newly diagnosed as being hypertensive may be concerned that sexual intercourse will increase their blood pressure and this will cause further problems. Providing the blood pressure is well controlled with appropriate therapy, hypertension does not contraindicate sexual activity.

Perhaps the most common situation where fear operates is in patients who are recovering from heart attack or cerebral vascular accident (stroke). The patient is reluctant to do anything which may bring on a second attack of these frightening life-threatening conditions. Many patients have heard rumours of patients dying from heart attack during sexual intercourse but in reality this is a very rare event. In one survey, only 0.6 per cent of sudden deaths occurred during sexual activity, half of which were attributable to heart disease (Ueno, 1963). Extramarital sexual activity, the use of alcohol and sexual situations in which there is excessive anxiety or guilt are probably associated with a greater risk of death than sexual intercourse with a familiar partner in a stable relationship.

Counselling of patients who have suffered a heart attack or stroke should start as soon after the event as is practical. It should be aimed at reducing the fear that sex is dangerous and encouraging a positive attitude towards sex in both the patient and the partner. Following myocardial infarction it is usual for the patient to undertake a programme of increasing exercise over the course of several weeks. Usually, the patient can resume sexual activity once he or she can climb two flights of stairs without getting breathless or chest pain occurring.

Many patients are not advised about the resumption of sexual activity following surgical operations, particularly those on the genital organs. There is the fear that sexual intercourse either will damage the surgical scars or that the operation has made intercourse difficult. In general, surgical scars are usually well healed within six weeks of genital surgery. A careful vaginal examination by the surgeon following operations on the vagina, such as in the repair of prolapse, should reassure the patient that the operation scars are healed and that the vagina is still capable of being penetrated. It will also enable the surgeon to break down any adhesions that might have formed and which might cause discomfort or difficulty during intercourse. Time spent in reassuring the patient about her capability for intercourse at the 'post op' follow-up will reduce anxieties and facilitate an early and successful resumption of sexual activity. Sometimes it is the partner who has excessive anxieties about the effects of intercourse, and he should be counselled as well. Diagrams are often useful in helping the patient understand the nature and effect of the operation. Resuming intercourse in a female superior position so that the woman is in control of the rate and depth of penetration is sometimes helpful in reducing penetration anxiety.

Patients who have recurrent urinary tract symptoms which they can relate to coitus sometimes avoid intercourse for fear of bringing on another attack. Emptying their bladder before and after intercourse may reduce the risk of postcoital urinary infection. Some of these female patients are oestrogen-deficient and replacement oestrogen treatment improves the situation considerably.

RELIEVING MECHANICAL PROBLEMS

Some medical conditions may make intercourse difficult by causing mechanical difficulties which affect either penetration or coital movements. Spasticity of the lower limbs, especially if affecting the thigh muscles, as may occur in multiple sclerosis, in a woman may prevent sufficient separation of the legs to enable penetration to occur. The spasm may be relieved by a muscle-relaxing drug such as diazepam or baclofen taken before attempted intercourse. Severe arthritis of the hips may also limit movement of the thighs and cause difficulty with penetration. Hip replacement will solve the problem but until this is undertaken penetration can sometimes be attained with a rear entry lateral position. Taking a warm bath before intercourse may reduce immobility.

Arthritis affecting the hands may make masturbation and sex play difficult. The use of a vibrator may be helpful although the diameter of the handle may have to be enlarged to facilitate holding by the severely arthritic hand (Riley, 1985).

Amputation of a limb or loss of function of limbs resulting from a stroke may cause difficulty in effecting coital movements, particularly when the affected person is in a superior position. The couple should be encouraged to experiment with alternative coital positions.

The effective size of the entrance to the vagina (introitus) may be reduced following operations on the vagina and vulva and especially after radiotherapy. Gradual dilation, ideally undertaken by the patient's partner using his fingers, with adequate artificial lubrication may overcome this problem.

Very rarely a further operation is required to enlarge the introitus.

Arousal dysfunction in women resulting from damage to the pelvic nerves or blood vessels during pelvic surgery or injury, spinal injury or neurological diseases may bring about a failure of lubrication and consequential dyspareunia. This obviously can be overcome by the use of an artificial lubricant but some patients need advice on this. Failure of lubrication and thinning of the lining of the vagina, which results from oestrogen deficiency, is best treated with oestrogen replacement.

RELIEVING PAIN

Chronic pain can be extremely debilitating and may cause loss of interest in sex. Painful conditions in the pelvis are often aggravated by intercourse and lead the patient to avoid sex. Specific medical or surgical treatment must be prescribed for these conditions. The most common cause of chronic pain is arthritis. Chronic pain originating in the lower spine may be made worse by the movements of intercourse and can be helped by placing a pillow under the back. Painful limbs due to arthritis may also be supported on pillows. A hot bath and the use of analgesics before intercourse help to relieve the arthritic pain. Some people find that they suffer pain and immobility more severely at particular times of the day, such as in the morning, and they should be counselled to avoid intercourse at this time.

Headache occurring in relation to intercourse is not uncommon and can cause considerable distress and fear of suffering a stroke. In the majority of cases this symptom is benign, but medical assessment is required and specific treatments are indicated (Davies and Clifford Rose, 1986).

IMPROVING EFFORT TOLERANCE

Normal sexual activity involves the expenditure of varying amounts of effort. Any medical condition that reduces the patient's ability for physical exertion can impair normal sexual functioning. Patients with heart or lung disease or anaemia may become breathless during intercourse. Many chronic debilitating illnesses may cause the patient to experience muscle aches and pains brought on by coital movements which limit further sexual activity. It is obviously important to treat the primary condition but even with treatment reduced effort tolerance may continue. All too often patients afflicted in this way try sex, find that they cannot complete intercourse and give up. The patient will require advice (usually not asked for directly) on how to minimize the effects of reduced effort tolerance on sex.

It is often necessary to state the obvious during counselling. The unafflicted partner should be encouraged to play a more active role in sex. This may necessitate a complete reversal of sexual roles. The patient should be made to feel at ease if he or she has to interrupt sexual intercourse because of physical discomfort, perhaps completing the act by mutual masturbation if the occurrence of symptoms preclude further strenuous exercise. Factors which aggravate reduced effort tolerance should be avoided. These include being overweight and smoking. Advice on coital positions may also be required in view of the fact that patients with heart disease may find that they get more breathless if they lie flat on their back. Intercourse should be avoided for two to three hours after large meals.

Specific symptomatic treatment may be necessary. The asthmatic who finds that coital exercise induces wheezing will find an inhaled dose of one of the bronchodilating drugs (such as salbutamol) taken before intercourse helpful in preventing this distress. Patients whose effort tolerance is reduced by the occurrence of angina may be helped by taking a long-acting nitrate preparation or a beta adrenoceptor blocking drug (e.g. propranolol) before sex (see Chapter 8). However, the adverse effects of such treatment on sexual responses must be considered.

ENHANCING SELF-ESTEEM

Disease can be an alienating experience with devastating social and psychological consequences. Loss of independence which occurs frequently with chronic debilitating diseases, disfigurement and defects of the special senses or speech often result in reduced self-esteem which in turn will cause the patient to feel less confident sexually. In the case of the breadwinner reduced self-esteem is intensified further by loss of employment and the financial hardship this may cause, which may necessitate drastic changes in lifestyle. The more unworthy a patient feels the more difficult it is for him or her to initiate and maintain satisfactory interpersonal relationships. The negative feelings about sex that the patient may have are often confounded by negative feelings in the partner.

Counselling, involving the patient's sexual partner, aimed at promoting a positive body image and enhancing feelings of self-worth is essential and frequently results in successful sexual re-adjustment. Patients with loss of speech, such as following a stroke, may require help with developing non-verbal communication.

Conditions that cause the most profound loss of self-esteem are those that destroy or disfigure secondary sexual characteristics. Mastectomy, for example, is followed by adverse emotional effects which may persist for many years. Maguire *et al.* (1978) reported that 33 per cent of postmastectomy patients had severe or moderate sexual problems after one year and had either stopped having intercourse or had ceased to enjoy it. Counselling should start before the operation or as soon after it as is possible. Encouraging the patient and her partner to examine and touch the scar is important so that they can both learn to accept the situation. Sexual activity in positions in which the breasts are not dependent (thus the absence of the breast is not emphasized) is sometimes helpful in establishing intercourse after mastectomy. Some patients prefer to wear a prosthesis during sex but this is not recommended as it delays acceptance of the situation.

TREATING DEPRESSION

Depression is a common consequence of chronic ill health and is sometimes not readily recognized and goes untreated. Loss of sex drive, diminished perception of sexual arousal and reduced satisfaction often occur in association with depression. It is sometimes difficult to ascertain whether the patient is depressed because they are experiencing sexual difficulties or whether the sexual problems result from depression. Knowing the patient's level of sexual interest may provide a clue. In general, the presence of a normal level (for the patient) of sexual interest in a depressed patient suggests that the depression is secondary to the sexual difficulty whereas interest is often lost when the sexual difficulty results from depression.

Depression should be adequately treated. Sometimes a trial of antidepressants in chronically ill patients who are not obviously depressed results in a dramatic improvement in their general well-being and enhancement of their sexual functioning.

AESTHETIC CONSIDERATIONS

Perhaps linked with loss of self-esteem patients may find the consequences of their diseases unaesthetic or embarrassing which leads them to avoid sexual relationships. Patients who suffer urinary or faecal incontinence will require advice on how best to cope when the bladder or bowel empties during sexual activity. Manually emptying the bowel and bladder before embarking on sexual activity is sometimes helpful. The patient who has a colostomy or ileostomy (operations which result in the bowel opening onto the abdominal wall) may be anxious about it working during intimacy. Time spent with the couple explaining the mechanics and care of ostomies frequently helps to promote a positive attitude to them. Advice may be needed on coital positions to avoid direct pressure on the stoma bag.

Partners of patients with chronic bronchitis and other chronic lung conditions which readily become infected may be put off by halitosis, coughing and the production of copious sputum. A mouth wash before sexual activity may help to reduce the bad odour and coughing and sputum production can be suppressed by a cough suppressant.

OPTIMIZING RESIDUAL FUNCTION

When disease results in permanent impairment of peripheral sexual responses it is important to make the patient and partner realize that it does not automatically mean the end of their sexual relationship. Patients need to be counselled to identify ways of optimizing whatever residual sexual function they may have. This may require giving the couple 'permission' to do things that they had previously not thought of or which they had considered were wrong or harmful. The emphasis should be on making love rather than having sex.

CONCLUSION

There are two situations confronting the sex therapist concerning sexual difficulties and medical problems. The first is the management of the patient who presents with a sexual difficulty and who is known to have a medical disease or physical defect. The trap is to assume that the two are causally related. Patients with medical diseases can develop sexual difficulties for all the same reasons as a physically fit person, the medical disease being a concurrent but unrelated problem. The second situation is where the patient presents with a sexual difficulty which the therapist suspects may be caused by an as yet undiagnosed disease or organic factor. These patients obviously require medical assessment and opinion. It is our opinion that referral to a medical specialist should occur early in the patient's management thereby allowing for the diagnosis to be made and the direction of therapy defined before the patient becomes demotivated by inappropriate counselling. Early referral would be facilitated by greater collaboration between sex therapists and physicians. Fortunately there is a move in this direction.

ACKNOWLEDGEMENT

The authors are grateful to Miss Wendy Phillips for the preparation of the manuscript.

REFERENCES

Abramov, L.S. (1976) Sexual life and sexual frigidity among women developing acute myocardial infarction, *Psychosomatic Medicine*, Vol. 38, pp. 418–25.

Davies, P. and Clifford Rose, F. (1986) Headaches related to sexual activity, *British Journal of Sexual Medicine*, Vol. 13, pp. 143–5.
Maguire, G.P., Lee, E.G., Bevington, D.J., Kuchemann, C.S., Crabtree, R.J. and Cornell, C.E. (1978) Psychiatric problems in the first year after mastectomy, *British Medical Journal*, i, pp. 963–5.
Riley, A.J. (1985) Painful joints and sexual function, *British Journal of Sexual Medicine,* Vol. 12, pp. 129–30.
Ueno, M. (1963) The so-called coition death, *Japanese Journal of Legal Medicine,* Vol. 17, pp. 333–40.

CHAPTER 16

SEX THERAPY FOR INDIVIDUALS

Martin Cole

Individuals presenting for therapy on their own with a sexual problem, whether they are single, divorced or separated, bereaved, or even married are severely disadvantaged. It is generally agreed that it is difficult to treat people with sexual problems unless they have a partner: indeed, one of the central doctrines of Masters and Johnson (1970) was that 'the relationship is the patient' and few facilities or expertise exist where an individual can be accepted for treatment for a sexual problem without a partner either privately or on the NHS. Thus, they find themselves in the classical 'Catch 22' situation of having a problem which may prevent them from forming a relationship but at the same time needing a relationship to help resolve the problem.

To make matters worse we live in a maritally mobile society with a very high divorce rate. For example, if this rate is measured as the ratio of the number of divorces over the number of marriages entered into in any one year then in 1984 there was a 41 per cent divorce rate (OPCS, 1985). However, even this high figure is almost certainly an underestimate since marriages entered into now, because of the upward secular trend in divorce, will be more at risk than those which took place say ten years ago but are now appearing as the current divorce statistics. Thus, in addition to the very large number of never-married patients who are beginning to seek help together with those who have lost their partners through bereavement there will be an increasing number of those who are separated or divorced some of whom may also need help.

A variety of therapeutic strategies have been designed for men and women with sexual problems but who present without a partner. Group therapy (see Chapter 9) has frequently been reported as an effective means of intervention by several authors. Reynolds *et al.* (1981) used teaching, role-play and homework assignments to help dispose of sexual myths and establish behaviours which would be more likely to lead to effective sexual functioning. They reported a significant improvement in 11 men originally without partners and who previously had difficulties with dating-skills and with erection, but who finally established sexual relationships. They maintained their progress over a six-month follow-up period. Using similar techniques Lobitz and Baker (1979) reported earlier that they were able to help six out of nine men with erectile problems but who, at the time of presentation, had no regular sexual partner. However, Price *et al.* (1981) using a control group designed to test the effectiveness of group therapy in the treatment of erectile dysfunctions in men without partners found that whilst some improvements were noticed there was no significant difference in the final outcome between the treatment and control groups with respect to erectile function. They attributed this to the older mean age of their clients and a lack of emphasis on dating-skills training in this particular programme.

Zilbergeld and Ellison (1979), to whom the reader is particularly referred, argue that social-skills training in either group or individual format plays an essential part in sex therapy for individuals without partners, and draw attention to the increasing need for this facility as sex therapists work more frequently with individuals. Bancroft (1983) devotes considerable attention to the needs of the patient who presents without a partner and describes the use of methods such as individual sensate focus, masturbation and fantasy-training and other covert methods of desensitization. Stravynski (1986) specifically reports on the successful treatment of a patient with erectile failure and premature ejaculation in a man without a partner. His treatment involved social-skills training by a regimen of behavioural interventions. Successful intercourse was achieved after six weeks of treatment and was maintained for a further six months at follow-up.

Of late considerable attention has been focused upon the sexual needs of those who have either a physical or mental handicap (see Chapter 12). Since these patients will normally present without a partner then some of the methods outlined in this chapter will be of particular interest.

Heterosocial-skills training is not readily available in the UK, and where facilities do exist there are often long waiting lists. In the best of all possible worlds it works well (Altman *et al.*, 1985) but it is unlikely to become a standard procedure until there is a vast increase in the resources available in this field of therapy.

THERAPEUTIC METHODS

Cognitive, psychoeducational and behavioural methods have an important and integrated part to play in social- and sexual-skills training where in the absence of a partner the presenting individual has to take much more responsibility for his or her therapeutic progress. Cognitive therapy depends upon the principle that an individual's thoughts, beliefs and expectations of himself or herself and the outside world (*cognitions*) will influence his or her feelings and emotions (*affect*) and hence behaviour (Beck, 1976; Kowalski, 1985a; 1985b; 1985c). Thus, to change maladaptive emotions and inappropriate behaviours, thoughts and beliefs need also to be changed and put in a rational and realistic perspective.

Closely allied to and overlapping with these cognitive methods is the psychoeducational approach of Ellis (1983). This also aims to increase self-awareness and knowledge of the world at large though here greater emphasis is placed upon providing appropriate *information* and *instructions* so that new lifestyle strategies can be initiated by the patient. Behavioural methods (see Chapter 7) are also important and are used to help modify the patient's maladaptive behaviour so as to improve his or her social and sexual functioning.

Much of what is written in this section is directed towards the individual *male* who is seeking help. Up to now there is no doubt that because of biosocial pressures to take initiatives in the processes of relationship formation the man is particularly disadvantaged. Thus there are very many men who have had neither a relationship nor any sexual experience because of the high levels of anxiety triggered by the prospect of courtship, sex play and coitus. These individuals are heterophobic (Cole, 1986). However, there are also many anxious women who can also benefit from this approach though it has to be said that women are less likely to be disadvantaged heterosocially, at least at the present time, if only because normally they will have the advantage of being exposed to the more assertive sociosexual behaviour of the male which will serve as a natural desensitizer to the female heterophobe. It could also be argued that the woman is intrinsically less vulnerable to stress of this kind (see Chapter 3).

MOTIVATION

Before any work is done with the man seeking help it is essential that he is encouraged to examine his own motivation to change. Many heterophobic men with little or no sexual experience live at home with an ageing parent and have evolved a secure and comfortable lifestyle. They may then present asking for help to find a partner, and assistance in reducing their sexual anxieties with the long-term objective of forming a relationship and perhaps of eventually getting married. In some cases, however, the patient has not fully examined the consequences of having a close relationship and he needs to be encouraged to do this carefully so that he can be sure that this is really what he wants.

In the remainder of this section the use of this *cognitive-behavioural-psychoeducational* approach is described firstly in connection with the need to acquire a partner and secondly in relation to more specific sexual strategies that need to be undertaken.

STRATEGIES FOR ACQUIRING A PARTNER

Initially the male patient needs to change his attitude towards himself in such a way that he can view himself and the world at large in a more positive way. He is urged to accept himself as a valuable and lovable human being, yet at the same time these changes must be made in a reasonable manner so that his expectations of himself and of the world at large remain realistic. So, for example, a man who is deeply introverted and dislikes crowds and has never danced a step in his life should not be encouraged to go to a disco, at least until he feels much more confident.

To achieve the goal of meeting people and eventually forming a relationship the patient should be encouraged to sit down with pen and paper and work out an overall strategy over a time scale of approximately six months to a year. The details of this scenario will vary considerably from individual to individual but so as to provide some idea of the value of such an approach some guidelines are set out below.

Purely as an intellectual exercise he should try and calculate the number of available potential partners 'out there' in his 'catchment area'. If he lives in a large urban community the number will be surprisingly large and if he lives in a small village or town his estimate might have to include neighbouring communities and towns.

He should disabuse himself of any idea that he is too old, too ugly, too poor, too anxious or too ineffectual to get a partner. He should be reminded that age in particular is much less important than it was for men, at least the older one gets the greater choice becomes.

His attention should be directed to his appearance, his clothing and his general social skills and often very simple changes in the style of clothes can produce dramatic changes. Slip-on shoes instead of lace-ups; clothes that fit, clothes that are new, clothes that are clean and clothes that are casual and fashionable all help. Sometimes contact lenses instead of spectacles reveal attractive eyes. Changes in hair style, even changes in underwear can prove rewarding. All wool, loosely fitting vests and pants more appropriate to the 1940s can have a very negative effect on a potential sexual partner. Above all, attention to body cleanliness and the use of underarm deodorants is very important as is sometimes a visit to the dentist.

His attention should also be drawn to the fact that not all women want a 'macho' male and that there is a great demand for the sensitive, emotionally perceptive man.

If he is unemployed it is obviously very important that if at all possible he tries to get some paid employment. Not only will this put some money in his pocket it will also increase his sense of self-esteem and improve his standing with potential partners. If paid employment is not possible then he should try to obtain a position on a 'job-start' programme or any of the current government training schemes. If this fails he should then attempt to get a voluntary job so that his time is occupied and he has an opportunity to meet people.

If his financial resources allow he should get himself a car so that he is mobile.

If he is living at home with his parent(s) he should seriously consider moving out. Sometimes this makes economic sense if he can afford a mortgage; it certainly makes good psychological sense because once away from home he can learn to be independent and perhaps the inevitable loneliness will increase his motivation to find a partner. (Care should be taken that his isolation does not lead to depression and further isolation.) Then there is the obvious advantage of having a place of his own in which to entertain.

He then needs to address himself to the ways and means of meeting a partner. He might make a list of the commonest ways by which men and women meet their partners. These are at parties and dances and other social events; at work; through agencies and of course by chance encounters. These various alternatives should be examined and as a man he must realize that he has to get out and face the world, no one will come knocking at his door saying 'I have found you, darling.'

Most local authorities publish a local *What's On* magazine listing local clubs, societies, social and sports activities. Evening classes are also advertised and these provide another useful way of meeting people. Language classes often have a good mix of the sexes whereas computer programming and car maintenance will be largely for men, therefore, it is important to make an intelligent choice of subject area.

Searching for a partner on one's own can sometimes be a lonely activity so if this search can be done in company it makes the exercise much more rewarding. Therefore it is important if possible to form friendships of any kind and with either sex.

He needs to be reminded that relationships between the sexes are of many types and levels of intensity and where there may or may not be a strong sexual element present. As part of the rehearsal and acquisition of social and sexual skills a so-called 'platonic' relationship can be extremely valuable. Prospective partners therefore should not be excluded simply because there does not appear to be any immediate erotic element in the friendship.

It should be remembered that there are two parts to the overall strategy – the first is to *meet* someone, the second to *form a relationship*. Therefore he should be continuously alert to new opportunities and be prepared to *act* and not let these chances become missed opportunities. He should therefore be encouraged to accept all invitations and not reject new experiences however unpromising they may appear or disillusioned he may become.

He should try at all times to dismiss rigid views of himself and other people and give any experiences a chance to work – most people improve on acquaintance and there is much in the view that *propinquity* is a very powerful element in the bonding process. If two people are thrown together, through whatever circumstances, they may discover a bond develop between them which otherwise would not have been forged. All relationships need time to mature – love at first sight is a rare event.

SEXUAL STRATEGIES

Sex plays a very large part in the initiation of a 'pairbond' (Morris, 1967). Of course there are some long-lasting relationships between individuals of the same or opposite sex where sexual attraction plays little or no part in the transaction but this is unusual outside the members of an extended family.

For those, therefore, who have problems with sex, relationship formation and its maintenance are likely to be difficult if not impossible. For example, for those who are deeply underconfident sexually and who may remain sexually inexperienced in their late twenties; for those who are victims of a broken relationship and where their sexual inadequacy had a part to play, and for those who have a clearly defined sexual disorder, establishing and maintaining a relationship may prove exceedingly difficult.

Naturally, more responsibility falls upon the male than upon the female in relationship formation, for reasons which have already been discussed (and see Chapter 3). Moreover, to add to his problems the male needs to get an erection and last at least a minute or two before ejaculation in order to, as he sees it, 'have sex' and 'please' his partner. The penis is a particularly sensitive barometer to a man's feelings about himself and his partner and the sexually precarious man can soon enter a self-perpetuating cycle of non-responsiveness. Feeling so deeply humiliated by the possibility of failure he may opt out of all potential sexual encounters and therefore cease even to look for a partner. Even men who know themselves to be popular with the opposite sex and who have more than adequate social skills may not seek out a serious relationship for fear of the possibility of failure and humiliation.

One way for these men to gain confidence and deal with their performance anxiety in the absence of a suitable partner of their own is to seek surrogate therapy (see p. 282). However, this form of therapy is expensive and not readily available, at least in the UK. Alternatively one has to rely upon the *integrated cognitive-behavioural-psychoeducational* approach, already referred to, using whatever procedures are available to motivate and prepare the individual for his first (or next) sexual encounter. This is not easy and clearly the *in vivo* methods implicit in surrogate therapy are to be preferred. Nevertheless, much can be done to help the sexually precarious man overcome his fears and learn how to initiate and respond sexually in a relationship. Though there is a considerable overlap between the three elements of the cognitive-behavioural-psychoeducational triad these have been separated, somewhat arbitrarily, simply in the interest of clarity. The ideas presented below do not claim to be exhaustive, but I hope will serve to indicate the value of this kind of approach.

THE PSYCHOEDUCATIONAL MODE

Ellis (1983) specifically describes what he means by the psychoeducational approach. 'Therapy however it is done, consists largely in *teaching* people how to look after themselves, how to undefensively see the way in which they are sabotaging their own basic goals and interests' (p. 37). An important part of this psychoeducational process is to help the individual dispose of what Zilbergeld (1980) described as sexual myths, that is, false ideas and expectations of himself and the opposite sex. To illustrate how this didactic approach can be used, listed below are a number of elementary facts about which men (and women), often misinformed, can be re-educated.

Men don't always want sex nor are they always ready for it – they are not sex machines. Indeed it is not essential that all physical contact should lead to sex, or should it do so then sex does not necessarily mean intercourse.

Men remain sexually responsive throughout their lives and though advancing age may slow down their responses there is no particular cut-off point at which a man's capacity to respond sexually disappears altogether.

As men age they require more direct and prolonged physical stimulation to the penis. It is important that they communicate this need to their partners verbally or non-verbally instead of hoping that his partner will discover this fact by telepathy or intuition.

It is often thought that by not masturbating a man can save himself and ensure a stronger and more long-lasting erection when the opportunity for intercourse arises. If anything the reverse is true since the neurohormonal mechanisms are then unprepared if there has been a long interval between ejaculations.

Quantity is not quality. It is not the length of intercourse that matters but the quality of the total sexual experience. A man's attention should be drawn to the more subtle physical and emotional rewards afforded by extending precoital sex play. Most men, once they have penetrated, last only three or four minutes, indeed, some women will complain that men go on too long.

A large number of women, perhaps as many as one in two (see Chapter 2) do not achieve an orgasm in intercourse without some manual assistance. This is a fact of life and it does not reflect badly either on him or her. Communication between them later can help to solve any difficulty that may arise though he must be reminded that both he and she can have good sex without her being orgasmic.

Men tend to project their own preoccupations about genital sensations and performance on to their partners. Although some partners are clearly very demanding sexually, there are many who are not, but who instead are often more nurturing and protective and hence more accepting of a man's problem.

Apart from providing *information*, the psychoeducational approach may involve giving *instructions*, for example:

If a man has a specific sexual problem that he feels may interfere with his sexual responses he should share this information with his partner before attempting intercourse. He should not 'soldier on' hoping that he will not fail this time. If he keeps his guilty secret he will be preoccupied with the risk of failure which will in turn raise his anxieties and make failure a self-fulfilling prophecy.

Though for each couple in a new relationship the point of readiness for intercourse is often arrived at intuitively, nevertheless there is little point in putting off the time when sexual intimacy begins because of the fear of failure. The longer it is put off the longer there is for the man's fear to incubate and gain strength. The various ways of deciding when to have sex with a new partner should be explored. The British are particularly reticent about communicating feelings but there is no harm in talking about sex and one's intentions with a partner beforehand. There is the myth that seduction needs to be spontaneous if it is to be romantic, but there are very many alternative options such as deciding to share a bed non-sexually to start with as a means of getting to know someone better.

THE COGNITIVE MODE

There is little doubt that the perception and evaluation of our sexual responses will in turn influence our own sexual behaviours. Indeed the whole meaning and value that we attach to erotic events is profoundly influenced by the cognitive activity of the brain; activity which in turn will either potentiate or inhibit particular patterns of sexual behaviour (Wolfe and Walen, 1982). Indeed, this may be the basis to what is described as *permission-giving*. Therefore, by using the cognitive approach the therapist aims to change the cognitions of the male patient (i.e. his thoughts, beliefs and expectations of himself, his partner and the outside world) so as to foster positive, adaptive and pleasurable sexual experiences.

Listed are a number of suggestions to illustrate how the cognitive approach might be used to help the man without a partner to change his self-evaluation and assist him in achieving a successful sexual experience.

He should become aware that his sexual partner is probably just as anxious about his first encounter as he is.

His attention should be drawn to the fact that if he can produce a good, hard erection himself by masturbation then it also follows that he should be able to produce an equally good hard erection when he is with his partner.

He needs to know in advance that if he loses his erection in sex play this is not 'terrible, awful or horrible'; that it is indeed a probable event particularly in a new relationship and that it is simply a consequence of him not being sufficiently relaxed. He knows from previous experiences (see pp. 281–2) that if he loses an erection he can regain it and that this is only a temporary setback.

In the same way, early ejaculation in intercourse must not be evaluated as a catastrophe. He needs to be reassured that it is not necessary for him to have prolonged intercourse to enjoy sex and to satisfy his partner.

The fear of rejection needs to be challenged cognitively. This fear is almost always found in those with heterosocial- or heterosexual-skills deficiencies (Zilbergeld and Ellison, 1979). For example, patients should be asked to try to balance in their minds the pain of rejection against the rewards of taking some risks such as initiating the early stages of sex play. Their attention should also be drawn to the fundamental behavioural principle that every time they back off from a threat or a feared experience this avoidance behaviour is reinforced because of the temporary relief felt as they withdraw from the threatening experience. If this happens, then the next time it becomes even more difficult to face the fear and the rewarding avoidance follows again until approach behaviour becomes so difficult that it stops.

THE BEHAVIOURAL MODE

Behaviour therapy plays a very large part in the treatment of sex disorders in couple therapy. It is therefore not surprising that it will also have an important place in the treatment of partnerless individuals.

However, there is often a larger cognitive element involved in individual behavioural therapy than in couple therapy to compensate for the lack of a partner. For example, Stravynski (1986) used both cognitive and behavioural methods in his treatment programme for erectile failure. In his package he used modelling, instruction-giving, desensitization, role-play, feedback from patient and self-monitoring to produce the appropriate behavioural change.

Most of the following procedures described are discussed elsewhere in this book (see Chapter 7).

Role-play

Role-play is a very effective means of preparing a male patient for an eventual sexual encounter. By providing him with an opportunity to role-play courtship and sex play he can rehearse a variety of behaviours in advance. For example, he can learn how to communicate his fears, practise elementary courtship skills and rehearse communicating requests or questions to partners such as 'Will you hold my penis?' 'What gives you pleasure?' or 'How do you like your clitoris stimulated?' and so on.

Masturbation- and fantasy-training

To a greater or lesser extent a man has some control over his sexual fantasies. By indicating to him how he might modify his existing masturbatory fantasy and substitute another provides a useful therapeutic technique. For example, some heterophobic men with little or no sexual experience do not fantasize themselves having intercourse, instead they limit their fantasies to sex play (or they may not fantasize at all). In these cases they should be given instructions to introduce a graded series of appropriate fantasies which will eventually include the target behaviour. This kind of approach is particularly useful where, for example, the patient may be ambivalent about the direction of his drive and reports a mixture of homosexual and heterosexual fantasies. Finally, if the patient's repertoire of fantasies is somewhat limited he can be taught, perhaps with the help of magazines and films, to switch from a 'performance mode' to an 'erotic mode' so that he can rehearse perceiving sources of pleasure other than from simple genital stimulation.

More specifically, masturbation-training can be used in the treatment of erectile failure and premature ejaculation. In the former, for example, the patient should rehearse gaining, losing and finally regaining his erection and in the latter he should practise the stop-start and squeeze techniques.

The role of masturbation-training in women for the treatment of orgasmic dysfunction is well-documented (Heiman *et al.*, 1976) and is used both in couple and individual therapy. Less is known about the effectiveness of fantasy-training in women, no doubt because it is often more difficult to initiate masturbatory fantasies in women. However, it would clearly have a role to play not only in the treatment of orgasmic problems but also in the treatment of vaginismus in conjunction with the use of a graded series of dilators.

Individual sensate focus

Individual sensate focus is simply a modified application to an individual format of the well-known programme of couple sensate focus (Masters and Johnson, 1970). The patient is instructed to proceed through the graded series of exercises beginning with self-stimulation and caressing over the whole of his or her body. By focusing on this non-demand means of self-arousal he or she can learn not only to relax but to switch attention away from performance-oriented behaviours. Eventually self-stimulation of the penis or the vulva can be incorporated into the programme.

SURROGATE SEX THERAPY*

Introduction

Sex therapists have been forced into using what must be regarded as less efficient methods of therapy because of the legal, ethical and practical difficulties involved in providing suitable partners for single patients. *In vivo* methods, whatever their nature, possess many advantages over those which attempt to intervene solely by psychotherapy and where the individual patient has, sooner or later, to transfer his 'modified behaviour' to a real partner without any previous opportunity for practical rehearsal. If this fact is not self-evident to therapists then it certainly is to those patients without partners who present for help with a sexual problem.

Masters and Johnson (1970) were probably the first to use substitute sexual partners. They called them 'partner surrogates' and treated 54 single men and 3 single women with various sexual problems in this way. Between 1959 and 1970 they achieved an overall 'success' rate of 78 per cent but they eventually stopped using surrogates because of the bad publicity which

* Parts of this section appear in Cole (1985). Throughout this section it has been assumed that the surrogate is female and the patient male. In practice, of course, male surrogates are able to help female patients equally well.

resulted from their use, though more recently they have accepted patients for surrogate therapy provided that the patient supplies his own surrogate.

As early as 1972 the Institute for Sex Education and Research's (ISER) clinic in Birmingham used surrogate sex partners in sex therapy and since then over 400 patients have entered treatment (see p. 290).

The role of the surrogate partner in sex therapy is complex. Briefly however, her role is to help the patient acquire sexual skills, previously deficient. She will attempt to help him to reduce his anxiety about the prospect of intimate sexual situations and in general provide the very best form of psychotherapeutic help by listening, talking and sharing feelings, fantasies and fears. As Masters and Johnson (1970) put it, the surrogate is 'someone to hold on to, talk to, work with, learn from, be a part of and above all else give to and get from' (p. 147).

On the West Coast of the US surrogate therapy is widely practised. The International Professional Surrogate Association (IPSA) provides training programmes, legal advice and ethical guidelines for surrogates and continues to flourish. However, even in the States there are some reservations. Malamuth *et al.* (1976) reported that although only 28 per cent of the professionals they questioned in the US had used surrogates 87 per cent said they would only do so if they were certain about the legality of the practice. In the UK where, for example, neither prostitution nor adultery are unlawful there should be fewer problems – though the basic conservatism of our culture has done little to encourage their use here.

In spite of their widespread use there has been very little published on surrogate therapy. Somers (1978; 1981) reports his experience in treating a group of 12 male patients with surrogates. After completing a programme of a mean of 10 sessions, lasting 4 months, there was a 'marked improvement' in 9 patients, 'improvement' in 2 patients and 'equivocal improvement' in 1. These results were maintained at follow-ups over a mean period of 7.5 months. Jacobs *et al.* (1975) reports on 2 female and 1 male surrogate and describes how their sessions were organized and Wolfe (1978), in a somewhat cynical account of surrogate therapy in the US, highlights the difficulties in their use. Apfelbaum (1977) goes even further when he argues that the whole idea of the surrogate playing a therapeutic role is a myth. I shall try to suggest otherwise.

The methods used and the outcome of treatment programmes using surrogates at the institute's clinic have been reported elsewhere (Cole, 1982); the only other publication in Britain was a report on the outcome of one patient of this series who had presented with severe heterophobia (Brewer, 1978). This chapter up-dates the work of the institute's clinic in this area of sex therapy reporting on 425 patients who have presented for surrogate therapy.

How does it work?

The manner in which a surrogate partner intervenes to help a patient cannot be presented simply: each treatment programme will be unique depending upon the personality of the surrogate and the patient and the nature of the presenting problem. The surrogate is confronted with a very difficult and complex task. Here she is meeting for the first time a complete stranger with a sexual problem who is often very apprehensive about what is in store for him. He will be worried about his own performance and in particular about the person who has been chosen to help him.

If one can encapsulate the advice that is given to the surrogate in her training it would be this. She must be prepared and able to take responsibility for this patient. Without being overtly assertive she must be able to provide a supportive context in which he can begin to relax. He must be able to disclose to her any pressures that he might have, for example, the conflicts he may experience about taking initiatives, or his need to please her and particularly his need to perform. She must try to convey to him that the meetings they will have must be to do with pleasure and not performance. Above all she must accomplish this role of taking responsibility in a way which is still compatible with her femininity. She must create an atmosphere which leads to the reduction of anxiety in the patient, but at the same time she must not forget the important role that sexual arousal plays in the therapeutic process. Too much emphasis on relaxation may lead the patient either to fall asleep or cognitively to spectate; too much arousal, too soon, will almost inevitably lead to performance-oriented fears.

The role of the surrogate in the therapeutic process

The simplest way to try to understand the role of the surrogate in the therapeutic process is to see her as occupying a variable point somewhere on an imaginary line between a prostitute and wife or girlfriend. Some surrogates will approximate more closely to the prostitute role whilst others more to the role of wife (or princess).

Whether the patient already has a relationship or is on his own and whatever the nature of the presenting problem, the intervention of a surrogate can provide a uniquely valuable asset to sex therapy. For example, where the patient has no available partner the surrogate provides the opportunity for practical therapeutic intervention which would otherwise not be available. Where previous or current relationships exist there may have been a long history of sexual failure or habituation may be playing a part in blocking sexual responses. Clearly in these circumstances the intervention of a surrogate will be invaluable. Paradoxically, surrogate therapy works often because there is no involved relationship between the patient and surrogate. Incestuous feelings do play a part in blocking sexual arousal and clearly these will be minimized in surrogate therapy. The absence of a significant relationship between the patient and surrogate will also mean that the patient's need to please his partner will be reduced and any failure experienced will not result in a dramatic loss of self-esteem which is more likely to happen in a serious relationship where performance fears can reach crippling levels.

The surrogates – who are they?

The 43 surrogates (34 women and 9 men) who have worked in my clinic over the past 13 years have been drawn from a wide cross-section of society. Though no attempt has been made to research their motivations or quantify their psychological profiles it is quite apparent that they are all very different people with their own quite private reasons for wanting to be a surrogate. The women range from their early twenties to their late forties and the men to their late fifties. Of the 34 women, 15 are married, 13 divorced, 1 separated and 5 are single. Of the 9 men, 4 are married, 4 divorced and 1 is single. The majority of the surrogates had heard of our work through the media and approached the clinic on their own initiative. One or two had been patients or the wives or husbands of patients and a few were approached personally and asked if they were interested in working as a surrogate. All the applicants were interviewed and generally required to satisfy three main criteria. The surrogate needed to be sufficiently intelligent to understand the basic ideas behind sex therapy; though they were not required to have a professional interest in the subject. Secondly, it was important that they were relatively uninhibited sexually so as to be able to engage in a fairly full sexual repertoire – so as to be able to give patients adequate permission to be sexual themselves. Lastly, it was very important that they were relatively free from the resentments that the sexes so often harbour against each other. Naturally, any evidence of a recent or recurring psychiatric history would also have to be considered carefully. Beyond these considerations there was a great need to obtain a wide spectrum of personality and appearance in order to allow the therapist (myself) as much flexibility as possible in assigning the surrogates appropriately – a process which is of considerable therapeutic importance.

Masters and Johnson (1970) reported that they rejected 60 per cent of the volunteers they interviewed as potential surrogates. Moreover, they only chose a woman for this role who was able to 'convey pride and confidence in her own innate femaleness' (p. 151). I am sure that if we had insisted upon such a criterion in Britain it would have proved very difficult to find even one surrogate. And it is of doubtful value. Good ego-strength may sound excellent in theory – in practice it can be therapeutically counterproductive since it is very important that the patient is able to perceive, albeit intuitively, an element of sensitivity, even vulnerability, in his partner if he is going to be able to relate to her sufficiently to attempt to solve his own problems.

The motivations of each surrogate are likely to be complex and individually different. For some the financial incentive is likely to be a powerful one. However, by accepting a fee she may be able to give herself permission to be sexual in exactly the same way as the patient is enabled to respond by paying a fee. This contractual agreement, though different in degree from that of the prostitute and her client, nevertheless does play an important role in the therapeutic process. More important, however, is the opportunity that being a surrogate provides her with the chance to meet people. Allied to this need for people, in someone who is otherwise quite reserved, is the protective drive and the need to help at a purely altruistic level. Thus, without belabouring the point, one can picture a relationship between the surrogate and her patient which is not quite as skewed as it might first appear. Instead, we have two people trying to help each other, and each reciprocally providing permission for the other. In practice this symmetry may be concealed in the surrogate-patient contract but it is there as an underlying and important dimension.

In her contract of employment the surrogate is asked to accept responsibility for her own fertility control. Where the surrogate is male no treatment of a female patient is undertaken without the most scrupulous attention to her contraception. The surrogate in her contract is also requested to be responsible for informing the clinic and seeking treatment for any infectious condition which is likely to be transmitted to the patient. The risks of sexually transmitted disease are small but continual vigilance is required. Generally the surrogates are in stable relationships and since the patient's sexual history will be known in detail, and moreover he will have been examined, sexually transmitted disease has not been a problem. The crisis created by the arrival of AIDS (HIV) has meant that even more scrupulous attention must be paid to the sexual histories of the patients and lifestyle of the surrogates before a treatment programme is started.

Most of the skills required of the surrogate are intuitive. Assuming that care has been taken in her selection then extensive training is not required. She is asked to familiarize herself with the basic ideas in sex therapy, for example, by reading Bernie Zilbergeld's (1980) book *Men and Sex*. She will have seen the institute's videos on sex therapy and had an opportunity to discuss problems she is likely to meet. Most of her skills however will be acquired once she has started seeing patients. Then she will have to learn how to follow an optimal strategy taking decisions to modify a programme which will have been outlined beforehand by the therapist in charge. In addition, ongoing support is provided by 'round table' discussions throughout the treatment programme. The surrogate, patient and the supervising therapist (myself) will monitor progress and introduce changes as and when necessary.

Ethical issues

There are two separate yet overlapping areas of ethical concern: those to do with the patient and those to do with the surrogate, though the chief objection is that because the surrogate is identified as a prostitute in the public eye moral objections to prostitution are levelled against the surrogate. In seeking a surrogate sex partner the patient is bypassing the biosocial constraints of courtship and its accompanying agonies and anxieties and will hopefully achieve intercourse. Thus the surrogate (like the prostitute) is seen as an overtly sexual woman instead of the societal stereotype of a sexually coy female.

Concern for the patient centres mainly on the fear that he (or she) will bond with the surrogate and hence the whole exercise will be counterproductive or that even with the knowledge and consent of his or her partner, where they exist, the exercise must of necessity be immoral because the professional is condoning adultery. However, the sex therapist involved in surrogate therapy can go some way to satisfy rational criticism of his or her methods. For example, one should obviously ensure that the patient and surrogate are over the age of 18, that it is heterosexual therapy and that consents are obtained, whenever possible, from both the patient and the partner, though treatment is not normally withheld if the partner's consent is not given. Reasonable precautions should naturally be taken to prevent the chances of pregnancy and reduce the likelihood of sexually transmitted diseases to a minimum. Confidentiality must be preserved at all costs and finally the therapist must be prepared to take responsibility for what he or she does.

Legal issues

There are at least three sections in the *Sexual Offences Act, 1956* where a successful prosecution could be secured against a sex therapist using surrogates in a therapeutic programme. They are an offence of procuring (*section 22*), an offence of living off (wholly or in part) the immoral earnings of a prostitute (*section 30*) and the offence of keeping a brothel (*section 33*).

Statute law, quite properly, cannot recognize motives. Thus, though there are clearly mitigating circumstances in the use of surrogates which might be accepted by the courts the deterrent effect of a possible conviction remains. However, the police exercise, as part of the Briton's insatiable need for compromise, a large measure of discretion.

Thus, prosecutions under the *Sexual Offences Act, 1956* and the *Street Offences Act, 1959* are episodic. They depend very much upon circumstances and in particular the mood of public opinion. So far no legal proceedings have been taken against a bona fide professional who has used surrogate partners in sex therapy and assuming that there were no legitimate complaints it is very probable that such a practice would be tolerated in the same way that termination of pregnancy was tolerated before the *Abortion Act, 1967* as long as the abortion was performed by a qualified medical practitioner in a proper place.

Though I think it would be safe to say that no professionally qualified person need fear prosecution under existing legislation in Britain, nevertheless the risk, however small, might well deter (and indeed has probably deterred) many professionals from openly using surrogates.

Therapeutic factors

Much of the time the patient and surrogate are together is spent talking – or more specifically with the patient talking and the surrogate listening. Naturally (with some exceptions) most of the surrogates have not had any professional training in psychotherapy. However, they can call upon a wealth of intuitive and practical experience of relationships that prepares them for this role. More important is the way in which they can provide the patient with an opportunity to off-load perhaps hitherto undisclosed experiences and fears, and in providing a listening ear give support and reassurance when necessary. However, their main function will be to provide the patient with as much warmth and empathy as is compatible with their role as a surrogate and this must take precedence if there is any risk of the relationship becoming too clinical.

Informational input

Many patients who present for help are poorly informed about their own and the opposite sex. The surrogate is in the unique position of being able to provide sex education in the very best sense of the word. Her body may be a complete mystery to the patient and the most basic of steps in courtship and sex play may be uncharted territory. Although such comments apply particularly to the inexperienced heterophobe most men and women with sexual problems can benefit from the educational aspects of therapy, such as those referred to earlier in this chapter (see p. 278). They should, naturally, be encouraged to ask questions, though the surrogate should always be aware of the individual variation in sexual needs and responses, and the patient should not go away with an oversimplified account of sexual behaviour (see Chapter 2).

The cognitive approach

In the use of cognitive methods perhaps the surrogate's role should be limited to helping the patient adopt a rational view of his problem and discourage him from 'catastrophizing' (Dryden, 1984). For example, many single patients with sexual problems overinvest in relationships and suffer the many unfortunate consequences that follow emotional rejection. If the dangers and the self-sabotaging nature of their behaviours are spelled out and they can be taught how to perceive the situation more sensibly (Hauck, 1981; 1982) then much can be done to help whatever sexual difficulties they may have.

However, particular attention should also be drawn to a large group of men with sexual problems who are best described as 'low-affect' males. These men have a highly developed cognitive approach to life and are well represented in those occupations who present most often for help with a sexual problem, for example, accountants, solicitors and electrical engineers!

An overdependence upon the use of cognitive methods throughout treatment with this group is likely to be counterproductive, where instead the purpose of therapy in these cases would be to try to develop their affect and put them in touch with their feelings (but see Barlow [1986] and Chapter 18).

The behavioural approach

The behavioural approach plays a prominent part in sex therapy and the surrogate needs to have at her disposal a basic understanding of the principles and practice of the main behavioural methods and be familiar with the work of Masters and Johnson (1970). In particular she should be familiar with the concepts of desensitization, stimulus-fading, sensate focus, the squeeze and stop-start techniques and understand the roles of anxiety-reduction and arousal in eliciting sexual responses (see Chapter 7).

A good surrogate, therefore, will be one who, whilst providing warmth and empathy, can also skilfully call upon and use those elements of the cognitive-behavioural-psychoeducational approach (see p. 275) appropriate to her partner's needs.

RESEARCH AND OUTCOMES OF SURROGATE THERAPY

The patient sample of the Institute for Sex Education and Research (ISER)

The sample is made up of every patient who was offered surrogate therapy (with the exception of two for whom there was inadequate information) who attended the ISER clinic between 1970 and the autumn of 1986. The majority of patients are male (see Table 16.1). The reason for the preponderance of men arises largely from the publicity that the clinic has received over the years from the media which has emphasized its role in

Table 16.1 Characteristics of patient sample

Total sample size (n)	425	100%
Mean age	36.6 ± 10.9* years	
Males	390	91.8%
Females	35	8.2%
Marital status: Single	287	67.6%
Married	97	22.8%
Divorced	20	4.7%
Separated	11	2.6%
Widowed	10	2.3%

* Sample standard deviation

Table 16.2 Treatment programmes

Total sample size (n)	425	100%
Diagnostic only programmes	27	6.3%
Treatment terminated by patient	57	13.4%
Treatment terminated by therapist	25	5.9%
Final treatment sample size (n)	316	74.4%
Location of treatment: clinic	347	81.5%
elsewhere	78	18.4%
Mean no. of sessions per programme	4.1 ± 3.8*	

* Sample standard deviation

providing surrogate therapy and which to the general public has usually meant the provision of 'surrogate wives'! Even though many women have been accepted for treatment and offered male surrogate partners it is not easy for a woman to present on her own, break with tradition and request help of this kind. Not surprisingly the majority of patients are single but their presence has highlighted the needs of this previously neglected group. (Cole [1985] provides an account of surrogate therapy for those who are married.)

Table 16.2 identifies the three categories of patient who were excluded from the final analysis. They were those who attended for only one or more diagnostic sessions and where the therapeutic contract was only to establish the nature and quality of the patient's current sexual behaviour without the prospect of further treatment (6.3 per cent). Included in this diagnostic category would be patients who, for example, wished to establish whether they were likely to ejaculate prematurely with another partner (i.e. the surrogate) or those who had had no sexual experiences for many years and wished to find out how they might respond sexually after a long period of abstinence. Then there were those patients who terminated treatment before its conclusion (13.4 per cent). This group dropped out for any number of reasons which may have been financial, patient-surrogate incompatibility or for an undisclosed reason. Finally, there were those whose programmes were terminated prematurely by the therapist (myself) (5.9 per cent). The reasons for this were where it was discovered that surrogate therapy was inappropriate, perhaps through a misdiagnosis, or where (rarely) the surrogate felt she could not proceed further with treatment with a particular patient. The final sample size, after these categories of patient had been removed, was 316.

Most of the therapy was conducted on the clinic premises (81.5 per cent) though 78 patients have been treated elsewhere, for example, in the surrogate's or patient's home, where long distances would be otherwise involved in travel. Recently, however, most therapy has been practised in the clinic because of the necessity for careful supervision which is not easy elsewhere. The mean number of sessions per patient was 4.1 ± 3.8 though there is a large variance.

Presenting problems

The men who sought help from surrogate therapy presented with 1 of 14 fairly distinct disorders, some of which (e.g. erectile dysfunction) were again subdivided (see Table 16.3). The women presented with 1 of 7 disorders (see Table 16.4). These conditions will be familiar to most sex therapists though some amplification may be helpful.

Because of the difficulties in making an accurate diagnosis, particularly in the early years, a majority of men presenting with erectile disorders were classified as either having primary (1°) or secondary (2°) erectile dysfunction of no known origin. This is clearly unsatisfactory since no attempt has been made to identify whether the condition is predominantly biogenic or psychogenic. This deficiency also accounts for the poor outcomes of patients in these categories. Indeed, even at the time of writing, it is proving very difficult to obtain, on the NHS, facilities which would enable an accurate biogenic/psychogenic diagnosis to be made and one is often only able to assess the hormonal status of the patient and little else. Absolute retarded ejaculation (one patient only) describes the condition where ejaculation has not been achieved even in self-masturbation.

The category of heterophobia represents the second largest group of males (after erectile dysfunction) and the largest group of females. This is a condition which is well represented in this clinic but is rarely, if ever, identified elsewhere (Cole, 1986). The main reasons for this are because in the absence of a suitable treatment programme (*viz.* surrogate therapy) patients with this condition will not normally present for help or when they

Table 16.3 Therapeutic gain by sex disorder in men

Presenting problem	*Total sample size (n = 390)*	*Treatment sample size (n = 289)*	*Per cent (n)*		*Mean presenting score*	*Mean outcome score*	*Therapeutic gain*
Erectile dysfunction (ED):							
1° biogenic*	7	6	2.1		0	1.3	1.3
1° psychogenic	1	1	<1		0	0	0
1° idiopathic	36	27	9.3	43.6	0.4	1.6	1.2
2° biogenic*	7	6	2.1		0.3	1.8	1.5
2° psychogenic	12	10	3.5		0.5	3.2	2.7
2° idiopathic	65	46	15.9		0.5	1.8	1.3
Premature ejaculation (PE)	47	30	10.4		0.6	2.9	2.3
Retarded ejaculation absolute	1	1	<1		0	2.0	2.0
Retarded ejaculation coital	19	17	5.9		0.3	1.6	1.3
Heterophobia absolute	95	74	25.6	35.3	0.2	2.7	2.5
Heterophobia partial	36	28	9.7		0.5	2.3	1.8
Low sex drive	1	1	<1		0	0	0
Heterophobe/homophile	12	8	2.8		0.3	2.6	2.3

Gender identity role conflicts	1	1	<1	0	0	0
Sexual variation	9	5	1.7	1.0	1.4	0.4
ED and PE co-presenting	5	4	1.4	0	1.5	1.5
Desire dysfunction	15	9	3.1	1.0	3.9	2.9
Handicapped	7	5	1.7	0.2	2.6	2.4
Medical indication	5	3	1.0	0	2.0	2.0
Non-consummation	4	4	1.4	0	2.3	2.3
Medical (psychiatric)	3	2	<1	0	0	0
Other	2	1	<1	0	0	0
Mean scores (all men)				0.46	2.26	1.80
Total sample (both sexes)	425	316		0.44	2.32	1.88

* Including iatrogenic; 1° = primary; 2° = secondary.

do, the condition will not be recognized by therapists because of the difficulties experienced in providing effective help.

Previously, men and women showing these high levels of anxiety in courtship and sex play, strong enough to prevent the formation of a sexual relationship which characterize the heterophobe, have been told to return only when they have a partner or occasionally they may have been accepted for social-skills training (Lobitz and Baker, 1979; Zilbergeld and Ellison, 1979; Reynolds *et al.*, 1981; and see Chapter 9). At least now attention can be focused on this large group of men and women who clearly need help since they have the double burden of being without both sex and a relationship. Giving the condition a name, *heterophobia*, has been a big step forward.

The *absolute heterophobe* is an individual who has not experienced intercourse and may, in many cases, have had no sexual experience whatsoever. It may seem surprising that there are an unknown number of men and women in their third and fourth decades who have never kissed or been kissed – and in many cases, without the provision of a surrogate, their condition would be permanent.

The *partial heterophobe* may have achieved intercourse intermittently on rare occasions, but the experience has usually been unrewarding because of an inadequate response and/or because of the very high levels of anxiety experienced. As a result, relationship formation has not been possible. In the heterophobe both courtship and sexual skills are markedly deficient but experience using surrogates, specifically in sexual-skills training, has shown that there is a concomitant improvement in social skills whereas the reverse is not so readily observed.

The *heterophobe-homophile* is a man who has had no heterosexual or homosexual experiences and is unsure of the direction of his sex drive. His masturbatory fantasies will be bisexual and he elects to proceed with surrogate therapy, often initially as a diagnostic experience, simply to find out what heterosexual intercourse is like and whether or not it is rewarding. If it proves to be he may then proceed with a longer programme aimed at reducing his heterosexual anxieties and at the same time attempting to extinguish his homosexual fantasies.

The men who presented with a medical (non-psychiatric) condition (5 patients) included those with diabetes, and those with endocrine (hormonal) abnormalities. Those with a psychiatric condition (3 patients) were all borderline psychotics.

OUTCOME OF TREATMENT

It is very difficult to quantify the effectiveness of any therapeutic technique

Table 16.4 Therapeutic gain by sex disorder in women

Presenting problem	*Total sample size (n = 35)*	*Treatment sample size (n = 27)*	*Per cent (n)*	*Mean presenting score*	*Mean outcome score*	*Therapeutic gain*
1° (GSD) arousal dysfunction*	1	1	3.7	0	3.0	3.0
2° (GSD) arousal dysfunction*	1	0	0	—	—	—
1° orgasmic dysfunction	10	6	22.2	0	2.0	2.0
2° orgasmic dysfunction	—	—	—	—	—	—
1° vaginismus/dyspareunia	6	5	18.5	0	3.0	3.0
2° vaginismus/dyspareunia	—	—	—	—	—	—
Heterophobia	8	8	29.6	0.1	3.9	3.8
Low sex drive	—	—	—	—	—	—
Desire dysfunction	7	5	18.5	1.2	2.6	1.4
Non-consummation	2	2	7.4	0	3.5	3.5
Handicapped	—	—	—	—	—	—
Medical indication (physical)	—	—	—	—	—	—
Medical (psychiatric)	—	—	—	—	—	—
Mean scores (all women)				0.26	3.00	2.74
Total sample (both sexes)	425	316		0.44	2.32	1.88

* Singles; 1° = primary; 2° = secondary; and GSD = general sexual dysfunction.

and many therapists do not even attempt to do so. In some instances it would be impracticable even to consider it, particularly where there is no clearly defined therapeutic contract. However, in sex therapy it is usually possible to measure therapeutic progress and though subjective errors will be quite large, the results though not dramatic, sometimes can give cause for satisfaction.

The method adopted here was to score the patient before he entered treatment and then score him again at its termination. Five point scores (0–4) were constructed for erectile dysfunction, heterophobia and premature ejaculation (see Table 16.5). These scores were then used for all the other presenting conditions, reinterpreting the scale so as to allow for the behavioural change appropriate to that condition. Thus in the case of desire dysfunction or orgasmic dysfunction the scale would read to measure the degree of renewed interest in sex or an increasing capacity to achieve an orgasm.

Initially all the scoring was done by myself but latterly the final score represents the mean of three independent scores, that of myself, the patient and the surrogate.

A detailed analysis of the therapeutic gain for men and women is presented in Tables 16.3 and 16.4. The grand mean for all patients gave a presenting score of 0.44, an outcome score of 2.32 and an overall mean therapeutic gain of 1.88 points which is in effect a shift of nearly two points out of a range of 5, that is, 40 per cent.

Some conditions respond better to surrogate therapy than others, as would be expected. For example, in men, absolute heterophobia showed a gain of 2.5 points and 2° psychogenic erectile dysfunction a gain of 2.7 points, conditions one would expect to have a good prognosis with a surrogate. On the other hand, 1° idiopathic erectile dysfunction and sexual variation, for example, showed only gains of 1.2 and 0.4 points respectively – conditions which would be expected to have a poor prognosis however they were treated. In women, heterophobics once again responded well (a shift of 3.8 points) though desire dysfunction did not with only a 1.4 point shift.

Follow-ups are notoriously difficult to obtain even in couple therapy. When, however, one is dealing with a group of usually self-referred, single patients sometimes it is quite impossible to obtain any information about their progress once they have finished treatment. A large proportion of patients are living at home with their parent(s) or have no permanent address. To try to correspond with them in these circumstances not only is likely to be unprofitable but may cause deep embarrassment – particularly if treatment has been successful! Only 42 (13.3 per cent) patients have been followed up successfully and most of these reports were unsolicited. The

Table 16.5 Scores used in the assessment of therapeutic gain for erectile dysfunction and heterophobia, and premature ejaculation

Score	*Erectile dysfunction and heterophobia*
0	An absolute block to intercourse operating either in courtship or in sex response cycle resulting from actual or expected lack of erection.
1	Poor performance, intercourse possible only very rarely. Very high levels of anxiety associated with all sociosexual or sexual encounters. Erection never firm in presence of partner though penetration possible occasionally.
2	Sexual behaviour precarious: performance unpredictable which, though not disabling, is likely to affect adversely existing or potential relationships. Sudden loss of erection after penetration not unusual – erection once lost is difficult to restore.
3	Sexual performance adequate but elements remain which reflect the patient's inadequacy from time to time. Erection once lost can be restored.
4	Sexual performance good, falling within normal range of behaviours: anxiety when present not limiting. Relationship formation and maintenance unimpaired.
Score	*Premature ejaculation*
0	Intercourse not possible because of early and uncontrolled ejaculation at or before penetration.
1	Only a brief period of intercourse is possible (a few seconds, at most 10 seconds) because of early and uncontrolled ejaculation.
2	Sexual behaviour precarious: performance unpredictable; ejaculation within one minute. Relationships adversely affected, patient conscious of sexual inadequacy, performance fears still present.
3	Sexual performance adequate but patient still reports uncontrolled ejaculation from time to time. He can last 2–3 minutes though rarely longer and he ejaculates sooner when stressed. (Relationship not seriously affected by condition.)
4	Sexual performance good, falling within the normal range of behaviours. Anxiety, when present, not limiting. Relationship formation and maintenance unimpaired.

mean score of this small group was 3.6 and in most cases they had formed a permanent or semipermanent sexual relationship.

CONCLUSION

Sex therapy for individuals without partners is never likely to be easy and will remain a challenge for those engaged in this area of work. There are, however, both theoretical and practical resources available and clearly with the increasing number of partnerless patients requiring help this challenge must be recognized and met.

REFERENCES

Altman, I., Gahan, P. and Jehu, D. (1985) Psychoeducational treatment of impotence, *British Journal of Sexual Medicine*, Vol. 12, pp. 55–7.

Apfelbaum, B. (1977) The myth of the surrogate, *The Journal of Sex Research*, Vol. 13, pp. 238–49.

Bancroft, J. (1983) *Human Sexuality and Its Problems*, Churchill-Livingstone, London.

Barlow, D.H. (1986) Causes of sexual dysfunction: the role of anxiety and cognitive interference, *Journal of Consulting and Clinical Psychology*, Vol. 54, No. 2, pp. 140–8.

Beck, A.T. (1976) *Cognitive Therapy and the Emotional Disorders*, International Universities Press, New York.

Brewer, C. (1978) Cure of heterophobia by sexual surrogate therapy, *British Medical Journal*, i, p. 1055.

Cole, M.J. (1982) The use of surrogate sex partners in the treatment of sex dysfunctions and allied conditions, *British Journal of Sexual Medicine*, Vol. 9, pp. 13–20.

Cole, M.J. (1985) Surrogate sex therapy, in W. Dryden (ed.) *Marital Therapy in Britain. Vol. II, Special Areas*, Harper & Row, London.

Cole, M.J. (1986) Socio-sexual characteristics of men with sexual problems, *Sexual and Marital Therapy*, Vol. 1, No. 1, pp. 89–108.

Dryden, W. (1984) *Rational-Emotive Therapy: Fundamentals and Innovations*, Croom Helm, Beckenham, Kent.

Ellis, A. (1983) Does sex therapy really have a future? *Rational Living*, Vol. 18, pp. 3–6.

Hauck, P. (1981) *Why Be Afraid*, Sheldon Press, London.

Hauck, P. (1982) *Jealousy*, Sheldon Press, London.

Heiman, J., LoPiccolo, L. and LoPiccolo, J. (1976) *Becoming Orgasmic: A Sexual Growth Program for Women*, Prentice-Hall, Englewood Cliffs NJ.

Jacobs, M., Thompson, L. A. and Truxshaw, P. (1975) The use of sexual surrogates in counseling, *Counseling Psychologist*, Vol. 5, pp. 73–7.

Kowalski, R. (1985a) Cognitive therapy for sexual problems: part I, *British Journal of Sexual Medicine*, Vol. 12, pp. 64–6.

Kowalski, R. (1985b) Cognitive therapy for sexual problems: part II, *British Journal of Sexual Medicine*, Vol. 12, pp. 90–3.

Kowalski, R. (1985c) Cognitive therapy for sexual problems: part III, *British Journal of Sexual Medicine*, Vol. 12, pp. 131–5.

Lobitz, W.C. and Baker, E.L. (1979) Group treatment of single males with erectile dysfunction, *Archives of Sexual Behavior*, Vol. 8, No. 2, pp. 127–38.

Malamuth, N., Wanderer, Z.W., Sayner, R.B. and Duknell, D. (1976) Utilization of surrogate partners: a survey of health professionals, *Journal of Behavior Therapy and Experimental Psychiatry*, Vol. 7, pp. 149–50.

Masters, W.H. and Johnson, V.E. (1970) *Human Sexual Inadequacy*, J.A. Churchill, London.

Morris, D. (1967) *The Naked Ape*, Jonathan Cape, London.

Office of Population Censuses and Surveys (OPCS) (1985) *Monitor* (October), London, Government Statistical Service.

Price, S.C., Reynolds, B.S., Cohen, B.D., Anderson, A.J. and Schochet, B.V. (1981) Group treatment of erectile dysfunction for men without partners, *Archives of Sexual Behavior*, Vol. 10, No. 3, pp. 253–68.

Reynolds, B.S., Cohen, B.D., Schochet, B.V., Price, S.C. and Anderson, A.J. (1981) Dating skills training in the group treatment of erectile dysfunction for men without partners, *Journal of Sex and Marital Therapy*, Vol. 7, No. 3, pp. 184–94.

Somers, F.G. (1978) Treatment of male sexual dysfunction in a psychiatric practice integrating the sexual therapy practitioner, in *Medical Sexology*, PSG Publishing, Littleton MA.

Somers, F.G. (1981) Some considerations on the psychodynamics of the psychiatrist, patient and the sexual therapy practitioner (surrogate) relationship in modern sex therapy, *Proceedings of the Fourth World Congress of Sexology*, Mexico City.

Stravynski, A. (1986) Indirect behavioral treatment of erectile failure and premature ejaculation in a man without a partner, *Archives of Sexual Behavior*, Vol. 15, No. 4, pp. 355–61.

Wolfe, L. (1978) The question of surrogates in sex therapy, in L. LoPiccolo and J. LoPiccolo (eds) *Handbook of Sex Therapy*, Plenum, New York.

Wolfe, J. and Walen, S. (1982) Cognitive factors in sexual behavior, in R. Grieger and I. Grieger (eds) *Cognition and Emotional Disturbance*, Human Sciences Press, New York.

Zilbergeld, B. (1980) *Men and Sex*, Fontana/Collins, Glasgow.

Zilbergeld, B. and Ellison, C.R. (1979) Social skills training as an adjunct in sex therapy, *Journal of Sex and Marital Therapy*, Vol. 5, No. 4, pp. 340–50.

PART 4

RESEARCH AND TRAINING

CHAPTER 17

SEX THERAPY TRAINING

Windy Dryden, Charmian Bollinger and Paul T. Brown

The extent of sexual dysfunction, difficulty and dissatisfaction is hard to gauge, but, without doubt, it is considerable. After reviewing a number of studies, Bancroft (1983) concludes that if all those experiencing dissatisfaction were to present for help, the health services would be overwhelmed.

Training courses for sex therapists are therefore to be welcomed and in this chapter we review four of those that are currently available. The chapter focuses on extended sex therapy training. While it is true that different groups of helping professionals receive briefer training in sex therapy as part of their education, this is outside the scope of the present chapter. The history of training for sex therapy in this country has been reviewed by Brown and Dryden (1985). Partly, its origins are indigenous, largely beginning with the dissemination of skills which had been acquired by psychologists and psychiatrists with a behavioural orientation who were inspired by the publication, in 1970, of Masters and Johnson's *Human Sexual Inadequacy*. Partly, they came from the United States, mainly brought by the Reverend David Mace to the National Marriage Guidance Council (NMGC), by Dr Elizabeth Stanley from Professor Harold Lief of the University of Philadelphia, and by the visit of Dr and Mrs Sarrel, who had been trained by Masters and Johnson, to Dr John Bancroft at Oxford.

In the United States, enthusiasm following Masters and Johnson's publications led to the establishment of large numbers of sexual dysfunction clinics, many of them staffed with therapists with no grounding in other mental health work. It seemed as though a new profession of 'sex therapy' would emerge. However, more recently, considerable doubts and anxieties about this trend have been expressed (see the discussion in Brown and Bollinger, 1985). Some writers express the view that psychotherapy is an essential element of sex therapy and hence sex therapy trainees should already be trained and experienced psychotherapists or counsellors. Others take the view that sex therapy is an essential part of psychotherapy and that every psychotherapist and counsellor should be trained in it. In California, under a law in force since 1978, for licensure, or renewal of licence, all physicians, psychologists, social workers and marriage/family/child counsellors must produce evidence of training in human sexuality.

SELECTION CRITERIA

In the United States, the American Association of Sex Educators, Counselors and Therapists grant a certification for individual sex therapists. In Britain, the Association of Sexual and Marital Therapists (ASMT) offers accreditation of sex therapy training courses. Criteria for accreditation include a selection procedure: 'Trainees should ideally have had training and experience in one of the recognised health care professions or counselling' (ASMT, 1985). In addition, the selection procedure should 'exclude candidates obviously unsuitable' for training in sexual therapy. It is generally agreed that the two elements of professional background and personal suitability are essential for selection of sex therapy trainees.

It is appropriate that a group of sex therapy trainees should encompass a number of professional disciplines. Sexual problems are presented in a wide variety of settings, especially gynaecology, urology, infertility services, psychiatry, family planning and general medical practice. It seems likely that, at present, many people are discouraged from seeking help with their sexual problems by the response of the professional to whom they first speak. Burnap and Golden (1967; reported by Bancroft, 1983) found that, in medical clinics and general practice, if the clinician asked questions about sex routinely rather than waiting for the patient to raise the subject, twice as many sexual problems were reported.

When Masters first lectured on human sexuality in 1960, 25 per cent of medical students refused to attend the lectures. Bearing in mind the wide range of specialisms in which physicians may encounter sexual problems, there is a case for the inclusion of a sex therapy training course in the general medical curriculum. In the absence of this, doctors, especially general practitioners, should be encouraged to apply for sex therapy courses. In Britain the majority of patients with sexual problems approach their general practitioner in the first instance and they are the commonest referral source to most sexual problem clinics (Bancroft, 1983). In addition, although the majority of cases may be of psychological origin, the role of physical and medical factors in sexual dysfunction is increasingly being recognized (Hawton, 1985).

Since writers commonly express the view that sex therapy is an integral part of psychotherapy and/or psychotherapy an integral part of sex therapy, courses should clearly be offered to psychologists, psychiatrists, psychotherapists, social workers and counsellors. Nurses should also be included, in particular those specializing in family planning. It would be appropriate for marital and family therapists to be trained in sex therapy, although there is disagreement in the literature about whether sexual and marital therapy should be combined or done separately (cf. Bancroft, 1985, and Hawton, 1985). For example, NMGC tends to see these as two different activities, but encourages some counsellors to train also as sexual dysfunction therapists.

The personal attributes required for this training are much more difficult to specify. Indeed, although one encounters in the literature expressions of strong feelings about suitability and unsuitability, it is more difficult to find clear descriptions or definitions of the qualities or attitudes referred to. The most important seems to be an attitude to sex which is relaxed, open and non-judgemental, or even 'creative' (Kaplan, 1977). However, to some extent these attitudes can be taught. Ayres *et al.* (1974, quoted by Brown and Dryden, 1985) bombard trainees with specially devised explicit film material, in a process they call 'sexual attitude restructuring'.

The characteristics of successful psychotherapists are clearly also relevant. In a recent reappraisal of Truax and Carkhuff's (1967) much quoted criteria of accurate empathy, non-possessive warmth and genuineness, Mitchell *et al.* (1977) conclude that the recent evidence, although equivocal, does seem to suggest that they are related in some way to client change but that their potency and generalizability are not as great as was once thought. There is evidence that these attributes, of empathy, warmth and genuineness, can also be learned. Mitchell *et al.* (1977) suggest that there are three key elements for this: a therapeutic context in which the supervisor communicates high levels of all three to the trainees themselves; a highly specific didactic training, 'shaping' trainees' responses towards high levels of all three; and a focused group experience that allows the emergence of the trainee's own idiosyncratic therapeutic self, through self-examination and consequent integration of his or her didactic training with his or her personal values, goals and lifestyles.

The study which needs to be done but which, to our knowledge, has not been, would relate the various characteristics which trainers consider important in a sex therapist to the actual success and failure rate of the therapist, once trained. Until this is done it is probably safest to accept the widely held view that sex therapists should be able to talk easily and openly about sex and be relatively free from guilt and conflict, at least in relation to sexuality, and show accurate empathy, non-possessive warmth and genuineness towards their clients.

FOCUS

Since the present-day practice of sex therapy in Britain originates from various sources historically (Brown and Dryden, 1985), the focus of different trainers varies considerably. The eclectic position was first taken up in 1974 by Helen Singer Kaplan (1978). She restricted the goals of sex therapy to the relief of the patient's sexual symptom and employed a combination of prescribed sexual experiences and psychotherapy. A prospective trainee needs to be satisfied that a course either has the focus preferred, for example concentrating more on the behavioural or more on the psychodynamic approach, or that course directors will create the freedom to find the right balance for himself or herself. In addition, a course may place less or more emphasis on the physical causes of dysfunction.

More generally, there needs to be a relationship between the backgrounds of trainees and the topics or techniques most focused on. If a course is accepting a multidisciplinary mix of trainees, with varying backgrounds, it may also be necessary to offer some individual variations in programme.

ACADEMIC/THEORETICAL

It is generally agreed that a knowledge of the anatomy and physiology of sexual function and dysfunction is essential for a sex therapist. Other topics would include different aspects of sexuality and various therapeutic approaches. ASMT (1985) gives a core curriculum for training courses (see Appendix).

Although it is not intended to be a complete list, the topics most noticeably absent from the ASMT's core curriculum relate to the theoretical bases of the various methodologies, notably, learning theory. Also, the study of behavioural psychotherapy is not mentioned, which seems curious when behavioural methods are so widely used. Other topics which might well be included would be sex-role stereotyping and the changing role-relationships between the sexes.

In such a rapidly moving field, we feel that there should be considerable emphasis on reading and evaluating research reports, in addition to gaining knowledge through lectures and/or seminars.

TRAINING IN THERAPEUTIC SKILLS

Trainees need to have skills modelled, practise them themselves and receive feedback on their performance of them. The kinds of skill-training that need to be offered will depend, to a large extent, on the selection of trainees for a course. Depending on the different professional backgrounds of trainees, different aspects of therapeutic skill will need to be stressed. Arentewicz and Schmidt (1983) describe the reactions of different professional groups to sex therapy training. Each professional group had very different strengths and weaknesses.

Doctors and nurses had difficulty accepting that they were treating problems in a relationship, not patients, and this was especially true of gynaecologists. They also had difficulties with transference and countertransference. Psychiatrists, especially those who had been psychoanalytically trained, had difficulties in giving instructions and in focusing on the sexual symptom rather than the relationship alone.

Those trained in client-centred therapy had difficulties with history-taking and with giving instructions. Trainees from other professional backgrounds showed less bias, especially social workers from family counselling centres and psychologists trained in behaviour therapy. It may be that trainees with a background of non-directive therapy/counselling need to be taught how to be directive when necessary, whereas those with a more directive style, such as doctors and nurses, may need extra training in learning to deal with transference, countertransference and resistance.

In addition, certain problems were shared by all professional groups and, in the light of these findings, it seems that for all groups training should particularly focus on: questioning clients in intimate areas to establish a sexual history; formulating the aetiology of the dysfunction in a way that is convincing to the clients; giving information and instructions; questioning clients in detail about homework exercises; avoiding the formation of a special alliance with the 'non-dysfunctional' partner; being responsive to clients' physical experiences without judging them; praising clients continually for small successes; giving positive reinforcement for homework done rather than criticism for homework not done; and dealing with clients' resistances, such as ignoring the coitus prohibition in the early stages of therapy.

PRACTICAL EXPERIENCE

It is generally agreed that clinical skills take a long time to be acquired. Sadock *et al.* (1975) allow a year for clinical training, during which time trainees treat an average of four dysfunctional couples. Stanley *et al.* (1986) hold that two years is the minimum length of time in which most trainees can develop their clinical skills sufficiently to work unsupervised. It depends, of course, on the level of clinical skill a trainee has achieved before embarking on the course. For ASMT accreditation, a course must require a minimum of 120 hours of supervised client contact over a one- to two-year period.

Some courses require trainees to work with co-therapists, who may be members of the training staff or other trainees. As evidence mounts that co-therapy does not produce better results than single therapy (e.g. Mathews *et al.*, 1983), co-therapy is seen more and more as a training device, rather than as a model for therapy.

However, studies which have investigated the single- vs. co-therapy dimension (Mathews *et al.*, 1976; Brown, 1979; Mathews *et al.*, 1983) have used co-therapists who were either of unequal experience (as in training situations) or established as co-therapists for the purposes of the study. Whether co-therapists of long-standing and shared experience would produce different treatment outcomes from those of equal therapeutic experience but less time together as co-therapists is a question that has not been pursued yet, though it might be a better test of whether co-therapy is more effective than single therapy.

SUPERVISION

An important issue in methods of supervision concerns their appropriateness to the end in mind. Trainees need to develop both skill and understanding. Case discussion in a group may develop understanding, a broad perspective on case management and vicarious learning through other trainees' experience. It is, however, ill-suited to determine or develop the level of trainees' skills.

For skill development, one-to-one supervision may be more effective. Skill development needs to be appraised and developed through 'live' supervision, through a one-way screen or the supervisor's actual presence, or by supervision using trainees' audio- or video-tapes of therapy sessions. Video-tapes will be necessary if non-verbal aspects of therapeutic skills are to be examined and supervision is not live. Sadock *et al.* (1975), for example, give supervision on a one-to-one, hour-for-hour basis. It is unlikely, however, that any British course would have the resources to provide such intense supervision.

PERSONAL LEARNING

Some of the theoretical techniques, such as transactional analysis or gestalt therapy, which trainees may be learning, are usually taught in an experiential situation, as well as didactically, and it is appropriate to do the same on a sex therapy course. In addition, sexual attitude restructuring, using films, lectures, discussions, perhaps on a weekend retreat (Sarrel *et al.*, 1982) can be useful. There should be opportunities for trainees to explore personal issues and, in particular, sexual issues. Some trainees find it helpful to be in personal therapy, though this might best be optional. Since the therapist's richest source of information about what goes on in other people may well be what goes on in himself or herself (Smail, 1978), it is clearly an advantage for trainee therapists to explore their own personal experience. Some knowledge of personal dynamics may help to prevent or overcome blocks to the practice of effective therapy.

Ideally personal learning should be facilitated by someone who is not concerned with the evaluation of trainees' academic and clinical work and who does not communicate to those who are so concerned. This is important if trainees are to feel able to disclose personal material freely. However, a dilemma for such facilitators may arise if they consider a particular trainee to be unsuitable for the work. They may need to reserve the right to communicate with the evaluators in extreme circumstances.

PARTNER INVOLVEMENT

Arentewicz and Schmidt (1983) note that a number of trainees' intimate relationships broke up during training. There could be a number of reasons why this should happen, including the trainee's changing attitude to sexuality. These authors, however, imply that part of the reason is the relationship which builds up between co-therapists (which may be to confuse cause and effect). They suggest that co-therapists may act out the kind of harmonious and exciting relationship which they would like to see in their patients.

Even without regular co-therapy partners, the training programme may seem very threatening to the trainee's marital or sexual partner. Therefore, although some trainers would think it paternalistic, most consider that it is appropriate to include some partner involvement in the course. Partners might, for example, be invited to participate in a sexual attitude-restructuring day or other workshops or discussion groups. Some trainers would go so far as to suggest that the partner must be fully in agreement with the trainee over the taking of the course, but, again, most would consider this to be a personal decision for the potential trainee alone.

RESEARCH

There is a paucity of outcome studies in the field of sex therapy and those that there are do not usually isolate which aspects of the therapy were the most effective. The validity of the very high success rates quoted by Masters and Johnson (1970) has recently been questioned (e.g. Hawton, 1985), but whatever their success or failure rate, it is not clear which elements in their programme were most responsible. In particular, since their original (1970) book underestimated the importance Masters and Johnson attached to the psychotherapeutic component of their method, it has been assumed by many that their method was purely behavioural and that they achieved their results without considering cognitive or emotive aspects in any depth. Bancroft (1983) concludes that they were skilled psychotherapists who, until recently, were unwilling or unable, to describe their psychotherapeutic technique.

Some recent research is reviewed by Hawton (1985), but much more needs to be done. It would seem appropriate, then, for sex therapy training courses to include some teaching of research methods, for those not familiar with them, in order to encourage future generations of sex therapists to do research. Trainers can encourage research by, for example, awarding more marks for a dissertation than for a set paper.

Even for those unlikely to carry out research of their own, it is necessary, in such a constantly changing, fast-growing field, for therapists to be able to read and evaluate research reports and sufficient course time needs to be allocated for them to learn to do so. However, it may be argued that actually carrying out research is a better way to learn to do this critically.

ASSESSMENT AND ASSESSMENT CRITERIA

Assessments may be made upon completion of a course or from time to time or continuously. They may be made by trainers, clinical supervisors, the peer group of trainees, or by the trainee himself or herself. In some cases, an assessment of academic learning is made before the trainee is allowed to go on to clinical work, or there may be an assessment at the end of each year which will screen out those considered unsuitable to continue. At the end of the course, an internal or external examiner will consider all the assessments made and judge whether the trainee can be considered to be a competent sex therapist.

The most valid assessment of a therapist would be an assessment of the improvement of the therapist's clients after the period of study. Any other assessment must be considered an assessment of the process of learning and these assessments may or may not be related to the outcome assessment, which is positive or negative client change. Truax and Mitchell (1971) would go so far as to say that process assessments are important if and only if the process variables can be related to positive or negative client change. For example, Brown (1979) demonstrates that an increase in sexual knowledge during training was associated with increased diagnostic accuracy.

There are practical problems in making outcome assessments. Upon returning to their own agency, individuals will be working in different settings, with different kinds of clients. Sarrel *et al.* (1982) did, nonetheless, use measures of the trainee's impact on his or her own agency.

Most trainers, however, fall back on the use of process assessments, most of them not demonstrably connected with client outcome, although the assumption is made that such a connection exists. Most trainers use written examination, *viva voce* and/or case presentations at the end of the course.

In addition, many trainers find it helpful to make assessments as the course progresses. Sarrel *et al.* (1982) required trainees to fill in a postmeeting response form after every seminar and these were used to guide the programme directors' preparation of subsequent class meetings. Supervisors met regularly and if it emerged that several co-therapy teams were having difficulty with a particular concept or strategy, this material was retaught during a later seminar. A knowledge test of 75 items was given halfway through the two-year course, as well as at the beginning and end. Attendance records and supervisory assessments were also used. The authors found that, to be effective, feedback should be given immediately and be compulsory. This procedure was seen as evaluating the course, as well as the trainees.

A problem with ongoing assessment, however, is the extent to which trainees will feel free to express their difficulties and problems if they know they are undergoing constant assessment. We suggested earlier that sessions devoted to personal learning or therapy should not be subject to scrutiny by those making assessments.

DESCRIPTIONS OF THE TRAINING COURSES SURVEYED[1]

As noted earlier, in preparing this chapter a number of training organizations were visited to discuss their extended courses with staff directly responsible for training. In this concluding section, descriptions of four such courses are provided with some critical comment.

1. St George's Hospital Medical School (University of London). (Medical School) Diploma in Human Sexuality: Two years (part-time)

In the first year the course is held on one full-day per week for 40 weeks of the academic year. The second year consists solely of clinical work.

Selection criteria

Applicants should possess one or more of the following: (a) a medical qualification; (b) other university degree – one with a health care focus is particularly favoured; (c) other qualifications or clinical experience judged of sufficient depth and relevance by the training committee. Previous training in counselling or psychotherapy is now a prerequisite. Applicants are required to attend two separate interviews with members of the Selection Committee, an interview with the course director, an informal lunch and a one-hour group experience when reasons for applicants wanting to do the course are discussed. The selectors are looking for people who are warm and empathic with an obvious capacity for insight, who would be likely to create an immediate favourable impression with clients and able to function well in a group setting.

Up to 10 people are accepted yearly onto the training programme.

Focus

Sex problems are seen in the context of the couple's wider relationship. Effective sex therapy is considered to be short-term and involves the enhancement of communication skills, particularly in relation to resolution of conflict. The approach offered to trainees is eclectic. It has a psychodynamic base into which are integrated both behavioural techniques and the innovative methods pioneered by the course director.

Cost (at the time of writing)

£930 for the first year; £120 for the second year.

Academic (theoretical) strand (offered only in the first year)

Term 1: Aspects of sex therapy. The first lecture/seminar covers history-taking and assessment, in which role-play and video-feedback may be used. The basic concepts of sex therapy are then covered over the next 4½ weeks using video-tapes of an entire sex therapy case. At the instigation of either trainer or trainees, the video-tape is frequently stopped to make teaching points and discuss aspects of content and therapeutic process. Particular reference is made to the ways in which the St George's model may differ from others.

Other areas covered in the first term include basic counselling skills, psychoanalytic concepts, transactional analysis, the cognitive therapies and marriage guidance counselling.

Term 2: Sexual function and dysfunction. Psychosexual development and gender identity; embryology and anatomy of the genital tract; physiology of sexual response; effects of ageing on sexual response; pharmacological agents affecting sexual response; medical aspects of sexual problems; surgical aspects of sexual problems; urological aspects of sexual problems; gynaecological aspects of sexual problems; sexuality and physical handicap; sexuality and mental handicap. The following topics are presented by trainees: erectile dysfunction; premature ejaculation; retarded ejaculation;

loss of libido; anorgasmia; vaginismus; sex variation or deviation; homosexuality; transexuality.

Term 3: Specific issues. Pregnancy; contraception; infertility; menopause; urological problems in the female; venereal disease; neuroses; psychosis; the Judeo-Christian ethic; Eastern religions; sex and the law; pornography; ethical issues; ethology; surrogate therapy; 'sex aids'; methods of physical and psychological assessment; epidemiological methods; assessment of treatment outcome; research design; ethical approval in sex research; how to prepare research results; how to submit papers for publication; further lectures on topics of trainees' choice.

Training in therapeutic skills

Deliberate skills training occurs in the following areas: basic counselling skills (two weekend workshops plus three two-hour sessions); initial assessment; history-taking. Role-play methods with feedback are employed. In addition therapeutic skills training is continually taking place both in small and large groups and in individual supervision sessions based on trainees' audio-taped casework.

Practical experience

Trainees are given client responsibility from the sixth week in the first year of the course. They see clients in the Sexual Dysfunction Clinic of St George's Hospital and, if relevant, in their own work setting. They are not formally assessed as to their readiness to see clients. Initially they work in trainee pairs but soon see clients on their own if they are considered competent to do so. If thought necessary, a trainee may also work in co-therapy with a trainer. They are expected to do a minimum of 120 hours of clinical work seeing at least 10 cases over the two-year period. They are expected to have a caseload that does not exceed two cases per week during the first year, though this is greater in the second year.

Supervision

In Year 1 supervision is carried out weekly both in groups (1¼ hours) and individually (1–1½ hours). In individual supervision, the focus is on audio-tapes of trainees' actual sex therapy work with clients. Here trainees are helped to formulate accurate clinical hypotheses, devise relevant therapeutic strategies and implement effective techniques. The general emphasis is on improving trainees' therapeutic skills. In group supervision the focus is on the therapeutic process, the dynamics of the therapist-client relationship and on the personal concerns of the therapist as they arise in the conduct of sex therapy. In Year 2 trainees receive monthly individual face-to-face supervision (2–3 hours) based on the audio-tapes of their clinical work which are sent weekly to their supervisors. They also maintain weekly telephone contact with their supervisor to discuss the general progress of their cases.

Personal learning

The personal learning of trainees is a theme that runs throughout the course. It is particularly addressed in the following ways: (a) trainees attend one 'Sexual Attitude Restructuring' workshop where the focus is on an exploration of trainees' attitudes to sexuality and sexual issues; (b) one-day workshops are held where the focus is on the trainees' personal learning, the context of which varies according to the interest of trainees (e.g. transactional analysis, bioenergetics); (c) personal issues are frequently discussed in group supervision; (d) trainees are allocated an individual tutor with whom they can discuss personal issues that arise out of the work. Trainees do not have to be in personal therapy but this is recommended if any trainee experiences enduring personal blocks to the practice of effective sex therapy.

Partner involvement

Partners are invited to attend the 'Sexual Attitude Restructuring' and other one-day workshops.

Research

Research issues are addressed in Term 3, Year 1. Trainees may do an optional project which may be a piece of research, but in practice rarely is.

Assessment

At the end of the first year of the course trainees who are judged to have made satisfactory progress in their clinical work (based on supervisor and trainee rating forms) gain entry to the examination. This involves answering 3 out of 5 questions from an essay paper, a multiple-choice question paper on the academic content of the course and attending two 20-minute *viva-voce* examinations.

In Year 2, trainees are continually assessed on their clinical work (as judged on supervisor, and trainee rating scales) and a final assessment form is completed by the second year supervisor at the end of the year. In addition trainees submit a written case presentation with an accompanying audio-tape of a therapy session from the case and receive a 30-minute *viva-voce* examination on the case. The External Examiners also assess the trainees' casebook consisting of summaries of every session of clinical work carried out during the two years. Trainees who successfully meet the examination requirements are awarded the Diploma.

Assessment criteria
Extensive written 9-point rating scales are completed by both the trainees and their supervisors in the ongoing assessment of the former's clinical work. These assess the trainees' ability to: take a good history; communicate effectively with clients; facilitate emotional interaction in therapy; recognize and evaluate interaction with clients; establish a therapeutic contract; be directive and maintain sensitive control of therapeutic interviews; effectively use therapeutic strategies and aids and form an effective co-therapy team.

In the final assessment of trainees' clinical work written 7-point rating scales are used. In the audio-tape of the therapy session these focus on: the ability to establish rapport; use of therapeutic skills; use of therapeutic tools and stratagems; ability to direct and control the interview; ability to facilitate emotional interaction when relevant; ability to help clients confront and deal with painful issues when relevant. In the written case history these focus on: the ability to take a comprehensive yet relevant history; the ability to identify the problem and recognize possible causes and contributory factors; the ability to formulate an appropriate treatment strategy, the ability to use specific sex therapy techniques appropriately; demonstration of an understanding of the therapeutic process; the ability to make realistic evaluations of the treatment programme and the client's prognosis; and general presentation of the case write-up.

Written rating scales, based on the trainee's performance in the written examination (i.e. the essay) and in the *viva-voce* examinations, are not used at the time of writing.

Course director's evaluation
The course director considered the following to be strengths of the course: its practical training orientation; the emphasis placed on intensive supervision; the focus on skills in supervision sessions; the wide range of topics covered in the lectures/seminars; the expertise of lecturers; and the emphasis on personal growth as an integrating feature of the trainee's learning. She considered the following to be weaknesses of the course: lack of time in Year 1 for informal staff-trainee contact; lack of time in Year 1 for comprehensive discussion of theoretical material; lack of time available to encourage trainees to undertake research; lack of balance between Years 1 and 2 (due to the fact that the course has a yearly intake and limited staff resources).

Comments
This course which began in 1981 is the only course in Britain with a multidisciplinary intake established within a medical school. We echo the course director's comments about the strong emphasis on intensive supervision. In particular, the use of audio-tapes as a base for individual supervision is praiseworthy. We agree with the course director's evaluation of the course's

weaknesses and concur that this is attributable to organizational constraints. If the course had a biannual intake some of the material covered in Year 1 could be dealt with in Year 2 making for a less pressured curriculum in the first year with more time devoted to discussion of course material. Perhaps this could also be realized if the course were to be upgraded to MSc level, or at least to University of London Diploma level which would serve to protect its annual intake and possibly give it more resources.

Much of the skills training on the course is covered in the supervision sessions. More time could possibly be devoted (outside supervision) to deliberate skills training – role-playing such skills as forming therapeutic contracts and facilitating therapeutic communication in therapy triads (one therapist – 2 members of a couple) – before trainees are given client responsibility. This would enable trainees to start clinical work with greater confidence in their level of skills. It is our view that the monthly face-to-face supervision (albeit 2–3 hours) offered to students in Year 2 may be of insufficient frequency considering their trainee status (despite weekly telephone supervisory contact). Again this may be a feature of limited resources.

The course makes excellent use of written assessment criteria applied to trainees' clinical work.

Considering the organizational constraints within which the course functions, it provides a most adequate training for prospective sex therapists.

Further details

Further information about the course can be obtained from: The Postgraduate Secretary, St George's Hospital Medical School, Cranmer Terrace, London SW17 ORG.

2. National Marriage Guidance Council*. Course in Sexual Therapy: a 16-month training programme (part-time)

The course comprises attendance at five residential courses at Rugby, work with clients, supervision of clinical work (both group and individual) and attendance at regional training days.

Selection criteria

This course is presently open to trained marriage guidance counsellors. MG counsellors should have satisfactorily completed their basic training and have had 300 hours of counselling experience. They should have the backing of the MG Council, their current tutor, and their region's tutor consultant. They should be willing to commit themselves to practising sexual therapy in

* Now known as Relate: National Marriage Guidance.

their MG Council for at least two years after completing the training course. They should also have the positive support of their spouse or partner. Counsellors who meet the above criteria attend a selection day at NMGC's headquarters in Rugby conducted by the Marital Sexual Therapy (MST) training officer and two tutor consultants. At this selection day the following take place:

(a) A group discussion on myths and taboos about sexuality and how these have affected the applicant.
(b) A 20-minute interview with the MST training officer.
(c) A group role-play exercise to determine the applicant's ability to 'talk sexually' and to stay with the sexual focus of a presented case.
(d) Discussion of one of the applicant's cases which had a sexual component.

The successful applicant is one who is free of major sexual conflicts, can demonstrate that they have their partner's support, has the necessary energy to cope with the active aspects of the work and displays the ability to communicate clearly and non-defensively about sexual matters.

Up to 16 people are accepted into the training programme which is run with two trainers.

Focus

The focus of the course is mainly on the treatment of sexual symptoms using a behaviourally oriented modified form of the approach pioneered by Masters and Johnson. Couples who are accepted into Marital Sex Therapy (MST) should have a sound, stable relationship. The dynamics of their relationship are considered (from a psychodynamic perspective) when progress on set behavioural tasks does not occur.

Cost

The training programme is free to marriage guidance counsellors.

Academic (theoretical) strand

The following are covered from a theoretical perspective:

Course 1.

(a) Criteria for MST
(b) Differences between MST and counselling
(c) A general overview of sexual dysfunction
(d) Anatomical aspects of sexual functioning

Course 2.

(a) Conducting an initial assessment – criteria of suitability for MST

(b) Conducting a history-taking interview with each partner (behavioural analysis)
(c) Conducting a 'round table' interview with both partners
(d) Principles of behaviour therapy (with reference to MST)
(e) Forming contracts with clients
(f) Sensate focus
(g) Giving information to clients
(h) Medical causes of sexual dysfunction

Course 3. More detailed coverage of sexual dysfunction and with special reference to treatment.
(a) *Male* – Premature ejaculation; secondary impotence; retarded ejaculation; inhibition of sexual desire (trainees are not encouraged to use MST with this group)
(b) *Female* – Vaginismus; dyspareunia; orgasmic dysfunctions; inhibition of sexual desire (trainees are not encouraged to use MST with this group)
In addition relaxation and self-focusing methods are covered.

Course 4. Review and self-assessment of sexual knowledge.
Course 5. Review of MST treatments.

Training in therapeutic skills
Course 1. Not covered
Course 2. Role-play methods (using a 'Visiting Couple' role-played by two experienced sex therapists) with provision of feedback are used in a group session, after trainees watch and discuss videos where skills are modelled. Trainees practise the following skills: conducting an initial assessment interview; executing history-taking interviews; conducting a round-table interview where behavioural analysis results are communicated to the couple; explaining sensate focus methods and dealing with emerging issues. In addition the trainees watch and discuss a video on forming a treatment contract. A medical practitioner with special interest in sexual medicine teaches about medical aspects of sexual dysfunction.
Course 3. Trainees practise the skills of carrying out treatment of various sexual dysfunctions (outlined in the section on academic strand – Course 3) and receive feedback from the trainers. They also practise relaxation and self-focusing methods.
Courses 4 and 5. Review of skills learned in Courses 2 and 3.

Practical experience
(a) Between Courses 1 and 2, trainees observe a minimum of three MST sessions (in the early stage of treatment) conducted by trained MST therapists.

(b) Trainees begin to see their own clients a week after Course 2 (unless clear evidence emerges from the role-plays during Course 2 that they are not ready). They are given a caseload of two or three clients who may be screened for the purpose (depending upon how well-established the MST clinic is in their local council or clinic). It is hoped that they will treat a broad range of sexual dysfunctions during the practical experience period. They will gain vicarious experience of treating other dysfunctions through participation in supervision groups.

Supervision
(a) Attendance at fortnightly (1½ hours) supervision groups during term time. Case discussion is the most frequent method of supervision used although other methods may be less frequently employed (e.g. audio-tape supervision).
(b) Termly meetings with an individual tutor (1½ hours per tutorial).

Personal learning
Trainees participate in a one-day Sexual Attitude Restructuring workshop during Course 1 where they examine their own attitudes to sexuality and sexual issues. During Courses 3 and 5 trainees participate in discussion groups where they reflect on their personal feelings which have been engendered by the work. During Course 5 some fantasy work that has a 'personal' focus is done.

Partner involvement
Trainees' partners are strongly encouraged to attend the first MST course. Here opportunities are provided for partners to confront their fantasies about the nature of sex therapy. A very high proportion of partners take advantage of this opportunity and (according to the training officer) find it a very valuable experience.

Research
Reference is made on each of the courses to research work relevant to topics under study.

Assessment
Reports on each trainee are compiled by (a) the residential trainers after each course; (b) the individual tutor after each tutorial and (c) the case discussion leader at the end of the course. In addition each trainee provides a self-assessment report of their own performance during the course. At the end of the course the training officer reviews all these reports before making a decision concerning whether or not the trainee can be considered a trained sexual therapist.

Assessment criteria

Loose criteria are employed based on a trainee's theoretical knowledge, degree of therapeutic skill and range of experience with clients. No formal written criteria are used at the time of writing.

Training officer's evaluation

The training officer considered the following to be a particular strength of the course: NMGC counsellors who start training as sexual therapists do so as experienced marital counsellors who have a deep understanding of the dynamics of relationships – deemed an essential component of sexual therapy by NMGC. They can thus make informed decisions concerning how best to help people with sexual problems and can, with experience, move readily from a 'counselling' approach to a 'behavioural' approach (and vice versa) as needed – even though they may find it difficult to maintain a 'behavioural' focus early in their training. In addition, partner involvement at the initial training weekend is regarded as a strength in that it dispells any anxieties partners may have about this kind of work.

The training officer considered the following to be weaknesses of the course: (a) Since the amount of time volunteers are able to give is limited, they may not have direct personal experience during the training period of working with each of the male and female sexual dysfunctions. This is counteracted, to some degree, by the vicarious learning they derive from listening to more experienced colleagues discussing their cases. (b) At present, the small number of MST clinics creates some practical problems. For example, it is sometimes difficult for trainees to observe trained therapists working, when the latter are located at a distance. This problem should become less acute in time as more clinics are established in more councils.

The training officer considered that the strengths of the training overwhelmingly outweigh the weaknesses.

Comments

The course has a sound and thorough set of selection procedures (although other trainers have commented that it is rather paternalistic to have applicants demonstrate that they have their partners' support for the training). Within the constraints of a residential training programme coverage of the theory and practice of sexual therapy is more than adequate and the sequencing of the training modules is logical with space intelligently devoted to revision sessions. The emphasis on skills training is particularly commendable and trainees have the opportunity to practise skills at each stage of the therapeutic process. However, a point raised in Dryden and Brown's appraisal of the NMGC's Basic Counsellor Training Course is also pertinent here: 'The training's . . . attention to the skills of counselling is not matched by the use of supervisory methods best designed to assess skill (i.e. supervision of video- and audio-tapes of actual counselling sessions)' (Dryden and Brown, 1985, p. 315). We thus recommend the increased use of audio-tape recordings in supervision in conjunction with case discussion methods.

We agree with the training officer that it is difficult to ensure that volunteers get sufficient direct practical experience with a broad range of cases, but do not consider that the vicarious learning derived from listening to experienced therapists discuss their cases goes far enough to make up for this 'shortfall'. We would like to see the course develop more precise criteria concerning the amount of clinical experience trainees should have before being considered a trained sexual therapist. At present explicit guidelines are not laid down on this point. Finally, we would like to see the training team develop more explicit assessment criteria than exist at present.

Further details

For further details of the training programme, write to Alison Clegg, MST Training Officer, NMGC, Herbert Gray College, Little Church St, Rugby CV21 3AP.

3. Edinburgh Human Sexuality Group. Training Programme in Human Sexuality: twenty-one months – six terms (part-time)

The Edinburgh Human Sexuality Group is a multidisciplinary group of professionals involved in sex therapy and counselling, training and sex education. Its terms of reference are to co-ordinate the provision of clinical services for sexual problems in Edinburgh and the Lothian Region, to provide teaching in human sexuality for medical students and other professional groups, to facilitate collaborative research projects, to provide information to other bodies, to arrange meetings and workshops and to organize training schemes in sexual counselling for those within and outside the area.

The course is in three parts. The first part provides an introduction to sexual counselling with an emphasis on counselling skills. The second part provides training in sexual counselling with an emphasis on clinical experience using a modified Masters and Johnson approach. The third part provides supervised clinical work, usually in the trainee's own work-setting.

Selection criteria

Applicants are selected on the basis of appropriate professional training, counselling experience and some limited experience of working with sexual problems. There is an introductory training seminar in Edinburgh each year and applicants who have not had any clinical experience with treating sexual problems are encouraged to attend this for one year before coming on to the full training course. Applicants should demonstrate an interest, an aptitude and an emotional suitability for this kind of work. They also have to show where they would use the training after the course within a work-setting which is not private. Opinions of referees on these issues are taken into consideration and applicants are interviewed by the training committee.

Five people are accepted on to the course.

Focus

Sexual problems are seen as (a) occurring within a relationship and are treated within the context of that relationship and (b) arising for individuals which impede relationship formation. In the latter case, individual and group counselling are best employed. The course has an eclectic approach to sexual counselling based on the use of a modified Masters and Johnson approach. Behavioural tasks are assigned as diagnostic tools and are viewed as providing a good treatment framework. Psychodynamic interventions are employed to help couples understand where their difficulties lie when behavioural tasks are not completed.

Cost (at the time of writing)

£750 for the entire training programme.

Academic (theoretical) strand

The academic material is covered in one-hour tutorials, held fortnightly (in term-time) for the first four terms of the course. Trainees are given prior reading and are expected to discuss the material in tutorials. This format is used to promote active learning on the part of trainees.

The following topics are covered:

Term 1. Anatomy and physiology of sexual response; classification and causes of sexual dysfunctions; sexual aspects of fertility control; counselling and therapy; introduction to marital counselling; initial assessment; principles of the behavioural approach.

Term 2. Patterns of sexual behaviour; physical examinations; physical assessment; sexual problems in the gynaecology clinic; medical conditions, drugs and sexuality; sexual development.

Term 3. Hormones and sexuality (including the menopause and ageing); sexual abuse; venereal disease and sexuality; sex and disability, homosexuality; transvestism and transexualism; cultural factors including sexual taboos.

Term 4. Evaluating research; ethical issues; other therapies; individual therapy; infertility and abortion; sterilization; sexual problems and childbearing; management of sexual offenders.

Theoretical learning is also acquired in the weekly supervision group and trainees are also encouraged to read widely for the preparation of their casebook.

Training in therapeutic skills

Deliberate skills training occurs over the first four terms of the course. During the first term the emphasis is on basic counselling skills when modelling, role-play (with feedback) methods are used. Training occurs in a weekly group setting and videos are used and a one-way screen is employed.

During Terms 2, 3 and 4 the emphasis is on sexual counselling skills. This occurs in two settings. First, in weekly 1½-hour group supervision the focus is on role-playing, the skills of history-taking, interpreting, task-assignment and information-giving. Trainees are given feedback on their skills development and also learn to understand likely client responses to these interventions through enacting the client role. Second, skills training also occurs in fortnightly individual sessions with their trainer.

Practical experience

During the first three months of the course trainees are assigned to one of five clinics in Edinburgh and the Lothian Region where they directly observe sexual counselling as conducted by experienced training therapists using a modified Masters and Johnson approach. Trainees are then attached to one of these clinics for a six-month period (at least three hours per week). Here trainees initially take on one or two cases where they work as a co-therapist with their own trainer or another trained member of the clinical staff. Trainees and trainers decide together when the former is ready to see couples on their own (or in co-therapy with another trainee). Trainees' caseloads will usually not exceed four cases at any given time and will span a broad range of sexual problems.

After this six-month period, trainees may elect to remain in the same clinic for another six months or to change to another clinic for six months in order to broaden the range of their experience. In any event, trainees are likely to have a minimum of 135 hours of counselling experience during the 12 months' experience in their training clinic(s). They will also likely be seeing cases in their own work-setting during the same period, which they also bring to individual and group supervision.

After the 12-month period in the training clinic(s), trainees are assessed concerning whether they can counsel independently in their own work-setting for the remaining six months of the course (while receiving individual supervision) or whether they require an additional period in a training clinic.

Supervision

Supervision is conducted individually and in a group setting. Individual supervision (1 hour, fortnightly) occurs with the trainee's clinic trainer (Terms 1–4). The initial focus is on the co-therapy team (since the trainer is also likely to serve as co-therapist). When trainees work on their own or with another trainee a case discussion format of supervision is used where the trainees discuss each of their cases. Audio-tapes of cases are usually introduced during the third term of the course and become an additional focus for supervision. Clinic trainers are also available during the clinic session to consult with trainees on different aspects of their clinical work.

In group supervision (1½ hours, weekly, during Terms 1–4) some of the trainees' cases are followed-up over time. Here case discussion and role-play methods are used. It is here that supervision and skills training are integrated.

In Terms 5 and 6 when trainees are conducting sexual counselling in their own work-setting, they are allocated a different supervisor (from the training team) with whom they have individual supervision at least one hour per fortnight. Taped sessions are used as much as possible here and trainees send supervisors their tapes in advance. Regular telephone contact is also maintained between trainees and their individual supervisors during this period.

Personal learning

Each trainee is allocated a personal tutor (Terms 1–4) with whom they are expected to meet on average one hour per fortnight. Such meetings provide an opportunity for the trainee to deal with any personal issues (anxieties, interpersonal difficulties, etc.) arising out of the course or raise questions about any aspect of the course. The role of the personal tutor is supportive. He or she is *not* invited to submit a report on the trainee's progress to the training committee because the latter does not wish there to be any barriers to the facilitation of personal learning. He or she does not serve as the trainee's therapist but might direct the trainee to a therapist by mutual consent if the need arises. Trainees are not required to be in therapy during the course.

All applicants for the course are encouraged to attend a sexual attitude workshop where they explore their attitudes towards various aspects of human sexuality (including homosexuality, sex and disability and child sex abuse). A similar workshop is held during the fourth term of the course. Both workshops are open to other professionals but in the latter workshop the course members work together in their own group.

Partner involvement

None required, although partners may attend a sexual attitude workshop.

Research

Trainees are encouraged to consult the research literature while preparing their casebook. There is one tutorial on 'evaluating research' in Term 4. The main emphasis of the tutorial is on how to read research papers and how to assess their validity and importance. As with all tutorials the tutor and trainees will decide whether more time is needed to discuss matters further with the tutor; in which case an additional tutorial will be arranged.

Assessment

While trainers discuss progress with trainees on a regular basis, three more formal periods of assessment occur. At the end of Term 3 (mid-year assessment) trainees are assessed by the training committee on the basis of their performance and progress in their individual supervision sessions with their trainer and in the weekly supervision groups. In addition, each trainee will be expected to present a casebook, in which each case treated by the trainee is briefly described and one or two cases described at length, with a full discussion of the aetiological aspects and process of treatment, and a review of the relevant literature. After this assessment the view of the training committee about the trainees' progress will be fed back to the trainees.

At the end of Term 4 (end-of-year assessment), the assessment takes a similar form to the mid-year assessment and again the trainee will be required to produce a casebook. In addition, at this assessment, the training committee are concerned to look for areas of the trainee's work which would benefit from further learning or development. The trainee would be encouraged to concentrate on these areas during the final six months of the course.

At the end of the course (final assessment) the training committee will discuss the trainee's progress in the light of a report from the trainee's supervisor, a log-book kept by the trainee and tapes of the trainee's clinical work. Trainees may be: (a) deemed competent and able to work independently and accept referrals; (b) told they require further supervision; or (c) told they require further training and supervision.

Trainees are not asked to assess themselves or their peers but are given an opportunity to rate their trainers and supervisors.

Assessment criteria

At the mid-year and end-of-year assessment, members of the training committee collaborate to award marks on the following aspects of the trainee's performance:

1. *Conceptual ability* (the ability shown in supervision sessions to think intelligently about clinic problems and therapeutic issues)

2. *Clinical performance* (as reflected in the actual conduct of therapy rather than in supervisory discussions about the conduct of therapy)
3. *Personal learning* (as reflected in the approach to supervision and *not* based on any report from the personal tutor), and
4. A composite rating based on the above three marks

At the time of writing no final decision had been taken on what assessment criteria would be used at the final course assessment although it is likely that similar criteria to the above would be employed.

The following marks are used: 70+ outstanding; 60–69 very good; 55–59 good; 50–54 competent; 40–49 weak; below 40 not passable.

While there is, in the strict sense of the term, no external examiner employed to moderate the assessment procedure and the standards, a member of the Edinburgh Human Sexuality Group, who is not concerned with the training programme, serves in this capacity.

Training team's evaluation

The training team considered that the strengths of the programme are that (a) trainees are given a lot of clinical experience and are exposed to a wide range of problems in the area of human sexuality and (b) that the programme emphasizes trainees taking responsibility for their own learning.

The training team considered that the programme's weakness lay in practical time constraints so that trainees' work is not directly supervised (via tapes) as much as would be desirable.

Comments

It should be noted at the outset that this appraisal was undertaken before this training programme had actually been run. In its original form the training programme had run for six years and lasted for ten months. The original course had received accreditation from the Association of Sexual and Marital Therapists (ASMT). The present course has been expanded to enable trainees: (a) to receive an introduction to counselling in weekly seminars at the beginning of the course; (b) to have an extended period of observation in a clinic before they began their clinical work; and (c) to be supervised in their own work-setting for a six-month period after the formal part of the course has ended. As such it is an improvement over the previous programme and will, in all probability, maintain its ASMT accreditation when this is reviewed.

Our view is that its particular strengths lie in its emphasis on supervised clinical work throughout although, given their trainee status, weekly face-to-face supervision in the final six months of the course is desirable. This may not be possible given the distance most of the trainees have to travel. We particularly like the following elements: First, we like the fact that applicants without clinical experience of treating sexual problems are directed to attend an introductory training seminar for a year to determine their own suitability for the work before being considered for the programme; Second, we appreciate the careful exposure of trainees to clinical work: trainees have a three-month observational period in a clinic before they see clients and when they do have a direct clinical role this is initially undertaken in conjunction with a trained clinic member in a co-therapy arrangement; only when they have shown competence in this arrangement can they take direct clinical responsibility; this careful exposure to clinical work is one feature that other courses would do well to emulate. Third, we consider that the 'pastoral' role of the personal tutor is a facilitative one given that the tutor does not have assessment responsibilities although, as noted in our section on personal learning, this may raise certain dilemmas for the tutor if he or she has decided reservations concerning a particular trainee's suitability for the work. Finally, we consider that the course has devised a helpful and clear set of assessment criteria.

We think that further improvement could take place in the following areas. First, although the course is designed for practitioners, perhaps more emphasis on the academic (theoretical) strand of the course is necessary. We wonder whether one-hour group tutorials occurring fortnightly are sufficient to cover the syllabus adequately. Perhaps weekly tutorials would be an improvement. In addition, perhaps evaluation of trainees' theoretical knowledge could play a more central role in the assessment procedure. Second, the course could pay more attention to covering research design and methodology if it expects its trainees to make an informed evaluation of the literature, a review of which is expected to form part of the trainees' casebook. One (or at most two) one-hour tutorials is insufficient to cover adequately the complexity of this material. Third, perhaps trainees could be introduced to the method of audio-taping interviews at the outset of their training rather than during the third term. In our experience as trainers, such early exposure does seem to facilitate trainees learning from audio-tapes of their own work.

However, despite the preceding observations EHSG has designed a well-constructed course, which if it lives up to its promise may warrant the status of a diploma.

Further details

For further details of the above training programme, write to Dr Agnes Begg, Honorary Secretary, Edinburgh Human Sexuality Group, Family Planning Centre, 18 Dean Terrace, Edinburgh EH4 1NL.

4. London Institute for the Study of Human Sexuality. Two- or three-year professional training. Diploma in Sex Therapy (Theory) and Integrative Sex Therapy (Clinical) (part-time)*

This course has two major tiers: Tier 1 involves training in basic counselling skills (one year) – offered in conjunction with Metanoia Group and Therapy Training Institute; Tier 2 involves training in sex therapy and education (two years).

Selection criteria
Applicants who have already undertaken a course in basic counselling skills may proceed directly to Tier 2 (beginning in the second year). Applicants who lack such training are advised to seek it either at Metanoia – a training organization with links with the institute, which runs a 24-day course in basic counselling skills – or elsewhere.

Applicants are assessed by a personalized curriculum vitae, references, and at an individual interview with the Institute's medical director. At this interview, those who rate highly on the following criteria are likely to be accepted for training: (a) keen motivation for the work; (b) relevant training background in the helping professions; (c) intention to use the training in their future career; (d) personal maturity and relevant life experience, and (e) experience in (or willingness to undergo) personal therapy.

Approximately ten students are accepted into the second tier of training each year.

Focus
Sexual problems are framed in the widest possible context of humanistic psychotherapy. The focus of the course seeks to integrate transactional analysis (TA) and gestalt therapy with standard behavioural approaches to sex therapy. The course is geared specifically to the needs of practitioners.

Cost (at the time of writing)
£700 per annum for Years 2 and 3. The Metanoia basic counselling skills course currently costs £500.

Academic (theoretical) strand
Year 1. At the time of writing the London Institute is running a basic counselling skills course in conjunction with Metanoia Institute which offers a diploma in counselling.

* This course has undergone a considerable change since the time of writing, due in part, to the impact of this review.

Year 2.
(a) Thirty-six 2-hour sessions on a wide and comprehensive variety of topics pertaining to sexual functioning and dysfunctioning and the practice of sex therapy. The following topics are covered: anatomy of the genital tract; physiology of sexual response, including the sexual response cycle; the history of sexology; personality development/psychosexual development; sex and ageing; non-psychogenic factors in sexual function including the effects of drugs; physical and mental handicap in relation to sexuality; pregnancy, contraception, infertility in relation to sexual problems; venereal disease; gynaecological disorders; homosexuality; transexuality; gender identity; transvestism and other variations, paraphilias or deviations; cross-cultural and religious aspects of sexuality; surrogate therapy and social-skills training; ethical issues in sex therapy; principles of evaluation of outcome of therapy; psychological causes of sexual problems; dynamics of interpersonal relationships; psychological approaches to the treatment of sexual problems; other psychotherapeutic approaches of relevance to sex therapy, e.g. TA, cognitive therapies, gestalt, psychoanalysis, group process.
(b) Attendance at a minimum of six weekend workshops chosen by the student (from a selection of 18).
(c) Optional attendance at the institute's monthly 'Friday Forum'*.
Year 3. Thirty-six 3-hour sessions of integrative sex therapy relating TA and gestalt concepts to the concepts and practice of sex therapy.

Training in therapeutic skills
Year 1. See comments on Year 1 in previous section.
Year 2. Thirty-six 1-hour sessions on the practical aspects of the theory sessions discussed above. In particular, role-play, peer counselling sessions and tutor-modelling are employed.
Year 3. See academic strand Year 3.

Practical experience
In the third year of the course, students are expected to treat a minimum of six cases over the full course of therapy – clients being seen at the institute's clinic. One completed case should be seen with a co-therapist. Trainees are also attached, in the third year, to a general medical practice for a period of six to nine months. This attachment is arranged by the London Institute in conjunction with the Department of General Practice at Charing Cross Hospital. This attachment is intended to give trainees experience of a wide variety of relationship problems and of working as a member of a primary health care team.

* Now the Monday Forum.

Supervision
In Year 3 students receive (a) supervision in pairs (minimum 20 hours) or supervision individually by arrangement – they have a choice of supervisors although 50 per cent of such supervision is conducted by the Institute's medical director, and (b) group supervision (2 hours for 36 weeks) run by the medical director and a co-supervisor. Students are encouraged to present audio-tapes of their cases as well as discussing their therapeutic work.

Personal learning
Students are required to have personal therapy during their training. They are expected to attend at least one series of Sexual Attitude Restructuring workshops where they examine their own attitudes to sexuality and sexual issues.

Partner involvement
Active support for trainees' partners is recognized to be important, as the nature of the training course is such as to lead to changes in the trainees' attitudes to sexuality and to facilitate personal growth. Trainees' partners are, therefore, invited to join trainees in the workshop programme, and in particular, the workshops on 'Attitudes to Sexuality'.

Research
Students do not study the research literature on sexual functioning/dysfunctioning or sex therapy in any depth. Where research-oriented sessions are held the emphasis is on pointing to gaps in present knowledge.

Assessment
At the end of the second year, students engage in a peer-group assessment exercise to decide whether course members will proceed to Year 3. The emphasis is on a consensus view of whether each student has met individualized criteria negotiated earlier in the year with the medical director.

In the third year, students' work is assessed through the evaluation of three case studies and the presentation of prepared answers to theoretical questions in a group *viva-voce* examination. Students are prepared earlier through the use of mock examinations. A peer consensus view of level of performance as a practitioner is also used. It is hoped to make increased use of an external examiner in the future.

Assessment criteria
Individualized assessment criteria are used as are adaptations of five-point transactional analysis rating scales to the arena of sex therapy. These scales assess knowledge of theory, treatment planning, clarity of making assessments, level of creative and effective practice and degree of professionalism.

Course director's evaluation
The course director considers that the following are strengths of the course: (a) the emphasis is on practical effectiveness; students are helped to set up in practice after the course and are educated to this end; (b) the small numbers of students facilitate a high level of enthusiasm and support within the group and enable the course to be tailored somewhat to individual students' needs; (c) the Institute provides continuing peer and professional contact through its ongoing educational programme; (d) fees for the training programme are spread throughout the course.

He considers the following to be weaknesses: (a) as the course is not part of a larger organization students have recourse to a variety of outside resources of expertise only in so far as this is specifically arranged; (b) because of its independent status the Institute's course will take time to establish credibility in the eyes of other professionals.

Comments
The course started in 1982 and has undergone a number of changes since its inception. It perhaps needs a period of stability to consolidate its curriculum. While it does cover core areas of sexual functioning/dysfunctioning and sex therapy, we are concerned that the one timetabled hour allocated to skill training in Year 2 is not enough to provide each student with sufficient individual attention necessary for effective skill acquisition. More specifically, more time should be devoted in Year 2 to the psychological approaches to the treatment of sexual problems and in particular to associated training in these approaches' skills before students are given client responsibility in Year 3.

The course's emphasis on placing sex therapy within a broad framework of humanistic psychotherapy is to be commended and for students wishing to pursue interests in TA/gestalt therapy, the staff seem eminently qualified to provide training within this specialization. The third-year course in Integrative Sex Therapy is a particularly interesting and welcome recent addition to the course. The fact that the Institute provides a varied programme of continuing education for its students is important in providing access to a professional reference group and students may (and many do) develop extra expertise by attending more than the minimum number of weekend workshops (they will, of course, have to pay extra for the privilege).

The emphasis on integrating personal learning into the curriculum could be further developed and students could perhaps be encouraged more to read the research literature to enhance their practical effectiveness.

Given the implementation of the above recommendations the course would be an attractive one for those not eligible for or not wishing to seek training within an academic institution.

Further details

For further details of the training programme, write to Dr Michael Perring, Medical Director, Flat C, Langham Mansions, Earls Court Square, London SW5 9UH. Details of the Metanoia course can be obtained from Course Registrar, 13 North Common Road, London W5 2QB.

APPENDIX

Criteria for ASMT Accreditation of Sexual Therapy Training Courses*

1. *Selection of trainees*
   (a) There should be a selection procedure to exclude candidates obviously unsuitable for training in sexual therapy.
   (b) Trainees should ideally have had training and experience in one of the recognized health-care professions or counselling and have the opportunity for working with sexual/marital problems in that professional setting.
   (c) Exceptions to (b) may be made at the discretion of the course director, but such exceptions may not always be acceptable to ASMT. To maintain ASMT accreditation evidence of the validity of making such exceptions may subsequently be required by the training subcommittee.

2. *Theoretical knowledge*
   (a) There needs to be a syllabus for each course which specifies the knowledge to be acquired by trainees by the end of the training programme which should include the topics listed below.
      1. Anatomy of the genital tract.
      2. Physiology of sexual response.
      3. Psychosexual development and sexuality throughout the life-cycle.
      4. Organic causes of sexual problems including effects of medical illness, surgery and drugs.
      5. Psychological causes of sexual problems.
      6. Physical and mental handicap in relation to sexuality.
      7. Pregnancy, contraception and infertility in relation to sexual problems.
      8. Dynamics of interpersonal relationships.

* Reprinted with permission of the Association of Sexual and Marital Therapists (ASMT).

9. Psychological approaches to the treatment of sexual problems.
10. Other psychotherapeutic approaches of relevance to sex therapy, e.g. gestalt, TA and cognitive therapies.
11. Homosexuality.
12. Transexuality.
13. Transvestism and other 'variations' or 'deviations'.
14. Cross-cultural and religious aspects of sexuality.
15. Surrogate therapy.
16. Ethical issues in sex therapy.
17. Principles of evaluation of outcome of therapy.

(b) This knowledge will be gained through lectures and/or seminars in addition to guided reading.
(c) Formal testing of the acquisition of such knowledge is not currently required but may become so at a later date.

3. *Minimum client contact time*
(a) A minimum of 120 hours of supervised client contact time over a 1–2 year period is considered essential.
(b) Although it is felt that ideally two years should be the minimum length of client contact time, it is generally thought that at this stage in the development of training programmes in the UK, one year could be considered sufficient. This will be reviewed by the training subcommittee in three years' time.

4. *Supervision*
(a) Both individual and group supervision should be an integral part of any ASMT accredited course. Supervisors must have professional standing and experience, at least of a standard which would meet the requirements for full membership of ASMT.
(b) At present, one year of supervised clinical practice is considered as sufficient in any ASMT accredited training programme. At the next training subcommittee review in three years' time, this is likely to be extended to a minimum of two years.

5. *Assessment of clinical competence of trainees*
(a) There should be a clearly defined method of assessing the trainees' clinical competence throughout the course.
(b) There should also be a clearly defined method of assessment of the trainees' clinical competence at the end of the course by an assessor who has not been directly involved in their training. Assessors must have professional standing and experience at least of a standard which would meet the requirements for full membership of ASMT.

(c) As yet there is no prescribed method of continuous or final assessment of clinical competence. This is currently under consideration.

6. *Selection of cases for therapy by trainees*
It is recognized that the course director has some responsibility for the selection of suitable cases with whom their trainees will work.

7. *Accreditation procedure*
(a) Completion of the application form.
(b) A site visit by two members of the training subcommittee where the course is not held on premises of the NHS or other nationally recognized organization. A report on this visit will be sent to the course director.
(c) An interview of the course director by the training subcommittee. Their report on this interview will be sent to the course director.
(d) Payment of a standard fee which will be charged for the process of accreditation.

8. *Accreditation reviews*
(a) Accreditation will be subject to review at three-yearly intervals, or earlier if there is a change of course director or premises.
(b) Visits will be made to accredited courses by two members of the training subcommittee. This will form the main part of the accreditation review process. A report on this visit will be sent to the course director.
(c) A standard fee will be charged for accreditation review visits.

9. *Ethical code*
All therapists training in or by accredited courses will be expected to adhere to the ethical code of ASMT and sign an undertaking to this effect.

10. *Appeal procedure*
If course accreditation is refused, appeal may be made to the committee of the ASMT.

11. *Withdrawal of accreditation*
The committee reserve the right to withdraw course accreditation under exceptional circumstances.

Training programmes in marital/sexual therapy accredited by ASMT
Edinburgh Human Sexuality Group Training Scheme

Marital Sexual Therapy Course, National Marriage Guidance Council
Sheffield Marital and Sexual Postgraduate Training Course
Manchester Psychosexual Counselling Course
Diploma in Human Sexuality, St George's Hospital Medical School, London

NOTE

1. We wish to thank the following for their views concerning the training programmes with which they are associated and for their comments on our descriptions of these programmes: Judy Bury of the Edinburgh Human Sexuality Group, Alison Clegg of the National Marriage Guidance Council, Michael Perring of the London Institute for the Study of Human Sexuality and Elizabeth Stanley of St George's Hospital Medical School.

REFERENCES

Arentewicz, G. and Schmidt, G. (eds) (1983) *The Treatment of Sexual Disorders*, Basic Books, New York.

Association of Sexual and Marital Therapists (1985) Criteria for ASMT accreditation of sexual therapy training courses. Unpublished manuscript.

Ayres, T., Lyon, P., McIlvenna, T., Myers, F., Rila, M., Rubinstein, M., Smith, C. and Sutton, L. (1974) *SAR Guide for a Better Life*, Nation Sex Forum, San Francisco.

Bancroft, J. (1983) *Human Sexuality and Its Problems*, Churchill-Livingstone, Edinburgh.

Bancroft, J. (1985) Marital sex therapy, in W. Dryden (ed.) *Marital Therapy in Britain, Vol. 2. Special Areas*, Harper & Row, London.

Brown, P.T. (1979) Practical modifications of Masters and Johnson's approach to the treatment of sexual dysfunction. Unpublished PhD thesis, University of Leicester.

Brown, P.T. and Bollinger, C. (1985) Training non-psychologists in the treatment of sexual dysfunction with special reference to the training of marriage guidance counsellors, in H. Davis and P. Butcher (eds) *Sharing Psychological Skills*, The British Psychological Society, Leicester. First published in *The British Journal of Medical Psychology* (1985) Vol. 58, pp. 257–65.

Brown, P.T. and Dryden, W. (1985) Issues in the training of sex therapists, in W. Dryden (ed.) *Marital Therapy in Britain, Vol. 2. Special Areas*, Harper & Row, London.

Burnap, D.W. and Golden, J.S. (1967) Sexual problems in medical practice. *Journal of Medical Education*, Vol. 42, pp. 673–80.

Dryden, W. and Brown, P.T. (1985) Issues in the training of marital therapists, in Dryden (ed.) *Marital Therapy in Britain, Vol. 2*, Harper & Row, London.

Hawton, K. (1985) *Sex Therapy: A Practical Guide*, Oxford University Press, Oxford.

Kaplan, H.S. (1977) Training of sex therapists, in W.H. Masters, V.E. Johnson and R.C. Kolodny (eds) *Ethical Issues in Sex Therapy and Research*, Little, Brown & Co., Boston.

Kaplan, H.S. (1978) *The New Sex Therapy: Active Treatment of Sexual Dysfunctions*, Penguin, Harmondsworth. (First published in Great Britain by Baillière Tindall, 1975, and in the US by Brunner/Mazel, 1974.)

Masters, W.H. and Johnson, V.E. (1970) *Human Sexual Inadequacy*, J.A. Churchill, London.

Mathews, A., Bancroft, J., Whitehead, A., Hackmann, A., Julier, D., Bancroft, J., Gath, D. and Shaw, P. (1976) The behavioural treatment of sexual inadequacy: a comparative study, *Behaviour Research and Therapy*, Vol. 14, pp. 427–36.

Mathews, A., Whitehead, A. and Kellett, J. (1983) Psychological and hormonal factors in the treatment of female sexual dysfunction. *Psychological Medicine*, Vol. 13, pp. 83–92.

Mitchell, K.M., Bozarth, J.D. and Krauft, C.C. (1977) A reappraisal of the therapeutic effectiveness of accurate empathy, non-possessive warmth and genuineness, in A.S. Gurman and A.M. Razin (eds) *Effective Psychotherapy*. Pergamon, Oxford.

Sadock, V.A., Sadock, B.J. and Kaplan, H.S. (1975) Comprehensive sex therapy training: a new approach, *American Journal of Psychiatry*, Vol. 132, pp. 858–60.

Sarrel, P.M., Sarrel, L.J. and Faraclas, W.G. (1982) Evaluation of a continuing education program in sex therapy, *American Journal of Public Health*, Vol. 72, pp. 839–43.

Smail, D.J. (1978) *Psychotherapy: A Personal Approach*, Dent, London.

Stanley, E., Kellett, J., Falkowski, B., Ramage, M. and Sketchley, J. (1986) St George's Hospital Medical School Course for the Diploma in Human Sexuality, *Sexual and Marital Therapy*, Vol. 1, pp. 75–88.

Truax, C.B. and Carkhuff, R.R. (1967) *Toward Effective Counseling and Psychotherapy*, Aldine, Chicago.

Truax, C.B. and Mitchell, K.M. (1971) Research on certain therapist interpersonal skills in relation to process and outcome, in A.E. Bergin and S.L. Garfield (eds) *Handbook of Psychotherapy and Behavior Change*, Wiley, New York.

CHAPTER 18

SEX THERAPY: A RESEARCH OVERVIEW

Martin Cole and Windy Dryden

The study of human sexual behaviour is of necessity a multidisciplinary pursuit. As such it has suffered because of the inevitable fragmentation of research programmes, which are often unco-ordinated, underfunded and hence by and large, at least in Britain, relatively unproductive. The fact that sex research is inevitably controversial does not help, particularly when even well-respected academics are misrepresented in the media if it is discovered they are doing sex research. However, in spite of these difficulties there is a tradition of excellence in much of the early research centred largely in the US with the occasional invaluable contribution in the UK and elsewhere. Amongst the most notable were Bancroft (1983), Kaplan (1974; 1979), Kinsey *et al.* (1948; 1953) and Masters and Johnson (1966; 1970; 1979). In addition there are a number of journals specialising in sex research such as *Archives of Sexual Behavior*, the *British Journal of Sexual Medicine*, *Journal of Sex and Marital Therapy*, *Sexual and Marital Therapy* and *The Journal of Sex Research*.

The success of any therapy, and sex therapy is no exception, depends upon a good academic base and the funding of research into human sex behaviour is essential if sex therapy is to flourish. There is, however, a distinction between research in human sexual behaviour and research in sex therapy. The former recognizes the rigours and constraints of the experimental method whereas the latter, as is evidenced by some publications, is less disciplined and is subject to the aspirations of therapists and objectivity is often sacrificed at the altar of therapeutic wishful thinking. The former is exact, reproduceable and predictive – the latter, more often than not, is inexact, ideational and involves approximations which would be unacceptable elsewhere. However therapy, in the final analysis, deals with the often elusive dimensions of the relationship between the therapist and the patient and to expect sex therapy to conform to the rigours of the scientific method may be demanding a lot. However, if a proper validation of therapeutic programmes is to be achieved then the highest standards must be set.

There has been little dramatic change in sex therapy since Masters and Johnson (1970). This has been said to result from the major influence these authors had on sex therapy which inevitably limited subsequent contributions to small innovations on the Masters and Johnson approach (Barlow, 1986). However, it could equally well be argued that the momentum created by the impact of Masters and Johnson's work might have stimulated equally imaginative contributions to sex therapy, but they did not. Nor has any real improvement been made in reported success rates. It seems that approximately one half to two thirds of sexually dysfunctional patients will show 'some improvement' immediately following treatment, though the results for erectile dysfunction are in general much poorer than this (Barlow, 1986; and see Table 18.1).

One of the explanations for this lack of progress may be the scant attention that is paid to pure research into human sexual neurophysiology and psychophysiology particularly in Britain. Moreover, even when research data are available they take a long time to filter down and influence practitioners at the working face of therapy. For example, it would be very interesting to enquire of the members of the Association of Sexual and Marital Therapists (or the Institute of Psychosexual Medicine) as to whether they were aware of Barlow's (1986) important research findings into the role of cognition and anxiety in sex behaviour, findings which may have substantial implications for treatment. Indeed, it has been shown that helping practitioners do not cite research findings as a major source of influence in their therapeutic practice (Morrow-Bradley and Elliot, 1986).

WHAT IS A SEXUAL PROBLEM?

To provide a simple definition of a sexual problem is a near impossibility and recourse to a list of sex dysfunctions (see Chapter 1) may not be as helpful as it might appear.

For example, quick ejaculation is perfectly acceptable to some couples and intolerable for others. A low frequency of intercourse is normal for some and disruptive for others. Some couples never consummate their marriages because of vaginismus or erectile problems yet happily stay together for a lifetime, yet for others this prospect would be unthinkable – the examples are endless. Clearly the only satisfactory way of defining a sexual problem is to focus not on a rigid definition of a sex dysfunction but instead on whether the behaviour is evaluated as a problem by the individual or couple in question. If one accepts this approach then by helping patients to see their problems in a different perspective can be very helpful. As a starting point for this process availability of information on the incidences and frequencies of sexual behaviour is esential. Cole, in Chapter 2, attempts to provide some of this data and it can be used as part of a cognitive and psychoeducational approach to therapy (Ellis, 1983).

THE CAUSES OF SEX DISORDERS

It has been suggested that organogenic (or biogenic) diagnoses of sexual disorders will grow at the expense of those which are psychogenic (Cole, 1985). Whilst this simple dichotomy between the organic and the psychogenic is both inadequate and somewhat misleading (see Chapter 7) nevertheless the distinction has sufficient clarity for it to be retained. Evidence for this shift from the psychogenic to the organogenic is nowhere better illustrated than in the aetiology of erectile dysfunction. It had been generally accepted until quite recently that up to 90 per cent of erectile failure was due to psychological problems (e.g. Johnson, 1968; Kaya *et al.*, 1979). However, of late there is abundant evidence that organic conditions may be implicated in up to 50 per cent of those presenting with erectile dysfunction (Fisher *et al.*, 1979; Kaya *et al.*, 1979; Melman *et al.*, 1984; Spark *et al.*, 1980).

Some of this shift in opinion has come from an increasing use of the measurement of nocturnal penile tumescence (NPT), (Fisher *et al.*, 1979; and see Chapter 6). Originally it was assumed that the absence of nocturnal erections indicated an organic basis to erectile dysfunction and the regular appearance of night erections a psychogenic basis. However, the interpretation of the results is more complex than it first appeared. For example, increases in penile circumference do not measure penile rigidity, an important component of erection. Moreover, the duration of nocturnal erection is important, NPT only confirming psychogenic erectile dysfunction when a rigid erection of at least five minutes is obtained (Melman *et al.*, 1984). The monitoring of sleep patterns is also an important part of the procedure and the use of portable NPT monitors and other devices are regarded as unsatisfactory for this reason (Conte, 1986). However, whilst NPT evaluation needs to be treated with caution because of some false positives and false negatives there is no doubt that it has provided a fairly effective means of detecting organogenic erectile failure.

The attention given to NPT studies in men has somewhat overshadowed comparable measurements in women. It is possible to measure changes in the blood flow to the vagina (vasocongestion) by photoplethysmography and hence obtain a physiological measure of sexual arousal. A photoplethysmograph measures light reflected off the vaginal wall which provides a means of estimating blood flow and hence arousal (Hatch, 1979; 1981). Clearly the use of vaginal plethysmography would be invaluable in helping to distinguish between impaired sexual desire and impaired sexual arousal. Evidence obtained so far supports the view that some forms of arousal dysfunction in women have an organic basis and one might predict that as diagnostic measures improve so, as has been found with men, organogenic diagnoses will grow at the expense of those which are psychogenic in women also.

It is important to understand that the issues raised and answers obtained are not only of theoretical interest but will have a significant impact upon treatment programmes. Because sex therapy, at least initially, was undertaken by practitioners who largely had a training in psychology, counselling or psychiatry the importance of biogenic elements in the causation of sex disorders was, and still is, underemphasized. For example, there is a general consensus of opinion that premature ejaculation is largely learned or contingent upon a poor relationship (Kaplan, 1974; Masters and Johnson, 1970; Trimmer, 1982). Bancroft (1983) had hinted that it was misleading to attribute premature ejaculation solely to psychological factors, but only recently did Goodman (1986) and Hong (1984) suggest that it may well have an innate component. Unfortunately very little has been published about the personality of premature ejaculators though Cooper (1968) found, compared with other males with sex dysfunctions, evidence of raised anxiety. Cole (1986) was able to identify certain characteristics associated with premature ejaculation. In particular the premature ejaculator, when compared to those patients with erectile dysfunction, showed a significantly lower adult masturbation rate and a significantly higher incidence of self-reported REM erections (NPT) and wet dreams. These results are consistent with the view that there is a biogenic element in the aetiology of premature ejaculation.

Thus, in general terms, it seems likely that stress, or more particularly sex stress, will result in different psychosomatic responses in different patients (Pervin and Leiblum, 1980). Thus in the male, sex stress, either 'remote' or 'immediate' (Kaplan, 1974), would lead to premature ejaculation, retarded ejaculation or erectile dysfunction, whilst in a woman the results of stress might express themselves in either orgasmic dysfunction, vaginismus, vaginitis or lubrication dysfunction. Often these symptoms are mutually exclusive and patient-specific and will depend amongst other things upon the individual's neurohormonal framework (Johnson, 1968). The overwhelming expression of premature ejaculation amongst Asian patients (see p. 349) could be explained, at least in part, by this idea which assumes a constitutional or biogenic element in all sex disorders, each individual having a specific somatic response on which the stress targets itself (Cole, 1985). What is urgently required is a series of up-to-date research programmes providing a full multivariate factor analysis of all the common sex dysfunctions: an analysis which must include both the biological and psychological determinants.

THE SOCIOBIOLOGICAL VIEWPOINT

The inclusion of a chapter on the sociobiological basis to sex dysfunctions (see Chapter 3) may seem somewhat perverse to some in a book on sex therapy. Indeed, many sex therapists may not have even heard of sociobiology. In essence sociobiologists have proposed that much of human social behaviour and even the structure of human societies have a biological basis and hence can be explained in evolutionary terms – 'genes have culture on a leash' (Ruse, 1979; Symons, 1979; E.O. Wilson, 1975; 1978; G. Wilson, 1979). Naturally such a view implies that in therapeutic terms there are limits to an individual's capacity for change and that human behaviour is not infinitely modifiable. From the aetiology (causation) standpoint naturally sociobiologists will attach more importance to biogenic (organogenic) factors, a view which appears to be gaining increasing acceptance (see p. 339).

It does no harm for sex therapists to be reminded that there may be limitations to the efficacy of their methods. And the ongoing debate between 'determinists' and the 'environmentalists' can only benefit sex therapy if it adds to an overall understanding of sex dysfunction. If certain questions are never asked, answers will never be found.

By attempting to understand the evolutionary origin of human sexual behaviour in general and the sex dysfunctions in particular the therapist is in a better position to put these 'disorders' in perspective. For example, Symons (1979) (and see Chapter 3) suggests that female orgasm should be regarded as a byproduct of mammalian bisexual potential. He argues that orgasm may only be possible for female mammals because it is adaptive for males. Thus, because the threshold for female orgasmic reflex is set at a higher level, coital orgasm for the woman will be a less predictable and more precarious event. Sexist as this may sound, this information can be used therapeutically by helping, for example, to reduce performance anxiety and at the very least this cognitive-psychoeducational approach should be used in conjunction with the other behavioural strategies used in the treatment of orgasmic dysfunction (Heiman *et al.*, 1976; Hooper, 1984). Awareness of this point of view might also stimulate more research into the organic basis to orgasmic dysfunction for which there is increasing evidence (Brindley and Gillan, 1982; Hoon *et al.*, 1981).

Sociobiology also makes a number of constructive contributions to the understanding of other aspects of human sexual behaviour, in particular the paraphilias (sexual deviation) and homosexual behaviour. Opinions are deeply divided on these sociobiological interpretations (Bancroft, 1983) and no doubt the debate will continue.

THE ROLE OF ANXIETY IN SEXUAL FUNCTIONING

Kaplan (1974; 1979), Masters and Johnson (1970), Wolpe (1958) and others have taken the simplistic view that anxiety reduction has a beneficial and global effect upon all sex disorders in all patients. This somewhat naive position arose from the misguided view that because *performance anxiety* had rightly been judged to have a devastating effect upon sexual responses then the reduction of *all* anxiety, however caused, would have a therapeutic effect comparable to that achieved when performance fears were reduced.

Recently there have been a number of studies showing that anxiety is either independent of or even has potentiating effect upon sexual arousal. For example, Wolchik *et al.* (1980) show that anxiety-provoking stimuli enhanced sexual arousal in functional men and women. Norton and Jehu (1984), in their review of the role of anxiety in sexual dysfunction, again support the view that consciously experienced anxiety is so commonly a feature of good sex that it would not be sensible to regard it as always being a liability. Chambless and Lifshitz (1984) report that sexual arousal and anxiety were uncorrelated and concluded that there was no obvious relationship between self-reported sexual anxiety and arousal. There is now a wealth of clinical and experimental evidence to support the view that anxiety may facilitate sexual arousal. For instance adolescent boys reported non-erotic erections where fear or excitement such as near accidents or being chased by the police acted as the stimulus (Bancroft, 1970; Ramsey, 1943). Sarrel and Masters (1982) likewise describe men who were able to achieve intercourse when molested by women, in spite of the fact that these men were threatened with knives and other weapons if they failed. Further support for the view that anxiety plays a part in sexual arousal comes from the well-established fact that men who engage in the paraphilias (voyeurism, exhibitionism and paedophiles e.g.) are often aroused as much by the fear of the forbidden and the risk of being caught as by the practice itself (Stoller, 1976). Laboratory experiments also support this view. Hoon *et al.* (1977) and Wolchik *et al.* (1980) describe how the initial exposure of women and men to an anxiety-producing film led to an increase in sexual arousal when the subjects were later exposed to an erotic film. Such an increase in arousal was not observed when the subjects had viewed a neutral film before the erotic film.

The idea that anxiety may potentiate as well as block sexual responses is clearly of considerable importance to sex therapists since it means that the global and uncritical use of the methods of anxiety-reduction, a main plank in the armamentarium of sex therapists, can no longer be relied upon in all circumstances (Cole, 1985). Fortunately some evidence is beginning to emerge about the way in which different individuals respond to sexual stress and anxiety. For example, subjects who have a sex dysfunction appear to be inhibited by anxiety whereas those who function well sexually are aroused by anxiety (Barlow, 1986).

There are a number of other correlates reported by Barlow that discriminate between those who are sexually dysfunctional and those who function well sexually (see Chapter 5). However, perhaps the most significant point that emerges is that different individuals showed different sexual responses to stress. This conclusion should have been self-evident, but it has been (and remains) a weakness in many clinical and therapeutic strategies to disregard the variation among individuals to the same stimuli.

One of the dimensions of personality that Barlow (1986) identifies as being important in sexual behaviour is that of the cognitive-affect variable. This dimension does not appear to have received much attention by sex therapists though personal experience supports the view that those with 'high affect' (the feelers), that is, those who experience and are usually conscious of their emotions, have a better prognosis in sex therapy than those who are highly cognitive individuals (the thinkers). Indeed, one might go even further and suggest that the expression of a sex disorder varies according to whether the individual is of high or low affect. For example, psychogenic erectile dysfunction and vaginismus appear to be more frequently found in high-affect individuals, whereas premature ejaculation is more a feature of those with low affect. Experimental tests of this hypothesis are urgently needed.

Barlow (1986) starts from the premiss that there are likely to be differences in the role of cognition between his sexually functional and sexually dysfunctional men and shows, for example, that the sexual dysfunctional group of males display a negative affect in sexual situations whereas those who function well sexually display a positive affect.

However, in order to try to improve therapeutic efficiency it is equally important to examine, conversely, the different ways in which 'high-affect' and 'high-cognition' individuals respond to standard therapeutic programmes. Barlow (1986) hints at this approach when he says 'detailed assessment of affective and cognitive functioning in a sexual context may predict a degree of improvement as well as long-term outcome' and later 'emphasizing anxiety-reduction operationalized as decreasing physiological arousal may be counterproductive in view of the effects of anxiety on sexually functioning subjects' (p. 147). In other words, a careful choice has to be made between cognitively based and affectively based therapies, a choice which should be made depending upon the personality of the patient and the presenting condition.

OUTCOMES IN SEX THERAPY

Research and therapy make strange bedfellows. The one requires discipline, measurement and accurate recording, the other requires empathy, spontaneity and wisdom. It is not surprising therefore that the accurate recording of data, the measurement of outcome and the relentless pursuit of follow-ups has never been a particular preoccupation of psychoanalytic and humanistic therapists. The notable exception to this observation has been the way which the cognitive-behavioural school of therapies has attempted to report on outcomes and follow-ups (Hollon and Beck, 1986).

Sex therapists, because of the eclectic nature of their discipline (see Chapter 7), have also faced the need to reconcile research and therapy and many reports appear on outcome and follow-up (see Table 18.1). Poor results may mean an inaccurate diagnosis, inappropriate therapeutic contracts, that the therapist is not very good at his or her job, that the methods available are not working very well, or perhaps that the outcome cannot be quantified in an objective manner. The most likely of these explanations for poor outcomes is that the methods are inappropriate or ineffectual and if this is the explanation for unsatisfactory outcomes then every attempt should be made to remedy the situation.

Unfortunately there are many obstacles to obtaining reliable data on outcome and follow-up in sex therapy. For example, the description of a disorder has to be precise if data from different sources are to be comparable. There are many ways of defining premature ejaculation or orgasmic dysfunction and each author will have his or her own (and sometimes an undisclosed) way of doing so. Added to this are the often uncontrollable variables of the relationship, imponderables associated with the intervention of the therapist (Truax and Carkhuff, 1967) and above all those difficulties met in attempting to measure therapeutic change objectively. Finally there are likely to be logistic problems in obtaining follow-up data from a sample of patients with sexual problems (Milne and Cordle, 1984; Kuriansky and Sharpe, 1976; Pervin and Leiblum, 1980).

Table 18.1 reveals considerable variation in reported success rates and clearly some must be accepted with great caution. Apart from the difficulties already mentioned some data will be suspect because of the biased nature of the sample (Masters and Johnson, 1970), the absence of follow-ups (Crown and d'Ardenne, 1982; Kaplan, 1979) or the subjectivity in recording outcomes (Heisler, 1983). The literature on outcomes is littered with near

Table 18.1 Outcome of treatment

Author	*Sample*	*Sex disorder*	*Treatment programme*	*Outcome after treatment*	*Outcome at follow-up*
Masters and Johnson (1970)	US couples	PE (n = 186) RE (n = 17) 1° ED (n = 32) 2° ED (n = 213) 1° ED (n = 193) 2° OD (n = 149) V (n = 29)	Masters and Johnson	Initial failure rates PE 2.2% RE 17.6% 1° ED 40.6% 2° ED 26.2% 1° OD 16.6% 2° OD 22.8% V 0%	At five years (overall failure rate) PE 2.7% RE 17.6% 1° ED 40.6% 2° ED 30.9% 1° OD 17.6% 2° OD 24.8%
Kockott *et al.* (1975)	Three groups of eight males – mean age 31 (n = 24)	Primary and secondary ED	Comparison of: systematic desensitization (SD), medication and advice (M+A) and waiting list (WL)	SD 25% 'cured' M + A 25% 'cured' WL no 'cure' 'cure' = maintenance of E for one minute after penetration with ejaculation before loss of E	Planned but no data
Ansari (1976)	Men with sex problems	ED	Comparison of: modified M/J chemotherapy and no treatment	No difference between two treatments and controls	No data
Bancroft and Coles (1976)	Men and women consecutive patients at sex problem clinic mean age 38 yrs (n = 78)	ED PE RE V OD LL	Modified Masters and Johnson programmes	'successful outcome' 37% 'worthwhile improvement' 31% 'no change' 13% 'dropped out' 19%	No data

Table 18.1 (contd.)

Author	*Sample*	*Sex disorder*	*Treatment programme*	*Outcome after treatment*	*Outcome at follow-up*
Levine and Agle (1978)	US couples age 25–29 wide cross-section (n = 16)	Secondary psychogenic ED	M/J and Kaplan programme	'potent' 38% 'improved' 25% 'no change' 37%	Only 6% (one patient) maintained full function after one year
Mears (1978)	(n = 1373)	OD V ED PE RE	The Balint approach 'brief interpretative psychotherapy'	Successful outcome: OD 26% V 45% ED 30% PE 30% RE 28%	No data
Kaplan (1979)	Wide spectrum (n = c. 1000)	All problems	Kaplan's methods	'cured' 63% 'improved' 7% 'failed or drop-out' 30%	No data
Crowe *et al*. (1981)	Couples with sexual problems (n = 48 couples)	ED OD LL	Comparison of Masters and Johnson (one and two therapists) and marital therapy based on 'discussion'	Statistically significant improvement using validated scales – no difference between programmes	Improvement persistent for one year at least – no difference between programmes
Crown and d'Ardenne (1982)	UK couples (n = 51)	ED PE RE V OD LL	Modified Masters and Johnson programmes	♀ positive change 59% some improvement 23% ♂ positive change 38% some improvement 26%	No data

Hawton (1982)	UK couples (n = 100) 70 completed treatment	ED PE RE V OD LL	Modified Masters and Johnson programmes	Problem largely resolved 63% ♀ 70% ♂	After three months ♀ 52% ♂ 63%
Watson and Brockman (1982)	UK couples (n = 116)		Comparison of various treatment formats		53% follow-up (n = 61) 42% (n = 26) of whom maintained improvement
Heisler (1983)	NMGC clients (n = 684)	All problems	Modified Masters and Johnson programmes	'some improvement' 6% ♂ 23% ♀ 'sufficient improvement' 5% ♂ 8% ♀ 'total improvement' 31% ♂ 26% ♀	(n = 460) 36% response improvement 20% no change 42% deterioration 38%
Pryde and Woods (1985)	UK couples (n = 56)	All problems	Modified Masters and Johnson programmes	'drop-outs' 23% 'worse' 2% 'unchanged' 2% 'slightly improved' 16% 'improved' 20% 'much improved' 38%	

Source: Reproduced with permission from Cole (1985) *The British Journal of Psychiatry*, Vol. 147, pp. 337–51.
For a review of outcome in 18 independent studies up to and including 1976 see Wright *et al*. (1977).
Key: PE: premature ejaculation; RE: retarded ejaculation; ED: erectile dysfunction; V: vaginismus; OD: orgasmic dysfunction; LL: loss of libido.

meaningless categories such as 'total improvement', 'worthwhile improvement' or simply 'improved'. Are these better or worse than 'positive change' or 'problem largely resolved'? A further complication which makes meaningful comparisons of outcome data suspect is the fact that dropouts are sometimes included in the final percentages as failures and sometimes not. Since dropouts can represent as many as one third of presenting patients clearly the way the data are reported will dramatically influence the results.

Psychotherapists, even behaviour therapists, are not laboratory scientists but there should be an obligation upon them to strive for the best evaluation possible of the outcome of therapy – if only to be able to give some kind of answer to the questions 'Does it work?' and 'For how long?' Fortunately sex therapists now have at their disposal a large number of standardized questionnaires designed to measure sexual and marital satisfaction. If these are administered before and after therapy they can provide one way of achieving objective assessment of therapeutic change. A critical review of these questionnaires can be found in Conte (1986). Not mentioned in that review, but of particular use to British therapists, is the recent Golombok Rust Inventory of Sexual Satisfaction (GRISS) (Rust and Golombok, 1985).

To some this section may have appeared to have diminished the invaluable yet often immeasurable elements in the therapeutic alliance. The inestimable value of communication, trust, warmth and empathy in therapy is undisputed and often its benefits cannot be quantified. However, sex therapists, particularly because of their eclectic discipline and the wide range of problems they meet, must try to reconcile, as far as possible, their humanity with their obligations to science.

SEX THERAPY – NEW APPROACHES IN A CHANGING SOCIETY

In a changing society existing approaches to therapy need to be modified to deal with new situations. Often sex therapists are heard to ponder somewhat wistfully 'Where have all the easy cases gone?' and this observation may not be entirely based upon a misguided nostalgia – it may reflect the fact that in our more relaxed and open society there is a lot of self-help and personal reappraisal taking place without recourse to seeking professional help – leaving only the more intractable problems for the professionals. And to the extent that many sexual problems are partner-dependent (Cole, 1985) the rising divorce rate may solve some sexual problems.

The Gay Movement

However, more tangible changes are also taking place. The growth and recognition of the Gay Movement has led to the realization that gay men and women also have sexual problems (see Chapter 13). Moreover, it appears that their problems are not very different in form or frequency than those of heterosexuals (Masters and Johnson, 1979). Therefore the benefits that follow from research into the causation and treatment of sex disorders are likely to favour homosexuals as well as heterosexuals, though this will depend upon the existence of an adequate network of gay counselling centres where realistic and supportive advice can be obtained.

People with disabilities

Somewhat more recently there has been increasing attention devoted to the sexual needs of those with a physical disability (see Chapter 12), together with concern for the sex lives of those who have a mental handicap or mental illness. In my own experience the number of requests for help from these disadvantaged groups has increased dramatically in the past two or three years and this interest and concern for these minorities is a welcome development and may add to the credibility of sex therapy.

Ethnic minorities

Increasingly, sex therapists and their allied professions are being consulted by those from other ethnic groups. Often these professionals are unprepared and insufficiently flexible to deal with these minorities and new approaches have to be evolved (see Chapter 11). For example, Atkinson *et al.* (1978) and Sue (1981) stress that the unstructured nature of counselling may not be appropriate to Asians who prefer a more logical cognitive approach to counselling and do not respond to one which attempts to foster affect. This raises interesting theoretical issues as to which is the preferred treatment mode for those of different personality types (see p. 343). Whatever final conclusions are reached it is clear that the usual type of therapy offered in Britain needs to be modified considerably if they are to be used effectively with Asian patients (Ghosh *et al.*, 1985).

Little is known about the epidemiology of sexual dysfunction and work in this area is long overdue. One fact that has emerged is that premature ejaculation is extremely common in Asian communities (d'Ardenne, 1984; Cole, 1985). For example, I have found that 64 per cent (n = 36) of those Asian patients who have consulted me (Martin Cole) with a sexual problem are premature ejaculators compared to only 12 per cent (n = 130) of those of Caucasian origin from the UK (Cole, 1982). However one tries to explain this striking observation, and it would not appear that cultural differences alone are adequate, the answers should provide some insight into the causes of premature ejaculation and hence the evolution of more effective treatment programmes.

Sex offenders
Nowhere are the effects of a changing society more dramatically felt than in the increase in the reported number of sex offences. Despite the fact that sex therapy with sex offenders (see Chapter 14) is in its infancy in Britain, some of the results are promising. However, advances in pharmacotherapy may prove to be as useful, if not more useful, than some of the psychological methods currently used, if only because the latter demands high motivation on the part of the offender.

Patients with medical problems
A further group of patients who are presenting for help with sexual difficulties in increasing numbers are those who have coexisting medical problems (see Chapter 15). Anderson and Wolf (1986) in a recent report on the psychological issues involved in chronic physical illness provide some excellent guidelines for psychologists and health professionals when dealing with patients with sexual problems.

The first was that workers who are likely to meet these problems should feel comfortable dealing with these sexual issues; second, the problems created by interrupted sexual activity should be discussed routinely with patients so that permission can be given to restart sexual contact at the appropriate time; third, consultations should always be arranged so that the patient's partner is present; and, finally, that the simple yet positive benefits of touching can be explained before attempts at more demanding aspects of sexual interaction are begun; attempts which should only be embarked upon gradually. At a time in life when intimacy, comfort and support are often most needed it is essential that the couple should not neglect their sexual needs, even though considerable adjustments may have to be made.

THE FUTURE

It would have to be either a very wise or very foolish man who attempted to predict with any certainty what the future holds for sex therapy. Much depends upon the changes in the man-woman relationship and the way in which the family unit evolves. With a fair degree of marital mobility many of those sexual problems which are partner-dependent will be resolved and with the reduction of sexual guilt others, which are the product of remote causes (Kaplan, 1974), will also reduce in number. However, there is little doubt that many problems will remain.

Sex therapy at the moment comprises an armamentarium of four main approaches: medical intervention (e.g. diagnostic investigations, pharmacotherapy and surgery) and the analytical, behavioural and cognitive psychotherapies. Further understanding of the importance of the roles of cell biology and neurophysiology in the causation of the sex disorders will hopefully lead to a greater sophistication in the formulation of both diagnostic and therapeutic procedures. As a result, more accurate and realistic therapeutic contracts can be entered into with the effect that the psychotherapies can begin to play the increasingly important role, for which they were devised, of helping those where organogenic factors are no longer limiting.

At the present time sex therapy has profound limitations (Cole, 1985) and failure to recognize these may lead to their methods becoming devalued. It is therefore imperative that sex therapy urgently receives financial and political support so that society can recognize its work and in so doing attract the very best professionals into its fold.

It is a sad but inevitable fact that this book must end on a cautionary note. The arrival of AIDS (HIV) in Britain in 1979 (Daniels, 1986) sooner or later will influence the course of many lives – many tragically. Social and sexual behaviour will change and until effective prevention and treatment is available the consequences of this epidemic, though unpredictable in detail, will be far reaching.

For those of us involved in sex education and sex therapy there is a particular poignancy, since AIDS presents us with a paradox not easily resolved. On the one hand, there is the challenge to face the crisis and respond effectively and with compassion, encouraging, for example, the practice of 'safe sex' and fostering unprejudiced values, but at the same time there has to be a change of emphasis in therapy, a change which may not be easy for some.

The need to reduce anxiety and guilt about sexual feelings has always played an important part in sex therapy. Sex therapists have also tried to encourage their clients to take responsibility for their own feelings and decisions. The resulting 'personal growth' has led inevitably to sexual freedoms in men and women previously unheard of, freedoms which many of us regarded as good and desirable in the search for self-actualization. However, the pursuit of these goals, at least at present, can no longer be undertaken without a very long and serious look at the likelihood of any risks that AIDS might bring as a consequence of pursuing these ideals. Meantime we await the results of medical research with apprehension, impatience and hope.

REFERENCES

Anderson, B.J. and Wolf, F.M. (1986) Chronic physical illness and sexual behavior: psychological issues, *Journal of Consulting and Clinical Psychology*, Vol. 54, No. 2, pp. 168–75.

Ansari, J.M.A. (1976) Impotence: prognosis (a controlled study), *British Journal of Psychiatry*, Vol. 128, pp. 194–8.

Atkinson, D.R., Marruyama, M. and Natsui, S. (1978) The effects of the counselor race and counseling approach to Asian Americans' perceptions of counselor credibility and utility, *Journal of Counseling Psychology,* Vol. 25, pp. 76–83.

Bancroft, J. (1970) Disorders of sexual potency, in O. Hill (ed.) *Modern Trends in Psychosomatic Medicine*, Appleton-Century-Crofts, New York.

Bancroft, J. (1983) *Human Sexuality and Its Problems.* Churchill-Livingstone, Edinburgh.

Bancroft, J. and Coles, L. (1976) Three years' experience in a sexual problems clinic, *British Medical Journal*, i, pp. 1575–7.

Barlow, D. (1986) Causes of sexual dysfunction: the role of anxiety and cognitive interference, *Journal of Consulting and Clinical Psychology,* Vol. 54, pp. 140–8.

Brindley, G.S. and Gillan, P. (1982) Men and women who do not have orgasms, *British Journal of Psychiatry,* Vol. 140, pp. 351–6.

Chambless, D.L. and Lifshitz, J.L. (1984) Self-reported sexual anxiety and arousal: the expanded arousability inventory, *The Journal of Sex Research,* Vol. 20, pp. 241–54.

Cole, M.J. (1982) Surrogates and sexual dysfunction, *British Journal of Sexual Medicine,* Vol. 9, pp. 13–20.

Cole, M.J. (1985) Sex therapy – a critical appraisal. *British Journal of Psychiatry,* Vol. 147, pp. 337–51.

Cole, M.J. (1986) Socio-sexual characteristics of men with sexual problems, *Sexual and Marital Therapy*, Vol. 1, No. 1, pp. 89–108.

Conte, H.R. (1986) Multivariate assessment of sexual dysfunction, *Journal of Consulting and Clinical Psychology,* Vol. 54, No. 2, pp. 149–57.

Cooper, A.J. (1968) 'Neurosis' and disorders of sexual potency in the male, *Journal of Psychosomatic Research,* Vol. 12, pp. 141–4.

Crowe, M.J., Gillan, P. and Golombok, S. (1981) Form and content in the conjoint treatment of sexual dysfunctions: a controlled study, *Behaviour Research and Therapy,* Vol. 19, pp. 47–54.

Crown, S. and d'Ardenne, P. (1982) Symposium on sexual dysfunctions. Controversies, methods and results, *British Journal of Psychiatry,* Vol. 140, pp. 70–7.

Daniels, V.G. (1986) *AIDS Questions and Answers.* Cambridge Medical Books, Cambridge.

d'Ardenne, P. (1984) Sexual dysfunction in East London; a preliminary report. Unpublished paper presented to the Tower Hamlets District Department of Psychology.

Ellis, A. (1983) Does sex therapy really have a future? *Rational Living*, Vol. 18, pp. 3–6.

Fisher, C., Schiavi, R.C., Edwards, A., Davies, D.M., Reitman, M. and Fine, J. (1979) Evaluation of nocturnal penile tumescence in the differential diagnosis of sexual impotence, *Archives of General Psychiatry,* Vol. 36, pp. 431–41.

Ghosh, G., Duddle M. and Ingram, A. (1985) Treating patients of Asian origin presenting in the U.K. with sexual dysfunction. Paper presented to the Seventh World Congress of Sexology, New Delhi.

Goodman, R.E. (1986) How to treat premature ejaculation? *British Journal of Sexual Medicine,* Vol. 13, p. 6.

Hatch, J.P. (1979) Vaginal photoplethysmography: methodological considerations, *Archives of Sexual Behavior,* Vol. 8, pp. 357–74.

Hatch, J.P. (1981) Psychophysiological aspects of sexual dysfunction, *Archives of Sexual Behavior*, Vol. 10, pp. 49–64.

Hawton, K. (1982) Symposium on sexual dysfunction. The behavioural treatment of sexual dysfunction, *British Journal of Psychiatry,* Vol. 140, pp. 94–101.
Heiman, J., LoPiccolo, L. and LoPiccolo, J. (1976) *Becoming Orgasmic: A Sexual Growth Program for Women,* Prentice-Hall, Englewood Cliffs NJ.
Heisler, J. (1983) *Sexual Therapy in the National Marriage Guidance Council*, National Marriage Guidance Council, Rugby.
Hollon, S. and Beck, A.T. (1986) Research on cognitive therapies, in S.L. Garfield and A.E. Bergin (eds) *Handbook of Psychotherapy and Behavior Change*. 3rd edn, Wiley, New York.
Hong, L.K. (1984) Survival of the fastest: on the origin of premature ejaculation, *The Journal of Sex Research,* Vol. 20, pp. 109–22.
Hoon, P.W., Coleman, E., Amberson, J. and Ling, F. (1981) A possible physiological marker of female sexual dysfunction, *Biological Psychiatry,* Vol. 16, pp. 1,101–7.
Hoon, P., Wincze, J. and Hoon, E. (1977) A test of reciprocal inhibition: are anxiety and sexual arousal in women mutally inhibitory? *Journal of Abnormal Psychology*, Vol. 86, pp. 65–74.
Hooper, A. (1984) *The Body Electric*, Unwin Paperbacks, London.
Johnson, J. (1968) *Disorders of Sexual Potency in the Male*, Pergamon Press, Oxford.
Kaplan, H.S. (1974) *The New Sex Therapy*, Brunner/Mazel, New York.
Kaplan, H.S. (1979) *Disorders of Sexual Desire*, Baillière Tindall, London.
Kaya, N., Moore, C. and Karacan, I. (1979) Nocturnal penile tumescence and its role in impotence, *Psychiatric Annals,* Vol. 9, pp. 426–31.
Kinsey, A.C., Pomeroy, W.B. and Martin, C.E. (1948) *Sexual Behavior in the Human Male*, W.B. Saunders, Philadelphia and London.
Kinsey, A.C., Pomeroy, W.B., Martin, C.E. and Gebhard, P.H. (1953) *Sexual Behavior in the Human Female,* W.B. Saunders, Philadelphia and London.
Kockott, G., Dittmar, F. and Nusselt, L. (1975) Systematic desensitization of erectile impotence: a controlled study, *Archives of Sexual Behavior*, Vol. 4, pp. 493–500.
Kuriansky, J.B. and Sharpe, L. (1976) Guidelines for evaluating sex therapy, *Journal of Sex and Marital Therapy*, Vol. 2, pp. 303–8.
Levine, S.B. and Agle, D. (1978) The effectiveness of sex therapy for chronic secondary psychological impotence, *Journal of Sex and Marital Therapy*, Vol. 4, pp. 235–58.
Masters, W.H. and Johnson, V.E. (1966) *Human Sexual Response*, Little, Brown & Co., Boston.
Masters, W.H. and Johnson, V.E. (1970) *Human Sexual Inadequacy,* J.A. Churchill, London.
Masters, W.H. and Johnson, V.E. (1979) *Homosexuality in Perspective*, Little, Brown & Co., Boston.
Mears, E. (1978) Sexual problem clinics: an assessment of the work of 26 doctors trained by the Institute of Psychosexual Medicine, *Public Health,* Vol. 92, pp. 218–33.
Melman, A., Kaplan, D. and Redfield, J. (1984) Evaluation of the first 70 patients in the center for male sexual dysfunction of Beth Israel Medical Center, *Journal of Urology,* Vol. 131, No. 1, pp. 53–5.
Milne, D. and Cordle, C. (1984) Evaluating sex therapy, *British Journal of Sexual Medicine,* Vol. 11, pp. 110–14.
Morrow-Bradley, C. and Elliot, R. (1986) Utilization of psychotherapy research by practicing psychotherapists, *American Psychologist*, Vol. 41, No. 2, pp. 188–97.

Norton, G.R. and Jehu, D. (1984) The role of anxiety in sexual dysfunctions: a review, *Archives of Sexual Behavior,* Vol. 13, pp. 165–83.

Pervin, L.A. and Leiblum, S.R. (1980) Conclusion: overview of some critical issues in the evaluation and treatment of sexual dysfunctions, in S.R. Leiblum and L.A. Pervin (eds) *Principles and Practices of Sex Therapy*, Tavistock, London.

Pryde, N. and Woods, B. (1985) Brief directive co-therapy in a psychosexual clinic, *British Journal of Sexual Medicine*, Vol. 12, No. 4, pp. 104–8.

Ramsey, G. (1943) The sexual development of boys, *American Journal of Psychology,* Vol. 56, p. 217.

Ruse, M. (1979) *Sociobiology: Sense or Nonsense,* D. Reidel, London.

Rust, J. and Golombok, S. (1985) The Golombok Rust inventory of sexual satisfaction (GRISS), *British Journal of Clinical Psychology*, Vol. 24, pp. 63–4.

Sarrel, D.M. and Masters, W.H. (1982) Sexual molestation of men by women, *Archives of Sexual Behavior*, Vol. 11, pp. 117–31.

Spark, R.F., White, R.A. and Connolly, P.B. (1980) Impotence is not always psychogenic, *Journal of the American Medical Association,* Vol. 243, pp. 750–5.

Stoller, R. (1976) Sexual excitement, *Archives of General Psychiatry,* Vol. 33, pp. 899–909.

Sue, D.W. (ed.) (1981) *Counseling the Culturally Different*, Wiley, New York.

Symons, D. (1979) *The Evolution of Human Sexuality,* Oxford University Press, Oxford.

Trimmer, E. (1982) Practical problem-solving in sexual medicine III: premature ejaculation, *British Journal of Sexual Medicine*, Vol. 9, pp. 26–8.

Truax C.B. and Carkhuff, R.R. (1967) *Towards Effective Counseling and Psychotherapy,* Aldine, Chicago.

Watson, J.P. and Brockman, B. (1982) A follow-up of couples attending a psychosexual clinic, *British Journal of Clinical Psychology*, Vol. 21, pp. 143–4.

Wilson, E.O. (1975) *Sociobiology: The New Synthesis,* Harvard University Press, London.

Wilson, E.O. (1978) *On Human Nature,* Harvard University Press, Cambridge MA.

Wilson, G. (1979) The sociobiology of sex differences. *Bulletin of the British Psychological Society,* Vol. 32, pp. 350–3.

Wolchik, S.A., Beggs, V.E., Wincze, J.P., Sakheim, D.K., Barlow, D.H. and Mavissakalian, M. (1980) The effects of a subjective monitoring task in the measure of genital response to erotic stimulation, *Archives of Sexual Behavior*, Vol. 9, pp. 533–45.

Wolpe, J. (1958) *Psychotherapy by Reciprocal Inhibition,* Stanford University Press, Palo Alto CA.

Wright, J., Perreault, R. and Mathieu, M. (1977) The treatment of sexual dysfunction – a review, *Archives of General Psychiatry,* Vol. 34, pp. 881–90.

INDEX

Index compiled by Peva Keane